YOUTH MINISTRY
CAMPING

By Bob Cagle

Group
Books

Loveland, Colorado

Dedication

To Brenda and Hoke

Youth Ministry Camping

Credits
Illustrations by Norman Kittens
Edited by Eugene C. Roehlkepartain
Designed by Judy Atwood

"Travel Standards" and "Tripping Standards" from *Camp Standards With Interpretation*. Copyright © 1984 by the American Camping Association. Condensed by permission.

"Bus Games," "Bus Safety and Operation" and "Pre-Trip Inspection Checklist" are used by permission of Fellowship of Christians in Action, 3585 Alan Drive, Titusville, FL 32780.

"Wilderness First Aid" by Pat Stone. Condensed with permission from Mother Earth News American Country. Copyright © July 1987 by The Mother Earth News. All rights reserved.

"The Parable of the Sower" from Transforming Bible Study: A Leader's Guide by Walter Wink. Copyright © 1980 by Abingdon Press. Used by permission of the publisher, Abingdon Press.

"Leading the Pack: The Role of the Group Leader in Canoe Tripping" by Cliff Jacobson. Copyright © 1979 by Canoe Magazine. Used by permission.

Excerpt from *The American Wilderness: The Grand Canyon* by Robert Wallace and the editors of Time-Life Books. Copyright © 1972 by Time-Life Books Inc. Used by permission.

Scripture quotations are from the Holy Bible, New International Version. Copyright © 1973, 1978, 1984 International Bible Society. Used by permission of Zondervan Bible Publishers.

ISBN 0-931529-37-9
Printed in the United States of America

Acknowledgments

Camp is a storytelling place—a special place where the church tells its story and where campers create their own stories to tell. The past 15 months of preparation and writing have been an adventure in uncovering my own camping story. In thanking the many who have shared their gifts so freely with me, I tell you part of my story:

The research for *Youth Ministry Camping* actually began 40 years ago behind the Smyrna, Georgia, grammar school in the paper house where newspapers and magazines had been collected for the "war effort." Now we call it recycling. I didn't know it at the time, but when my older brother Earl and I scavenged through tons of newspapers searching for hunting and fishing magazines, my camping journey was underway. So, the first person I want to acknowledge is one of those magazine writers, the late John Jobson, former camping editor of Sports Afield magazine. I never met him, but when I eventually did throw away those musty magazines, I cut out and filed all of his articles. Years later those articles led me and my wife, Brenda, and our church youth groups to many backcountry places in Wyoming, Colorado, Maine and Canada.

When I was 13 we moved to the mountains where my dad, Freeman Cagle

Jr., taught me to seine minnows, set a trotline, skin catfish, boil steel traps in walnut hulls, track wild game and pull a crosscut saw. It was in tagging along with him and my uncles that I heard stories of their fathers and grandfathers and learned to "live" outdoors.

My journey in ministry also began outdoors. My pastor, Charles Shaw, honored me as a teenager by asking me to teach him how to trout fish. I did, and it was on one of our trips that I told him I felt God was calling me to be a preacher.

I went to summer church camp only once as a youth—to take Brenda to senior high camp. We married in college, splurged on an 8-by-8-foot tent and camped together for our honeymoon. My first camp leadership came in seminary when George Dunbar, a fellow seminarian, and I rented our conference's pioneer site and co-directed a camp for kids from six rural churches.

My next leap into camping was as conference coordinator of youth ministries for the North Georgia Conference of the Methodist Church. We lived at Camp Glisson for nine weeks each summer directing camps for more than 200 young people each week. The program included junior high and senior high assemblies, pioneer camps and backcountry adventures. The staff and volunteers there were valuable partners in ministry for me.

It was with my wife, Brenda, that I discovered the adventure of cross-country travel. Her inspiration came largely from the slide presentations of one of her pastors, the late George Erwin, a former missionary to Russia. Later his son Henry Erwin taught us a systematic approach to teaching outdoor living skills to youth, American Camping Association style. To them we're both indebted and grateful.

There are many others who have been guides for me on my camping journey— mentors who have taught me formally and experientially. I especially thank Edie Klein, who trained me in camp administration and Courtney Skinner, who showed me how to live comfortably in the winter Wyoming wilderness.

The big adventure in camping came for Brenda and me in 1977 when we accepted positions in central Oregon at Suttle Lake Camp, a year-round United Methodist retreat in the Cascade Range. There we learned firsthand to manage a camp facility and to direct summer and winter programs. Working at the camp also gave us the opportunity to work with Presbyterian, Catholic, Assemblies of God, Baptist, Disciples and independent church programs as well as special outdoor education for clubs, schools and religious groups. I deeply appreciate the staffs and volunteers with whom I shared ministry at Suttle Lake.

In 1979 camping took us on an even different journey. I succeeded Mel Moody as national director of junior high and outdoor education for the United Methodist Church. To Mel and my successor Chuck Kishpaugh I offer my greatest admiration. Together, the three of us have led 10 national camp conferences that span 20 years— an affirmation of church camping's power to sustain relationships.

Now our eight-year-old son, Hoke, has set his heart on hiking the Appalachian Trail. Beginning at the southern terminus, Springer Mountain, we've already hiked and camped 40 miles together. Next time we'll pick up at Hog Pen Gap and head north again.

In addition to those who have touched my past, I want to express my appreciation to those who have provided special information, consultation, assistance and critique in preparing this book: Paul Petzholdt, Eliot Wigginton, James Turpen, John Farmer, Mary Beth Fuller, Will Schutz, Ruth Cohn, Jim Black, Paul McNeal, Jeff Ross, George Holland, James Thompson, Clifford Knapp, Gary Fawver, Dan Waters and Jon Waters. The American Camping Association, Christian Camping International/USA and Fellowship of Christians in Action also provided valuable information.

I also want to thank Thom Schultz and Lee Sparks of Group Publishing for believing in youth ministry and my ability to create this resource.

Finally, I want to spotlight Gene Roehlkepartain for his gentle pressure, insightful questions, careful reorganization and meticulous detail on every chapter. Gene acted as lead safety person on hikes I led in Estes Park, Colorado, for GROUP Magazine's National Christian Youth Congress. He has demonstrated his care for this book the same way he looked after young people on the mountain.

Youth Ministry Camping is not my story alone. Like most camp stories, it is a gift, which I am giving back to the camping community.

Contents

Foreword 8
By Richard Chamberlain
Introduction 10

Part One:
Planning Youth Camps

1. Finding Roots and Coming Home 13
A First-Time Place 13
Coming Home 14
Uprooting to Reroot 15
Why Christian Camping? 16
Why Take Teenagers to Camp? 17
Understanding Camping 18
Church Camping on the Boundary 21
Rethinking Youth Ministry Camping . . . 22
Discussion and Action 24

2. Planning a "Boundaryless" Youth Camp 27
Beyond Previous Barriers 28
The Planning Process 29
Creating the Camp Theme 32
Discovering Resources 35
Designing the Program 39

3. Campsites, Support Services and Transportation 45
Finding Nearby Camps 46
Finding Long-Distance Campsites 50
Securing Support Services 52
Getting to Camp 53

4. Communicating the Good News About Camp 62
Who Will Hear Our Story? 63
How Will We Document Our Camp? . . 64
Who Will Document Our Camp? 64
How Should We Tell Our Story? 66

Part Two:
Camps in Action

5. Residential Youth Camps 72
Elements of a Residential Camp
Program 72
Evaluating Residential Camp 83
The Camp Director-Manager's Role 83

6. Backpacking 86
Guidelines for Backpacking Trips 87
Choosing Your Gear 90
Planning Your Menus 91
Planning Your Program 92
Trail Etiquette 92
Getting Your Group Ready to
Backpack 96
Backpacking Evaluation 101

7. Canoe Camping 103
Successful Canoe Camping 104
Canoeing Equipment 105
Basic Canoe Techniques 109
Canoe Safety and Rescue Techniques . 113
River Techniques 117
Training Teenagers for Canoeing 121
Planning Your Canoe Trip 128
Canoe Camp Evaluation 132

8. Snow and Winter Camping 134
Types of Winter Camps 134
Winter Camping Activities 140
Winter Wilderness Camping
Techniques 148
Preparing Your Group for a Winter
Camp 153
Winter Camp Evaluation 154

9. Specialty Camps and Adventures 156
Bicycle Camps 156
Foxfire Camps 160
Sailing Camps 164
Workcamps 166
A Winter Wilderness Survival
Adventure 168

Part Three:
Camp Leadership

10. Recruiting and Training Camp Leaders 174
  Recruiting Counselors and Leaders ...174
  Training Counselors and Leaders 176
  Leader Training Episodes 181

11. Developing a Group Spirit at Camp 190
  Leadership That Enables Growth 191
  The Group Development Process 193
  The Definition Stage 193
  The Discovery Stage 198
  The Direction Stage 201
  Questions for Discussion and
    Reflection....................203

12. Leading Campers 204
  The Dynamics of Action-Based
    Leadership 204
  Styles of Action-Based Leadership 206
  Using Action-Based Leadership Skills ..209
  Leading Campers With Special Needs .214

13. Leading Camp Worship and Bible Study 217
  The Importance of Worship and
    Bible Study 218
  Uniqueness of Camp Worship 219
  Elements of Camp Worship 221
  Types of Camp Worship 222
  Planning Camp Celebrations 226
  Camp Celebration Ideas 228
  Leading Camp Bible Studies 232
  Transforming Bible Study..........232
  Conversations With Scripture.......234
  Questions for Discussion and
    Reflection....................236

Part Four:
Camp Programming Ideas

14. Group-Building Activities 240
  Camp Catalog Game 240
  Family Fact-Finding Mission 241
  Secret Friends 241
  Friendship Lanyard 241
  Rhythmic Speaking 242
  Group Life Diagram 242
  Group Journal 243
  No Questions Asked 243
  Picture Framing..................243
  Care Cards.....................244
  Swamp Ladder..................244

  Morning in a Tree 244
  Detaining Stone 245
  Powwow Blanket 245
  Breakfast in Bed 245
  Feather in Your Hat 246

15. Trust-Building Activities ...247
  Stretching and Balancing 247
  Push, Pull, Lean and Fall 248
  One-Legged Balancing 249
  Spider Web 250
  Hand In 251
  Sharing Circle 251
  Lineups 251
  Sensory Meal 252
  Web of Life 252

16. Nature Awareness Activities 254
  Nature IQ Test 254
  Sense of Wonder.................255
  The Wilderness Is a Sanctuary 255
  Listening Pictures 255
  Color Hike.....................256
  True North 256
  Animal Map 256
  Talking Across the Water 256
  Balloon Voyages 257
  Night Hike 257
  Viewing Party 258
  Stalking Circle 258
  Thread Circle 259
  Spider Web Tour 259
  Bark Weavings..................259
  Shadow-Tracing.................260
  Rubbing Collage 260

17. Games and Fun Times 261
  How Many Ways? 261
  Circle Soccer 262
  Meltdown Relay 262
  Running Water Relay 262
  Boot Shuffle 263
  Coconut Tag 263
  Spud.........................263
  Circle Jump Rope 264
  Line Jump 264
  Square Tug Standoff 264
  Quick-Change Artist 264
  Clock Race.....................265
  Heavy Canoe Race 265
  Rescue Relay 265
  Bag Drama 266
  Indoor Cross-Country Ski Relay.....266
  Gully Washer Day 266

Part Five:
Backcountry Living Skills

18. Teaching Backcountry Living Skills 270
Create Interest in Outdoor Skills 271
Introduce Skills in Small Segments ... 271
Develop Subgroups for Personal Support 272
Help Campers Visualize a System of Outdoor Skills 272

19. Backcountry Judgment and Safety 274
Backcountry Living Demonstration ... 274
Backcountry Safety Guidelines 278
Discussion and Reflection 283

20. Personal Gear and Packing 287
Bags and Packs 287
Sleeping Bags.................. 290
Clothing...................... 291
Group-Building Activities for Packing . 293
Personal Gear Lists 295

21. Ropes, Knots and Hitches 301
Basic Knots and Hitches 301
Rope Activities 303

22. Tents and Emergency Shelters 306
Choosing Tents 306
Tenting Tips 307
Other Backcountry Shelters 309
Tent-Pitching Activities 311

23. Wood-Cutting and Fire-Building 312
Gathering Wood Safely............ 312
Minimum-Impact Fire-Building 317
Group-Building Through Fire-Building 321

24. Food and Cooking 322
Menu-Planning Guidelines 322
Backcountry Cooking Methods 323
Backcountry Cooking Safety 325
Keeping Utensils Clean and Dirty 327
Backcountry Cooking Tips 327
Neat Treats for the Backcountry 328

25. Map and Compass Navigation 331
Using Maps 331
Using a Compass 333
Using a Map and Compass Together .. 335
Map and Compass Group-Building Activities 338

Afterword 341
Camping Resources 343
Camp Planning and Leadership 343
Understanding Teenagers 344
Campers With Special Needs 345
Camps in Action..................... 345
Camp Activities and Crafts............. 346
Nature Awareness 347
Backcountry Living Skills 348
Camp Readings and Reflections 349

Foreword

A Gift to Camping

When I think about Bob Cagle, I think about the enormous impact he has had on the personal growth of hundreds of camping and outdoor ministry volunteers and staff throughout the United States.

When I think about Bob Cagle, the words "professional," "innovative," "caring," "family," "youth activities," "backcountry camper" and "Christian lifestyle" spring to mind.

I first "experienced" Bob when the American Camping Association's Council of Religiously Affiliated Camps asked him to keynote a national workshop on "commonalities in outdoor ministries" across many faith groups. It was a masterful presentation that later became a well-read article in A.C.A.'s Camping Magazine.

Then I experienced Bob as he led more than 100 church camp leaders in a service of worship that focused on visualizing a canoe trip. Yes, we were worshiping in a building, but Bob led us to feel that we were really in that canoe in the midst of the wilderness!

Then I experienced Bob and his young son Hoke in a leadership presentation at a national denominational gathering for outdoor ministry. There I saw firsthand the affection and respect Bob and Hoke have for each other. And, in the way Bob "lives out" being a dad, I saw his sensitivity to respecting young people as persons.

Over the years in meetings across the country, I've been in many conversations, discussion groups and planning sessions with Bob. Again and again, I and others have benefited from his wisdom and insight.

Taking Notes

So, with all those positive thoughts about Bob, wouldn't you be excited to read his first book on outdoor ministry? I sure was. And as I read the manuscript, I wasn't disappointed! *Youth Ministry Camping* is a gift to youth ministry, the church and the camping community.

Bob Cagle's presence permeates this book, chapter by chapter. I know of no other book in the field that compares in the way this book weaves "people-wisdom," camping knowledge, spiritual insight and professional development.

Youth Ministry Camping isn't a book to read quickly from cover to cover. It's a vast storehouse of helpful information, plans, facts, exercises and detailed help. In fact, I defy the reader to move through this book without taking notes!

Here Bob shares camp programming ideas that have grown out of his experience with young people in camp, retreat and church settings across the country. The ideas are fun and innovative for teenagers.

Bob also tells us about backcountry living skills—about backcountry judgment, gear and packing, shelters, fires and cooking. He tells us out of his vast experience as a backcountry trip leader and out of his leadership in the American Camping Association in developing workshops and standards for backcountry living skills.

His youth ministry philosophy shines as he writes about leadership training, group development and planning youth camps. Unfortunately, some camp leaders still think they just need a lovely site and a well-intentioned staff, and—as if by miracle—any camper dropped into that match will be significantly changed within a week. Not so! Bob knows that staff need training, the setting needs interpretation, and that the "magic" is most often the result of long, hard, skilled planning.

But I believe Bob is most helpful to us when he shows how the church can utilize camping and outdoor skills to enhance its ministry with youth. As outdoor leaders discover—and as Bob aptly shows in his book—outdoor ministry relates to every aspect of Christian ministry. *Youth Ministry Camping* gives concrete guidance to youth ministers, camp directors, and regional and national camp leaders on bringing alive our faith priorities in outdoor settings.

As Bob talks, writes, promotes and lives out his own youth and camping ministry, he constantly draws on the best of religiously affiliated, agency and private, independent camping. He understands that no one segment of camping has a market on the "camping truth." As a result, his book is a valuable collection of camping wisdom from camping experts, church youth leaders, Appalachian Mountains folk, Native Americans and others.

In *Youth Ministry Camping*, Bob challenges us to a commitment to excellence as we reach for ways to enhance young people's personal growth and spiritual development.

Richard Chamberlain is the national outdoor ministry consultant for the United Church of Christ and a consultant for several other denominations. He was president of the American Camping Association from 1986-1988.

Introduction
Kissing the Flowers

It was early one morning high in the Wind River Range of Wyoming. The late-June sun draped the purple peaks, like a flowing mantle sliding down from the summits, shining on the craggy rocks and snowfields. Downward and outward it moved, till the lofty, frosty meadows sparkled as the sunlight touched flowers and tender aspen leaves.

All was silent on the mountain—except for our 18-month-old Hoke, who'd been awake since before dawn. Bundled up and outside, he was running through the knee-deep grasses, slowing, then ambling flower to flower, bowing like a miniature monk to smell each one.

It was a perfect picture. I pulled out my camera, crept closer, knelt, lowered my head to get a good angle, focused. Then I stopped. To my amazement, Hoke wasn't smelling the flowers; he was kissing them.

As I recall that time in 1981 camping with more than a dozen outdoor leaders, I'm struck by the notion that any of us can learn from all of us. The night before, Paul Petzholdt, founder of the National Outdoor Leadership School, had bounced Hoke on his knee beside the glowing embers of the campfire. All of us reveled in Paul's outdoor wisdom. But come morning, the child among us was the teacher. In all my life, I'd never thought of kissing flowers!

I hope that reading *Youth Ministry Camping* will be for you a similar experience—a spontaneous discovery of some new flower that leads to another flower then another—until some new vision for ministry with youth is born in you.

Let me invite you to the many meadows of camping with youth groups—planning, leading, learning and experiencing. I've organized the book as follows:

Planning youth camps. This section introduces you to the "boundaryless" possibilities of camping with youth groups.

Camps in action. These chapters describe the ins and outs of specific types of youth camps—residential camps, backpacking, canoe camping, and snow and winter camping. The final chapter introduces possibilities for less common specialty youth camps.

Camp leadership. In this section, I introduce camp leadership skills.

Camp programming ideas. Here are dozens of unique camp activities designed specifically for youth groups to use.

Backcountry living skills. The final section of the book details a host of backcountry living skills for youth groups.

May God bless your dreams as you venture out with the young people of your church—our church! May you and your campers kiss the flowers and blossom within.

Part One
Planning Youth Camps

Chapter 1

Finding Roots and Coming Home

"It is a strange paradox of modern life that for members of a family to really be together, they have to leave home."[1]

Tony was the child of migrant workers, and I was director-manager of Suttle Lake Camp in central Oregon. The week at Suttle Lake with his sixth-grade class was Tony's first camp.

Tony stayed on the fringes of the group and group activities until midweek. The only memory I have of him before Wednesday was watching him stand between the storage and maintenance buildings with his hands in his pockets, his elbows tucked in, and his eyes focused somewhere in the distance—as if he were thinking about something or someone far away.

Then on Wednesday Tony's counselors finally talked him into joining a small group that was going to canoe and explore a mountain lake. He rode in the van, while I hauled the canoes with a four-wheel drive vehicle. We ferried the group to a tiny island where we talked, lounged in the sun and explored. Tony enjoyed paddling and looking through the big end of the binoculars; I still can see him clutching the binoculars to his eyes.

That afternoon Tony began relaxing, but he didn't talk much. At the end of the day I invited him to go with me to bring the four-wheel drive around the lake to load the canoes.

When the engine roared to life, Tony said, "You know what, Bob?"

"No. What?"

"This is the first time I ever rode in a Jeep!"

Tony smiled, and I smiled. The silence ended. Tony talked about camp and home and himself. He joined the camping experience.

A First-Time Place

For Tony camp had become what it is for most campers: a "first-time place." Whether it's a weeklong cabin camp, backpacking expedition, canoe trip, wilderness survival experience, bicycling trip or winter cross-country skiing adventure, camp has a dramatic and unique impact on its leaders and campers. Over and over the Tonys of our churches and communities discover in camp a place for personal affirmation and renewed self-esteem. What happens at camp that makes it a first-time place for campers? Let's look at some of the life-changing experiences campers have:

Campers are known and valued as

individuals. At camp young people find—sometimes for the first time—a place they're known and valued as individuals when they otherwise may feel undefined and unrecognized.

At camp personal history takes on a sacred dimension as campers are introduced to one another and tell their life stories. Age makes little difference. To be listened to, known by others, and affirmed by counselors and friends make camp an uplifting and unique experience for many young people. As many life streams—each with a unique source—converge at camp, young people learn to see themselves as important members of the Christian community.

Campers are initiated into adulthood. At camp young people break barriers that have kept them from feeling free and responsible as maturing young people. Camp is often the first time teenage campers experience themselves in adult roles. Although parents may give teenagers freedom and responsibilities at home, camp responsibilities and freedom—without parental supervision—are highly prized experiences for campers. Young people who feel put upon to set the table at home will proudly undertake the task at camp. We see that setting and serving tables is important to kids in their promptness, their desire to create neat table arrangements and their enthusiasm for being table runners during meals.

Everything young people do at camp—skillfully paddling a canoe through rapids, building a fire, cooking a meal, cleaning a mess or doing a job over—is a step toward adulthood. The tasks may not be earthshaking rituals of passage, but they're important initiations that build self-esteem, identity, trust and independence.

Campers are initiated into childhood. For some people camp is an initiation into childhood. Campers and counselors whose home experiences minimize play, leisure and fun for fun's sake may discover within themselves a childlike self who can "cut up" and "carry on"—overriding the constraints of playing only to learn, compete, achieve and succeed socially.

Campers discover they can be more than they are now. Finally, at camp young people discover that "I can be more than I am now." As a result, they find themselves yearning to invest their lives in something important. Something about life at camp draws them to look beyond themselves. It lets them be "at home" with themselves, and it beckons them to sing a song they've never heard before.

Sooner or later every camper yearns "to be more than I am now." Campers may have felt this before—at home, at school or with a close friend. At camp, though, it always seems like the first time. In a new, first-time way, campers consider and explore how to invest their lives in something significant.

What makes the camping experience have so much potential for changing the lives of teenagers and other campers? Two images or themes capture camping's impact: coming home and uprooting to reroot.

Coming Home

Coming home is a camp theme that's easy to image. Camp provides memories that carry us back and stories that lead us forward. Remembering, knowing and discovering tie life together. In the camp setting, campers are reminded of who they are and whose they are. They find acceptance and comfort that make them feel at home.

I once worked with a church camp counselor, Victor, who was also an international student. In reflecting on the camping experience, he remembered this song, which he taught to campers throughout the summer:

> Cho boy, cho-o-o boy-ye-e
> So jai a ya qua bo
> Za-ma na-ma-na za-ma na-ma-na
> Ya qua bo Hey!

"The song," Victor explained, "is from my country, Ghana. It's a welcoming song, originally a war song sung by my grandmother and all the village when the men came home from war. But we no longer celebrate battle victories, so we sing it as a 'coming-home song.'"

He continued: "That's why I'm here: to help you come home to camp. I'm a long way from my home, my mother and my father. So are you. But we can feel at home because that's what camp is—a home away from home."

The words of Victor's coming-home song haven't faded from the hearts of those campers. Now, 20 years later, some of them still sing "Cho Boy" to help a new generation of campers discover the spirit of camping—the coming home spirit.

The challenge for camp leaders is to create a climate where campers feel at home and among friends. Creating this climate may involve identifying and celebrating the times and places outdoors when simply being together supersedes campers' desires to collect experiences. Or creating the climate may involve reaching lonely, unwilling teenagers who were pressured into going to church camp. Then, through the week, the campers discover they can contribute and receive love even though they didn't have a choice in where and when they went to camp.

To live simply in the face of complexity. To be valued no matter what you wear or whom you know. To feel you've come home. These experiences may be the greatest adventures the church can provide

through camping. Everything we do at camp involves a quest for home—to be one; to be whole; to be with God, ourselves and others; and to be with God's creation.

Uprooting to Reroot

Camp is also significant in the lives of teenagers because of their own quest to be rooted when so many feel uprooted. "At camp we uproot in order to reroot," church historian-theologian Martin E. Marty told a group of camp leaders. "[Camp] intentionally relocates people and creates a different set of circumstances so that they are in some sense different people than they are the rest of the time. We uproot to reroot. We change locale in order to recreate."[2]

Camping is an experience similar to everything we do yet different from anything we do. In leaving home for camp—uprooting—we truly experience coming home—rerooting—to ourselves, to others and to God. In camping we realize anew that we're truly a pilgrim people, a "tenting" community of Christians—which we're apt to forget if we worship too long within brick walls without being uprooted.

At camp young people discover and rediscover their roots and make decisions about their futures. Scott, for example, had a long history of camping and retreating. During college he was a counselor in senior high camps. In early adulthood he taught school and then volunteered to spend a summer doing camp maintenance.

These summers at camp shaped Scott's life plans. He began traveling throughout his state promoting camps in local churches. Then he headed to seminary, a part-time camp management position and two years as a full-time youth minister in California. Scott is now an associate pastor in Idaho and an active camp and youth ministry leader in his area.

Why Christian Camping?

When we think of camping, we usually think of fun times, recreation and "getting away from it all." While these characteristics are present in church camping, there's more to church camping than having fun.

The camping themes of finding roots and coming home naturally connect with our Christian faith. Jesus' wilderness experience was a desert of discovering—a coming home to God's purpose in his life and ministry. And remember the Exodus story of the Hebrew people's wilderness experience? In many senses, that story was one of camping as the Hebrew people were uprooted from everything they knew in order to wander through the wilderness toward a promised land. The Israelites were challenged and tested as they camped in the wilderness year after year. There they discovered who and whose they were, and they were rerooted in the Promised Land.

The spiritual analogy of these experiences makes them more than just stories from the past. They become personal encounters with God—experiences in which campers recall, rehearse and respond to the Christian message. In camping, campers can be taught through experience the meaning of the Greek word for incarnation, "skenoo." Though it's usually translated "He dwelt among us," it literally means "He tented with us." By living a parable in their camping experience, campers discover in new ways how the Christian faith is a spiritual journey—a journey that continues today.

Camping provides an ideal setting for teenagers to explore, test and shape their personal faith journeys. In church camping, the "wilderness" and "journey" are shared corporately by campers and staff. The camp experience becomes a life-size allegory for campers to "act out" their faith and theology. Let's look at the Christian beliefs that teenagers, leaders and others experience at camp:

Creation (Genesis 1:27). Camping affirms that God is the source of all that's possible. By understanding our relationship to and the sacredness of God's creation, we remember our responsible interdependence within the created order.

Freedom and fall (John 8:32 and Isaiah 53:6). Humanity is free to choose and therefore vulnerable to hurt, brokenness, alienation, hostility and wrong choices. The Christian camp provides an alternative to our fallen, distorted experience of freedom and reinterprets our freedom as a hopeful experience of trust.

Grace (Ephesians 4:7). Accepting individuals as they are and where they are is central to the experience of Christian groups. This unmerited, unconditional love is the underlying assumption that unifies campers and counselors. The shared camping experience shifts our focus to several of God's gifts—earth, sky, water, food and friendship—and exposes the falseness of our efforts to earn and manipulate acceptance.

Covenant community (Genesis 31:44). The camping experience provides two unique learning opportunities. Campers learn to be responsible to, for and with others. They also learn to create covenants together. In these experiences, campers discover that the camp community is a microcosm of life where they learn new ways to relate to their parents, siblings and friends.

Confession and reconciliation (2 Corinthians 5:18). In living our covenants at camp, we realize we often break the covenants we make in our everyday lives. Recalling daily events and opening ourselves to one another establishes confession, forgiveness and reconciliation as a natural experience of Christian living.

Faith and love (Galatians 5:13). Camping deepens love and faith because life at camp is fresh and real. When dislocated from everyday living patterns, campers learn to affirm and value one another. When counselors help campers connect camp life with home life, they discover that accepting and loving are as important as being accepted and loved. This acceptance generates a capacity to serve one another and the community at camp and back home.

Hope (Romans 15:13). The previous points about freedom, grace, faith and love at camp may seem idealized and romanticized. It's not always that easy. Strangers who come to camp may leave as strangers. A lonely person who comes may leave just as lonely—if not lonelier. "This time" camp didn't elicit these important Christian themes. The strangers and lonely people didn't experience the love, community, faith, reconciliation or grace that camping is supposed to offer.

But the key is "this time." Christians live in hope. We know God is still creating and his grace is still breaking through. Whatever happens in our present efforts, we know we can look to the future for deeper relationships and greater wholeness. Thus the last word at our camps isn't a tearful farewell, self-congratulation or self-criticism. Rather, the last word is hope—hope for the future, hope for what God is still creating.

Why Take Teenagers to Camp?

In addition to the theological insights young people gain through camp, the experience speaks directly to teenagers' specific needs and concerns. The camp setting provides a significant contrast to the hurried, often impersonal world in which teenagers live. Let's contrast a teenager's everyday world with camp life:

Community versus isolation. Many teenagers feel isolated and lonely. One study found that teenage girls are lonelier than any other segment of the American population.[3]

Camp breaks teenagers' loneliness and feelings of isolation through the sense of community and cooperation that develops during the week. The closeness between campers becomes a parable for them to see what relationships can be like in families and other groups.

The closeness campers experience in small groups away from everyday routines also provides a mirror in which they re-evaluate their relationships with family members and friends. In some cases the camp experience confirms those relationships. In other cases it creates dissonance, challenging campers to re-evaluate and strengthen their relationships. In both cases teenagers experience the joy of close relationships with Christian brothers and sisters.

Relaxation versus hurried living. One of the most revealing descriptions of teenagers is found in the title of David Elkind's landmark book, *All Grown Up & No Place to Go: Teenagers in Crisis.* Teenagers and families are busier than ever. Detailed date books—which used to belong only to high-powered executives—are now part of the stack of books students carry to high school. Young people are hurried—pushed to achieve quickly in all areas of life. They fill their calendars with school, work, extracurricular activities, socializing and church.

Camp life sharply contrasts with this hurried life. It has a different time frame—a different rhythm. At camp teenagers have a chance to stop. They listen to themselves. To others. To creation. To God. In the process they gain a new, fresh perspective on life.

Cooperation versus competition. A teenager's life often revolves around competition. Our culture says that the only way to succeed is to outdo others. Grades, sports, money, hobbies and even relationships make teenagers compete. I'm better. I'm first. I'm faster. I'm stronger.

The camping experience changes the equation for success. As duties are divided among campers, all campers discover they must depend on one another. Setting up a tent only succeeds if teenagers work together. The only way for the group to reach the mountain peak is for everyone to support one another. If campers want to succeed, they must cooperate. Those cooperative experiences become an important model of servanthood for life after camp.

Nature versus technology. The world of human inventiveness contrasts dramatically with the world of God's creation. Unlike cars and appliances that age, rust and stop working, nature is an ongoing process of death and rebirth with the changing seasons.

At camp teenagers sense this cycle of rebirth as they see new, young sprigs among old timbers. They perceive the continuity of time as they discover relics and symbols of previous times and generations. The world becomes a holy place as they see God's handiwork in nature.

Awe and wonder versus mass production. Many things teenagers value are the products of human inventiveness. Everything appears to be explainable, understandable and reproducible.

But camp introduces teenagers to a sense of awe and wonder. Running the rapids in a canoe, climbing to a mountain peak or looking at the bright stars while lying in a sleeping bag outdoors reminds teenagers that the world and universe are full of mystery and wonder. Teenagers discover the world is bigger and greater than they ever imagined. In the process of interpreting their experiences to one another, they develop a reverence and sense of awe for the world and its Creator.

Understanding Camping

Just as each generation's teenagers are different, contemporary camping is different from camping in previous decades. Since the 1960s, we've seen a subtle yet radical reshaping of North America's leisure mind-set and camping spirit.

Many influences have inspired our culture to reach life's physical and spiritual boundaries. The camping environment is a natural setting for this quest. It's important to understand the trends and shifts in order to continue to provide positive growing experiences for teenagers.[4]

To understand these shifts, think of trends in camping as waves that wash onto the beach, each one shifting the sand subtly but significantly. Each wave changes the methods and emphases in the camping experience. Let's look at major trends, or waves, in recent decades and then consider what the future holds for church camping and outdoor recreation.

By the mid-'50s most major denominations had established campsites and assembly grounds for youth conferences, assemblies and small group rustic camps. Yet even at remote sites, camping was a "front yard" experience. The grandeur of nature was distant, with campers venturing only beyond the lodge, ball field or waterfront for a special vesper or sunrise service. Connecting with nature—close up—wasn't really a concern. As a result, church camp was compartmentalized, and a gulf separated those who *camped* (assembled themselves indoors at camp) and those who *camped out* (in tents in the woods).

But during this time the seeds were sown for greater relational, ecological and theological concerns. The next 20 years brought a revolution to camping and a new emphasis called "outdoor ministry." Camping began to grow in many directions. Camp counselors became skilled in nature awareness, experiential theology and group dynamics. Play was reshaped as a venture in cooperation rather than a contest to become champions. Campers and counselors grew up and wanted camping events and places for their children and families. The stage was set for major changes—and they came.

High-tech camping. A recreational tidal wave swept across North America in the late '60s. Brought on by a quest for freedom and the human potential movement, this tidal wave consisted of "up trips," "out trips" and "in trips." People longed to be "real" and free. Campers were motivated by questions such as "How far?" "How high?" "How deep?" and "How personal?"

In the wake of this freedom quest came the technological quest for space. Alpine shops replaced Army-Navy stores. Campers equipped themselves with Space Age gear and shelters: tubular aluminum pack frames; arrows; laminated rafts and canoes; fluorescent plastic bows; skis; freeze-dried ice cream; breathable, waterproof clothing; and sporting shoes with five densities of rubber in a single sole.

The high-tech camping equipment wave was paralleled by a high-tech quest for fitness and adventure: jogging, aerobics, weight training, and a worldwide enterprise called "adventure travel," which explored, rafted, climbed and toured almost every conceivable nook on the planet. Professional guides, outfitters and explorers pointed campers to hundreds of new adventure frontiers.

Camp directors discovered untapped outdoor resources at their back doors: rivers, lakes, deserts, and state and national parks. They'd been there all along, but now they'd been discovered—not by map and compass but by television and magazines. The demand for competent leaders and the necessity of risk management skills and emergency training were—and are—unparalleled.

The quest for simplicity. Technology provides things, not relationships. Not everyone was ready to ride the recreational tidal wave on a high-tech surfboard. Those caught up in the fervor discovered that bigger, more, farther and faster didn't necessarily mean better.

Simplicity became the new watchword for a growing number of camp leaders. Even founders of major high-tech equipment companies began saying the best wilderness education isn't created by Space Age equipment but by simple approaches to experiencing the outdoors.

Reflective travelers began to balance what they learned from Space Age technology with a new spiritual quest to know nature. Earlier writings of simplicity advocates such as John Muir, Henry David Thoreau and Ernest Seton found a new place in outdoor enthusiasts' hearts. Wilderness associations grew and focused their energies on acquiring and preserving wilderness areas and isolating natural islands in big cities.

The simplicity tide required overtime effort by the U.S. Forest Service and the National Park Service. Crowded campsites and waterways and increasing traffic on fragile wilderness areas demanded radical rethinking of maximum group sizes, numbers of annual users and camping techniques to preserve the backcountry. An area-by-area study of year-round use and heavy-use times resulted in regulations tailored to each park or wilderness area. Group sizes for the backcountry were reduced 20 to 30 percent during the '70s, and some places stopped issuing backcountry permits to groups of more than six members.

Minimum-impact camping techniques marked a new wave of government-produced outdoor education leaflets, films and filmstrips. Many of the approaches to wilderness behavior and ethics pioneered by Paul Petzholdt and the National Outdoor Leadership School were adopted by national and state agencies. These approaches also influenced the practices of outfitters and private, church and agency camps across North America.

During this time, the recreational ventures shifted from high-tech extravaganzas to simplicity-oriented activities, such as cross-country travel, orienteering, whole-food cooking, low-impact aerobics, walking and gardening. These activities were combined with an interest in pioneer crafts of wool, wood, leather and survival lore. All these earthbound simplicity pursuits coexisted with the continuing quest for a new experience in a high-tech age.

Campers at risk. Paradoxically, amidst the wave of technology and a consciousness of the natural environment, a phrase evolved to describe a growing segment of the adolescent population: youth at risk. It refers to more than nine million young people who have difficulty functioning in normal day-to-day routines—runaways, dropouts, throwaways, abused children and delinquents. They've tried everything, and nothing seems to work.

The camping community discovered that it—like no other institution—could make a difference in these young people's lives. Actually, the seeds for reaching these kids who were lost to their families, communities and churches were sown in the '20s and '30s by pioneers in therapeutic camping. Year-round camping for emotionally troubled youth was established and refined in six locations in the United States and Canada between the '40s and mid-'60s.

Then, in the early '70s, camp leaders developed stress-challenge education—a framework for outdoor training and living that transforms both adults and young people, including the youth at risk. Adapted from survival skills used in British, American and Australian military training, stress-challenge education was designed to help people discover and believe they can be and do more than they dreamed possible. Campers discover themselves and their potential through challenge, group problem-solving, personal and group initiatives, and values clarification.

One camper involved in a weekend stress-challenge camp to develop church youth leadership remembers being transformed by the experience: "If I had to pick out a more meaningful place to learn, experience and try, I don't think I could," he wrote. "It was a learning experience—not like school, but through trial and error . . . As we overcame the 'high ropes,' I found that encouragement had a great deal to do with my accomplishment."

Almost every contemporary camp program has spinoffs from stress-challenge education programs such as Project Adventure, New Games, Outward Bound and the National Outdoor Leadership School.

Boundaryless camping. The changing tides and crosscurrents of the '80s created a camping style for the future: boundaryless camping. The camping experience is no longer limited to tenting in a national forest or hiking in the mountains. Contemporary camping is boundaryless—open to the creative visions of camp planners, program designers, directors, counselors and leaders.

Camping may be a bicycle trip, a wilderness survival experience or a canoe trip with teenagers with disabilities. It may take place in any season of the year. It can be an inexpensive and simple Foxfire camp or an extravagant rafting expedition. Opportunities and possibilities are limited only by the creativity of camp leaders and planners.

While the freedom of boundaryless camping offers youth groups significant camping experiences, it also confronts church, agency and private camp leaders with major challenges. For boundaryless camping to maintain its impact and significance in young people's lives, leaders must use the freedom responsibly. They face challenges such as:

● Knowing their reasons for camping.

● Utilizing technological innovations responsibly out of commitment to the community and to the wholeness—mental, spiritual and physical—of individuals.

● Appropriating the insights of camp planners and the National Park Service who—for ecological and spiritual reasons—are moving cabins and tents further from water sources, providing greater space between structures, and lowering group size.

Church Camping on the Boundary

Like other kinds of camping, church camping has grown and changed tremendously in recent decades. Not only has church camping changed, but church camp leaders have learned the important skills and emphases that reshaped camping.

In the early '70s the church experienced a surge in conference family camping along with the specialized "getting out there" trend. These denominational and regional camps taught youth workers and families that they could lead camps and retreats with their own members, friends and neighboring youth groups. As a result, denominationally sponsored family camps, backpacking, canoeing, bicycling, rafting and other specialized events dwindled in the mid-'70s, while self-directed adventures and conference facility use grew.

As local churches organized their own camping events, denominations and interdenominational groups developed large group residential camps, conferences, personal-growth weekends and workcamps. These events have attracted hundreds of youth groups from across the country.

Perhaps more significant than the shift in camping styles in the church is the shift in emphasis. Let's look at some of the changes:

Higher standards. One of church camping's brightest horizons is the partnership of denominations and camps to provide high standards for programs, staffing and camp administration. Never before have churches and denominations been more aware of the need for safe and loving environments, quality faith experiences and competent leadership at camps.

Biblical application. Church camps balance the surge of human potential training and environmental education with global mission issues, Bible study and spiritual disciplines. Resources for training and processing camp experiences biblically and theologically are available to church leaders now more than ever before.

Focus on camping's impact. Today's church camp leaders reaffirm that—through all the years and all the changes—camping is most effective when it equips campers for their ministry back home. An overwhelming number of church leaders point to a church camp experience as the time they received their vocational call, resolved major faith struggles or met their lifetime mate.

This highlights the tremendous impact camp has on the church's future. Church camp leaders recognize this positive impact and foster it in the camp setting.

Rethinking Youth Ministry Camping

Just as changes in camping have led the church to re-evaluate the role of camping in its ministry, changes in our understanding of teenagers demand that we rethink how we lead teenage campers. Youth workers, camp leaders, teachers and mental health professionals are rethinking adolescent development, and the changes have important implications for camping.

Until the mid-'80s, most professionals based their perspective on teenagers on surveys and studies of a narrow, troubled segment of the teenage population. Very little was said or studied about "normal" teenagers. The resulting images in the media of delinquent, depressed, distressed and degenerate teenagers played havoc with parents' and youth workers' fears—even in the healthiest groups and communities. In the words of one tearful mother: "We have two daughters—an eighth-grader and a ninth-grader. They are absolutely wonderful in every way . . . But I live in constant fear that any day the bottom is going to fall out."

Camp staffers who model this storm-and-stress approach to adolescent development limit their ability to provide warmth and acceptance for campers. When counselors are preoccupied with campers' struggles, problems and negative behaviors, they're unlikely to affirm the campers' strengths, character and capacity for good. This perspective becomes a self-fulfilling prophecy, which reveals itself in poor counselor-camper relationships.

Despite the dismal picture of teenagers' and parents' plight, a new realization dawned in the mid-'80s as a result of several unprecedented studies of normal teenagers. These studies showed that most teenagers aren't on the verge of trouble. While all teenagers experience the stress and strain of adolescence, young people also have many strengths to sustain them. The most extensive study—conducted by Search Institute of Minneapolis—highlighted the strengths of average, churchgoing kids and their parents.[5] These strengths included:

● They considered their faith to be an important influence on their lives.

● They generally felt loved and trusted in their families.

● They valued relationships, family approval, world peace and others' welfare more than money and popularity.

At the same time, the study showed critical areas that call for thoughtful reflection and action by those who work with young people. These areas include:

● Sexual experimentation among many average teenagers.

● Teenagers' concern about sexual and physical abuse.

● Family tension that may result in family violence and marital conflict.

● Social alienation experienced by some young people.

The Search Institute study and other recent studies about teenagers haven't painted a glossy picture, but they've given a more accurate portrait of young people. The studies show a generation of young people growing up; struggling with issues and identity; solving problems; and, for the most part, coping rather well with the stresses they face.

This balanced view of adolescence leads to important questions for camping with teenagers—questions to ponder while sitting around staff campfires. I ask the following questions as conversation starters to prompt youth workers and church leaders to consider the most appropriate ways they can use the camping experience to meet teenagers' needs. None of the questions has a definitive answer, but each will help you explore possibilities for you and the young people you serve.

• **Can we free ourselves from previous youth stereotypes?** In a study reported in *The Adolescent: A Psychological Self-Portrait*, researchers argued that a major problem for parents and professionals who work with young people is conceptualizing the self-image of a normal, mentally healthy young person. When mental health professionals were surveyed, researchers discovered that these experts saw normal adolescents as significantly more disturbed than normal teenagers saw themselves. The researchers wrote, "The professionals even saw the normal adolescent as having more problems than were reported by samples of either psychiatrically disturbed or delinquent adolescents."[6]

As church youth workers, we're undoubtedly caught in the same stereotyping snare that traps many parents and professionals who work with teenagers. To identify and clarify our personal assumptions about teenagers could minimize the unconscious barriers we bring to camp.

• **Can we utilize and build on young people's strengths?** By understanding that teenagers—particularly those who attend church camps—are generally healthy, value-oriented young people, we're reminded that our ministries are not *to* campers but *with* campers. Teenagers do have stresses, but they also have strengths—strengths that can be tapped for the good of other campers as well as counselors.

This understanding can reshape our camp leadership style and priorities. We begin to see camp not only as an opportunity for counselors to help kids but as a shared ministry experience in which campers help campers and campers help counselors. Young people become planners and leaders for their peers.

Nowhere is this emphasis on shared ministry more dramatic than in the grow-ing number of workcamps in which young people spend camp time serving less fortunate people.

• **Can we identify and explore significant life issues with campers?** Search Institute's study demonstrated that teenagers' worries and concerns shift drastically from grade to grade, from community to community and from denomination to denomination. In one congregation I used a portion of the same survey with 60 teenagers and 50 of their parents. I found that several of their values were significantly different from the composite national study as well as denominational samples.

These differences remind camp leaders that teenagers aren't alike. Your young people may or may not reflect the concerns of national samples. The challenge is to discover and address the needs of the unique young people who participate in camp.

• **Can we recognize new expressions of the faith when they surface in teenagers and ourselves?** In *All Grown Up & No Place to Go*, David Elkind talks about the intellectual development that occurs during adolescence—a development that's often overlooked. He describes it as "thinking in a new key."[7]

As I thought about Elkind's emphasis, I suddenly made the connection between this new thinking ability and teenagers' faith. That connection led me to ask myself what's become the most important question I've dealt with in youth ministry: If young people think in a new key, do they also pray in a new key? If so, how are those prayers different from childhood prayers? How are they prayed?

As I listened to interviews I conducted with teenagers for the Search Institute study, I realized that some questions I asked over and over elicited responses that were like prayers. Young people openly expressed themselves to me, an adult, and to other teenagers on a wide variety of topics. Their ability to share and support others emotionally was incredible.

Maybe a mark of new-key prayer is to engage in honest, open conversation with God about how life is and how we want to change it. It's not so much asking for things as clarifying where we are and listening to God's direction for change. Those interviews helped me see that prayers form in us constantly, and sometimes we pray them best in intimate conversation.

Many faith expressions go unnoticed at camp and elsewhere—even by the religiously trained. How can we as camp leaders listen for these prayers in a new key? Can we learn to accept and affirm these prayers so that young campers with new thinking abilities can make the Christian faith their own?

Discussion and Action
Questions for Leaders and Campers

Use the following questions to guide you as you apply this chapter to your situation and camping experiences. If you're alone, write your thoughts in a journal. If you're in a group or leading a group, invite others to share their responses in small groups of three or four. Then open a discussion for everyone.

1. What do you think of when you picture "church camping"? Is there a single image? Or do many different settings and activities come to mind?

2. From your church camp experiences, which of the following memories do you have? Tell the group about them. Camp is a:

● Place of corporate rebirth for the camping group.
　● Reconciliation experience.
　● Faith-sharing place.
　● Place of forgiveness and healing.

● Place of challenge and new direction.

3. How can or does camping contribute to your youth group?

4. How have the places you've camped changed?

5. How have program themes and activities changed over the time you've been camping?

6. What hasn't changed about camping that should continue to be treasured?

7. What aspects of camping do you wish you could change?

8. Reread the questions and challenges for church camps in the "Rethinking Youth Ministry Camping" section (page 22). What's your response to the author's perceptions? What questions would you add to the list? How has your youth camping program responded effectively to these questions? How could it respond more effectively?

Activities for Leaders and Campers

Understanding the "kid next door." Distribute a photocopy of "The Kid Next Door" handout (Camp Notebook 1) to each camp leader. Have the leaders list current TV shows and movies that include teenage characters. Ask them to think of words and phrases that describe the strengths young people have and the stresses they experience. Have them list each one as portrayed in the media in the appropriate column. Then have the leaders list your church youth group members and describe them using the same process used for the TV characters. (You don't need to share these thoughts openly unless it can be redemptive for ministry.)

When leaders finish their charts, have them compare the image they have of TV characters and youth group members. What are the similarities? differences? What do the differences say about our image of

Camp Notebook 1

The Kid Next Door

List several current teenage TV and movie characters: _____
_____
_____
_____

Major Strengths   **Major Stresses**

List several youth group members you know well: _____
_____
_____
_____

Major Strengths   **Major Stresses**

young people?

Surveying. Have counselors and other camp staffers complete the youth values or worries section of the survey in *Determining Needs in Your Youth Ministry*[8] as they think young people would. Compare the leaders' results with the results of a survey of campers, the results of a survey of your youth group members, or the results in *The Quicksilver Years: The Hopes and Fears of Early Adolescence*. Discuss the implications of the leaders' perceptions and the teenagers' responses for camping ministry.

Use the same survey questions in a small group of campers. Have the groups take the survey and then discuss their priorities together. Then tally the results from all the groups, and lead a discussion based on the results.

Thinking out loud. Invite camp leaders to write 10 assumptions or truths they hold about youth campers. Ask each person to share his or her thoughts, and discuss the similarities and differences of the assumptions. If you're a camp director, include the kitchen and maintenance staff.

Invite campers to write three to five things they feel are most important to teenagers. Have the young people share and discuss their thoughts. Remind campers that they're expressing and hearing personal viewpoints that vary widely. Encourage them to discuss and test one another's perceptions sensitively.

Building an agenda. Ask leaders to create a list of "baggage free" interview questions for conversation starters with campers. For example: "What makes a good conversation with your friends or parents?" "If you could change one thing,

Use a similar rethinking process to help develop questions around the camp theme. what would it be?" "What are the most important decisions you've made up to now?" "What's important to you now that won't be important to you five years from now?"

In twos or threes, have campers compile lists of what they'd like to talk about at camp. List their ideas on newsprint. Categorize the topics into short-term questions, lifelong subjects, religious topics and topics for prayer. Invite campers to pair up and choose one of the topics they'd be willing to discuss together.

Notes

[1]Mihaly Csikszentmihalyi and Reed Larson, *Being Adolescent: Conflict and Growth in the Teenage Years* (New York, NY: Basic Books, 1984), p. 145.

[2]Martin E. Marty, *Forming the Future— Church Camping in the '80s*, keynote address at an American Camping Association symposium for church camping leaders, (Elizabethtown, KY, 1979).

[3]"The Loneliest People: High School Girls," Campus Life Leaders Guide (March 1987) p. 10.

[4]For a detailed history of organized camping (including church camping), see Eleanor Eell, *A History of Organized Camping: The First 100 Years* (Martinsville, IN: American Camping Association, 1986).

[5]Peter Benson, Arthur Johnson and Dorothy Williams, *The Quicksilver Years: The Hopes and Fears of Early Adolescence* (San Francisco, CA: Harper & Row, 1987).

[6]Daniel Offer, Eric Ostrov and Kenneth Irwin Howard, *The Adolescent: A Psychological Self-Portrait* (New York, NY: Basic Books, 1981), p. 126.

[7]David Elkind, *All Grown Up & No Place to Go: Teenagers in Crisis* (Reading, MA: Addison-Wesley, 1984), Chapter 2.

[8]Peter L. Benson and Dorothy L. Williams, *Determining Needs in Your Youth Ministry* (Loveland, CO: Group Books, 1987).

Chapter 2

Planning a "Boundaryless" Youth Camp

Last spring our youth group took its first camping trip. There were seven people altogether—mostly eighth- and ninth-graders. We left after the worship service on Palm Sunday and drove all afternoon. We had three group goals as we traveled—each to be completed between two towns about 20 to 30 miles apart. First we divided ourselves into three leadership teams—without voting. Actually it was simple. The group listed all the boys for one team and divided the group of girls into two teams. We made sure each team included one person who could cook.

Then each team had to plan meals and make shopping lists. Each team came up with its own ideas, and each team was responsible for determining what was needed to prepare the meals.

Finally, we developed a theme for the four days using books, worship resources and our own ideas. We boiled down five or six ideas to one theme: "A Time to Reflect."

Supper was Dutch treat in a small, one-stoplight town followed by a night's rest at Adventures Unlimited, a camp on the banks of the Coldwater River. The next morning

we canoed, waded, swam and picnicked along the wild, sandy-bottom river. Then we headed on, taking time for a long shopping stop at a Piggly Wiggly. An hour later we parked the van and U-Haul at a camp overlooking the Atlantic Ocean and headed for the beach. Real sand and cold, salty surf. Before the sun went down the tents went up.

For the rest of the week teams took turns cooking breakfast and dinner and leading morning and evening reflection times. (We used "reflection" whenever possible.) Right after breakfast we decided what to do and where to go that day. We played on the beach and toured a historic fort and the Naval Aviation Museum. We walked nature trails, explored dunes and shorelines, and froze in the surf. One night we went to a movie. We ate lunch at fast-food stands as we toured and explored.

The last night we played Capture the Flag in the dark on the beach. Our closing campfire was a candlelight celebration on the eve of Maundy Thursday. We read about the woman who anointed Jesus, and we talked about extravagant love. Most of us were reminded of our parents.

That camp wasn't a typical youth camp. Our youth minister called it a hodge-podge camp since we did a little of everything. But despite being somewhat unorthodox, that spring camp was like a family vacation for me. We ate all our meals together, and we helped one another learn to cook, set up tents and keep coons out of our food box.

And, like family vacations, we had funny stories to take home. The funniest story was about Elizabeth trying to paddle in the stern of the canoe. She had never canoed before and it really showed!

Another youth group sponsored a "Do-Nothin' Camp." At first group members objected because the camp conflicted with a Friday night ball game. But the leader wasn't fazed. "No problem," he said. "It's a do-nothin' camp anyway, so we'll leave after the ball game."

The planning method reflected the theme. The group did nothing until everyone decided as a group to do something. The purpose was tied to a single rule: Anything's possible; everything's negotiable. Each morning the campers negotiated what to do that day using consensus decision-making.

One whole day was spent in a water balloon battle. The event wasn't planned; it grew out of a reprimand from the previous night when a camper threw a water balloon in the cabin. The next morning the incident was the topic at the "negotiating table." "I thought anything was possible," the camper said. The youth leader replied: "Yes, but not when it's inappropriate. Water balloons can only be part of a negotiated event."

That explanation was the key to the daylong event. The campers asked the camp manager for permission—which was granted on the condition that the group would clean up every balloon scrap. Then the 12 teenagers and the adult leaders spent two hours driving to three small towns to buy every balloon available—more than 300. After lunch, team selection and an elaborate rules-making session, the balloon battle was underway.

The rest of the week was fairly normal—negotiated sharing times, recreation, field trips, pack-out lunches, a field game taught by the camp manager and a group-led communion celebration.

The camp's group journal documented an honesty and openness the group had never before experienced. Participants shared about their families and growing spiritually. After the camp two teenagers were baptized and began confirmation classes. A third young person transferred her membership to be in church with her do-nothin' friends.

How did this group grow so much in such an unusual setting? Perhaps anything really is possible when "anything's possible and everything's negotiable." The adult leaders attribute the growth to the decision-making process that all group members were involved in.

Beyond Previous Barriers

These two youth camps—like many youth camps—defy traditional camping labels and stereotypes. Youth camps can encompass all outdoor experience styles. "Boundaryless camping" more accurately describes the many possibilities for youth group camping.

Many boundaries of previous years have been pushed back by more integrated camping styles and changes in our society. Camp activities are no longer limited to opportunities at a particular campsite. The list of options mushrooms when groups develop a boundaryless viewpoint toward ministry beyond church buildings and camp properties.

Moreover, long distance travel by youth groups has become a common summer venture, so distance to camp is no longer a barrier. Finally, camp leaders may be recruited from other states or even other countries for special camp programs, thus adding expertise—and thus new opportunities—to a camp program.

What identifies a boundaryless camp is not place, method or style, but purpose. Many camping events integrate elements of retreats, backcountry camping, institutes, classroom learning and vacation tours. Youth workers' and camp planners' challenge is to choose from various possibilities to design an appropriate event for everyone involved.

Boundaryless camping is flexible and open. It defines its purpose based on the group's life and needs, and it refines that purpose through the dynamic group experience.

Sometimes the same activities have different goals and emphases, depending on the group's goals. A Georgia church took its senior high and college kids to New Brunswick and Maine for a canoeing and mountain-climbing adventure. The return route included a two-night stay at a Toronto church. While at the church, the group received an unexpected invitation to help the congregation's youth group with its work-service project.

A youth group from Illinois went to West Virginia for a weeklong workcamp to repair an elderly couple's home in Appalachia. On the way back to Illinois, the group went rafting and camping on the Gauley River.

Both the Georgia and Illinois groups experienced wild, white water adventure; outdoor and indoor camping; and service through hard work. But each achieved its own unique purpose through a different approach. The first group wanted to grow

in Christian faith through outdoor adventure and learning outdoor living skills. The work-service project was a happy discovery—something to celebrate. The second group sought Christian growth through loving service and outreach. Rafting and camping weren't designed for skills training but for celebration and debriefing.

The camps I've just described share the purposes of boundaryless youth camping: discovery and growth. These elements are integral to Christian camping's purposes, themes and goals.

Discovery. The camping experience is by definition experimental. It generates a spirit of self-discovery, pushing back boundaries and stimulating growth. For campers the event is a new experience in a new place among friends. Campers discover more about themselves, their gifts, their friends, their faith and their God.

Growth. Moments of discovery are magnified by campers' lack of experience and their inclination to want to know and do for themselves—even if they need a friend to do it with them. The central question at camp is not, "How are they doing?" but "How are they growing?" Campers who make the most mistakes may also grow the most.

Use Camp Notebook 2, "For Reflection and Discussion," to think about the priorities of discovery and growth with other camp leaders.

The Planning Process

How do youth workers plan camps that foster self-discovery and growth? No single planning formula adequately meets every need in every situation. Different groups are different sizes. Different teenagers have different needs. Different communities have different resources. Community-life dynamics vary from church to church and from year to year. As

Camp Notebook 2

For Reflection and Discussion

Read the following story and think about the importance of discovery and growth in the camping process. What other responses could there be for this situation? Write your ideas, and discuss the hoped-for outcome of each response with other camp leaders.

A longtime canoe instructor once said: "I've been on 52 canoe trips, and never has anyone played a radio— ever! That's my rule!" He said this to two campers who were listening to top-10 cassette tapes in their tent. Other campers who were spending free time by the campfire and in other tents couldn't hear the music.

Earlier that day all the campers had a two-hour debate on Christian rock music versus popular rock music. The wilderness rockers actually were continuing that debate. The campers had the cassette recorder to conduct interviews, and to record camp songs and nature sounds.

a result, each camp requires creative and resourceful planning. Providing appropriate experiences that are grounded in an overarching purpose of personal and corporate growth is simultaneously a calling, a task and a ministry.

All leaders undoubtedly have an ideal planning process in mind as they prepare for a new event. But, in truth, every event is different, and each begins at a different point. Many factors influence where the planning begins. A new facility is discovered. A new person joins the church staff and takes initiative. A youth group needs a unifying experience away from the church. Last year's camp evaluation contains suggestions for "next year's theme and activities." These and other factors provide camp planners with different springboards from which to dive into the planning process.

Because of the unique dynamics of each camp and each group of campers, it's important to begin the camp planning process by scheduling an unhurried time for camp leaders to sort the group's needs, interests and wishes. The planning group

needs to dream for the group and create a vision of life together at camp.

One way to identify starting points for planning is to visualize the resourcing and designing process as two ends of a constantly moving Slinky (see Diagram 1). Each part of the Slinky is connected to the others, and choices about one element affect all others.

To understand how the planning process fits together, let's stop the Slinky and carefully consider each wiggly part. The rest of this chapter will examine each of the following planning elements:

Purpose/theme. The dreams and vision, discovery and growth that motivate planning.

People resources. Everyone who influences and is influenced by camp programs—campers, parents, congregations, counselors, staff, neighbors and camp friends.

Place resources. The camp's immediate living environment.

Public resources. The environment beyond the campsite with cultural, historical, recreational, educational and human

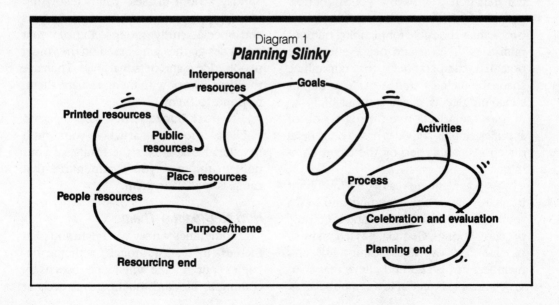

Diagram 1
Planning Slinky

Interpersonal resources

Goals

Printed resources

Public resources

Activities

Place resources

People resources

Process

Purpose/theme

Celebration and evaluation

Planning end

Resourcing end

resources.

Printed resources. Books, scriptures, curricula, videotapes, films, cassette tapes, posters, journals and training resources.

Interpersonal resources. The emerging interpersonal group curricula—group experience, ideas, memories, skills and insights.

Goals. Plans that say what the group hopes to accomplish during camp.

Activities. What campers and staff do together to promote discovery and growth.

Process. The arrangement and sequence of activities and group living experiences that constitute the camp journey plan.

Celebration and evaluation. How campers say "yes" to the journey plan; naming and affirming personal and community discovery and growth.

Creating the Camp Theme
Who Plans a Theme?

The nature of each camping event usually determines when and how the theme is created and who develops it. Your congregation may have a youth council, outdoor ministry committee or family ministry team responsible for planning outdoor ministries. Interest and needs surveys of potential campers help the committee shape the theme. Often a smaller group or subcommittee is given responsibility to nurture the selection and progression of specific camping activities based on general directions established by the larger committee.

As you plan your camp, it's important to share leadership, planning and—as a result—ownership. Youth worker Jeff Ross of Sandy Springs, Georgia, has led many of his church's "Love Week" camps. Ross and members of his church believe that sharing ownership is crucial to a camp's success.

They make the following recommendations for youth leaders who want to have church camps:

Make camp the church's idea, not the youth director's. Parents and teenagers must share in ideas and planning. Talk with teenagers about the idea. Then go through the official structures to help camp become a churchwide, church-owned idea.

Use a layperson as camp director. A camp shouldn't depend on the paid youth worker. Lay leadership should claim youth camping goals as it represents the congregation's youth ministry. Such an approach avoids setbacks when a particular youth leader leaves the church.

Let young people set up and run your camp. Pride and team spirit grow when youth are given the chance to be leaders. Otherwise you spend energy trying to sell teenagers on adult-led programs. For your camp leadership, use members of your existing youth leadership structure and add other young people with special interests in the camping event.

Ask all young people to complete a camp interest sheet. Gather data from Sunday school classes, youth fellowship meetings, youth choir, church sports teams and special study groups. Explain that you'll design the camp based on the young people's ideas and personal goals. Then use the ideas—work with them, reshape them, respond to them.

Report back. A first step in camp publicity is to run an article in your youth newsletter that shows the results of your poll. In this way you communicate that camp is made for them.

How to Dream a Theme

Sometimes we say we dream and plan themes. In reality, though, a theme becomes "our" theme when it chooses us by coming to life and touching our deepest yearnings. The secret to having the theme choose the staff and campers is to foster openness throughout planning, preparation, staff training and camper involvement. Daily opportunities for counselors and campers to work together to create a morning watch, evening recreation, campfire program or camp celebration keep the theme growing and coming true in leaders and campers.

Themes usually grow out of a group's need or purpose. They symbolize unrealized hopes, destination and promise for campers. Leaders discover these issues in many ways: through surveys, interviews, brainstorming sessions, informal conversations, and previous camp and event evaluations. Whatever method is used, gather information early and include teenagers in the planning process.

The camp theme visualizes in three or four words the "why" of the camp. By choosing a theme carefully to fit campers' and counselors' needs and interests, an important step is taken toward helping the theme choose the campers.

Having a strong theme is an important element in your camp's success. Here are some of the purposes themes serve:

● They tell campers what to expect during camp, thus helping campers prepare for fun, growth and learning.
● They speak to campers' imaginations.
● They keep speakers, Bible study leaders and discussion group leaders on track.
● They keep planning and publicity on track and consistent.
● They enhance group ownership.
● They unify the different activities.
● They make each camp unique, giving young people something to anticipate—even if the schedule is identical to previous years'.

Many subtle elements contribute to a theme's strength. Strong camp themes are action-oriented and open-ended. They are symbolic, giving leaders flexibility to take a theme several directions.

An example is a Lenten theme developed by a group of junior highers: "Building a New Trust—Shedding Doubt." "Building" and "shedding" are action words: How do you build? How do you shed? "Trust" and "doubt" are faith words—common words that communicate everyday experiences. "New" is a word of hope and possibility.

This theme is also open-ended. It doesn't confine the camp to dealing with a set doctrine or truth (though many elements of doctrine and truth influence and grow out of the theme). Finally, the theme is broad enough to be explored through involving activities—trust games, case studies, role plays, Bible exploration, and listening to hymns and contemporary music for accounts of people who doubt and trust.

Activities for Developing a Theme

There are many useful processes for developing camp themes. Here are two activities to help groups start dreaming and visioning:

Theme dreaming. This planning exercise uses a "theme board" to help the planning group brainstorm themes and then decide a camp theme.

1. Before the planning meeting, design a theme board similar to Diagram 2 out of posterboard, newsprint or cardboard. Place it on a table or the floor with the planning group seated comfortably around it.

2. Before talking about themes as a group, distribute several small slips of paper and a pencil to each person. Ask group members to write as many ideas as they think of based on the theme board sub-

---

Diagram 2
Theme Board

Purpose   PLACE   Album/song titles

Most important   book-titles   MOVIE TITLES
world issue

SEASON   CHRISTIAN SEASON   Group's main
concern

Scriptures you can visualize   Main activity
of the event

---

jects. Participants might write: "Our group's main concern is to get dropout members active again" or "The main activity I want at camp is a good concert on Saturday night."

Request 10 minutes of silence while people write. Suggest that group members each write one idea on each subject before adding a second or third idea on the same topic. As they complete each slip, have them turn it face down on the theme board beside the appropriate subject.

3. Turn all the slips face up. Read them aloud, or ask group members to look through the slips to inspire them for a new theme. Have them list possible themes on sheets of paper. Then post a sheet of newsprint that says:

Strong themes contain:
Action words
Visual words
Promising words
Biblical words
Faith words
Value words
Concept words

Ask group members to evaluate their ideas based on these guidelines. Allow ten minutes for writing.

4. Ask participants to suggest possible themes. Record their ideas on newsprint, and see which ideas are similar. Invite the group to combine and sharpen suggested themes and spontaneously add new ones. Follow this process until the group seems "chosen by"—comfortable with—one theme.

If the group reaches an impasse, take a break, work on another camp aspect, play a game or have a snack. Then return to the theme-dreaming exercise to find the appropriate vision for your camp.

Themes begetting themes. Another approach to dreaming themes is to develop themes through word association. This activity uses a list of possible camp themes plus your own previously used themes to guide the planning process:

1. Write the following themes (plus any you've used) on newsprint or posterboard, but don't post the list until you've given directions to the group.

Camp Themes

Becoming God's family
Shedding doubt, building trust
Building bridges to the future
Celebrating our differences
Free to be you and me
Friends are friends forever
Getting to the heart of things
Jesus, a friend forever
Life is a mountain, and you can climb it
Life's rich pageant
Becoming the friend you'd like to have
Run with the wind
Seasons in the Son
Singing the Lord's song
Touch a new horizon
We all have destinations
We are the church

2. Distribute a 3×5 card to each participant. Explain that you'll display a list of camp themes for only 30 seconds. Then group members will have time to write the theme or themes they liked most. Show them the list, then give them time to write their preferences.

3. Ask participants to share the themes they chose. List their ideas on newsprint. See if their preferences cluster around certain themes. Then ask the group to brainstorm ways to improve or reshape the themes.

4. Now ask the group to think of new themes. List the ideas on newsprint. Encourage participants to let their imaginations run free, but set a time limit on the brainstorming.

5. When the brainstorming list is complete, ask each person to choose two themes that seem to "choose" him or her. Before the participants share their preferences with the group, have them write, "This theme seems to choose me because . . ." Then have them discuss their ideas.

Help the group come to a consensus on a camp theme by discussing each person's reasons and how those reasons meet the group's needs. While it might be quicker and easier to vote on a theme, waiting for a consensus provides a sense of group ownership.

Discovering Resources

Resources are vehicles for themes. They supply possibilities for bringing themes to life. Sometimes you know about or discover resources before you decide the theme. But once the theme is established, list all possible resources before you continue to plan. Here are the five major resource categories to consider:

● People resources: everyone involved in camp.

● Place resources: the immediate campsite.

● Public resources: the larger environment and human resources.

● Printed resources: tangible program tools.

● Interpersonal resources: existing and hoped-for group experiences.

People Resources

When some people hear "resources," they think of curricula. As a result, people resources—which are often the most available and most dynamic—are also the most often overlooked. By beginning our resource list with people resources, we reconceptualize resource possibilities and open new, creative planning possibilities.

The ages and experiences of campers and leaders significantly impact camp theme and program planning. By knowing and using participants' skills and interests, camp planners can enrich the camp experience for all campers.

One Colorado camp uses every counselor as a specialist—an idea that's easily adaptable for any camp length, type or size. On alternate afternoons, half the counselors lead elective interest groups based on their personal skills and interests. Activities include water sports, drama, movie-making, cooking, crafts, music and outdoor living skills.

As a result of this program, the camp offers more than 30 electives during each camp. The counselors benefit by being elevated to program specialists, and on alternate afternoons counselors have time to prepare for their own interest group.

In many camps—particularly residential camps—a special speaker or resource person may be one of the central programming resources. What characteristics should you look for in choosing a special speaker for a youth camp? Here are issues to explore with a potential speaker or resource person:

The speaker's personal faith journey. Teenagers don't want factual reports from camp speakers. They want to know the speaker as a person. Effective camp speakers are, most of all, articulate storytellers. They tell their story and God's place in their story. As high school student Nancy Wareham of Sandy Springs, Georgia, explains: "You don't want speakers just to go up there and read stuff from the Bible. You want them to give their witness. It's good when they give their stories and tell about their lives." When hearing those stories, young people identify with different parts and say: "That's me! She's talking about me!"

The speaker's willingness to be "with" young people. "Speakers earn the right to speak to kids, and they have to do that early in the week. The people who do that are the most effective speakers, because they earn the respect," Jeff Ross explains. "The kids look up to them, they enjoy them and want to hear what they've got to say."

In selecting a speaker, Ross urges leaders to find out whether the person will spend the week with the campers or use every free opportunity to go to town, head home or do something for themselves. Good camp speakers give themselves to the kids for the week. When this occurs kids will listen—even if the speakers can't preach.

Camp is a wonderful opportunity for teenagers to have significant face-to-face experiences with their pastor or another clergy member. Myths about pastors evaporate quickly, and young people build a new relationship with their pastor.

Dave Ballew, a young adult, enjoyed having his pastor at camp. "I always thought it was neat," he said, "because your opinion of a preacher is what you see on Sunday most of the time. They're wearing a suit and tie or their robes in the pulpit. They're talking a lot to you but also to a lot of adults. But out here they're wearing shorts and rolling in the dirt with you. They're relating on your level specifically. And that's always what we're looking for—somebody who can relate well with our age group and who understands what we're going through."

Compatible ministry goals. Are the speaker's goals and your youth program's ministry goals compatible and consistent? If not, your camp experience will be frustrating and unrewarding—both for you and the speaker.

The speaker's sense of image and role. Does the leader perceive himself or herself at camp as the person with all the answers? as a fellow learner and explorer with campers? as an active participant? as a distant observer and "expert"? These perceptions will impact the camp's tone and emphasis and must be dealt with before asking someone to speak at your camp.

The speaker's questions about camp. Once you've chosen a speaker, he or she has a tremendous responsibility in leading campers and counselors for an intense week. Even familiar pastors who are good camp speakers can feel overwhelmed. If possible, have the planning committee meet the speaker. Talk about the theme and expectations for the camp. Make sure the speaker knows your expectations and his or her responsibilities.

Thinking of people resources first also reminds leaders to consider program support from unusual—often untapped—sources. Camp and conference center staff are often skilled and available for specific programs. By visiting a campsite for advance planning, one church discovered that the camp cook and her husband were musicians. So the church scheduled an evening fireside concert that gave a new dimension to the family feeling at camp.

While camping on an island wildlife refuge, another youth group got to know the soon-to-retire caretaker, who had been born on a nearby island and still spoke an African dialect. He soon became a family friend to the campers. After the caretaker retired, the assistant pastor would contact him each year before camp. The lean island man would paddle across the tidewater creek and walk two miles to the campsite one morning of each six-day camp. He would recount the history of the island and his ancestors, and tell his faith journey from childhood.

You'll discover a wealth of people resources by "asking around" and creatively scheduling so that outside resource people don't have to make major time commitments to the camp. An open invitation for an hour or an afternoon, a morning or three short afternoons allows nearby pastors, educators, artists, musicians, professors, or forest service and natural resources personnel to add a new dimension to the camp theme.

Place Resources

As obvious as place resources may seem, they're often overlooked—especially if an advance campsite visit is only a hurried take-care-of-business trip. Each camp setting offers unique resources waiting to be tapped. By taking time to find the camp setting's hidden and unexplored places, planners discover readily available resources to enhance the camp's mood and theme.

The watchword is to move out, take time and let the theme help you choose the right places for specific camp experiences. A chapel in the woods, a particular cabin, a campfire, a playing field and an endless list of other elements of a camp can be wonderful settings for meaningful camp activities.

One group, for example, has a "Cross Service" the last night of its annual summer camp. Group members consider selecting the perfect place for the cross and the worship service the most important decision they make at a new campsite.

The emphasis on place resources also applies to trail camps. Arriving early enough to set up camp and look leisurely at possibilities helps planners discover a special place for worship or teaching that would otherwise be lost to the group.

Public Resources

The larger environment and surrounding community of any camp are also resources for your youth camp. These resources include nearby forests, waters, deserts, mountains or marshes—whatever's there. You also may have access to historical places, human institutions, agencies, businesses and factories, and each is a resource.

One camp never offered pottery-making classes until a new pastor leading his first conference camp asked, "What do people do around here that might interest the kids?" The discovery of a nearby large stoneware factory and the possibility of pottery-making at camp helped create the summer theme and pointed to previously untapped scriptures.

Another church always thought of horseback riding as an activity only for private camps. Then the church's education director realized church members owned a local saddle-manufacturing company. It was one of the few shops that still made saddles by hand. The family was delighted when asked to sponsor leather craft workshops for the church summer camp. And, at the family's suggestion, horse care and riding lessons were added to the camp activities as bonuses since the family owned horses.

Printed Resources

Printed resources—scriptures, music, drama, visuals and staff training resources—help hold the activities and theme together. Selecting the right printed resources to keep the camp theme growing is a great challenge for any camp leader.

Finding appropriate printed resources involves exploring religious and secular bookstores, catalogs, libraries and any place camping books are sold. Community colleges, state department of education film libraries, department of natural resources film libraries and the American Red Cross have many audio-visual resources both for training and camp programs. (The annotated list of resources on page 343 contains information on useful resources.)

One guest leader for an interdenominational camp training event in Missouri asked the leaders-in-training if they'd seen the state-produced film *More Than Trees*. No one had. A short drive to the Department of Conservation found the film and had it in hand before evening. That

night the group viewed a beautiful and uplifting tax-produced resource. But the local camp leaders discovered it only through an out-of-state guest who happened to notice the film's credits when he saw it at an ecology conference 800 miles away.

Sometimes printed resources don't fit traditional categories. One backpacking group used the theme "Being and Becoming." One resource for the theme was a "Being Bag"—a small, handmade burlap bag with a drawstring top for each camper. Inside each bag was a journal called the "Being Book," a pencil, one watercolor block, a short-handled artist brush, a magnifying glass and a different passage from 1 John.

The journal was made of 5×8 colored construction paper sheets interlaid with sheets of watercolor paper. Each colored page had a brief scripture or quotation based on what the group would see or encounter that day. The journal cover was designed from recycled outdoor magazine and catalog covers that were stapled and bound with binding tape used in libraries.

The Being and Becoming group members used the Being Bag twice each day to focus on the theme and their reflections on eight days of backpacking. In the mornings two group members led a "Being Time," and two other campers led an evening "Becoming Time." Leaders rotated each day and built on the previous leaders' work.

By midweek the group spoke of Being Time and Becoming Time as easily as breakfast and dinner. Soon campers were checking with one another to make sure they wouldn't duplicate activities. Options were developed, and group ownership deepened as young people traded ideas.

Interpersonal Resources

Interpersonal resources emerge and develop each day of camp. They are the living resources of the group—the curricula that's born each day as the product of living and learning together. Maximizing group life as a resource assumes a daily time for campers and counselors to identify and reflect upon their own growth, feelings, perceptions and insights.

It's easy to spot the physical skills campers acquire in a short time. Some campers' adeptness to assist others and pass on their skills may take time for leaders to recognize, but camper-to-camper interaction is a constant possibility for growth.

A group's growing awareness of each member's needs and contributions is a resource that comes only through coming to know one another through common experience. Remaining alert to feelings of isolation or attention-seeking is like reading an open book about the group. As camp leaders, you and other adult counselors are integral characters in this interpersonal curricula too.

Of course no one will say, "Here's the product of our experience in intentional Christian community." The interpersonal resource isn't easily named. But campers and counselors intuitively recognize the resource's presence.

I remember Janet. The first three days at camp she prefaced every statement with "Well, my friends . . ." One day at the table after she made a "my friends" statement, Kim put her arm around Janet and said, "You know, Janet, we're your friends too."

The growing product of group experience was present. No one named it, but everyone knew Kim had taken a risk to open a door for Janet. It was a turning point. From that incident until the end of camp, Janet was freer and not preoccupied with escaping from the group by talking about friends back home.

Designing the Program

The camp's purpose and theme are supported by the program. Think of the program as the camp's map or journey plan. Choosing a theme and exploring resources are like gathering the clues for a treasure map. Designing the program involves fitting together various clues to discover the route to the camp's hidden treasures.

The step-by-step plan for designing a camp program is found in the answers to four basic questions:

● Where are we going? (Goals)
● What will we do along the way? (Activities)
● How will we get there? (Process)
● How will we say "yes" to the journey? (Celebration and evaluation)

Goals

"Where are we going?" is a question about goals. Sometimes the camp theme clearly expresses the camp's overarching goal. But asking this question at every point in the program-designing process clarifies the theme and purpose. It reminds us to move in one direction.

The adage that "the highest mountain is climbed one step at a time" helps focus our attention on the small elements of a greater goal. But we must remember that the first step is to select a mountain to climb—to set a goal. Little steps in the right direction are possible only when we have a definite big destination.

The advantage of goal-setting with a theme in mind is the sense of progression of and interrelationship between different camp goals. Each day builds on the previous day's foundation. The test for goals—however big or small—is "Do they fit what comes before and after?"

A big goal for a camp week may be to create a deeper awareness of the gifts of

God's creation. A related one-day goal might be to develop appreciation for the gifts around us. A morning goal might focus on the gift of friendship, with the first hour focusing on helping campers get to know and appreciate one another.

Making each goal fit together with the larger camp purpose doesn't always occur through logical, step-by-step deduction and planning. Rather, it often occurs through thinking out loud, testing and making revisions until the small steps seem to be in concert with the large ones.

Activities

"What will we do along the way?" is an activities question—what to do to experience or accomplish goals. The question takes on deeper meaning when asked in the framework of specific goals. Moreover, choosing activities is easier once the goals convey the sense of progression, rhythm and flow, which gives activities a sense of "rightness" for a specific time and place.

Listing activities always results in an overabundance of ideas. Most must be set aside for another time and place. However, the value of putting many activity pieces on the planning table is that later, in sorting ideas, the right piece will suddenly show up—like the missing clue for the treasure map.

In addition to your planners' own creativity and experience, hundreds of resources are available with youth camp activity ideas. (See Section 4 for ideas specifically designed for church youth groups.) Many youth ministry ideas can be adapted to the camp setting, and ideas from any camp can be adapted for church camps.

Sometimes you'll discover activities in unexpected ways. The idea of a "Doo Dah Parade" jumped out of a magazine story as one camp director sat in a barbershop. It was the perfect activity for the closing camp celebration that year.

None of the ideas from past years seemed usable, and none of the "parade" ideas from the camp committee caught fire. Then suddenly there it was, hidden in a story of a little California town's annual Doo Dah Parade. Artists would paint big pictures and cut out holes just the size of a face. Instead of people walking around looking at paintings, the paintings would walk around looking at—and talking to—people!

In adapting this idea for camp, each camper was given a piece of white posterboard, scissors, markers and a face pattern to cut out a hole. Each person drew a poster-size portrait and cut out the face hole. When the right moment arrived in the closing celebration, campers gave their creations to secret friends as they paraded to music.

A brainstorming page in the camp leader's notebook is essential to developing appropriate activity ideas. When you sense that an idea or activity has potential or adaptability, jot it down along with an immediate hunch for how to use it. The list of tricks and gimmicks scribbled in margins often provides the magical seeds of an idea that will bear fruit at a camp many seasons later.

Process

"How will we get there?" This question involves arranging activities so they flow together in the best possible sequence to achieve your purpose. The camp journey must be carefully planned and revised in the hope that it will contribute to every participant's growth.

Process is concerned with variety and balance; with including everyone and giving individuals space; with creativity, continuity, unity, climate, feeling, color and spirit. It involves:

● The planned rhythm of physical activities and reflective times.

● The carefully designed contrast between easy, affirming activities and challenging activities.

● Keeping campers on the path toward the purpose without losing them along the way.

To illustrate sequence and flow, for example, let's think through some process questions about activities for younger teenagers:

● What is it about each activity that makes it fit with other camp activities?

● Is it a high-energy or low-energy activity?

● Does it involve concentration? competition? cooperation?

● Is it designed for the total group, subgroups or individuals?

Describing each activity makes it obvious when the activity will fit and when it won't. It isn't appropriate for campers to play high-energy running games right after dinner or right before worship for several reasons. However, those reasons don't diminish the value of the running games.

When do high-energy games work best? Do campers have to find their own space for quiet time in a busy schedule, or is it built in? When's the best time for crafts?

The greatest pitfall in designing the camp process is to plan sequentially by simultaneously developing process steps and activities. Even camps that follow the same basic schedule and activity pattern each year must fine-tune the process each year to develop an appropriate flow within and between activity blocks.

Each activity has a best place that creates a sense of balance in a particular camp's overall design. Finding that place involves working openly and diligently in the planning group.

No previous schedule can be adopted as ideal for all camps. New themes, goals and activities influence the flow and sequence of events at each camp. Sometimes a surprise event or activity that takes campers out of the ordinary is exactly what it takes to give a theme full impact. (For example, see "Breakfast in Bed," page 245.)

Celebration and Evaluation

"How will we say 'yes' to the journey?" Affirming life together as a gift and responsibility is the heart of celebration. Camp celebration incorporates evaluation, worship, devotion, reflection, trust, reconciliation and new commitments. Leaders who anticipate and plan for celebration give everyone a chance to say "yes" to the day's challenges and joys. Connecting the group's joy and accomplishment with God's joy and accomplishment is crucial to the group's self-discovery and growth.

Planned celebration. Planned celebration is an appropriate camp activity for a wide range of occasions: delighting in a new day; naming and claiming the day's events together; being supportive when a group member struggles to be faithful; or praying when the group grieves for a faraway family member. And celebration can involve seeking a word from scripture or sharing Holy Communion together.

Spontaneous celebration. Celebration also can occur spontaneously at camp in many ways. Campers may feel joy over accomplishments, relief after a crisis or struggle, or the impending separation at the end of camp. Each of these emotional times involves spontaneous celebration.

Even the most sensitive leaders sometimes miss the first clues for celebration only to awaken later to ask "Why didn't I realize . . ." Not noticing the need for spontaneous celebration or rushing campers to "stay on schedule" thwarts valuable celebration opportunities.

Think about a group that spends its last day at camp white-water rafting or rappelling on a vertical rock face. Putting out the campfire early so everyone can get a good night's rest for the long road home is out of the question. The celebration will occur regardless of or despite the leader's plans.

Celebration as evaluation. Evaluation is central to celebration, and every evaluation should cause celebration. Evaluation isn't labeling things, people and events as good or bad; it's individuals sharing their experiences of growth and learning at camp. Thus, completing a ranking sheet without conversation or reflection on the event is of little use to campers or leaders. But openly shared evaluations enable group members to grow together.

Role playing, using modeling clay or pipe cleaners, taping interviews to play for the group or making a collage to give away can help young people get involved in the evaluation-celebration process. The first four chapters in Part Two, "Camps in Action," include an evaluation process designed for sharing, celebrating and planning camp events.

Dealing With Details

Planning your theme and designing your program are the overarching tasks in planning your camp. To accomplish these tasks successfully, your camp planning committee must also deal with details, such as timetables, counselors and locations for specific programs. Diagram 3, "Sample Planning Timetable," suggests a format and planning schedule for the various responsibilities. Adapt the format to fit your planning needs.

Here are details you'll need to tend to in planning your camp:

Establish your camp budget. Determine how much money can be spent in each area of responsibility. Some areas can be revised as needs change and plans solidify.

Determine how many counselors you need. Base this decision on the expected number of campers, the type of camp and the age of campers. A good starting place is to have one counselor for every five young people.

Decide the composition of discussion or sharing groups. Will you divide the larger group by various ages? by boys and girls? randomly? with a different method? Will you keep the same groups throughout your camp or change them? Will you keep the same counselor with a group throughout the week?

Determine the role of the speaker or camp minister. If you're inviting a guest speaker or leader, what role will he or she have in the camp? Will he or she participate in discussion groups and learning activities? recreational events? a communion service? other activities?

Plan evening activities. If you're planning special evening activities (particularly for a residential camp), you need to arrange them. This could involve selecting and ordering a film; scheduling a live band or other "special" if your budget permits; choosing treats, such as popcorn, peanuts, soft drinks or watermelon; and determining areas for campfires.

Assign campers to cabins or tents. Will you assign young people to cabins or tents by age? grade? random matching? another method?

Choose music. Do you want the music to be structured with special music to learn? informal camp songs led by a guitar or piano player? a combination? What other options should you consider?

Decide a basic weeklong schedule. If you've had similar camps in previous years, review past schedules in light of

Diagram 3
Sample Planning Timetable

When to do	Task	Who's responsible	Date done
Eleven months before camp	Establish tentative budget.	Youth committee	
	Make camp reservations, specifying facility needs.	Youth minister	
Eight months before camp	Select camp director(s).	Youth minister	
	Select camp minister or speaker.	Pastor and youth minister	
Five months before camp	Arrange initial bus contract.	Camp director	
Four months before camp	Start planning committee.	Camp director	
Three months before camp	Determine camp theme.	Planning committee	
	Arrange final bus contract.	Camp director	
	Meet with camp minister or speaker.	Camp director and youth leader	
Two months before camp	Establish theme material and resources.	Planning committee	
	Begin poster promotion.	Planning committee	
One month before camp	Initial deadline for camp registration.	Planning committee	
	Make personal contact with potential campers who haven't registered.	Planning committee	
	Send letters to registered campers.	Church office	
One week before camp	Arrange final details (buy groceries, etc.).	Planning committee	
	Fine-tune recreation and evening activities.	Planning committee	
First Sunday after camp	Hold homecoming worship service.	Planning committee	
First week after camp	Write thank-you letters to speaker, leaders, camp staff and counselors.		

campers' evaluation forms. If you're staying at a cabin camp or retreat center, check with the camp manager about canteen or snack shop hours. Establish wake-up times and mealtimes for each day. Establish a basic framework for whatever activities you've planned. Make a working draft of the schedule.

Assign planning committee responsibilities. List all areas of responsibility for planning committee members. Leave blanks by each one, and find leaders and other volunteers for each area.

Clarify the director's responsibilities. Be sure church staff, parents and teenagers know that the camp director is "The Boss" at camp. Clarifying the director's role averts confusion and miscommunication.

Train counselors and leaders. Discuss responsibilities with counselors and leaders. Clarify their roles in keeping track of campers, supporting campers and participating in activities. Outline the purposes of the activities, including quiet time and free time. Focus on examples of sharing problems or issues appropriately with the director and staff.

The 3x5 Camp: A Planning Activity

Here's an activity to use as you plan a camping event. Divide your planning group into teams of two to four people. Give everyone a 3×5 card and pencil. Then say: "Imagine that everything we plan for this camp must fit on a 3×5 card. Each team must think of a theme and as many resources and activities as can be listed on one side of the card. You have only 15 minutes to plan the entire camp."

Give the teams time to brainstorm ideas. Use the results for actually planning your camp, as a springboard for outlining the planning process in more detail, or for both.

Chapter 3

Campsites, Support Services and Transportation

Choosing a campsite is a major decision for every type of youth group camp. While selecting a campsite is obviously a major task when planning a month-long, 4,000-mile journey, the task is no less important when choosing an overnight camp 50 miles from home. An appropriate and careful choice enhances the camp's mood, pace and purpose, but poor choices can compromise the most carefully planned camp program.

Before you select a campsite, you need to make several decisions that will influence your selection. Let's look at some of these decisions:

Camp goals. Your camp goals and purposes are the primary factors that influence your campsite choice. They determine what kind of camp you want (residential, canoe, backpacking) and the type of facilities you need (primitive, rustic, recreational).

Also think about the best place and type of camp for your group. Kids from a city church might want a remote, retreat-type campsite. Kids from an outlying area might want a camp near more activity and some off-site attractions.

Group size. The size of the camping group is an important consideration in choosing a campsite. A small group could feel overwhelmed at a large retreat center, while a large group might be cramped at a small one.

If you have a large group, remember that many national parks have regulations that protect the land by limiting the size of camping groups to 10 to 12 people. If you plan to use these public facilities, check the regulations and if necessary divide your group into smaller, separate camping groups for your time in the back country.

Once you know what you want in a camping facility, compare campsites to determine what's best for your group. There's no simple checklist that quickly ranks each camp from best to worst. Most camps have both advantages and disadvantages, depending on your group, your needs and your priorities. A denominational camp may be ideal for one group, while a private camp may be more appropriate for another. The challenge is to find just the right camp for your group for your particular purpose.

Shared or exclusive use. If you plan

a residential camp or another camp that requires special program resources, you must decide whether you want exclusive use of a facility or to share it with another group. Some camps require a substantial deposit for exclusive use, and other large facilities don't offer exclusive use.

Cost. How much can your group pay for its camping events? What type of camping is within your group's price range? Your choice will affect your budget and vice versa. If you want to cut costs, check national and state parks. If your budget is larger and you can subsidize campers' expenses, you could consider a resort, retreat center or the services of professional outdoor leaders.

Finding Nearby Camps

Many youth group camps take place within two to five hours of home. Groups sometimes repeatedly return to the same camp because "we've always gone to Camp Nearby." While the standard camp may have the exact facilities you need for your group, other camps may offer excellent options and opportunities—if you just knew about them. Here's how to discover nearby camps:

Talk with youth ministry colleagues. Regular questions among youth workers include: "Where did you go camping this year?" Or "How was your last retreat?" Fellow youth workers are usually pleased to tell you about their experiences—both good and bad—at nearby camps. Simply calling neighboring pastors and youth leaders from other denominations often leads you to a camp or retreat site you didn't know existed.

Denominationally owned camps—as well as many private camps—often lease their facilities to "outside" groups, particularly in the off-season. These facilities range from small, rustic operations to large, elaborate retreat and conference centers. Some camps have facilities to accommodate outside groups simultaneously with their own programs. Since many denominations publish directories of church-owned camps and retreat centers, colleagues from other denominations may be able to point you toward appropriate facilities for your group.

Contact the camp director-manager. Once you find a facility that merits further exploration, ask the camp manager to send brochures, group guidelines, maps, cabin diagrams, meeting space descriptions, food service information, sample menus, prices and information about program resources. Use the "Preliminary Facility Checklist" (Camp Notebook 3) to discover the basic information you need. Add other questions specifically related to your needs. These could include questions about special facilities (such as pottery-making), access for people with disabilities, or nearby attractions and natural wonders. Ask these questions in person, over the phone or through the mail.

Take an on-site tour. There's no substitute for actually seeing a camp and talking with its management. Visiting a camp helps you realistically evaluate its facilities and plan your program. You can adjust your expectations and needs as you visualize your group and program at a particular site. It also helps establish a healthy relationship between you and the camp management.

To ensure camper ownership, include teenagers in the on-site visit. Their presence not only adds insight into your evaluation, but helps you get a feeling for whether the camp director-manager likes young people. A camp director who gets to know kids and likes them will remember you and make it worth coming back to the camp. You can get similar impressions

Camp Notebook 3

Preliminary Facility Checklist

Name of camp: _____

Name of director-manager: _____

Address: _____

Phone: _____

General

How far is the camp from church?_____

What is the physical appearance of the camp?

    ☐ Excellent   ☐ Good   ☐ Okay   ☐ Poor

    Words that describe the physical appearance: _____

_____

What is the spirit or feel of the camp?

    ☐ Excellent   ☐ Good   ☐ Okay   ☐ Poor

    Words that describe the camp's spirit: _____

_____

What is the cost?

    Per person per day: _____

    For group:_____

    Does this cost include meals?   ☐ Yes   ☐ No

Is insurance available?   ☐ Yes   ☐ No

    Cost: _____

Lodging

How many people can the camp accommodate?

    Maximum: _____

    Minimum: _____

What are the sleeping conditions like (space, cleanliness)? _____

_____

What are the restrooms like (accessibility, cleanliness)? _____

_____

What do campers bring (sleeping bags, linens)?

    Other options: _____

Program Facilities

What indoor and outdoor program spaces are available? _____

_____

_____

How big are they? _____

_____

What rainy-day spaces are available? _____

_____

How big are they? _____

What recreational equipment is available? _____

_____

continued

Are indoor and outdoor campfire sites available?

Indoor   ☐ Yes   ☐ No

Outdoor   ☐ Yes   ☐ No

Does the camp provide program support for leasers?   ☐ Yes   ☐ No

What kind? _____

_____

_____

Cost: _____

Would our group have exclusive use of the camp?   ☐ Yes   ☐ No

If not, how are decisions made about when different groups have access to various program facilities? _____

_____

Food Services

Does the camp provide food service?   ☐ Yes   ☐ No

Can we do our own cooking?   ☐ Yes   ☐ No

What is the cost for food services?

Per day: _____   Per meal: _____

Per person: _____   Package cost: _____

Additional charges: _____

How are meals served?   ☐ Cafeteria style   ☐ Family style

Mealtimes:

Breakfast: _____

Lunch: _____

Dinner: _____

Are mealtimes negotiable?   ☐ Yes   ☐ No

Does the camp provide snacks?   ☐ Yes   ☐ No

Can we bring our own snacks?   ☐ Yes   ☐ No

Is there a camp snack store?   ☐ Yes   ☐ No

Do campers share in setup and cleanup?   ☐ Yes   ☐ No

Does the camp provide the following?

Cookouts   ☐ Yes   ☐ No

Pack-out meals for overnight camping   ☐ Yes   ☐ No

Pack-out lunches   ☐ Yes   ☐ No

Are meals nutritious? (Ask for sample menus.)   ☐ Yes   ☐ No

Other Information

Is the camp available when we need it?   ☐ Yes   ☐ No

Can we arrange an on-site visit?   ☐ Yes   ☐ No

Date: _____   Time: _____

Are there camp staff, local people or groups that might be program resources (musicians, folk game leaders, storytellers, craftspeople, artists, naturalists, recreation leaders, pastors, youth workers)?

Name	Specialty	How to Contact

by paying close attention to the wording of brochures and camp rules.

An on-site visit also has a surprise factor. Often the camp has more to offer than brochures or letters indicate. When two youth workers visited a wilderness school center, they discovered the center staff would lead low ropes and high ropes courses for a nominal fee. (Ropes courses are group and individual physical challenges involving platforms, boards, logs, cables, suspended beams and other apparatus.) Both churches decided to use the center—and the unique group-building experiences they wouldn't have known about otherwise.

It's important to visit a facility by appointment and if possible have a meal at the camp. Two church youth workers once toured a series of three camps with only brief conferences with each director-manager. Then the leaders went back to one camp with six teenage youth council members. However, the young people decided they'd rather stay in the open-air, rustic cabins than the lodge. Their youth director thought they'd opt for comfort—and they might have been stuck with the lodge if they hadn't visited the camp beforehand.

Another youth leader reserved a camp for two different events without ever visiting the camp. When he did visit, it was on the spur of the moment, in the winter, without the camp owner's knowledge or guidance. The impression he got of the camp (closed for the winter) was cold and negative. As a result of the unplanned visit, the group cancelled both camps.

An on-site visit also can alert you to potential problems. A church group planning to use one camp, for example, visited the camp and found limitations not mentioned in the brochure. The horseback riding program was routed along a public highway—putting campers at risk from oncoming traffic. And the camp had canoes on its small lake but didn't have life jackets. As a result, the group decided not to use the camp's horseback program and to have campers bring their own life jackets to make the canoeing program acceptably safe.

When you visit camps where you'll share the facilities with other groups, find out how decisions are made about using facilities such as pools, playing fields, kitchens or meeting areas. Ask about your options for using different facilities, and determine whether the arrangements fit your group's needs.

Most camp directors welcome on-site visits by potential users. Calling ahead to arrange a visit usually works best. Otherwise you may arrive on the manager's day off or when another camp is in session. If distances aren't too great, two or three campsites can be visited in a day with ample time to walk through the facilities and ask the director-manager questions.

If your planning committee visits the campsite, have each person (or pairs) fill out the "Preliminary Facility Checklist." This process focuses your discussion when people have differing perceptions. One person may be struck by the shiny tile pattern in a restroom, while another only notices spider webs in the same building's windows.

Reserve your camp location. Once you decide a particular camp is appropriate for your group, contact the manager immediately and pay the reservation deposit. Ask the manager to send a letter confirming your reservation and to include a copy of the camp's group guidelines.

Most groups should make camp reservations at least six months in advance. Nine-month reservations are preferable—particularly if you plan to use a good, popular campsite. Many groups have standing reservations every year at good camps, and it's difficult for new groups to make reservations if they wait too long.

Schedule an on-site planning session. If distance isn't a barrier, consider an on-site planning visit after you choose a facility. The planning committee or youth leadership team will get maximum use from a facility by going to the camp for preplanning. Many camp directors welcome such a visit—sometimes without charge—when the facility is available.

The central values of on-site planning are confidence in the facility and group ownership among everyone taking part in the camp program. The on-site visit should include touring the entire facility and visiting adjacent off-site program areas, such as overnight campout sites, beaches, parks, recreational facilities, and historical or cultural areas. If you share the facility with other groups, work out an understanding of when different groups will have access to various facilities. Groups planning rafting, skiing or other off-site adventures also will need to consult with managers of those facilities about program activities and group services.

Finding Long-Distance Campsites

When your camp is more than three or four hours away, most planning must be done long-distance. Thus youth groups setting out for a wilderness event, workcamp, choir tour or other long-distance trip must make all the arrangements by telephone or mail.

Despite more difficult logistics, many successful events take place without an advance visit of the destination or the campsites along the way. Here are tips for successfully locating and researching a route and destination for youth group trips:

Gather general information. If you plan a long-distance camping event in a general area (backpacking in the Colorado Rockies, or canoeing in the Florida panhandle or Minnesota's Boundary Waters), plan far in advance. If you plan a major trip, start at least a year in advance.

If you don't have specific locations in mind, contact state departments of tourism and local chambers of commerce for local information, brochures and suggested activities in the general area you want to visit. These resources not only help you plan your itinerary, they also add color and motivation to your planning sessions. Once our youth group took a trip to Isle Royale on Lake Superior. I bought $25 worth of small books on the island's geology, mining, wildlife and history. I also purchased 10 slides of the island. Interest among youth group members grew as we looked at the slides, plotted our itinerary on the map and talked about the area.

The following resources—which are available in most bookstores—are excellent guides for making preliminary plans:

● The annual Rand McNally Road Atlas. In addition to showing routes, parks and major landmarks, this resource lists the address and phone number of each state's department of tourism in the upper left-hand corner of each state map.

● The annual Rand McNally RV Park and Campground Directory. This resource points out specific campgrounds along routes and in specific areas.

● Mobil Travel Guide. Travel guides are available for the following areas of the United States: West; Great Lakes; Middle Atlantic; Northeast; Northwest and Great Plains; Southwest and South Central; and Southeast. In the introduction to each state, the address of the state's department of tourism is listed.

Each guide includes a description of the state, National Park Service area listings, National Forests, state recreation areas, major recreation information, highway information, weather statistics and a listing of additional resources with addresses.

The guides also list major towns with regional descriptions; chamber of commerce information; what to do and see; annual events; and information about local parks, hotels, motels, restaurants, attractions, guides and outfitters.

Gather specific information. Once you have a general idea of where to go, write to parks, campgrounds, national forests, national parks, state departments of natural resources, and historical and cultural centers in the area for more specific information. Here are items to ask for:

● Listing of campsites for groups.

● Camp guidelines, including minimum and maximum sizes.

● Group guidelines.

● Maps.

● Information about regularly scheduled interpretive and cultural programs.

● List of available books, topographical maps and area resources.

● Outfitters, guides and concessionaires licensed by the state.

Contact resident camps and retreat centers. Many church and private camps operate a complete summer program as well as an off-season weekend program. Contact camps and centers in the area you'll be visiting to see if they have the facilities and services you need. Use the "Preliminary Facility Checklist" (Diagram 3) to evaluate your options.

You can find camps listed in many places. Youth magazines, denominational offices and popular outdoor magazines often list residential camps and retreat centers. Most pastors can give you an address to write for listings of campsites sponsored by their denomination. Two major listings of residential camps and retreat centers are the following guides published by national camping organizations:

● *Parents' Guide to Accredited Camps*, American Camping Association, Bradford Woods, Martinsville, IN 46151-7902 (1-800-428-2267).

● *Official Guide to Christian Camps and Conference Centers*, Christian Camping International, Box 646, Wheaton, IL 60189 (312) 462-0300.

Contact needed guides and outfitters. If you need professional guides and outfitters for transportation, rafting, canoeing, horseback tripping, mountaineering or skills training, write to several of them. Ask about their services, costs and experience in working with youth groups. Request references to contact about their services to youth groups.

Obtain backcountry permits. Many national and state parks require permits for backpacking, building fires and other backcountry use. Often they limit the number of groups that can use the campsites or trails. For instance, the Superior National Forest regulates the number of people and canoes that can use the Boundary Waters Canoe Area Wilderness in Minnesota.

It's important, therefore, to know what permits you'll need and when to apply for them. Sometimes a park accepts applications beginning January 1 on a first-come, first-served basis. Avoid disappointment by knowing the regulations and acquiring the permits as early as possible.

Call an area pastor. Once you settle on your destination and basic travel itinerary, call a pastor in the town nearest your destination. If your group will be there on worship days, ask about local church services. If your group wants to meet young people from the area, explore the idea of the two youth groups getting together.

Great moments often grow out of a chance call to a pastor. One Georgia youth group spent the night at a church in Maine after its canoe trip and was treated to a genuine New England backyard clambake. Five years later a newly graduated college student traveled 2,000 miles back to Maine to marry a girl he met at the clambake!

Securing Support Services

Since the 1960s, professional touring, outfitting and guiding have moved into a new era of professionalism. Competent support services now enable people to raft white-water rivers; ride horseback into wilderness areas; and sail, ski and explore remote areas around the world that were previously considered off-limits or beyond budget. Youth groups can now arrange exciting river trips for a day or a week. And they don't have to travel very far—unless they want to.

The key to these new possibilities is the plethora of professional outfitters and guides who will provide supplies and services for youth groups. Churches don't have to furnish everything they need for a canoeing expedition or a backpacking wilderness trek. Outfitters can provide everything they need. Nor does a youth worker have to have special skills to lead a ski trip or mountaineering adventure. Professional guides will contract with groups to provide skills training, leadership and guidance.

How does a youth group find, evaluate and contract with a professional outfitter or guide to provide services for a camping adventure? Veteran professional outfitters Jon and Dan Waters have operated Canadian Waters, a canoe outfitting and guide service in Ely, Minnesota, since 1964. Their experience with countless church youth groups gives them particular insight into these groups' specific needs. In a special interview for this book, they offered the following suggestions for working with a guide or outfitter:

Contact outfitters early. Lining up outfitters and guides late in the season limits your options and your chances for getting the exact services and supplies you need. If you're too late, outfitters and guides are usually booked solid and have no dates to offer your group. Setting your plans with outfitters and guides early allows flexibility and offers the opportunity for better service. Contact outfitters and guides at least six months in advance (nine months is even better).

Define your expectations. Before your trip, talk with outfitters or guides about what's most important to your group. Are you interested in sightseeing, learning to canoe, fishing the rivers and lakes, learning to ride horses, hiking the back country, photographing wildlife and scenery, or relaxing? It's imperative to clearly understand priorities before you take your trip.

Also clarify how long you plan to be in the back country. Do you envision a physically challenging trip that requires endurance? Or are you more interested in a relaxed trip that focuses on group times and fellowship? How much time will it take to accomplish your purpose and goals?

Check potential outfitters and guides. You don't have to conduct an FBI investigation, but do ask the right questions about potential guides and outfitters. How long have they been in business? How much experience do they have with youth groups? What kind of reputation do they have?

Ask if the outfitters and guides have worked with other youth groups, and request youth worker references. Contact these youth workers about their experiences and what they'd do differently if they were taking the trip again.

Don't dismiss potential support people simply because they haven't been in their present business long. Many legitimate outfitters have just begun their present work but have excellent background experience as guides or outfitters elsewhere.

Look for professionalism. Avoid guides and outfitters with unprofessional attitudes and practices. A qualified outfitter or guide should have a professional manner in dealing with the public. Your questions—no matter how simple or complex—deserve warm and authoritative answers.

Professionals don't penalize youth group leaders who have their own gear, who want partial outfitting or who simply request advice on what's best for their group. True professionals are willing to talk with you and help you—whether or not you outfit with them.

Know what an outfitter can do. What can potential outfitters and guides provide that will improve the camping experience for everyone involved? Competent outfitters offer information and route planning throughout the year. They clearly understand and communicate what your group must do to plan its adventure. They know the back country and can advise you on portages, trail conditions, snow levels, water safety and weather conditions. They know the hazards of their area and the campsite conditions. If a guide or outfitter doesn't offer these services, look for someone else.

Professional outfitters also have quality, custom equipment that makes your trip a fun adventure, not a coping experience. They supply the appropriate equipment for your particular group and the adventure you have in mind. Rafting in a quality raft or packing your gear on horses instead of using makeshift, tattered equipment makes the adventure trouble-free and pleasurable.

Experienced outfitters have complete gear that's especially suited for their particular area and camping type. If they choose,

uninformed campers should be able to rely on an outfitter for everything they need—right down to matches and toilet paper.

Make sure you feel confident. Your feelings about particular outfitters or guides are the best indication of whether to work with them. If you don't have confidence in a particular guide or outfitter, look until you find someone you trust.

As you talk with outfitters, do you feel you're valued and being heard? Or do you just feel your group will be treated like more bodies to fill places in a raft? Discern whether the guide or outfitter really wants to meet your group's needs. Ask previous clients if the guides seemed happy around kids. Avoid being pushed into a deal. Wait until you find the outfitter or guide who's best-suited for your group and its needs.

Getting to Camp

It's often said that the journey is as important as the destination. This is certainly true in planning a youth group camping trip. A group needs to grow and maintain its life and spirit as a Christian community during the trip to and from camp—particularly on long-distance trips. Thus what you do along your route is as important to your group's total camping experience as the destination itself. A well-planned, well-paced trip becomes the agenda for Christian community, and the final itinerary must be evaluated based on how it builds up the group during its time on the road.

Pacing Your Travel Time

In planning your final itinerary, think through the rhythm of long travel days, layover days and short travel days and how these relate to your main camping event. Plan travel breaks that take advantage of the refreshing diversions you discover along the route as you gather and study resources for your trip.

As you plan your travel itinerary, keep the following guidelines in mind:

Long-distance days. On long-mileage days, it's easier to start early and eat simply than to leave late and drive late. Regular stops keep drivers and campers refreshed. Changing drivers every 50 miles and stopping for restroom and snack breaks every 100 miles lowers the fatigue. This procedure counteracts the danger that develops when one driver drives hours on end only to fall asleep when the next driver takes over.

Layover days. Every third day should be a rest day or a short travel day. Give time for rest, recreation, washing clothes, shopping and sightseeing. Plan one full day without any travel at least every fourth day.

Transition days. When on an outdoor adventure trip, such as hiking, canoeing, backpacking or biking, use the first day after your long-distance trip for orientation and preparation. Arriving late at night and starting the adventure early the next morning is exhausting, confusing and spiritually self-defeating.

Instead, refresh campers by spending time repacking gear, practicing skills, and meeting other campers and leaders at an easy, restful pace. Carefully reviewing trip plans, spending time alone and preparing a special pre-adventure meal are all important elements in the transition from the road trip to the adventure.

Celebration days. Allow campers and leaders time to celebrate before beginning the long trip home. The last thing campers want to hear after a challenging and successful outdoor adventure is "Now, let's get a good night's rest for the long trip home." Campers may certainly need the rest, but they need to celebrate first.

What sometimes appears to be rowdiness, inconsiderateness or general noisiness among campers at the end of an adventure is actually a misplaced expression of their need to celebrate the event. By recognizing this need, planning ahead and involving campers in inventing the celebration, you can end the adventure on a positive note.

Bus Activities

Nothing challenges a camp planning team more than planning for the long bus trip to camp. How can you promote group-building and growth in such a confined environment? Of course the group will grow informally in small groups and through one-to-one conversations. But how do you include everyone?

Despite difficulties, the trip to and from camp can be a valuable time. One group on its annual ski weekend used part of the five-hour trip to orient skiers about the weekend and to review basic techniques and safety. Before the orientation started, the youth leader announced that they'd use an orientation tape that was actually a comedy routine on skiing by a Christian comedian. Then the ski instructor led the orientation using the bus's public-address system.

Other ways to use the time include having the group sing along with a guitar played into the public-address system. Or "air" a creative traveling radio show by spontaneously asking two or three gregarious teenagers to use the bus microphone to be disc jockeys and play tapes for the group (with the bus driver's permission, of course).

Playing bus games is another way to use travel time. Great bus games can be adapted from traditional games. The same presentation style can be used. For example, quiz pages from Games magazine (available at large newsstands and bookstores) can be transferred to posterboard and held up so everyone can play together. Teams of two can work together to think of answers, and the first pair to answer correctly wins.

The Fellowship of Christians in Action in Titusville, Florida, provides year-round transportation and programming for church groups throughout the United States. It punctuates its trips with Bible quizzes, self-inventories, sharing guides, and dozens of other individual and team games. Two of the organization's popular bus activities are "Group Inventory" and "Pro Bowl IQ" (Camp Notebook 4, "Bus Games"), which were shared by the organization's president, Rudy Moberg.

Choosing Transportation

Choosing transportation is an important decision in planning your trip. Here are questions to ask yourself as you evaluate options:

● Is this transportation appropriate for the group size? Chartering a full-size bus is unnecessary for a group of 12 young people, but renting 10 vans could be a logistical nightmare for a large group.

● Is this transportation adequate to carry the camping gear? If you have camp stoves, tents, sleeping bags, skis or other bulky camp equipment, you'll need more luggage space than if you're going to a fully furnished retreat center. Be sure you have room for all the personal and community camping gear. You may need to take an extra vehicle or some trailers to carry the equipment.

● Are there enough qualified adult drivers for each vehicle? Using several small vehicles requires at least three drivers for every two vehicles. Plan transportation knowing whether you have adequate drivers.

Whether you rely on parent-driven caravans, church vans, a church bus or a chartered vehicle, the church has a partic- ular responsibility and liability when taking young people on trips and camp events. Careful and thorough plans avert misunderstandings, problems and even lawsuits.

Regardless of the transportation used or distance traveled, operate vehicles within the following guidelines:

● Use only mature adult drivers. Never use young people as drivers, no matter how much experience they have.

● Make sure all vehicles have full fuel tanks when you begin your trip.

● Give each driver a map and discuss the itinerary in detail. Clarify and answer questions about breaks and rest stops, meals and refueling.

● Never let campers ride in the back of pickups en route or at camp.

● Give campers clear instructions at stops before they leave the vehicle. Clarify returning times and places. Establish a buddy or small group system for on-your-own lunch breaks and touring cities and amusement areas.

Drivers. During travel time, the bus or van driver is the key person on the trip. The bus or van drivers are weather forecasters and route checkers—not to mention vehicle operators. They must be equipped mentally and physically and have the skills and judgment to travel in unknown territory under unexpected road conditions. Only experienced drivers with equipment in top condition should undertake extensive mountain driving.

Don't assume that someone who can drive a bus is also equipped to chauffeur a youth group on a long trip. To be a safe and effective driver for youth camping trips, a driver must also have a high tolerance for music, loud talking and people getting sick on the way. So choose your drivers with care! Every bus driver should have an assistant to help double-check systems and assist in navigation.

Camp Notebook 4

Bus Games

Group Inventory

Divide your group into teams of four. If possible, include equal numbers of boys and girls. Give the groups two minutes to think of the total of the following items within their group:

_____ Number of different states team members have lived in.
_____ Number of houses team members have lived in.
_____ Number of pictures of guys team members have in their wallets.
_____ Number of pictures of girls team members have in their wallets.
_____ Number of love letters team members have with them.
_____ Number of bedrooms team members have in their present homes.
_____ Number of brothers and sisters team members have.
_____ Number of speeding tickets team members have received (subtract 5 points for each ticket).
_____ Total score for your team.

The team with the highest number in each category, such as number of states, love letters, brothers and sisters, and speeding tickets, tells the whole group about that section.

Pro Bowl IQ

Test your memory by identifying the 28 professional football teams. To make the quiz more challenging, identify the last team by elimination. (For answers, see page 57.)

1. Six shooters _____
2. $1 for corn _____
3. Fish arms for a girl's toy _____
4. Loaders _____
5. Six rulers _____
6. Wise sunbather _____
7. Foolish sunbather _____
8. Protected species _____
9. King of beasts _____
10. Seven squared _____
11. Ewe's mate _____
12. IOUs _____
13. Credit card users _____
14. Midnight sneakers _____

15. Lubricators _____
16. Half bovine, half human _____
17. Indian leaders _____
18. Peter and Paul _____
19. Uncle's spouse in the army __
20. Type of tiger _____
21. Marine bird _____
22. Fundamental rules _____
23. Shoplifters _____
24. 747s _____
25. Equine rodeo participants ____
26. Chicken prisoners _____
27. Extra point goes wild _____
28. ???? _____

For long-distance trips, recruit at least two experienced drivers for each vehicle. Alternate drivers every 50 miles, and give them a one-minute walk-around-and-keep-driving stop. It's amazing how refreshed and alert drivers stay when given regular breaks.

It's also important for churches to have written guidelines for vehicle operation, road-check procedures, emergency management and defensive driving procedures. When followed, these guidelines protect the campers on board. The guidelines also ensure that operating procedures are properly documented to guide and protect the driver.

Camp Notebook 5, "Bus Safety and Operation Guidelines," is adapted from the Fellowship of Christians in Action's extensive drivers manual. These guidelines are beginning points for safe driving. Use Camp Notebook 6, "Pre-Trip Inspection Checklist," to conduct a thorough inspection before you leave on your trip.

Weather conditions. Checking weather conditions by radio, television or calling the State Patrol is critical every travel day. Drivers and camp leaders should know about local conditions and prevailing seasonal weather patterns to anticipate flooded roads, snow and ice conditions, and other weather problems that may exist, particularly in forest and wilderness areas.

Be cautious under adverse weather conditions and when traveling in flood or avalanche zones. If you have any questions about conditions or safety, it's better to spend an extra day waiting than to take a risk.

Travel Camp Standards

A good way to plan and evaluate your itinerary is to use the travel camp standards established by the American Camping Association. These guidelines, which are required for accreditation, apply to campers and staff who travel in motorized transportation for four or more consecutive days. This includes many church youth group camps. Camp Notebook 7, "Travel Camp Checklist," is based on the A.C.A.'s travel guidelines. These same guidelines are available with interpretation from the organization.

Answers to "Pro Bowl IQ" (Camp Notebook 4)

1. Indianapolis Colts	2. Tampa Bay Buccaneers	3. Miami Dolphins
4. Green Bay Packers	5. Minnesota Vikings	6. Cleveland Browns
7. Washington Redskins	8. Philadelphia Eagles	9. Detroit Lions
10. San Fransisco 49ers	11. Los Angeles Rams	12. Buffalo Bills
13. San Diego Chargers	14. Los Angeles Raiders	15. Houston Oilers
16. Dallas Cowboys	17. Kansas City Chiefs	18. New Orleans Saints
19. New York Giants	20. Cincinnati Bengals	21. Seattle Seahawks
22. Phoenix Cardinals	23. Pittsburgh Steelers	24. New York Jets
25. Denver Broncos	26. Atlanta Falcons	27. New England Patriots
28. Chicago Bears		

Camp Notebook 5

Bus Safety and Operation Guidelines

General Drivers Guidelines

1. Be sure the vehicle is free of physical or mechanical conditions that present apparent danger to the passengers.

2. Report all conditions that present apparent danger to the camp leader as soon as the problems arise. If there's immediate danger to the passengers, stop the bus at once.

3. Don't let anyone else in the driver's seat.

4. Always drive at a safe and legal speed.

5. Always use turn signals.

6. Have someone outside the bus to guide you as much as possible when backing the bus.

7. Keep full control of the front-door exit and its operation; never give a passenger this responsibility.

8. Never let the bus coast with the clutch depressed or the gears in neutral.

9. When leaving the bus, shift into neutral, set the parking brake, idle the bus for approximately 30 seconds and shut off the engine.

10. Always lock the bus when leaving it unattended.

11. Immediately report all accidents—no matter how small—to the camp leader, and fill out an accident-report form.

Safety Precautions

1. Drive ahead. Let your eyes scan the road in front of you. A good way to do this is to pace yourself with the vehicle in front of you.

2. Don't rush! "Better late than never" and "Safety first, schedule second" are always good mottos for drivers.

3. Start braking early. The less you use the brakes, the longer they'll last. When you do use the brakes, use them gently, allowing plenty of room for stopping. Then reduce the pressure on the pedal as you come to a stop.

4. Remember that roads are slippery when wet. You can't drive the bus the same way on wet roads as on dry ones. If the bus begins to hydroplane on a wet road, turn into the skid and then immediately recover.

5. Drive defensively. Many drivers you'll encounter won't be paying attention. Watch out for them!

Camp Notebook 6

Pre-Trip Inspection Checklist

Use the following checklist before each bus trip to ensure that your trip is safe and trouble-free.

Step One: Exterior Checks

	Okay	Needs Attention	Notes
Check the oil	☐	☐	_____
Check the water	☐	☐	_____
Check the battery	☐	☐	_____
Check the transmission fluid	☐	☐	_____
Check the power steering fluid	☐	☐	_____
Check the belts	☐	☐	_____
Check for fuel leaks	☐	☐	_____
Check all hoses	☐	☐	_____
Check for loose wiring	☐	☐	_____
Check the bus body for damage	☐	☐	_____

Step Two: Running Checks

	Okay	Needs Attention	Notes
Tires. Inspect for underinflated, flat, worn or damaged tires. Don't drive the bus unless the tires are in good shape.	☐	☐	_____
Wheels. Look for loose or missing lug nuts, excessive corrosion, cracks or other damage.	☐	☐	_____
Fluid leaks. If leaks are found, determine the source and correct the problem.	☐	☐	_____
Warning systems. Make sure the following work: running lights, reverse lights, turn signals, four-way flashers, brake lights, headlights, high beams, fog lights, reflectors, destination sign and license plate light.	☐	☐	_____
Windshield and windows. Make sure they're clean.	☐	☐	_____

continued

Step Three: Inside Checks

	Okay	Needs Attention	Notes
Gauges (air, water, fuel, oil, tachometer, speedometer and voltmeter)	☐	☐	_____
Telltale lights	☐	☐	_____
Turn signal operation	☐	☐	_____
Four-way flasher	☐	☐	_____
Headlight and highbeam operation	☐	☐	_____
Drivers light operation	☐	☐	_____
Indirect light operation	☐	☐	_____
Horn and horn foot-switch	☐	☐	_____
Air conditioning and heating system	☐	☐	_____
Drivers air conditioning	☐	☐	_____
Defroster (low and high)	☐	☐	_____
Dash lights	☐	☐	_____
Control lights	☐	☐	_____
Step light and bay lights	☐	☐	_____
Intercom system	☐	☐	_____
Citizens band radio operation	☐	☐	_____
Stereo system and headphone operation	☐	☐	_____
Drivers seat belt	☐	☐	_____
Drivers seat	☐	☐	_____
Fire extinguisher	☐	☐	_____
First-aid kit	☐	☐	_____
Emergency equipment (including reflectors)	☐	☐	_____
Lavatory (toilet paper, paper towels, working light and occupied sign)	☐	☐	_____
Cleanliness of bus	☐	☐	_____

Step Four: Miscellaneous Checks

	Okay	Needs Attention	Notes
Cargo-bay door operation	☐	☐	_____
Spare tire, jack, wrench, wedge	☐	☐	_____
Compartment doors on bus exterior	☐	☐	_____

Camp Notebook 7

Travel Camp Checklist

The following guidelines—adapted from the American Camping Association's guidelines—apply to all campers and staff who travel in motorized transportation for four or more consecutive days. Appropriate travel camps will answer "yes" to every applicable question.

Yes No

- ☐ ☐ Are all drivers at least 21 years old?
- ☐ ☐ Do the drivers each have a valid operators license?
- ☐ ☐ Is the camp leader at least 21 years old?
- ☐ ☐ Do living arrangements for all staff permit a reasonable degree of freedom and privacy from campers?
- ☐ ☐ Do campers participate in planning and preparing meals?
- ☐ ☐ Have you planned at least one rest stop every four hours of travel that includes relaxation and exercise?
- ☐ ☐ Does everyone have personal time in the travel schedule and program?
- ☐ ☐ Have you scheduled at least one full non-travel day between each four consecutive travel days?
- ☐ ☐ Do you have safe storage for all supplies and equipment in transit and at campsites?
- ☐ ☐ Have you filed a written itinerary with the home congregation?
- ☐ ☐ Have you set up ways to communicate the progress and condition of your trip to your congregation?
- ☐ ☐ Do you have a log to record each day's operation, including driving time, mileage, daily occurrences, maintenance records, fuel records, and trip expenses?
- ☐ ☐ Do you have documents with you that fully identify the group, its leadership, equipment ownership, purpose, insurance coverage, and congregation and other contacts?
- ☐ ☐ Do you have limited power of attorney from parents or guardians for each minor?
- ☐ ☐ Do you know how to obtain medical assistance on the trip?
- ☐ ☐ Have you established written procedures to follow when you must exclude someone from the travel program?
- ☐ ☐ Have you made provision for regularly laundering clothing?
- ☐ ☐ Do you have a minimum of one relief driver for every two vehicles?
- ☐ ☐ Do trailers comply with all state, local and national regulations for all travel areas?
- ☐ ☐ Are warm-water bathing facilities available for both campers and staff at least once each week?
- ☐ ☐ Has the physical condition of each camper and staff member been screened within 12 hours of departure and return by a licensed physician, a registered nurse or someone approved by a licensed physician?

Chapter 4

Communicating the Good News About Camp

Picture a church family-supper night. Eight sixth-graders lead the evening devotional. They use the Creation story from Genesis and a creation of their own—a slide show from their summer camp. Two dozen colorful slides illustrate a litany written and led by the campers themselves:

We See the Earth

Into the woods we went—
Eight of us—
To look, to seek, to study, to listen,
To make a few pictures of how we see the earth.
The waterfall
It seemed like rain coming down every second
Over big boulders.
Powerful, magnificent, huge,
Helpful, destructive.
Dear God, you are as mighty as the falls,
Yet you care about the earth,
Which is just a pebble in your dominion.
Thank you, Lord, for caring.
The stream
Wet, cold, swift, inviting,
Strong, moving, fun,

Trapping stones, hollowing circles and holes,
Transporting sand to the lake below.
Dear God, you are our source
Supplying life and joy.
Moving us to consideration and love.
Thank you, Lord, for caring.
The plants
Cattails, wading on the edge of extinction,
Casting a picture on the water.
Leaves changing colors,
Evidence of life and death—ordered change.
Dear God, you are present in our changing lives,
Present in life,
Present in death.
Thank you, Lord, for caring.
The little creatures
Spiders—balloonists, trappers, superarchitects.
Spinning trails from tree to tree.
Centipedes—many-legged, wet with dew,
Clinging to cave walls.
Dear God, you are equipping us to think,
To design,
To create.
Thank you, Lord, for caring.

The slide show wasn't slick. Some slides were mounted at angles so sprockets showed; the narration sometimes faltered; and the reading chorus needed more practice. But—despite the lack of polish—the short devotion effectively communicated the good news about camp. The campers' joy and excitement were unmistakable.

In this particular case, the campers took the slides themselves. Each person was given two shots. The group members decided together how to use the rest of the roll. Then a geology professor helped the campers develop the film in the church kitchen.

The young people also wrote the litany with the assistant pastor's help. The campers watched the slides three times while writing the litany. First they watched to see what "we" had done together. Then they created a list of words in response to each slide. After some suggestions about writing a prayer refrain (and some possessive arguments about the slide sequence), everything jelled. The campers couldn't wait to show their creation.

Campers tell their story best. But they aren't good with giving off-the-cuff reports or answering probing questioners. Instead, campers communicate best with the help of friends who guide them in planning and presenting their ideas.

Whether you're publicizing an upcoming camp or reporting on a recent camp experience, communicating the camp story requires careful planning. Such planning prevents laments, such as "Oh, I wish we had pictures of . . ." Unless you plan in advance, your presentation possibilities are limited to what you happen to end up with. You also avoid embarrassing situations, such as "I thought Harry said he'd bring a camera" or "All I have is print film; I didn't know we were doing a slide show."

Initial decisions that affect your presentation include:

- Who will hear our story?
- How will we document our camp?
- Who will document our camp?
- How should we tell our story?

Who Will Hear Our Story?

Knowing your audience is essential in preparing your presentation. Is your presentation for parents? young people? both? the whole congregation? Are you giving this presentation to celebrate the camp experience? share information? motivate and recruit campers?

In many cases, the answer to these questions is "all of the above." Unless you have lots of time, people and resources, you'll probably use one presentation several times with different audiences and purposes. It's important, though, to avoid a one-sided presentation by knowing the audience and presentation setting before you document the camp. Here are potential audiences and purposes to consider in planning:

Young people. Your youth group will want to hear about camp. Participants want to celebrate their experiences, and other group members will want to share the experiences vicariously. Your presentation also can be used to motivate and recruit campers for future adventures.

Strong pre-camp publicity is particularly important before your first year of camp when teenagers aren't sure what to expect. In subsequent years, tradition and person-to-person contact will tell the good news of previous camps, making recruitment easier. As camp leader Jeff Ross of Sandy Springs, Georgia, says: "When parents are really involved and a parent, as director, is responsible for getting the brochure out, all you have to do is say, 'Love Week [his church's camp] is this date.'

And as soon as you put that date down and put out the first publicity, 30 to 40 kids will sign up for it. Working on the rest of the kids isn't too hard because you already have 40 people going.''

Parents. Telling parents about camp is important for several reasons. It lets them celebrate and share the experience with their children. It also tells parents what happened and reassures them of the benefits—and safety—of the experience. Finally, it fosters their support—both moral and financial—for the camping experience.

The congregation. Other congregation members also may want to know about the youth camp. Telling them your camping story allows them to share in the experience, thus building relationships within the congregation. Your presentation also can build support in the congregation for youth ministry. By showing the congregation that important and meaningful experiences take place at camp, you affirm the importance of your youth program. Finally, if you ask congregation members to support the camp through special gifts or fund-raisers, your presentation shows them how you used their gifts responsibly and thanks them for their generosity.

How Will We Document Our Camp?

Unless your group is unusually large, you can't take advantage of all the types of documentation in capturing your camping story. Instead, choose the best way to tell your story based on your audience and the youth group's talents and skills. It's usually better to select the easiest ways for individuals to document the event. Otherwise they work so hard gathering information and images that they miss experiencing camp themselves.

You can gather information from camp in many ways. Diagram 4, ''Approaches to Documentation,'' lists options, equipment you'll need and ways to use the documentation. There are other ways to document camp that require special talents, such as art. Use these if they're available for your group.

Who Will Document Our Camp?

The people most likely to document your camping event are people who already have an interest or skills in photography, video or art. Ask youth group members with particular skills to contribute their talent to the group. Or ask an adult with expertise to share those skills while serving as a camp counselor.

One camp had a professional artist lead an art workshop. Camp leaders invited the artist to document the whole camp with action sketches. The resulting pages provided illustrations for the group journal, which was photocopied for the campers and leaders.

An experienced video-camera operator or photographer can cover a camp unobtrusively, providing quality documentation without distracting the campers. Blending a skilled photographer's work with campers' own photos provides a comprehensive picture of the camp.

An effective way to involve the whole camping group in documentation is to keep a group journal. Have campers write their thoughts, feelings and insights in the journal each day. The results will show not only the camp's events, but its moods, feelings and impact.

One group chose to create a group journal to document its week at a workcamp. During the week all the group members wrote in the journal. After the event group leaders condensed the journal accounts into a two-page youth newsletter article. They also used it as a bulletin insert so the whole congregation could learn about the youth group's mission trip.

Diagram 4
Approaches to Documentation

Approach	Equipment and Supplies	Uses
Print photographs	● 35mm camera with self-timer and flash unit (may be a single-lens reflex camera or a simpler range-finder model). ● Waterproof case for camera, film and lenses. ● Spare batteries for camera or light meter. ● Batteries for flash. ● 400 ASA black-and-white film, such as Kodak Tri-X pan film. ● 100-400 ASA color print film, such as Kodacolor. ● Lense-cleaning paper.	Bulletin boards; newsletters; neighborhood newspaper reports; folder for sanctuary or class display; or a complete album for the youth room, parent Sunday school classes, church library or parlor.
Slides	● Same camera equipment as for print photographs. ● Slide film, such as 100 ASA Kodak Ektachrome for daylight and 400 ASA for night. (If you plan to process slides yourself, don't use Kodachrome film, which can be processed only professionally.)	Youth group slide shows, family supper nights, camper reunions, parent nights and camper recruitment.
Tape recordings	● Portable cassette tape recorder (or micro-recorder with adapt-for transferring to standard cassettes). ● Remote microphone (if desired). ● Plenty of good, blank cassettes. ● Several sets of batteries.	Recording music, singing, camper interviews and outdoor sounds to use as sound tracks for slide shows.
Videos	● Portable video camera. ● Blank videocassettes. ● Extra batteries and cells.	Youth group presentations, family nights, camper recruitment and reunions.
Journals (personal or group)	● Spiral-bound notebooks or pocket-size booklets. ● Pencils, pens or markers.	Narrative for camp presentations, brochures and publicity; readings for reunions; and text for albums.

Here's the group's account of the final "Workcamp Sunday" service:

The chancel area had some new paraphernalia today: two sawhorses and some tools—a hammer, a saw and a nail apron. As Sally played the prelude, we processed with the acolytes.

We all wore our "roofing pants," our paint-splattered boots and our workcamp T-shirts. Without a word, we started on our "project." Scott cut a two-by-four into two pieces. Then Tim hammered the two boards together to form a crude cross, which we leaned in front of the communion table.

During the service we gave our testimonies of the week in the Virginia mountains. Each person told about a different aspect of the experience. We also passed folios of pictures and journal quotes from person to person in the pews.

The senior minister preached about our week. He tied our story to the story of the Master Builder, Jesus. We all felt a new kinship with our pastor, who made it a priority to be with us for a week of hard work.

How Should We Tell Our Story?

Taking time to think creatively of ways to communicate both the events and mood of camp makes a big difference in people's interest and support. Whatever methods you choose, keep the following points in mind:

Give leadership to young people. The youth group, parents and congregation will be most interested in your report if campers report their experiences. Help campers develop their own newsletters, slide shows and other reports, and support the campers as they present them to peers, their parents and the congregation. Giving campers ownership of their story is more important than producing slick, polished reports.

Keep reports brief. Few people will want to hear hour-long reports on all the details of your trip. Instead, present short reports that focus on your camp's highlights and mood.

Communicate activities and moods. Instead of just reporting everything you did, give the feel of camp. Tell about emotional highs and lows. Serve camp food as refreshments. Help people experience camp elements by simulating occurrences in a skit or other exercise.

Connect camping with the church's mission. In celebrating the joy and wonder of camping, it's important to show the relationship between outdoor experiences and Christian growth. In hearing about all the "fun we had at camp," some people may miss seeing the personal and spiritual growth that also took place.

With these guidelines in mind, let's look at ways to tell about your camp successfully in different settings:

Parent and family nights. Few settings outside camp itself help parents understand the camping experience better than a parents or family camp night. These nights have the parallel themes of reunion and recruitment. Reunion occurs as group members, parents and other church members see and hear young people tell their stories about camp. Recruitment takes place as parents and teenagers hear the stories, see the value of camp and decide that camp should be a family priority.

Snacks, potlucks, cookouts, songs, skits, group games, displays, and slide or video shows—in almost any combination—make these camp nights enjoyable. Testimonials and question-and-answer times with campers, staff and parents enhance and personalize camp's spiritual values.

Printed literature. Printed materials are particularly valuable in publicizing an upcoming camp. These can range from single-page, hand-typed leaflets to four-color, typeset booklets or posters. Whatever formats you use, prepare your literature with both campers and parents in mind.

Parents—especially mothers—are your primary readers. A simple survey of campers' mothers asking what they look for in a camp can be a valuable guide for designing your publicity. One five-year camp study found that mothers are responsible for more than 90 percent of the registrations, letters, checks and phone calls to the camp. Of the 7 percent of phone calls that fathers made, most began with "My wife asked me to call, and . . ."

Young campers seldom read brochures and other literature until they've actually registered for camp. Instead, they look for pictures and other attention-grabbing devices.

Use all forms of literature in promoting your camping event. Creative use of newsletters, bulletins, fliers and posters will attract interest in your camping event.

Here are six ways to enhance your printed publicity. Each tip's appropriate for publicizing upcoming camps (using information from previous years) and telling about a camp just completed.

1. Use pictures. Recent advances in photocopying let churches and camps use photographs in their bulletins, newsletters, brochures and fliers. Moreover, many quick-print shops effectively reproduce black-and-white pictures without the screening expense.

Other artwork also enlivens publicity. If there's an artist in your youth group, ask him or her to draw cartoons or sketches to tell the camp story. Or use clip art that conveys images from your camp.

2. Use variety. Plan pictures before camp so you can show a variety of settings, angles and activities when you publicize future camps. Plan panoramic shots and close-ups. Take pictures of activities, recreation, discussions, worship, mealtimes and one-to-one conversations. Use pictures that portray safe and appropriate techniques in recreational and skills activities. Stage pictures when it would be inappropriate to take photographs during actual events (such as worship services, prayer times or deep discussions).

3. Use few words. Describe your camp concisely. In publicizing an upcoming camp, say only what must be said, and leave the details for information sheets and packing lists. Mention the camp program's highlights and show the variety of activities. Include a simplified schedule, but don't list camp guidelines.

4. Quote campers. Glean quotes from group and personal journals for a "Here's What Campers Say" paragraph or panel in a brochure or newsletter. Carefully planned evaluation questions also provide valuable camper comments.

5. Quote leaders and parents. Parents value what other parents and leaders say about camp. Use letters, evaluation sheets and interviews with parents and camp staff to endorse your camp program. One camp reduces and reprints two to four letters from parents in its annual newsletter. These hand-written recommendations add a personal touch to the publicity.

6. Describe leaders. Too often church camping brochures, articles and registration materials list only the program director's name. As a result, parents often don't know who's leading the camp or the leader's qualifications. Supplying background information answers parents' concerns and gives the program credibility. Parents want to know their children are under the leadership of safe, competent and caring adults.

Albums and scrapbooks. Picture albums remain effective vehicles for your camp story. By paging through a well-designed album or scrapbook, parents see and feel what their teenagers experienced at camp. Group members will wear pages thin as they thumb through the collection of good camp memories. And as they recall stories, other potential campers will sense the enthusiasm and growth a camp generates.

An album or scrapbook can be used many ways. Circulating it in parent or youth Sunday school classes informally communicates the camp story. The church library, parlor or dining room are also key places to spark interest during gatherings or church meals. And if properly maintained, the album can be a creative record of the camp for years to come.

A striking scrapbook format involves selecting 10 to 12 black-and-white camp pictures along with quotes from personal or group journals. (Be sure to get an individual's permission before using one of his or her quotes.) Type the quotes and cut them in random shapes. Trim the photos in random shapes as well. Then arrange the quotes and photographs on four to six black-background photo album pages with plastic or cellophane covers. Bind the pages in a simple term-paper folder or three-ring binder. The result is an attractive record that people can easily view and read in two to three minutes.

Slides and videos. Our society is selectively visual. We're conditioned to see what we want to see and to tune out whatever doesn't immediately intrigue us. As a result, the visual camp presentation is most demanding. Even campers who attended the event will lose interest if the presentation is unnecessarily long or carelessly presented.

Artful visual essays are simple, short and spiritual. The spirit of camp can captivate the audience when thoughtful images are juxtaposed with music, song, verse or journal passages. Your goal is to touch the audience's imagination and spirit, paving the way for interaction, personal memories and celebrations.

One youth group used a camper's personal journal as the narration for its camp slide show. The journal wasn't exceptional, but it consistently reflected her daily impressions of camp. The resulting 12-minute slide show conveyed even deeper meaning because the slides pictured every group member. The presentation created enough excitement to encourage several young people to talk in depth with their parents about their week at the mountain workcamp. It also served as a great publicity tool for future camps.

Both video presentations and slide shows pose the same temptations: to be too long on visuals and too literal in narrative. Variety, mood and pace are more important than showing everything that happened at camp. Planned portraits, long-range shots and action sequences combined in a smooth order keep your audience anticipating more. Here are tips to follow in taking pictures and preparing your presentation:

1. Include people and nature. Close-ups of campers and camp leaders catch the camp's mood, spirit and flavor. Similarly, close-ups of nature—water lapping at the shoreline, detailed tree bark, sand patterns or rock formations—help viewers feel the camp setting. Focus on the tranquil moment, and give viewers time to be touched by the outdoors.

2. Long-distance shots need something special to give them impact. A lone camper reading on a dock or two young people walking by a lake adds dimension to scenic views. Night shots of a campfire or a candlelight procession reflected in the water dramatically capture the event's mood.

3. Close-up action shots should reflect the variety of camp experiences—meals,

study, worship or recreation—as well as campers' responses—playing, talking, relaxing, listening, or struggling to learn and achieve.

4. Take most of your pictures in the early morning, late afternoon and evening. Because of the light pattern and color, photographs taken during these times convey deeper color and feeling. High noon shots rarely turn out well; colors are washed out and shadows are unappealing.

5. Let the visual presentation speak for itself. Don't feel obligated to identify everyone in every photograph or to discuss the details of every activity pictured. Use surprise. People get involved with your presentation more quickly when they haven't been told what they're about to see.

Displays and bulletin boards. On every first Sunday of June, one church opens its summer season by arranging a fleet of canoes and a large tent on the church lawn. The display is a vivid reminder that it's time to sign up for summer camp. A statewide church association once spotlighted its outdoor ministry program at its annual gathering by assembling a complete campsite—right in a downtown convention center. The camping hospitality was complete with tents, rafts, backpacks, a fake fire, potted trees and artificial turf. Lemonade was served from blackened coffee pots.

Displays are lifelike pictures. They catch people's attention and build interest in the camp. Think of creative ways to use items from camp to pique youth group and congregation members' interest. What camp elements capture its flavor, spirit and excitement? What gear or supplies can you display to spark interest in and memories about camp?

If displays are lifelike pictures, bulletin boards are supersize brochures. Find bulletin board ideas in public visitors centers, popular magazine layouts or bulletin board idea books from school supply stores. Include brochures from your campsite and information from local chambers of commerce. Integrate elements into an appealing and organized display.

One bulletin board idea is to use topographic maps as the background for the display. Identify the camp and outlying areas on the map. The attractive display absorbs viewers as they trace camp activities on the map. When you return from camp, one-hour photo services allow you to design a camp bulletin board for the Sunday after the event—when excitement is still running high.

Personal letters. Everyone likes to receive personal, handwritten letters. When publicizing a camp, a brochure with an enclosed handwritten note is worth more than 10 impersonal brochures.

Personalizing a camp mailing is easy—if you have plenty of help. Orchestrate a big mailing party. Have envelopes, paper, pens, stamps, address lists, and lots of kids on hand to do the writing. One church youth council took 10 minutes of its annual planning retreat to write zany football post cards to 34 inactive young people in the church. They told about the camp and invited the "inactives" back to the youth group. The following Sunday four teenagers returned—talking about the unexpected post cards.

Communicating Your Good News

Telling the good news about camp is most effective when you use a combination of two or three documentation and presentation methods. For instance, at camp you could take slides, keep a group journal, and record campers' insights and wilderness sounds. You then could use these elements in a slide show, a newsletter or brochure article, and a bulletin board display. Decide which methods are primary and which are secondary for reaching potential campers and their parents. Concentrate your time and resources on the primary method.

Regardless of the methods you choose, remember that the key to effectively tell-ing campers and parents about camp is to convey the ministry of camping within the congregation's larger mission and ministry. With this focus, you ensure that your news about camp is indeed *good* news.

Part Two
Camps in Action

Chapter 5

Residential Youth Camps

"**B**efore I went, I thought it would be great that I'd get to go to the beach," ninth-grader B.J. McCrosky remembers. "I had just started in this church group. I had a couple of friends who went to church here. We played hockey and just ran into each other—it was a lot of fun. I didn't really think of it as a church thing." After the week, he saw it differently. "It was the most special week of my life," he said.

B.J.'s experience at his church's annual youth camp could be echoed by thousands of teenagers who participate in residential youth camps each summer. These camps represent the most common type of church youth camps—three- to six-day events known as camps, assemblies, conferences and institutes.

Residential youth camps give teenagers opportunities to break out of their daily routines for a week of intensive study, play, self-examination, friendship building, worship and personal growth. Whatever the week's format, many young people leave camp with their lives changed and new friendships formed. At camp leaders see teenagers make faith decisions and vocational choices that set the pattern for a lifetime of Christian growth and service.

The residential camp experience not only benefits campers, but it gives youth workers, parents and other leaders a new perspective on and relationship with youth group members. In camp's uniquely relaxing environment, adults listen to, understand and build relationships with teenagers.

Atlanta pastor James N. Thompson says his experience as a camp leader has affected his relationship with young people. "They would get to know me as a person who could have fun and sometimes get angry," he remembers. "And I got to know them. As I did, I became aware of their deeper struggles and hurts—as well as their fun and hopes. It opened avenues for counseling and strengthened relational bonds between me and the youth."

Elements of a Residential Camp Program

Whether a camp is congregation-sponsored or run by an interchurch or denominational group, its basic program elements haven't changed much since the mid-'50s. Most camps include the following elements in their daily program:

● Morning watch.

● Campwide morning event.

● Bible studies and group discussions.

● Downtime and free time.

● Mealtimes.

● Recreation.

● Elective workshops and activities.

● Campwide celebration and worship.

● Special evening events.

● The closing celebration (on the last day of camp).

Diagram 5, "A Typical Day at Camp," shows how these elements fit together.

Though the schedule may seem rigid, it isn't. The themes, group process, workshops, recreation and crafts shift dramatically from year to year. Thus while each camp includes each element, camps have their own character and spirit. Let's look at each of the basic program elements.

Morning Watch

A brief quiet time for reflection before or after breakfast sets the tone for a day at youth camp. A morning watch can take many forms:

Personal time alone. Developing a printed guide with suggested reading for time alone focuses prayer, meditation and scripture study on the camp's theme.

One-to-one guided sharing time.
Using a printed guide prepared for the week, pairs of campers study scriptures, meditate and pray together, adding an interpersonal dimension to their morning devotional time.

Small group devotions. Dividing the whole group into small groups adds a new dimension to worship and devotions—particularly at a large camp. Having smaller groups sing, pray and read scriptures together creates special bonds of Christian fellowship.

All-camp devotional time. These morning events include singing, meditation and prayer. They also become creative morning worship celebrations that use God's creation as their setting. (Chapter 13, "Leading Camp Worship and Bible Study," illustrates creative morning worship experiences.)

Campwide Morning Event

The campwide morning event usually revolves around the camp theme and the camp speaker's message. Music, calls to worship, scriptures and litanies focus on the day's theme.

The morning event can take many shapes, depending on the speaker's style or the theme. An inspirational message, question-and-answer time, open dialogue, drama, slides, panel discussion and daily

---

Diagram 5
A Typical Day at Camp

7:00 a.m.	Rise 'n' shine!		1:45 p.m.	Growth groups or workshops
7:30 a.m.	Morning watch			
8:00 a.m.	Breakfast		2:30 p.m.	Free time or electives
9:00 a.m.	Campwide morning event		6:00 p.m.	Supper
10:00 a.m.	Bible Study		7:00 p.m.	Rap groups or free time
11:00 a.m.	Free time		8:00 p.m.	Worship celebration
Noon	Lunch and rest hour		9:00 p.m.	Campwide special event
			10:30 p.m.	Cabin devotions
			11:00 p.m.	Lights out

discipleship assignments are effective in setting the tone, mood and focus for the day.

Bible Studies and Group Discussions

Away from the traditions and time constraints of Sunday school and church activities, camp provides an ideal setting for creative, in-depth Bible study and discussion. Young people are more relaxed and open as close community develops through the week. As a camp planner, you don't have to deal with the distractions of other programs. Your time frame is more relaxed, allowing for greater creativity and depth in Bible study and discussion times.

Action-oriented, experiential Bible study appeals to young people. Using role plays, making scripture passages contemporary and leading guided group interactions around biblical themes motivate campers to stretch themselves to learn more about the Bible and live its truth. (For more on creating camp Bible studies, see Chapter 13, "Leading Camp Worship and Bible Study.")

Topical discussions thrive at camp for the same reasons Bible study does. Because of the closeness and intensity that develops at camp, young people more naturally share their feelings, experiences and struggles. By planning discussions and activities that touch important concerns for young people, camp leaders provide rich growing opportunities.

Downtime and Free Time

Despite appearances of unending energy, campers (and leaders) need daily downtime and free time at camp. These respites in the midst of many activities help maintain a camp's rhythm and pace.

Though sometimes confused, downtime and free time are different in important ways. Let's compare them:

Downtime. Everyone—staff and campers—needs downtime in the middle of each day. During this time the entire camp rests, writes letters and journal entries, reads and quietly relaxes. This helps campers and leaders reflect on the morning and prepare mentally and spiritually for the afternoon and evening. (Calling this "downtime"—not "horizontal time"—meets less resistance from energetic campers who need rest.) Campers need more rest through downtime as the week progresses—an hour a day except for the first day of camp, which has a brief cabin time for groups to get better acquainted.

Younger campers require more rest than teenagers—an hour of downtime each day plus some afternoon quiet games, crafts or other activities that aren't physically demanding.

Free time. Free time is unscheduled time that lets campers choose what to do. Some campers may want to spend their free time as downtime. Many camps provide optional activities—sports, crafts, discussions, guided walks, meditations and counseling—designed to let campers be re-created at their leisure. These activities can be creative expressions of the camp theme. (Because free time is unstructured, camp guidelines must clarify that campers must not leave the campsite without permission and supervision.)

Mealtimes

Meals are special times at camp. Meaningful mealtime rituals—thanksgiving, singing, announcements and personal affirmations—create a sense of the camp family as a covenant community. (Chapter 13, "Leading Camp Worship and Bible Study," contains several ideas for celebrating Christian community at mealtimes.)

Some camps let groups do their own cooking. If your group elects to cook its own meals, visit the kitchen staff to check utensils and to learn kitchen procedures your group should follow in meal preparation and cleanup.

Involving campers in preparation, setup and cleanup can be a parable of Christian servanthood. When thoughtfully approached and interpreted, this camper involvement brings an important new dimension to residential camping—a common dimension of backcountry camping.

Diagram 6, "Sample Menus for Residential Camps," contains suggested camp meals that have been approved by state nutritionists. Use them as a beginning point. Adapt them, add your favorite, local tastes and involve the young people in creating final menus.

Recreation

In today's rushed and competitive world, most teenagers have few opportunities to play simply for the sake of playing. Games, recreation and sports usually have other goals—to get in shape, to beat the other team or to win a trophy. Moreover, because of competition only a few teenagers with particular athletic prowess actively participate.

Away from competitive routines and expectations, recreation at camp should focus on play for the fun of it, with only secondary (or less) emphasis on competition. Camp leaders can borrow the noncompetitive motto from the popular *New Games Book*: "Play hard, play fair, nobody hurt."

Some campers groan when they learn they aren't playing games with win-lose rules. But their disappointment is shortlived. Most campers are relieved when leaders make games easier and inclusive.

Making camp recreation inclusive doesn't mean you must stop playing competitive games. Softball, volleyball and flag football remain important parts of camp recreation. However, by creating a new spirit and atmosphere of play and by reworking rules to be less competitive, all campers can participate equally—whether they're athletic or not.

Here are guidelines for making camp recreation less competitive and more inclusive:

Introduce the spirit of play in orientation. Introducing camp leaders in comical ways and having snappy get-acquainted activities to kick off the camp set a tone of positive playfulness for the week. Laughing together is healthy, and it invites campers to play and have fun at camp. Remember, of course, that humor at someone else's expense detracts from community-building as one person becomes a scapegoat for others' pleasure.

Begin the week with easy and non-competitive games before moving to competitive play. As campers grow in personal confidence, group support, physical coordination and joy, you can introduce activities with friendly competition.

Use games that help groups learn and grow together. Invent games that help campers share and work together either by starting from scratch or recycling old games. Diagrams 8-11 include ways to adapt flag football, volleyball, water polo and softball to be more inclusive and less competitive.

Include all campers in games and recreation throughout the week. Unless everyone can participate, recreation builds walls, not community.

Plan games for large groups. A major challenge for leaders planning large camps is to organize recreation to include 50 to 3,000 campers simultaneously in sectional or campwide activities. It requires detailed planning, leadership orientation

Diagram 6
Sample Menus for Residential Camps

Breakfasts	Lunches	Dinners
1. One-eyed jacks Hash browns Cereals Juice Milk and hot chocolate	1. Sliced turkey and peanut butter and jelly sandwiches Apples Carrot sticks Oatmeal cookies Beverages	1. Pizza with cheese, olives, mushrooms, pepperoni and onions Mixed vegetables Gingerbread Beverages
2. French toast Butter, peanut butter and syrup Applesauce Cereals Milk and hot chocolate	2. Tuna sandwiches* Carrot and celery sticks Baked beans Brownies Fruit punch	2. Hamburgers** Toppings (mustard, ketchup, mayonnaise, tomatoes and lettuce) French fries Apple crisp Milk and other beverages
3. Scrambled eggs with bacon bits Bran muffins Pears Milk and hot chocolate	3. Grilled-cheese sandwiches Vegetable or tomato soup Crackers Orange slices Milk and water	3. Baked chicken Baked or mashed potatoes Green beans Raw vegetable sticks Chocolate cake Milk and water
4. Pancakes Butter, peanut butter and syrup Fruit slices Cereal options Milk and hot chocolate	4. Turkey hot dogs** Mustard, ketchup, relish Potato salad Fruit Jell-O Lemonade and water	4. Spaghetti with Parmesan cheese French garlic bread Tossed salad Watermelon Milk, ice tea and water
5. Scrambled eggs Cinnamon rolls Juice Milk and hot chocolate	5. Chili Crackers and peanut butter Raw vegetable sticks Ice cream Beverages	5. Baked pork chops Baked sweet potatoes Fruit salad Banana pudding Milk and water
6. Hot cereal Coffeecake Fruit slices Milk and hot chocolate	6. Macaroni and cheese Bread sticks Stuffed celery Coleslaw Peaches and cookies Fruit punch	6. Meat loaf Baked potatoes Peas Rolls Cobbler Milk, ice tea and water

*Optional picnic meal (requires refrigeration)
**Optional cookout meal

and adapting game rules to include all campers.

One organization that has successfully led large camps for 15 years is the Church Recreation Department of the Baptist Sunday School Board (Southern Baptist Convention). Through its Centrifuge camp program, it serves about 28,000 young people each summer. The Centrifuge approach accommodates a variety of games and traditional team sports. Slight rule changes and adaptations of traditional sports create a sense of play and community spirit.

In some events, "Spirit Teams" are the heart of the daily recreation program, affectionately known as "Peanut Patch Olympics." They're made up of one-fourth of the campers in a section or camp. Each team includes an equal number of young people from each grade. In area-wide events, campers from different churches are randomly mixed together to promote interaction.

Each day of camp the Spirit Teams work together to score points through team play, team cheers and team spirit. They also try to avoid having points deducted for being "unsports." Because of the point system, no one knows which team has won in each category except the game leaders. Winners are announced at the end of camp.

Through the week, each Spirit Team plays all the other teams in all the sports—called "Close Encounters"—on the schedule. But winning the Close Encounters isn't the only way to win the Peanut Patch Olympics. In addition to earning points for winning games, teams earn points with their team cheers, by having participants and spectators at games, and for showing team spirit. Points are deducted for poor sportsmanship. Diagram 7, "Peanut Patch Olympics Point System," shows the scoring system.

Elective Workshops and Activities

Elective workshops and activities are the backbone of many residential camp programs. They provide variety and substance to the camp program. They give campers opportunities to choose topics and activities that particularly interest them.

Electives can have many shapes and purposes. They might be one-day sessions or day-to-day sessions continued through the week. They may involve special guest leaders, creative projects, interest groups, wilderness experiences or field trips. They can focus on personal or spiritual enrichment; creativity; learning skills; group-building; or adventure. Thus camp leaders

---

Diagram 7
Peanut Patch Olympics Point System

Close Encounters
Win: 100 points
Loss: 50 points
Forfeit: 100 points to other team

Team Cheer
Best: 50 points
Second best: 40 points
Third best: 30 points
Fourth best: 20 points

Participation
10 points for each player and spectator

Team Spirit
25-50 points each day

Poor Sports
Points are deducted as judges see fit for poor sportsmanship among team members and spectators.

can choose specific electives to meet their group's specific needs.

In planning your electives, find out from the youth group members what workshops and activities they'd like to have. Not only does this focus your planning, but it helps the teenagers feel involved in planning.

One effective way to gather this information is to compile a list of all the reasonable and achievable ideas group members suggest for workshops. Then have teenagers each rank 10 workshops from the list, using one for their first choice and so on. Then compile the results for the planning committee.

Diagram 8
Flag Football Rules
Follow regulation rules with the following exceptions:
1. The field is 75 yards long and 50 yards wide. End zones are 10 yards deep, making the field a total of 95 yards long from end line to end line.
2. Players and substitutions: Each side has two 11-member teams—one womens team and one mens team. The two teams alternate quarters, playing another team of the same gender. On offense, seven men or women play on the line of scrimmage. Each team can make unlimited substitutions, but only when the ball's dead.
3. The game isn't designed for heavy contact. No regulation equipment is necessary. Players wear shorts and shirts. Whenever possible, players should wear basketball shoes. *Cleats are prohibited.*
4. Each game has four 10-minute quarters. Mens teams and womens teams alternate each quarter. There's a 10-minute halftime.
5. Kickoffs are made anywhere along the kicker's 30-yard line.
6. Scoring: six points for a touchdown; one point for a conversion; and two points for a safety.
7. No one may tackle the ball carrier, passer or kicker.
8. Each team has four downs to reach midfield, then four downs to score.
9. Forward and lateral passes follow standard football regulations. All players on the playing field—both offensive and defensive—can receive passes any time.
Other adaptations could be to require any team with a 10-point lead to change the backfield or have coed teams.

Diagram 9
Volleyball Rules
Follow regulation rules with the following exceptions:
1. No spiking is permitted.
2. All serves must be underhand.
3. Each team hits the ball only three times before returning it. At least one woman must hit the ball during a volley before it's returned. (Exception: A man may directly return the serve if he's on the front line and the ball fails to pass that line on the serve only. However, he cannot drift back to take advantage of this exception.)
4. Each team must have at least six players and at most nine. Teams can substitute players freely. Teams must have a minimum number of women as follows:
● Six-player teams: two women.
● Seven- or eight-player teams: three women.
● Nine-player teams: four women.

This process has a significant advantage over openly brainstorming ideas. In brainstorming, some suggestions are laughed at and dismissed when actually they're creative ideas. As a result, young people are reluctant to suggest anything unusual. Writing suggestions puts everyone's idea on an equal level, and no one knows who suggested what. Then young people take seriously the ranking, since they know it affects the options they'll have at camp.

As you plan workshops for your camp, use the following suggestions as springboards:

Guest leaders. Guest leaders enrich workshops with their unique perspectives,

---

Diagram 10
Water Polo Rules
Follow regulation rules with the following exceptions:
1. The play area is the full length of the pool.
2. Miniature soccer cages are used for goals at each end of the pool.
3. Each team consists of equal numbers of players.
4. Each game has two halves of 25 minutes. Teams switch ends at halftime.
5. Walking with the ball is illegal.
6. Goalkeepers may stand to defend the goal but can't throw the ball beyond the halfway point.
7. The goalie box extends two yards in front of the goal. No one but the goalie can enter the box except to pick up a loose ball. The player must immediately leave the box in this case.
8. No holding, grasping, pinching, prodding, pushing, slapping or other such illegal use of hands is permitted. Continual violation results in two minutes in the penalty box.
9. No shot-on-goal from inside the penalty box is allowed.
10. Shot-on-goal goes back to the goalie.

Diagram 11
Softball Rules
Follow regulation rules with the following exceptions:
1. The batting team provides its own pitcher.
2. Each batter receives two pitches (hit fair or an out).
3. The batting team may begin hitting when all its players have gathered.
4. The ball must be returned immediately to the pitcher's mound after the third out.
5. Pitchers may not play defense.
6. Any batted ball that hits the pitcher retires the batter. All base runners must stay on their base.
7. Left-handed boys entering the 10th grade and up must bat right-handed and vice versa. Boys ninth grade and under and all girls bat normally.
8. Defense must play in normal positions. No one may "edge in" before the ball's hit.
9. Games last 50 minutes rather than a certain number of innings.
10. No bunting is permitted.

specialized skills and diverse leadership styles. Including guest leaders multiplies the possibilities for enriching campers' lives.

Contacts with potential guest leaders seldom prove fruitless. Even when potential leaders aren't available during your camp, they often know another person who can work with your program.

Consider these options:

1. A naturalist from the state's Department of Natural Resources, a U.S. Forest Service specialist or leaders from the state Wildlife Federation can enhance a group's awareness of the local outdoors and environment in brief presentations or guided field trips.

2. Ministers, theologians, missionaries and other Christian professionals can lead appealing workshops for campers. Introducing young people to other ministers, ideas and expressions of faith broadens their perspective on the church. And since many clergy and other professionals trace their first sense of calling into professional ministry to camp experiences, they're usually delighted to help if they're available.

3. Local artists, musicians, writers, storytellers and artisans also enrich camp experiences with their diverse talents. Groups who travel long distances to camp often find talented local people through the camp director-manager, area pastors, or nearby state and campus offices.

Creative projects. Creative projects can be tailor-made for each camp. Plan both individual and group projects that relate to the camp theme and campers' interest levels. By planning carefully, you can include projects related to the camp theme that individual campers can share to enhance worship experiences for the whole group.

To provide variety and balance in projects for your camp, mix new projects with standbys that always create interest in your group. Also provide both short-term projects and projects that require work each day of camp; each appeals to campers' different interest levels.

Select a manageable number of projects, and have someone responsible for supervising each project. If the camp has a craft room or other suitable space, you may be able to set up your projects and leave them there throughout the camp. If counselors or camp staff have specific skills, ask them to teach their skills to campers.

Include young people when deciding what projects to offer at camp. Keep in mind a project's space requirements, portability, expense and time requirements. Craft stores and magazines have lots of ideas you can use or adapt. Diagram 12, "31 Camp Projects," lists projects that have worked well for many youth camps. Keep in mind that projects that don't work with some groups may generate great interest in others.

Interest groups. In addition to creative, hands-on project electives, many camps hold interest groups that focus on issues, information, survey and study. These groups may be experiential or seminar-oriented. Each approach appeals to different young people. Workshops are especially interesting to senior highers.

Involve young people in determining and shaping the interest groups and workshops at your camp. Use interest finders, camp evaluations and interviews to identify issues that appeal to campers and relate to the camp theme.

Workshops and interest groups can cover a variety of campers' personal, theological and social concerns. Or they might focus on learning new skills. Interest groups might include:

● Personal: getting along with parents, peer pressure, divorce, death, friend-

Diagram 12
31 Camp Projects

The following 31 projects have been used in many youth camps. Evaluate each project in light of your group's needs and interests. Remember that each factor can vary, depending on the approach you take on the project.

Each craft requires different space, materials and time to complete. It's easier to have a temporary or permanent camp craft shop with rotating groups than to move crafts between groups to different locations. Many crafts can be done outdoors on tables or in the open.

Advanced planning will dramatically cut expenses, since planning gives you time to gather materials from salvage shops and to ask church members for donations.

Check local bookstores for popular craft books. Some of the best ones are listed in the camping resources on page 343.

Ammonia blueprinting	Fabric painting (shirts,	Pottery
Banner-making	shorts, jeans,	Print-making
Basket-making	pillowcases)	Sand painting
Batik	Foxfire crafts	Screen printing
Belt-making	Kite-making	Sculpturing
Box-making	Macrame	Shrink art
Camp newspaper	Mask-making	Slide-making
Collage	Moccasin-making	Stained glass
Cornstalk carving	Mosaics	String painting
Creative cooking	Name tags and lanyards	Tie-dyeing
Drawing and sketching	Poster-making	Weaving and wall hangings

ships, sex, dating and vocations.

● Theological: Bible study, missions, creative worship, cults and meditation.

● Social: world hunger, peace, international relations, service projects and crime.

● Skills: drama, mime, music, clowning, outdoor living, photography, puppetry, interpretive dance and leadership skills.

Wilderness living skills and adventures. The area surrounding your residential camp may offer opportunities for campers to experience a taste of backcountry camping through short adventures and wilderness skills training. Multiple classes on a subject or classes covering a new subject each day expose campers to skills and experiences normally reserved for backcountry trips. Half-day or overnight adventures appeal to campers who want a challenge beyond camp boundaries. Some

camps couple off-site adventures with introductory on-site training seminars.

Breakfast or lunch cookouts, day hikes and field trips are additional ways to provide off-site adventure for small groups. Most camps are within driving distance of a national forest, state park, or historical or natural area—all public resources you can use at little or no cost.

Outdoor skills to consider for your camp include using gear and shelters; map and compass navigation; building fires; rope work; cooking; and survival training. Adventures could involve a variety of activities, depending on the location of your camp: deep-sea fishing, cycling, mountaineering, canoeing, sailing, cross-country skiing and rappelling. (For details on skills and adventures, see chapters 6-9 and 18-25.)

Ropes courses. With qualified instructors, a ropes course is a fun outdoor activity for group-building and skills development. Camps, colleges, schools and outdoor learning centers throughout the United States have established ropes courses that may be available for your camp.

There are usually three levels of apparatus:

1. Group initiatives. These courses involve platforms, hanging log beams, climbing walls and physical initiatives. They require ingenuity and teamwork for solving problems posed by the instructors. Many initiatives require no apparatus.

2. Low-ropes courses. More complex initiatives, low-ropes courses involve cables, ropes, and physical group challenges that require focus, balance and teamwork.

3. High-ropes courses. High-ropes courses involve personal initiatives on high cables, poles, suspended beams, zip lines and rope webs. While a course is usually done individually, encouragement from other team members is central to the experience. Most campers begin with group initiatives and low ropes initiatives before attempting high ropes experiences.

If you want to offer a ropes course for your camp, contact nearby camps, YMCAs, outdoor education centers, college recreation departments, residential treatment program centers, or public and private schools. Then visit the director or leaders. Be sure you feel confident about the leaders and their abilities. Explain your goals, and ask for a guided tour of the course elements. Openly ask any questions you have about safety, group sizes, process and cost.

Campouts and field trips. An overnight campout or field trip provides a unique opportunity for community-building and group learning among residential campers. One outdoor school camp provides a 24-hour experience for their camp-

ers from 11:00 a.m. to 11:00 a.m. The leaders plan hiking, group initiatives, meals, skills training, catnapping and a full range of nighttime adventures that add mystery and discovery to the outing.

The campout should be simple and based on the site, availability of camping equipment and leadership skills. By establishing a base camp within walking or driving distance of the residential camp, you can rotate groups throughout the week of camp.

Keep the four key ingredients of an overnighter in mind to keep the camp from becoming too complex: shelter, food, safety and fun. You'll need only basic camping equipment for an overnight experience: food, water, shelter and supplies. Campers can roll a change of clothes, a jacket, rain gear and personal articles in their sleeping bags or pillowcases.

Campwide Celebration and Worship

Celebration and worship are central to Christian camping. Formal worship can occur in mealtime blessings, morning watches, and small group and large group times.

Worship celebrations should revolve around the camp theme, and each subsequent celebration experience should flow from preceding experiences. Talk with the camp minister or speaker ahead of time to refine each worship time by carefully selecting music, scriptures, activities and other elements of the service.

If several people share leadership for campwide presentations, it's important that they build on one another's strengths. Encourage leaders to attend one another's sessions. Worship leaders who are aware of your camp's dynamics and incidents can often find unusual ways to connect with campers' experiences. This communicates the speaker's personal involvement and interest in the campers. (Chapter 13, "Leading Camp Worship and Bible Study," focuses on worship at camp and includes worship ideas for various times and settings.)

Special Evening Events

Each evening of a residential camp is a unique occasion to add variety and creativity to the camp's program. Campfires, skits, talent nights, special guests appearances, concerts and sing-alongs are standard evening treats at many camps.

The camp's theme, location and availability of talent (among campers, leaders and community people) can guide your planning. Each evening should conclude with a focus on the camper's faith experience through celebration and worship.

The Closing Celebration

Perhaps the most significant experience at camp is the closing worship celebration. As camp draws to a close, worship and celebration take on special meaning. Campers and leaders often feel called to make new commitments to Christ and the church's mission. Even campers who aren't outwardly expressive often respond emotionally in dedication, thanksgiving, forgiveness, reconciliation and determination to live life differently. See Chapter 13 for more on leading closing camp worship experiences.

Evaluating Residential Camp

One of the keys to planning successful residential youth camps year after year is to have campers evaluate their experience at the end of the week. Their comments about what they liked, didn't like and want next year help fine-tune your camp program.

Camp evaluations have several purposes. First, they help planners critique their work. This critique is a learning ex-

perience that helps leaders rethink their preconceptions and emphases. Second, evaluations give ideas for planning the next camp. These ideas surface through specific suggestions or by implication—what did campers like or dislike about this camp, and how can we better meet their needs? Finally, evaluations give campers an opportunity to express themselves. It's a way of reminding them that they're important and that the camp's designed especially for them.

You can evaluate camps in many ways. Each chapter in this section offers a model. Camp Notebook 8, "Residential Camp Evaluation," is an open-ended evaluation form that gives campers the freedom to express specific thoughts about the camp.

The Camp Director-Manager's Role

Whenever a youth group uses a camp facility, the camp's director-manager greatly influences the tone and success of the weeklong event. His or her attitude, reliability and helpfulness all contribute to a camp's success—and whether a group will return to the facility.

In an interview for this book, Jim Black, manager of Camp Lee in Andalusia, Alabama, explained what a camp manager can do to help churches in their youth camps. Here are his suggestions:

Have fun with campers. Black says he works hard to tell campers how happy he is that they've come to his facility. When campers first arrive, he sets a playful and friendly tone by mixing up his words during orientation. Not only does this get campers laughing, he says, "They also have to listen to make sure what I'm saying—like 'pimming swool' instead of 'swimming pool' or 'slock ride' instead of 'rock slide.' Pretty soon [the gimmick] catches on, and they use it all week long—'chied fricken,' 'ginger-ficking lood' or 'Let's go down to

Camp Notebook 8

Residential Camp Evaluation

We want you to tell us about your week at camp. Please use concrete statements, such as "We spent too much time . . . ," "I'd like for us to use our time . . ." and "What meant the most to me was when . . ."

You'll have a chance to talk about these evaluations, and the next planning committee will read all the comments when it begins planning for next year.

Answer each of the following questions. *Be as specific as possible.*

1. Look at your camp schedule and evaluate each day. Use the following questions as your guide:
● What was this day's best experience for you? Why?
● What part of this day would you like to forget? Why?
● What would you add or subtract from this day?

Monday: _____
_____

Tuesday: _____
_____

Wednesday: _____
_____

Thursday: _____
_____

Friday: _____
_____

Saturday: _____
_____

2. How did camp affect your idea of God, other people and your faith? Explain. If you don't think it affected any of these areas, explain why.
● Idea of God: _____

● Other people: _____

● Your faith: _____

3. If you could write a letter to someone attending camp next year, what would you say to help that person get the most from the experience? Write your letter on the back of this sheet.

4. How is youth camp an extension of our church's youth ministry? Explain.
_____

5. Now that you've reflected on your week, how has camp helped you personally? _____

the larkin' pot.' "

Love the camp. Black says it's important to love the facility, to want to keep it nice and to communicate these things to campers. He adds: "It's sort of like they have come home . . . When groups come back year after year, I tell them that I expect more of them. They love camp too and want to do a good job keeping it looking neat."

Remember names. "Knowing names and safety are the #1 concerns of camp for me," Black says. He explains that remembering individual campers' names is the most critical thing he does—"whether they're going to be there for one year or forever."

Remember that food service comes second. After knowing names and safety, camp managers should concentrate on serving good food, Black says. Don't cut corners in preparing and serving food. Campers remember the food at camp, and it greatly influences whether they'll return.

Make people feel at home. Black suggests that camp managers should always think of little ways to make campers feel at home. "I put the coffeepot on early and keep it on all day," he says. "I also run the canteen twice a day. Sometimes it's boring, but it gives me another chance to meet campers."

Do things with campers. "I take all groups to the rock slide the first time," Black says. "I go for safety, but they think it's for the fun of it. Sometimes I take groups on night hikes. That's a highlight for a lot of campers."

Concentrate on promotion. Black says that since he's not responsible for counselors or leading groups, he concentrates on relationships and promotion.

Give visitors a full camp tour. Black urges director-managers to give prospective campers a relaxed tour of the entire facility. He adds that it's important to clean the camp immediately after a group leaves. He explains: "If we have a visitor the next day, they'll see the camp as it will be when they come to camp. Waiting to clean camp up until before a group arrives gives a bad impression on a tour. I show them the showers especially, so they can see they are really clean. Then we go back to the dining hall to have some brownies and something to drink while we talk over their questions."

Chapter 6

Backpacking

FOOT TRAVEL ONLY
PURSUANT TO EXISTING LAW AND
REGULATION, THE TRAIL BEHIND THIS SIGN
IS CLOSED TO ALL FORMS OF MOTORIZED
VEHICULAR USE . . .

The stark U.S. Forest Service sign poses both an invitation and a warning. When youth groups pass such signs, they begin a fascinating and challenging adventure—backpack camping.

Backpack camping is more than just walking or hiking. It's thinking and searching as you cool your feet in a mountain stream. It's sharing your quest with others while reading the poetry nature etches on chestnut logs. It's asking "why?" to a thousand mysteries that mark the path you travel. It's an experiment in responsibility and Christian community.

Setting out for the high country on foot with a pack on their back fascinates and challenges teenagers. It fulfills their urge for freedom, and it invites them to test themselves beyond the boundaries of everyday life. It provides a living parable that allows them to measure themselves and reflect on their journey into adulthood.

One group's 30-mile outdoor adventure illustrates the possibilities of backpacking with a youth group. The eight hikers and two leaders began their five-day adventure in the Appalachian Mountains by hiking to the top of Springer Mountain. After a light lunch they descended along the trail into the Blue Ridge Wildlife Management Area.

Every bend of the trail brought new discoveries. The trail down Springer's eastern slope ran through almost endless fern beds. Then the ferns gave way to wildflowers. As the hikers turned north, they crossed a series of low ridges and clear mountain streams. The hikers fell silent as they walked, looked and listened to the world around them.

The day's end meant two things: rest and a hot meal. Each hiker carried a portion of the community supplies and two meals. When it was time to eat what a camper carried, he or she organized and led the cooking team. Dinner consisted of lightweight foods cooked on a small camping stove. (In five days these hikers built only three fires—two for fellowship and one for cooking.) Once the dishes were cleaned, the hikers gathered around a few burning logs to relive their five-mile trek and to celebrate with scripture readings, songs and stories. Finally they bedded down in improvised tarp shelters under the stars.

The new day brought fresh experiences and discoveries as the hikers pushed deeper into the forest—a wild turkey track, a crashing waterfall, a pioneer cemetery, a burned area and another church group hiking south. Each event drew the group together. At one point on a ridge, the campers used binoculars to see the ridges they'd cross in two days.

Leaving the high mountains, the group traveled downhill to set up camp for two nights. The next day was a layover day when campers took it easy, washed clothes, and took baths and afternoon swims. The day ended in celebration and reflection around a special campfire with singing and marshmallows.

On the fourth day the hike continued, offering still more trails and discoveries. That night campers talked intimately, each keenly aware that this was their last night together. Only six miles separated the hikers from the journey's end. The final day's hike was as beautiful as the first day. It ended in Woody's Gap Recreation Area, where families, fried chicken and potato salad greeted the campers.

Guidelines for Backpacking Trips

Leading teenagers in a backpacking trip introduces them to outdoor living and the resulting independence and interdependence. They experience the world without the amenities and distractions of everyday life. They challenge themselves physically, and they discover the importance of working together as a group. They learn how to live with only what they can carry—and their ingenuity.

Backpack camping has many variations. Different seasons, terrains, vegetation, groups, lengths, goals and required skills all shape the trip's mood, itinerary and outcomes. Backpacking can also be the vehicle for many outdoor interests: mountain climbing, cross-country skiing, fishing, caving, photography, survival training and outdoor education.

As you consider the shape of your group's backpacking trip, keep in mind the following guidelines:

Plan precisely. A successful backpacking trip requires precise planning. Gear selection, menu planning, personal conditioning and route selection must be carefully thought through to avoid last-minute changes, impossible itineraries, inadequate food, and other problems or disappointments.

In planning its first eight-day backpacking trip to an unseen area, one youth group originally selected a west-to-east route because it was easiest to reach. But careful research, map checking and information about local regulations revealed an obvious oversight. Only groups of six or fewer could qualify for backcountry permits in the area, so the group had to camp in established campsites, near the trail. However, the distance between the first two campsites was 11 miles—an impossible distance with eight days of food in your pack.

By studying more, the group learned that if it traveled east to west, the distance between the first two camps was only five miles. So the leaders reversed the original plan, putting the 11-mile hike at the end of the trip.

The seventh day followed a layover day. The group was rested, and since most of the food was gone, the packs were lighter. Everyone was stronger from packing and living outdoors. The group was revved to undertake its longest hike of the trip. The spirited backpackers hit the trail early and arrived at their last campsite by 2 p.m. By spotting a potential problem early, the campers enjoyed a well-paced trip instead of an impossible chore.

Seek assistance in planning. If you're planning a trip to a distant area, learn as much as possible about every aspect of the area. Find out about the weather, topography and local regulations. Contact a local pastor or camp director to find a local guide to help you plan and lead the trip. Having a competent guide becomes more critical as you venture into more challenging wilderness areas.

Know your group's limits. Nothing lowers campers' spirits or raises parents' ire more than a camping trip that's too difficult or dangerous for group members. Likewise, planning a trip that's too easy defeats one of the purposes of backpacking: to challenge and stretch campers. It's critical, then, to understand your group's level of experience and physical condition as well as the ease or difficulty of the trails you'll use.

Assessing group strength isn't easy. The best indicator of whether to include a teenager on a longer trip is firsthand experience. One way to guard against including teenagers who aren't ready is to require first-time campers to participate in a beginners backpacking trip that focuses on teaching skills. Mailing campers information about conditioning and requiring a physical examination before camp, which many camps routinely do, also helps.

However, there's no way to guarantee that all campers can undertake a backpacking trip. Thus the leader must exercise sound judgment throughout any backcountry event.

Knowing your group's growth and leadership skills is essential when undertaking a longer hiking event. A group with two experienced adult leaders and four or five experienced campers can afford to include four or five teenagers with less experience. But adult leaders with less leadership experience would be unwise to plan a long trip for a group of beginners—regardless of their ages.

This chapter concludes with a suggested process for introducing backpacking to your congregation if the youth group hasn't been backpacking before (page 96). The process consists of a backpacking workshop, a backpacking seminar, an overnight training trip and a residentially based backpacking trip.

Each backpacking experience builds on the others, and each offers new challenges and opportunities. After a few successful trips, many groups are inspired to venture further and longer in the wilderness. They may choose to climb a series of major mountain peaks or explore in depth an area with the assistance of a local guide. By understanding this growth, you can offer challenging experiences for campers year after year.

Don't push too hard. The following journal excerpt from a trip across the Grand Canyon emphasizes the mistake groups make when they push too hard to reach their destination without enjoying the journey itself:

The first afternoon we hiked to Widforss Point on the north rim of the canyon. The next day we hiked back to the North Rim Campground for another night. Then we descended the grand walls and camped on Bright Angel Creek. Two nights were spent at Phantom Ranch where the Bright Angel Creek flows into the Colorado.

At midnight on our first night at Phantom Ranch, a college geology class arrived. The class had packed from the north rim that day—a two-day trip for us.

The next morning was layover day—a time to explore the area and watch rafters going down the Colorado. At breakfast we met a photography team from Encyclopaedia Britannica that was making a geology filmstrip. The producer invited us to tag along as they took pictures of Indian ruins along the river.

We met the college students again. After a four-hour sleep most of the students were looking at the ground, slumped under their backpacks and bulky sleeping bags. The professor lectured rapidly, pointing out many things the geologists from Encyclopaedia Britannica had told us. The geology class wanted to reach the south rim by noon. It took the shortest and steepest trail in order to stay on schedule.

The next day we hiked out along the lower, not-so-steep trail and camped at Indian Gardens Campground. We spent our last evening talking with other campers and watching the sun burnish the limestone and shale temples to a deep red.

Much of our itinerary had been shaped through reading the Time-Life book The Grand Canyon. *In it we discovered the story of Gunnar Widforss the Swedish artist. The author made a striking statement about hiking across the canyon. He said, "A runner in top condition . . . once set a rim-to-rim record of three hours 56 minutes." Then he added, "It is also possible for a runner in top condition to pass by all the paintings in the Grand Gallery of the Louvre in about 28 seconds."*

Always have emergency plans. Establishing clear contingency plans and emergency procedures is mandatory, particularly on an extended backpacking trip. Leaders should know how they'll respond to injury, illness and inclement weather. Group equipment should include emergency gear.

Before the trip, think through access and evacuation routes in the wilderness area. Leave a marked trip itinerary with responsible people at the base camp or church and with local authorities.

One senior high camper arrived at a residentially based camp fully equipped to hike. She was energetic, a star student, a runner—a delightful person. Though she had an elastic brace on her knee, her doctor had assured the camp leaders that she'd be fine. Her mother said she "had looked forward to backpacking all year long."

The backpackers set out early the next day. By midmorning they'd crossed a moderate mountain. The girl was already in pain. The group took a break before tackling an even steeper ascent. The girl's boyfriend put her sleeping bag on top of his pack and encouraged her as the group set out again. Periodically on the steep climb she'd stop to rest as other hikers volunteered to lighten her pack. Before reaching the summit, she was limping, and a leader was carrying her pack.

The long lunch and exploring time at the summit gave the leaders time to slow their racing minds and think through alternatives. Then they proposed their plan to the group: Hike to the next road crossing to wait for transportation for the disappointed camper. If no one came along, they'd spend the night at the crossing and replan their route. There was silent commitment.

After a slow descent the group met a day-hiking family that agreed to drive the girl back to base camp where she could call her parents. Her boyfriend decided to continue the trek so the rest of the group wouldn't have to carry the extra community gear and food after two people dropped out.

As the afternoon wore on the group's silent grief for their hurting friend was replaced by excited talk, laughter and a quickened pace. The backpackers were determined to make up the lost time and reach the scheduled campsite. They did. Five days later they emerged 30 miles further up the trail—close, bonded and excited to see a smiling friend who waited with her parents and a basket of fried chicken for a trail-head picnic.

Choosing Your Gear

Having the right equipment doesn't guarantee a good hike, but it does prevent equipment problems from interfering with your trip's success.

If your group doesn't have experience backpacking, don't ask teenagers and the church to buy expensive gear until you've backpacked a few times. Instead, use borrowed or rented gear. Rent several types of packs and tents to help the group discover what best suits its needs. Then on your first trip, have leaders and teenagers try different types of packs and tents to learn what feels good and what seems most practical for the money. If your church wants to purchase equipment in quantity, rent equipment in the early stages. Then consult camp supply companies or manufacturers for discount purchases.

Making sure community and individual gear is adequate is particularly important for long-distance hikes. The longer the backpacking trip, the greater the demand on equipment and the possibility of equipment failure. A longer trip may also expose your equipment to a greater possibility for severe weather. In this case, not having appropriate gear could lead to serious problems.

Part Five of this book, "Backcountry Living Skills," discusses how to select and use the equipment you'll need for backpack camping. Here are the types of gear and equipment your campers will need:

Clothes. Having appropriate clothes is essential since hikers won't have cars and buildings to protect them from the weather. Campers must also remember that they carry whatever they wear, so they won't be able to take a change of clothes for every situation. Teach them how to layer clothing for the season and climate of your hike

(see Chapter 20).

Boots. Feet are your most important asset on a backpacking trip. Having boots that fit well and are broken in to conform to the hiker's feet guards against blisters and other sore spots. Chapter 20, "Personal Gear and Packing," discusses how to choose boots and how to break them in before your hike.

Backpacks. Backpackers use two types of backpacks: external-frame packs (most common) and internal-frame packs (soft packs). Internal-frame packs are used more for mountain climbing or cross-country skiing trips, and some hikers prefer soft packs because they're easier to load. However, they tend to be hotter in warm summer weather. See Chapter 20 for more about choosing backpacks.

Sleeping bags. Different sleeping bags have different constructions and insulation. Each has certain advantages and disadvantages. Using information from Chapter 20, catalogs and sporting goods stores, help campers select sleeping bags that fit their needs and budgets. They may choose to rent or buy their bag. Outdoor schools and rental dealers usually use washable sleeping bags that can undergo 30 or more washings. Frequent washings aren't necessary for a personal bag.

Tents. Even though many outdoor enthusiasts believe sleeping under the stars is the only way to enjoy a camp, a tent is still a good retreat from inclement weather or mosquitoes. For comparisons of tents and their uses and information on tent care, see Chapter 22, "Tents and Emergency Shelters."

Personal articles. Campers will want various personal items for their camp. While many of them are appropriate, don't let campers bring too much. The packs will only get heavier as the hike progresses. Diagram 13, "Hikers Personal Articles Checklist," lists items campers may want with them. Chapter 20, "Personal Gear and Packing," gives more details on equipment.

Planning Your Menus

Planning meals for an extended backpacking trip requires care and creativity. What foods are light? What foods will keep without refrigeration? What foods will ensure a balanced, healthy diet for tired hikers? These are the questions to ask yourself as you plan menus.

Determining menus as a group is an excellent opportunity to work together and build community before setting out on your trip. Divide the group into three or four teams for planning trail meals. Have them work together to plan meals that are lightweight, nutritious and easy to prepare. Encourage hikers to be creative and innovative. If possible, shop and repackage food as a group.

Diagram 14, "Sample Menus for Backpacking," gives a sample menu for three full days in the backcountry. In addition to food for the meals, carry a good supply of snacks, including cheese, crackers, jerky, raisins, nuts, dried fruit and candy. Chapter 24, "Food and Cooking" discusses cooking gear and methods. It also suggests some great backcountry treats.

Diagram 13
Hikers Personal Articles Checklist

☐ Folding knife   ☐ Batteries   ☐ Journal and pen
☐ Compass   ☐ 12-inch-by-12-inch Ensolite   ☐ Bandanna
☐ Water bottle   sitting pad   ☐ Camera and film
☐ Sierra cup   ☐ New Testament   ☐ Fishing tackle
☐ Flashlight   (see page 297 for personal gear checklist)

Diagram 14
Sample Menus for Backpacking

	Day One	Day Two	Day Three
Breakfast	Ham and eggs, hash browns, toast, juice, hot chocolate.	Applesauce, scrambled eggs, toast, coffee, tea, hot chocolate.	Oatmeal, bagels and jelly, dried fruit, juice, hot chocolate.
Lunch	Sandwiches, apples, cheese, celery, drinks.	Raisins, cashews, jerky, cheese, peanut butter, crackers, hard candy, drinks.	Saltines, peanut butter and jelly sandwiches, fruit drink.
Dinner	French onion soup, beef stroganoff, green beans, hot apple cobbler, drinks.	Macaroni and cheese, fruit, veggies, pudding, drinks.	Soup, Spanish rice, S'mores, Dutch oven cake, drinks.

Planning Your Program

Most of the "program" for your backpacking trip will consist of hiking, enjoying the outdoors, having informal conversations and doing camping chores. However, it's also important to plan opportunities for hikers to reflect on and celebrate their experiences together. These structured experiences include:

● Trail meditation for setting out.
● Campfire programs and celebrations.
● Morning watches.
● Closing celebration before leaving camp.

Programs for backpacking trips should be simple and portable. (You have to carry everything you need on your back.) Group or individual journals are often ideal vehicles for personal reflection. Other experiences could use nature itself as "props" for experiencing Christian truth.

As always, let campers plan and compile the program for your hike. Give them the freedom and encouragement to be creative. Supply program resources and examples from previous camps to get them thinking about how they want to do their program. Plan *with* them!

Camp Notebooks 9-11 are sample group devotional guides for the theme "Life Is a Mountain—and You Can Climb It." Use these as prompters to help your group develop its own theme and group times. Chapter 2, "Planning a 'Boundaryless' Youth Camp," suggests additional ways to plan themes and programs. Chapter 13, "Leading Camp Worship and Bible Study," gives additional insights.

Trail Etiquette

Most trails in the backcountry are shared with other individuals and groups—horse packers, riders, fishers, hunters, photographers, families, couples and picnickers—to name a few. Public lands belong to everyone, so it's important to learn to live together and appreciate other people's recreational pursuits.

Before embarking on your hike, think through your group's responsibility to the people you'll meet on the trail. Group singing, for example, can be a delightful experience—if you're the ones singing. But having another group marching up the trail in song can frustrate the individual or group whose primary interest is peace and quiet.

Here are a few guidelines for meeting people on the trail:

1. When meeting one or two people on the trail, the lead hiker should greet the smaller party then follow its lead. Some people want to talk—to know where you're going, where you've been or where you're from. Others prefer to move on in silence. If your group prefers not to stop and speak, your leader will know not to stop for conversation.

2. Follow the same principle when meeting another group. The lead hiker's first greeting should clarify whether to talk together or move on. The two groups may want to compare trail notes or take a break together.

3. When two groups meet on a steep slope, the group traveling downhill has the right of way. The group traveling uphill should step to the right and if necessary stop to let the downhill group pass or stop.

4. When stopping for a break or meal, choose a place where your whole group can move off the trail, take off packs and spread out to rest. Avoid places with fragile growth or creek banks that are easily eroded.

5. When meeting horseback riders remember that horses are easily spooked by the unknown. If possible move to the downhill side of the trail and lower back-

Camp Notebook 9

Life Is a Mountain—and You Can Climb It

Beginning the Climb

1. For a few moments remember some of the mountains you've seen or climbed. Tell other group members about your memories.

2. What words describe your experiences with mountains? Write them down. _____

_____

3. Have someone in the group read Luke 9:28-36. As a group list words that describe how the disciples felt. _____

_____

4. Compare the words describing the disciples' experience to the words from your experiences. Discuss the similarities and differences with your group.

5. Read in unison the following statement from René Daumal's classic work *Mount Analogue*:

> *You cannot stay on the summit forever; you have to come down again . . . So why bother in the first place? Just this: What is above knows what is below, but what is below does not know what is above. In climbing, take careful note of the difficulties along your way; for as you go up, you can observe them. Coming down, you will no longer see them, but you will know they are there if you have observed them well.*
> *There is an art of finding one's direction in the lower regions by the memory of what one saw higher up. When one can no longer see, one can at least still know.*

From *Mount Analogue* by René Daumal. © 1959 Vincent Stuart Ltd. Reprinted by arrangement with Shambhala Publications, Inc., 300 Massachusetts Ave., Boston, MA 02115.

6. Underline the parts of the quote you like best. Write down your own thoughts or responses about how life is a mountain. Share your thoughts with your group. _____

_____

7. Close with a prayer.

Camp Notebook 10

Life Is a Mountain—and You Can Climb It

Finding Your Way Together

1. Have two group members alternate in reading aloud the following story for the group:

When I met Dave in the Absoroka Wilderness of Montana, he was working for the Department of Interior's Geological Survey. His job was to verify or correct the readings on topographical maps that had been charted in the '20s and '30s. Dave told me that magnetic bearings are constantly changing. I remembered that early maps of the West were often miles and miles in error. Yet as inaccurate as older maps may have been, later travelers have been able to identify the major peaks and lakes and the routes that led to their summits and shores.

Dave also talked about geology. He explained that what appears to be bedrock holding back the waters of an Alpine lake is actually the remnant of an ancient beach. Two days later, from a peak 2,000 feet above the lake, it was easy to see the distinct difference in the formation.

We all spend our lives finding our way. At first, faint word-of-mouth markings lead us. And tracings—words of the Bible, the love of family and friends, the rituals of the faith community—give us courage to explore the boundaries of life. Line by line, contours are laid down, forming our inner maps. And we each choose our routes— sometimes familiar pathways, and, now and then, uncharted treks cross country.

2. Read Matthew 4:1-11 together. In your own words, write the obstacles (temptations) Jesus faced in finding his way:

verse 3: _____

verses 5-6: _____

verses 8-9: _____

3. Now think about the obstacles you face as you try to find your way in life. List them, then share your thoughts with the group. _____
_____

4. How can Jesus' answers to his obstacles help you in the obstacles you listed as a group?

verse 4: _____

verse 7: _____

verse 10: _____

5. Pray the Lord's Prayer together.

Camp Notebook 11

Life Is a Mountain—and You Can Climb It

Attempting the Summit

1. Use a rope to tie the whole group together at the waist. Then walk as a group to a nearby spot where you can sit comfortably together to follow this guide.

2. Have two group members read the following passage aloud while still tied together:

> In major expeditions, a large party of guides, packers and climbers travels together, packing the necessary supplies to a base camp midway on the revered peak. Most of them stop at base camp, and the remaining climbers set up a series of camps as they climb. Higher and higher, they alternately pack their precious essentials and then retreat to lower elevations for rest. Finally the last camp is set.
>
> Summit in sight, and rested as much as possible, only three or four are chosen to climb. They set out before morning light. The leaders kick a trail in the snow, spending their energy to make it easier for those who follow. As the day wears on and the cold wears away at the climbers, those who broke trail are exhausted, and they turn back while they have enough strength to return. Then the followers, whose energy was saved by their traveling companions, continue upward.
>
> Of the 30 or 40 or more who set out in the beginning, only two climbers— maybe just one—will reach the summit. But all share in the triumph. None is unimportant.

3. As a group, think out loud about the spiritual lessons in this passage.

4. Who are the guides, packers and climbers in your life? Name some. Tell other group members how they support you.

5. What are the base camps and the high camps you rely on?

6. Take turns reading the Beatitudes in Matthew 5:1-10.

7. Give names to the "summits" or "mountain experiences" found in these verses. For example, verse 3 could be "the mountain of spiritual poverty."

verse 4: _____ verse 8: _____
verse 5: _____ verse 9: _____
verse 6: _____ verse 10: _____
verse 7: _____

8. Write your own prayer to pray aloud when you leave this campsite. After everyone has written a prayer, pray them aloud one by one. Then pray the following prayer in unison:

God of our journeys,
We thank you for the trails that bring us home
*   again,*
For life coming full-circle,
For births and deaths,
For the memories of times and places
*   that you have made holy in our minds.*

Lead us back to those who have touched us,
*   and loved us,*
*   and set our feet upon the pathways of faith.*
Let us touch them in return. Amen.

packs to the ground until the horses pass. Refrain from making quick movements, talking or reaching out to touch the horses.

Getting Your Group Ready to Backpack

Youth groups that are new to backpacking need to learn as much as possible about backcountry living before they take their first extended trip. Allowing campers to touch and taste backpacking one step at a time prepares them to undertake longer treks realistically. Moving too far too fast frustrates beginners. Campers are easily turned off or burned out when a leader overestimates a group's motivation, experience or endurance. Training adult workers for backpacking also assures parents that their church's youth program will provide safe trips in the backcountry.

An introduction to backpacking should integrate fun, freedom and Christian friendship with an overview of living outdoors with your home on your back. By planning progressive experiences, feelings of security, fun and anticipation develop among participants. These experiences can include:

● A backpacking workshop (two to three hours).

● A backpacking seminar (all day on the trail).

● An overnight backpacking training trip.

● A residentially based backpacking trip.

The first three steps can be billed as an "Introduction to Backpacking" course in the fall to prepare for longer backpacking trips the following spring or summer.

A Backpacking Workshop

Backpacking workshops or interest groups invite potential campers and their parents to see the possibilities for Christian community in backpacking. They also help people get a feel for backpacking and alleviate fears. The two- to three-hour presentations should be succinct, with plenty of time for questions and answers. Save the last 30 minutes for discussion.

Setting. Generate excitement by displaying backpacking gear in a spacious, comfortable meeting place. Alpine shop owners and rental dealers will often gladly send a resource person with samples of the latest equipment.

Set up one or two tents in the meeting room. On carpet, use drapery hooks to secure the corners. Place heavy books inside each corner on a tile floor. Display sleeping bags, backpacks, kitchen items and personal gear on nearby tables. If available, include a video or slide show in the display. Serve backpacking snacks and drinks for refreshments to give participants a sense of backpacking fellowship.

Crowdbreaker. Begin the program by inviting participants to play a group-building game, such as "Camp Catalog Game" (page 240) or "True North" (page 256). If participants don't know each other, ask them to tell their name and to share their favorite outdoor memory.

Overview. Set a backpacking tone by showing a slide show, video or film. If properly presented, such an introduction raises countless questions to explore. Invite participants to imagine themselves backpacking as they watch. To increase participation in the show, give viewers a simple assignment before viewing. Then have them discuss what they learned after the show. Sample viewing assignments include: Watch for the scene that best portrays the purpose of backpacking for you, or look for something you'd like to know more about.

After the visual presentation, ask participants to identify the purposes of backpacking, specific areas that need more discussion or questions they have.

Demonstrations. Many of the participants' questions and interests will involve equipment: What's most practical? best? useful? Is it best to borrow? rent? purchase? Another important, sometimes unspoken, question is: Can I carry a pack for five miles?

Use equipment demonstrations to answer these types of questions. Demonstrations let participants have hands-on time with equipment. They also guide potential shoppers for wise shopping. Distribute printed handouts or information from manufacturers catalogs to help participants understand the equipment.

Demonstrations need not be exhaustive. You don't need to demonstrate a full line of gear from simplest to expedition quality. Instead, include two or three quality lines with midrange prices. Encourage potential campers to borrow or rent equipment and take time shopping before investing in new equipment. Workshop leaders and demonstrators should be available after the group session to talk with individuals.

You can lead demonstrations in different ways. If your group is small, you can keep the group together and demonstrate each aspect sequentially. If your group is large, set up different displays in different rooms or corners and have small groups watch different demonstrations. Then rotate so each small group sees each demonstration.

Here are things to include in your demonstrations:

1. Clothes. Help participants picture the clothing they already have and how it would work in the backcountry by having a personal demonstration, a clothing display or a picture display. Show campers layering techniques for summer, spring-fall and winter clothing combinations (see Chapter 20).

2. Backpacks. Have a fully packed pack of moderate weight (25 to 30 pounds) available for people to try on. Include samples of different backpacks, and explain the advantages and disadvantages of each. Show campers how to arrange a pack correctly.

3. Sleeping bags. Display two or three bags that supply the lowest comfort-range needed for your area. Use manufacturers descriptions and show the different types of construction—sewn through, layered and baffled. Demonstrate how to stuff a sleeping bag in a stuff sack and how to attach it to a backpack with straps (see Chapter 20).

4. Tents. Set up one or two tents in advance to create the feeling of camping out. Being able to take off their shoes and crawl into a tent with one or two other people helps campers and parents feel the space a tent provides.

Putting up and taking down tents seems like a big task to beginners. End your tent demonstration by taking the tent down, rolling it up and packing it on a backpack. This exercise helps people see how easy it is to move camp from place to place.

5. Kitchen equipment and community gear. Set up a backpacking kitchen on a table to illustrate what you'll need for group cooking on the trail (see Chapter 24). Briefly explain how to use each item. Talk about how to fill and light a stove safely, how to dip hot water, and how to handle hot pots and pans. Here's other community gear to include in your display and discussion:

- Hudson Bay ax
- Folding saw
- Folding shovel
- Rope

- Nylon or plastic tarp
- Maps
- Group first aid kit
- Small roll of duct tape
- Backpacking repair kit in a drawstring bag with the following:
  - ☐ Unpadded waist belt
  - ☐ Spare shoulder straps
  - ☐ Clevis pins and rings
  - ☐ Small roll of wire
  - ☐ Pliers or backpack tool
  - ☐ 10-inch section of 1-inch PVC pipe for a spring or stream water spout
  - ☐ 3-foot section of surgical tubing for a fire bellows

6. Personal articles. Personalize your workshop display by including a change of clothing, a ditty bag, rain gear and a jacket. Several other personal articles to include are listed in the "Hikers Personal Articles Checklist" (Diagram 13, page 91).

Conclusion. Conclude your backpacking workshop by reiterating the purpose and value of backpacking for Christian community-building and growth. Help refocus the group on the church's purpose for trekking into the backcountry by reading a scripture passage and a brief quotation from an outdoor book, such as the following thought by naturalist John Muir from Richard Cartwright Austin's *Baptized Into Wilderness: A Christian Perspective on John Muir*:

We seem to imagine that since Herod beheaded John the Baptist, there is no longer any voice crying in the wilderness. But no one in the wilderness can possibly make such a mistake, for every one of these flowers is such a voice. No wilderness in the world is so desolate as to be without divine ministers. God's love covers all the earth as the sky covers it, and also fills it in every pore. And this love has voices heard by all who have ears to hear.
John Muir, March 14, 1873

A Backpacking Seminar

A daylong outdoor seminar for would-be backpackers is a natural second step toward full-fledged backpacking. The freedom of a day on the trail without the tasks of overnight camping is an excellent way to introduce beginners to trail camping techniques.

Gear. Let backpackers feel what it's like to carry a pack by loading three backpacks for your seminar to be carried by the seminar members. Hikers then trade off carrying the pack throughout the day so everyone gets a chance to carry a pack without having to do it for long. Here's what to include in each pack:

Pack 1: Clothing for a three-day trip, tent, sleeping bag, 12-inch-by-12-inch Ensolite sitting pad, ditty bag, saw, ax, rope and map.

Pack 2: Snacks and ingredients for the noon or evening meal, extra water, stove, fuel, first aid kit, fire-building supplies and emergency kit.

Pack 3: Personal water bottles and rain gear for group members.

If your group is large or if you plan two trail meals, add a fourth pack or a couple of day packs for the extra supplies.

Ask everyone to carry a personal drinking cup—either a plastic cup tied by a thong or a wire-handle Sierra cup that attaches to a belt or pack. The experience of consolidating water and rain gear in one pack builds community by enabling everyone to assume responsibility for other group members.

The hike. Base the schedule, distance, pace and content of your walking seminar on your group members' fitness and experience. Carefully choose your route. You don't need to travel a long way to a popular backpacking area; many state parks and conservancy areas with established trails and picnic areas are adequate. It's better to spend your time on the trail than in a van. Neither do you need to cover a great distance on the actual hike; a two- to four-mile round trip is sufficient. The more you hike, the less time you have for teaching and processing the group's experience.

Teaching is imperative. Even though you're out for an enjoyable day, you're also there to learn. Use five minutes here and a sentence or two there to keep the group on track. Also stop for some focused, sit-down discussion times.

As organizer, model responsible leadership for your camping group. Rotate head and foot leaders (group members) on your hike. Take a midmorning foot check for hot spots. Help campers adjust their packs or learn to lock lace boots.

Schedule. The specific schedule for your hike will depend on the location and your group. As you plan, remember that it's most important for your group to have an enjoyable time together. Blend teaching episodes to fit the day's natural flow. Plan a route that provides resting times, discussion times and mealtimes near places that invite group members to explore.

Here are two possible seminar schedules. Consult Part Five for more details on trail technique. Use program ideas from Part Four where appropriate.

Option One

10 a.m. Arrive at the trail head. Assign head and foot leaders. Discuss trail etiquette. Begin your hike.

Rest stop. Take a rest stop on a steep hill. Talk about rhythmic breathing techniques. Demonstrate adjusting packs and helping others in shouldering and dismounting packs.

Noon. Have a picnic.

1 p.m. Set up "camp" using gear in Pack 1. Discuss no-trace techniques.

3 p.m. Take a nature-awareness hike.

4 p.m. Cook a no-trace supper. After supper have a closing celebration.

6 p.m. Return to the trail head.

Option Two

10 a.m. Visit a park nature center for a presentation by a naturalist. Check park regulations for hiking and cooking (even though you previously checked).

11 a.m. Discuss trail etiquette and hike through a natural area to a picnic area. Set up camp using gear in Pack 1.

Noon. Cook a no-trace lunch if possible and use soapless cleanup.

2 p.m. Take a cross-country hike. Introduce map and compass use.

4 p.m. Return to the nature center.

5 p.m. Lead a closing celebration.

An Overnight Backpacking Training Trip

An overnight backpacking trip is an ideal prelude for a longer adventure. Not only does it introduce leaders and campers to the skills and realities of outdoor living, but it helps create positive group interaction, which is essential as you plan a longer adventure.

Orientation session. About two weeks before your overnight training trip, you'll need to have an orientation session for all participants. Model this session after the backpacking workshop, but add time for checking gear, discussing logistics, planning menus and designing programs. Chapter 10, "Recruiting and Training Camp Leaders," includes another overnight backpacking trip orientation model.

1. Check gear. Develop an essential-gear checklist, such as the reproducible checklist in Chapter 20. Include every item on the list in a table display. Discuss the gear and answer questions. Find out who has equipment to loan and who needs to borrow or rent items. If the church has money budgeted to rent equipment or if

it has gear available to loan, include that information on the gear list.

2. Discuss essential information. Give each participant the backpacking route with directions. Distribute emergency contact numbers in the area (a forest service officer, a pastor or a camp director). Distribute necessary permission forms and additional information to each camper.

3. Plan menus. Divide the group into three or four teams to plan trail meals. An overnight hike usually involves the first breakfast and last supper in transit and four meals on the trail: two lunches, a dinner and a breakfast. Follow basic menu selection guidelines listed earlier in this chapter. Food weight is not a major factor on an overnight trip. Campers will learn more experientially by having the freedom to experiment.

4. Plan programs. Each menu planning team also can plan part of the program. Once the teams are organized they can do the planning work between the orientation and the trip. Ask each team to prepare a group time using a preselected theme or one the group develops. Programs would include a meditation for setting out; a campfire program and celebration; a morning watch; and a closing celebration before leaving camp. Encourage campers to be creative as they plan. Use the "Life Is a Mountain—and You Can Climb It" devotional guides (pages 93-95) as a guide for the groups.

Trip schedule. Each group and setting demands a unique schedule and emphasis. Develop your schedule based on your group's needs and strengths. Keep in mind the goals of group-building, training and having fun. Here's a sample schedule to get you started:

First Day

6:00 a.m. Check your gear, gather permission slips, load, and drive to the trail head or drop-off point.

8:00 a.m. Eat a Dutch treat breakfast on the road.

10:00 a.m. Have a group lead the setting-out meditation. Then begin hiking. At the first rest stop discuss trail etiquette. Check feet for hot spots after the first mile. Stop during the hike to learn map and compass basics.

Noon. Eat a trail lunch.

2:00 p.m. Arrive at the campsite. Let hikers explore the area and select program sites. Find a water source and set up water purification. Locate your latrine area. Select sites for several types of tents and shelters. Discuss knife, ax and saw safety, then gather wood.

5:30 p.m. Learn no-trace fire-building and stove use. Prepare supper.

6:30 p.m. Serve supper, then learn how to have a soapless cleanup. After supper relax and explore. Around your campfire, evaluate the day and outline the next day. Hold your program and celebration. End the evening with snacks, campfire conversation and sleep.

Second Day

7:00 a.m. Have the morning watch.

8:00 a.m. Serve breakfast and clean up. Have a nature-awareness hike. Lead a group time to discuss emergency procedures. Have time for open discussion about backpacking. Then pack and hold your closing celebration. Hike to the pick-up point or back to the trail head.

Noon. Serve lunch and have written and verbal evaluation. Spend the early afternoon hiking in the area.

3:00 p.m. Return home.

A Residentially Based Backpacking Trip

Another natural introduction to backpacking is through a residential camp program (see Chapter 5). Because many residential camp facilities are located near backcountry trails, they become a natural base for afternoon, daylong and overnight backpacking trips. And because campers are already together at camp, they can learn backcountry skills at base before heading for the backcountry. Chapter 5, "Residential Youth Camps," discusses the specifics of residentially based backpacking and ways to fit backcountry adventures into the camp schedule.

Backpacking Evaluation

As with all camps, evaluation is important after a backpacking trip. Through your evaluation you can learn what aspects of the trip contributed most to personal growth, whether you set a good pace, whether campers felt prepared and other information to help plan future adventures. Evaluation also allows campers to process the experience together, making it a learning experience for them too.

Camp Notebook 12, "Backpacking Evaluation," suggests one method for evaluating your camp. Adapt it to fit your specific group and adventure, or follow a format suggested at the end of another chapter in this section.

Camp Notebook 12

Backpacking Evaluation

1. In what ways was this year's backpacking camp an adventure for you?

2. What new outdoor skills do you have now that you didn't have five days ago?

3. What was the highlight of the week for you?

4. How has the week's theme, "_____," affected your thinking and living this week?

5. What faith words would you use to describe this experience?

6. Do you feel this backpacking adventure will affect your life back home?

7. If we could have this camp again, what would you change?

Chapter 7

Canoe Camping

During the late '70s and early '80s, Minnesota's Boundary Waters were the focus of an intense struggle to eliminate logging, mining and motorized backcountry travel in the wilderness area. Leading the environmentalists crusade was the late Sigurd "Sig" Olson, a renowned environmentalist and canoeist from Ely, Minnesota. Olson's writings are an enduring source of spiritual reflection and practical wisdom for paddlers of the Boundary Waters.

In the midst of the controversy, youth groups would visit Olson before they set out on their wilderness adventures. He'd share his stories and philosophy about the beautiful watery wilderness along the U.S. and Canadian border. One group heard Olson after he'd been hung in effigy the night before by logging advocates. The teenagers said hearing Olson was the most important part of the trip.

By listening to Olson, groups not only learned the importance of protecting the environment, but they also gained a sense of canoeing at its best. Here's how he once described the way his philosophy of canoe camping developed:

Once I tried to make McIntyre in one day from Basswood Lake . . . Determined to get there by night, I had told my party about the wonderful fishing, trout on the reefs, walleyes off the campsite, a lake within easy reach swarming with large-mouth bass. That day we fought the wind, were drenched with rain, passed up campsite after campsite thinking only of our goal, and by late afternoon were only on Caribou, ten miles away. Tempers were short, everyone thoroughly miserable, and regretfully I made camp, hoping to get an early start in the morning and . . . make our objective by noon.

The morning dawned cold and rainy, the wind was in our teeth. We could not go on, so I tried to make the best of it. Toward midafternoon and far too late for travel, the sun burst out; we took the canoes, left our sodden camp, and found a rocky reef with the finest fishing any of us had ever known. It was in the lee and away from the wind, and during the hour we spent there we were so intrigued we forgot all about McIntyre and decided to stay for an entire week.

That taught me a lesson: we could just as well have stopped in any one of the lakes on the way, and would have been happy. From then on my trips were different, and never again did I attempt the impossible to save my pride, or make a schedule more important than enjoyment.[1]

Olson's story and philosophy are important places to begin thinking about canoeing with youth groups. They point out both the challenge and beauty of canoeing. And they remind campers that the task, paddling a canoe, is a vehicle to other goals: appreciating creation, growing as a group and enjoying the wilderness's isolation.

Canoeing has a particular appeal to youth groups. Young people are intrigued with the possibility of feeling free and grown up in the backcountry. They enjoy the challenge of white water and the opportunity to master new techniques. They savor the idea of the cool summer activity—especially if they live in a hot, humid climate. It's a welcome backcountry alternative to backpacking, which some youth groups reserve for cooler spring and fall trips.

Canoeing is also an exciting possibility for youth groups, because churches can design trips to fit their group and its experience. Canoe camping can be easy, leisurely and laid-back, or it can be technically and physically demanding.

Successful Canoe Camping

The keys to a successful youth group canoe trip are careful planning, knowledgeable leaders and adequate preparation. In an article in Canoe magazine, Cliff Jacobson, an authority on canoeing with teenagers, tells a story that underlines the near-tragic consequences of incompetent leadership and poor preparation:

[In the summer of 1978,] a friend (Bob Dannert) and I, rescued several people and canoes from upsets on Wisconsin's Flambeau River. A steady headwind of about 30 miles per hour blew fine mist into our faces and made the day feel much colder than the 47° F my thermometer indicated. A check of the water temperatures revealed a chilling 48° F . . .

None of the kids in one group we encountered that day had gloves or woolens. A few wore shorts. All were clad in orange horsecollar-style lifejackets. The canoes were not outfitted with extra flotation.

It was not an ideal day for paddling. The cold high water and fierce wind suggested that the Flambeau was best run by experienced canoeists.

For a few moments I watched the "leader" explain to his flock of novice canoeists the basics of paddling: "Don't paddle on the same side," he said. "If you wanna go right, yell 'go right!' For left, yell 'go left!' " Bob and I could hardly suppress the laughter. Determined to be

free of this example of sheer incompetence, we hurriedly packed out canoes and put to sea, only to encounter the group again further downstream.

The first dumping occurred at Cedar Rapid—a solid class 2 pitch with a hard-to-spot narrow slot at its center. It was here we learned that the group's leader hadn't told the youngsters to bring a second set of dry clothes!

At Beaver Dam (not a true dam), things changed dramatically. Bob and I studied the old four-foot sluiceway for several minutes before we ran it, but the kids were ready to come right through, sight unseen. Thoughtfully, Bob signaled the leader to shore and politely suggested that the dam was no place for beginners. "No sweat," said the leader, "I've run it before." "I dunno," I said, "the water's pretty high."

Without much debate the fearless leader led the pack downstream. Like a gaggle of geese they followed, barely a canoe length between. After the first canoe capsized in the big swamper waves below the ledge, the show evolved into a comedy of errors. In quick succession, three other boats followed suit and dumped . . .

In the midst of it all, canoes continued to come through the drop: people, canoe paddles, lunches, rain gear, cameras and cans of pop floated downstream. Bob and I grabbed the nearest beached canoe . . . and shot into the current to help . . .

Ultimately, all the young paddlers made it safely to shore, though there was still one canoe well wrapped around a rock in midstream. Unhesitatingly, Bob drew some dry kindling from a plastic bag he carried and started a warming fire while I pulled dry clothes from our packs for the chilled victims. One young fellow had a cut ankle. "Get your first aid kit," I called to the group's leader. "I don't have one," he replied. "Get our kit!" I yelled to my friend.

An hour later the 35 "canoeists" were gone. Behind them lay a badly damaged canoe, a still roaring fire, and an odd assortment of trash and clothing . . .

Later, at trip's end, we checked with the group's outfitter: "The leader does this every year," offered the outfitter. "He's never prepared, but he hasn't had a serious accident yet."[2]

In this chapter we'll discuss the following keys to successful youth group canoe camping:

- Canoeing equipment.
- Basic canoe techniques.
- Canoe safety and rescue techniques.
- River techniques.
- Training teenagers for canoeing.
- Planning your canoe trip.

Canoeing Equipment

Appropriate equipment not only allows your group to have a trouble-free adventure, but it's also insurance against safety problems or even tragic accidents. Let's examine the equipment youth group canoeists need.

Personal gear. Camp Notebook 13, "What to Take Canoeing," illustrates basic articles canoeists need. Specific needs vary depending on season, length of trip, type of adventure and transportation to the waterway. Here are personal gear guidelines for campers to follow:

1. Always wear socks and shoes while canoeing. Wool socks are a must for cold waters. Use over-the-ankle boots on trips where you must portage between rivers and lakes.

2. Include clothing that's more than adequate to cover emergencies and extreme weather. Have wool clothing even on summer trips since wool insulates even when it's wet.

3. When planning a trip with portages, use Duluth packs if possible. The large pack will carry two people's gear or two sleeping bags and pads. If campers pack their personal gear to fit in a shopping bag, two people can share a Duluth pack.

4. On non-portaging trips, use duffel bags to hold an individual's personal gear, sleeping bag and pad.

5. Pack a complete change of clothes separately for the return trip.

Group equipment. Just as campers must limit their personal gear to the essentials, it's important to carry minimal group equipment. At the same time, you should be prepared to deal with emergencies, accidents and other unanticipated occurrences that might otherwise detract from your canoe trip's fun and success. Camp Notebook 14, "Group Equipment Checklist," lists the basic group equipment for canoeing, camping and cooking.

Paddles. Paddles come in many shapes, sizes and price ranges. It's important to choose the right paddle for your campers and trip. Paddles should stand about as tall as a camper's chin or nose.

To protect a paddle when you're not paddling, rest it on your foot or put it in a safe spot where no one will step or trip on it.

Paddles have three basic parts: the blade, the shaft and the grip. There are several types of grips and blades for different uses. Choose the right combination for your trip. The most popular paddle used by outfitters has an aluminum shaft with an ABS plastic blade and T-grip. It's durable and lightweight, and it will withstand rocks and hard use.

Canoes. Leaders and campers need to know basic canoe parts and terminology to communicate with each other while canoeing. Diagram 15, "Canoe Parts," shows the various parts of a canoe. Here's a brief description of each part:

1. Bow: the front section of the canoe.
2. Stern: the rear section of the canoe.
3. Amidships: the center section of the canoe.
4. Port: the left side of the canoe.
5. Starboard: the right side of the canoe.
6. Keel: the middle of the canoe

Camp Notebook 13

What to Take Canoeing

What to wear in spring or fall

- ☐ Sock hat
- ☐ Wool sweater
- ☐ Windbreaker or rain jacket
- ☐ Wet suit
- ☐ Wool socks
- ☐ Tennis shoes

What to wear in summer

- ☐ Windbreaker or rain jacket
- ☐ Swimsuit or cut-offs
- ☐ Tennis shoes
- ☐ Suntan lotion

Pack the following items in a double plastic bag *inside* a gym bag:

- ☐ Rain jacket
- ☐ Hat
- ☐ Dry clothes
- ☐ Sunglasses
- ☐ Canteen and cup
- ☐ Snacks

- ☐ Matches
- ☐ New Testament

Optional articles:
- ☐ Camera
- ☐ Glasses
- ☐ Fishing gear

Camp Notebook 14

Group Equipment Checklist

For canoeing
- ☐ Canoes (one for every two people)
- ☐ Ropes for painter lines
- ☐ Life preservers (one per camper)
- ☐ Paddles (one per person plus one spare per canoe)
- ☐ Bailing scoop and sponge for each canoe (see page 109)
- ☐ Group emergency kit
- ☐ Waterproof maps

For camping
- ☐ Tents and ground covers
- ☐ Nylon rain fly (8 feet by 10 feet or 12 feet by 16 feet)
- ☐ Ropes and cords for shelters
- ☐ Hudson Bay ax
- ☐ Folding saw
- ☐ Folding shovel
- ☐ Repair kit (pliers, small file, duct tape, small roll of wire, nails, twine and sewing kit)

For cooking
- ☐ 6- to 8-quart kettle
- ☐ 4-quart kettle
- ☐ Bucket
- ☐ Griddle or Maytag lid
- ☐ Fire grate
- ☐ Reflector oven
- ☐ Plates, cups and silverware (or bring your own)
- ☐ Camp stove
- ☐ Extra fuel (safely stored)
- ☐ Nesting mixing bowls
- ☐ Spatula, wooden spoons and wire whisk
- ☐ Cooking mitts
- ☐ Three plastic nesting dishpans (can double for packing storage)
- ☐ Optional: lantern, folding table, stools and ice chest

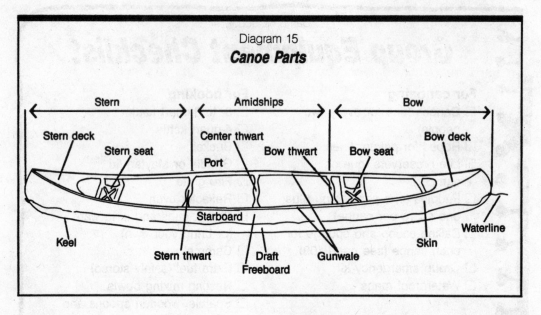

Diagram 15
Canoe Parts

bottom.

7. Thwart: the braces across a canoe.

8. Gunwale: the canoe's rim.

9. Skin: the canoe's outer covering or shell.

10. Freeboard: the canoe's height from the gunwale to the waterline.

11. Draft: the part of the canoe that's below the waterline.

Life preservers. There are three basic types of life preservers. Each has advantages and disadvantages. Whatever life vest you choose, be sure it has a "U.S. Coast Guard Approved" label. Let's look at the differences:

 1. Horsecollar vest: The most common type of life preserver, the horsecollar is inexpensive. It provides upright flotation even if a paddler is unconscious. However, its main disadvantage may be the reason people don't wear life jackets: It's bulky and uncomfortable. Also, it doesn't provide warmth or back protection.

2. Panel-style vest: Made from closed-cell foam, this preserver is more comfort-able and provides warmth and front and back protection. It is, however, more expensive than the horsecollar and less flexible than the vertical rib vest.

 3. Vertical rib vest: This is the least restrictive and the most comfortable life jacket. It provides vertical and horizontal flexibility. Though it's the most expensive, its comfort, warmth and high flotation make it worth the investment for groups and individuals.

Rescue bag. In swift water, throwing lines are essential for fast and effective rescues. In the past canoeists have used a 50-foot coil of floating rope. However, these ropes sometimes tangle. So the Navy began using rescue bags on its lifeboats instead, and they've become standard equipment for river guides, park rangers and professional rescue teams.

A rescue bag is easy to use. The rope is stuffed randomly into the bag and the top is closed. To use it, open the top, grab the end loop and toss the bag with a firm, underhand motion. You don't have to be strong or particularly skilled to use them. A few practice throws by every group member prepares everyone for throw-line setups at difficult rapids. And the bags can be stored for months without problem. Keep in mind, however, that rescue bags tend to have ropes that aren't quite as strong as the traditional throw lines.

Miscellaneous equipment. Here's other equipment that's useful on canoe trips:

1. Canoeists who float rivers where capsizing is likely should wear plastic helmets for added protection.

2. A three-eighths-inch Ensolite pad (a backpacking sleeping pad) section glued to a canoe's bottom provides remarkable comfort for a canoeist's knees. Kneepads serve the same purpose but aren't as comfortable as the larger pad that permits movement.

3. A sponge on a string and a plastic jug with the bottom cut out help with bailing water from the canoe (see Diagram 16).

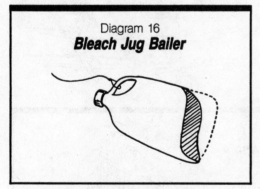

Diagram 16
Bleach Jug Bailer

Basic Canoe Techniques

Campers can easily avoid the frustration of not being able to steer a canoe by learning to use their paddles correctly to move forward and backward and to make turns. With a little practice they can create a specific response from the canoe by al-

tering each basic movement by a slight twist or turn. Or they can use a combination of paddle movements to hold a straight line. Novice campers can quickly learn how to use combination strokes to maneuver their canoe between rocks, over rapids and around tree trunks.

When teaching campers the basic canoe strokes, it's important for them to get a paddle in hand as soon as possible. It's remarkable how 20 minutes of experimenting increases campers' desire to learn proper strokes and techniques.

Campers can practice basic strokes by kneeling on a low dock, standing in midthigh-deep water, or kneeling or sitting in a canoe. Avoid the temptation to cover too much technique verbally without letting campers practice what they hear. (See page 121 for an outline of canoe training sessions.)

Here are basic tips for paddling:

Handling a canoe on land. Unless your campers are quite young, two people can carry a canoe on land. The two campers should stand at opposite ends and on opposite sides, holding the canoe under the deck. With younger campers, have two campers at each end. From this position, the campers can carry the canoe from the vehicle or trailer to the water's edge.

Any time campers lift or carry, they should be exactly opposite each other and grasp the canoe at exactly opposite points. Lifting from unequal positions turns a manageable 75-pound canoe into an unbalanced monster.

Putting a canoe in water. Canoes should always be placed in and taken from water without dragging them on the shore. To do this have two campers face each other and hold up the canoe on opposite sides at the center thwart. While balancing the canoe, lower the bow until it's in the water. Then walk hands backward toward the stern. Reverse the process for taking a canoe out of water.

Boarding and deboarding. Practice boarding and deboarding a canoe with a camper, or have two campers demonstrate. Take it step by step and emphasize teamwork. Camp Notebook 15, "Boarding a Canoe," shows the proper steps for boarding.

Emphasize to campers never to step into a canoe until it's free-floating. Walking into a canoe with one end propped on the bank can weaken and damage the canoe's keel.

Holding the paddle. Grip the shaft just above the blade with your lower hand, and hold the top of the grip with your upper hand. (It takes a little practice to discover which side is your strongest side.) Avoid the tendency to hold the paddle like a yard rake, since grasping the top of the grip lets you turn the blade any direction.

Feathering strokes. Feathering the paddle is one of the fine points to teach after campers have experimented with their own paddling "techniques." There are two keys to smooth paddling and continuous forward movement.

1. Place the paddle straight in the water perpendicular to the surface (see Diagram 17, "Paddle Angle").

2. Exit from a stroke to the side. Take the paddle edge out before the paddle leaves the water, keeping the edge forward as you return for another stroke. This technique cuts down wind resistance.

It's important to demonstrate paddle dynamics to campers. A paddle pulled flat from the water in the bow pulls the bow down. From the stern it pulls the stern down. Both slow forward motion.

The mark of a smooth side feathering stroke is an arch of water drops pouring off the end of a paddle without splashing. The mark of a flat paddle exit is an upward sucking splash behind the paddler.

Varying basic strokes. All strokes can be performed in varying degrees: quarter sweeps or full sweeps; hard or light J-strokes; shallow or deep draws; slow, deep strokes; or quick, dipping strokes. The following pages show how to do each of the basic canoe strokes:

Forward Strokes

Stroke: Bow stroke.
Use: To give power.

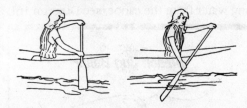

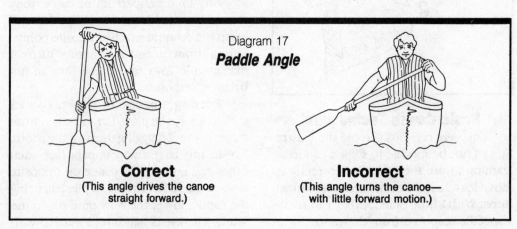

Diagram 17
Paddle Angle

Correct
(This angle drives the canoe straight forward.)

Incorrect
(This angle turns the canoe— with little forward motion.)

Camp Notebook 15

Boarding a Canoe

1. The stern person holds the canoe by the center thwart parallel to the shore with the canoe free-floating.

2. The bow person enters the canoe at the bow seat. He or she holds both gunwales and keeps a low center of gravity. He or she steps into the center of the canoe over the keel line to keep the canoe balanced.

3. The bow person kneels in front of the bow seat with paddle in hand.

4. Once the bow person is in place, the stern person swings the bow into the water (point it upstream in a river).

5. The stern person climbs in the canoe as the bow person did: holding the gunwales, keeping low and placing one foot in the center at the keel.

6. Then the stern person pushes off from shore with the other foot and kneels in front of the stern seat.

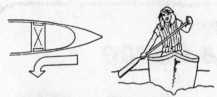

Method:

1. Lean slightly forward and place blade in water parallel to the bow.
2. Pull blade straight back in the water by pushing upper hand forward and pivoting the paddle with lower hand.
3. Feather stroke to the side when the paddle nears the surface behind you.
4. When blade leaves water, bring forward to begin next stroke.

Stroke: J-stroke.
Uses: To steer canoe and give power. (Make on opposite side from bow stroke.)

Method:

1. Place paddle in water forward, parallel to gunwale.
2. Push upper hand forward and turn thumb down to turn blade when paddle is parallel to canoe seat.
3. Use lower hand to pivot paddle and assist the upper hand in twisting and pushing the paddle outward.
4. Feather the stroke to the side for a smooth exit from the water.
5. Return for another stroke.

Turning Strokes

Stroke: Bow sweep.
Uses: To turn and avoid obstacles. When used on the right, it turns the bow left; when used on the left, it turns the bow right.

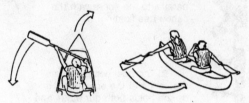

Method:

1. Reach forward at a shallow angle.
2. Pull the paddle in a large arch. Use the lower hand to pull as you push forward with the upper hand.
3. Feather the stroke and return for your next stroke.

Stroke: Stern sweep.
Uses: To steer and correct course. When used on the left, it turns the stern left and the bow right; when used on the right, it turns the stern right and the bow left.

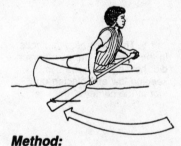

Method:

1. Reach forward at a shallow angle.
2. Sweep paddle in a large arch as in a bow sweep.
3. Feather and exit for your next stroke.

Stroke: Draw and cross draw.
Uses: To maneuver bow in white water or to move stern sideways. Can use on either side without changing hands.

Method:
1. Reach straight out and "stab" your paddle in the water.
2. Pull paddle toward you in one motion.

Stroke: Pry—with draw or cross draw.
Use: To move to the side to avoid an upcoming rock.

Method:
1. Reach far out over the side and put blade under canoe.
2. Pull back with upper hand using gunwale as pivot point.
3. Caution: Place lower paddle hand above gunwale to avoid a pinched thumb.

Brace Strokes

Stroke: High and low brace strokes.
Use: To stabilize a leaning canoe and to slow down for turning into eddies (calm waters).

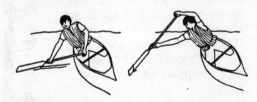

Method:
1. Low brace: Lean out over water and place paddle on water surface like an outrigger to counteract tilt.
2. High brace: Reach out over water and

"stab" water with blade to counterbalance tilt in the opposite direction.

Canoe Safety and Rescue Techniques

While canoeing is an exciting and challenging experience for teenagers, it also can be dangerous—particularly if basic safety precautions aren't implemented. Camp Notebook 16, "Dangers of River Canoeing," lists the major dangers of river canoeing and how they can be prevented. Let's look at specific safety precautions and techniques.

Life preservers. Everyone knows canoeists "should" wear life preservers. Too often, though, they don't. For example, a popular canoeing guidebook admonishes readers to "wear life jackets at all times" in three sets of guidelines. Yet not a single paddler in the book's 32 photographs is wearing a life jacket. How easy it is to override our best judgment!

The greatest danger in the wilderness is your inability to calculate the risks. It's not enough to say all the campers have "passed lifesaving tests" or they're "all good swimmers" so they don't need the jackets. Canoeing without life preservers multiplies the risk of injury or drowning. Frantic rescue attempts risk swamping additional canoes, but wearing life preservers dramat-

If anyone forgets to wear a life preserver, every camper has a responsibility to remind that person to put on the jacket. And all travel should be stopped until everyone is wearing a jacket and is ready to proceed.

Camp Notebook 16

Dangers of River Canoeing

Danger or problem	How to prepare for it
1. Not wearing a life preserver.	Require all campers to wear life preservers when paddling.
2. Hypothermia, precipitated by improper clothing and rain gear, pushing too hard, improper eating and drinking, cold or fatigue.	Require wool socks, warm clothing, and wind and rain gear. Carry extra dry clothing in a waterproof bag. Plan a reasonable and flexible itinerary. Plan balanced meals.
3. Running unfamiliar waters without scouting the rapids.	Always reconnoiter a river before your training event or trip, and teach campers how to reconnoiter rivers as you travel.
4. Attempting rapids beyond the paddlers' skill levels.	Choose rivers appropriate to your group's experience. Know safe river levels and where river gauges are located. Use a gauge to teach campers how to tell when a river is safe.
5. Ignorance of appropriate rescue techniques.	If weather and river conditions permit, select areas to demonstrate and practice self-rescue and canoe rescue.

For insurance against many different problems, carry the following items as a group emergency kit. Pack everything in double plastic bags inside a sturdy duffel bag. Keep the kit in the drag canoe.

☐ One or two wool blankets.
☐ Group first aid kit.
☐ 10-foot-by-12-foot nylon or plastic tarp.
☐ Assorted nylon cords for shelter.
☐ Small roll of silver duct tape.
☐ Fire-building materials (tender kindling, candles and lighter in a small plastic container).
☐ One or two spare rain parkas.

☐ Hudson Bay ax with sheath.
☐ Small trail stove with fuel.
☐ Coffeepot or #10 can with bail.
☐ Bouillon cubes, tea, Jell-O, hot chocolate and snacks.
☐ White water rescue bag (or a 60- to 70-foot coil of floating rope strapped on top of the bag).

ically reduces the panic—even in white water. When everyone wears a life preserver, there's a greater sense of security in setting up a rescue. Each canoe-trip leader has a responsibility to every camper and every camper's family to insist that everyone wears life preservers.

Self-rescue techniques. Knowing self-rescue is most important when a canoe capsizes or is swamped on a hanging rock. Here are two dangers to avoid:

● Getting downstream from the canoe. A canoe filled with water can pin a paddler against a rock.

● Being swept down rapids back first or head first.

The advantage of group travel is that a rescue party is always ready to rescue campers and canoes—in that order. Self-rescue involves three priority steps:

1. Get on the upper side of the canoe and hold onto the canoe. Stay with the canoe as long as you're safely holding on upstream.

2. If you get separated from your canoe, float downstream feet first. If your feet strike rocks, your knees act as springs to push off and move on downstream. Work your way toward shore.

3. Let other paddlers rescue your canoe and pick you up. Don't swim back across the river. Rest before proceeding, and dry out if it's cold.

Canoe rescue techniques. What do you do when a canoe capsizes in the middle of a deep lake? The canoe-over-canoe rescue technique allows campers to work together to rescue a canoe without going to shore. It's also a great camp training and group-building exercise (see page 127).

The rescue technique involves draining and turning the swamped canoe over another canoe. The keys to the operation are balance and practice. A single demonstration won't teach rescue. To learn the

technique thoroughly, campers and leaders must experience the cold water, physical struggle, teamwork and, sometimes, panic of rescuing a swamped canoe.

I once led a September training trip in Minnesota. The cold water meant that the leaders gladly would've settled for a single demonstration! But everyone practiced the technique anyway, and it turned out to be the event's best group-building experience. Everyone got wet and cold, but everyone was successful—and we celebrated our success for eight days!

Camp Notebook 17, "Rescuing a Canoe," outlines the steps in this process.

Throw lines. Setting up a leader with a throw line below a rapid provides a back-up safety measure for running more difficult rapids. When a paddler loses his or her canoe and ends up floating through the rapids, a throw line can rescue him or her. Throw the line across and above the swimming paddler, and let it float downstream within his or her reach. Then pull the paddler to shallow, safe water. When running a difficult rapid, the first paddlers through should wait in the eddy waters until all paddlers have gone through.

With a little practice campers can throw a 50-foot floating rope or a rescue bag. It's important to involve campers in learning this safety and rescue leadership even on their first trip.

"Broached" canoes. A stuck or "broached" canoe is the most common dilemma on a rocky river. Paddlers don't clear a rock or boulder, so the canoe bellies up to the rock amidships. Since the canoe is leaning upstream without capsizing, it hangs on the rock and fills up with water. The force of the moving water combined with the water that fills the canoe makes it difficult to unlodge the canoe from the rock.

If the water is shallow and it's safe to

Rescuing a Canoe

1. The rescue canoe approaches the swamped canoe at a right angle. The rescuing paddlers should talk through the process as they work with the swamped campers.

2. Lift the end of the swamped canoe upside down over the center thwart of the rescuing canoe. Swamped canoeists hold and move the swamped canoe exactly opposite each other to maintain balance.

3. Pull the upside-down swamped canoe until it's completely balanced across the rescuing canoe's center thwart. All the water will drain from the swamped canoe. The swamped canoeists should hold the upright canoe's bow and stern to help maintain balance.

4. Then carefully turn the canoe upright, return it to the water and turn it parallel to the rescuing canoe with the center thwarts side by side.

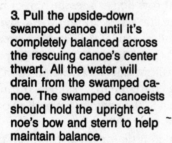

5. While rescuers hold the inner gunwales of the two canoes tightly together, the swamped campers climb into their canoe one at a time over the outside gunwale.

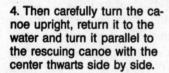

wade to the canoe, several campers can work together to push one end of the canoe upstream while others pull downstream on the other end. Thus you roll the canoe off the rock and back into the current where it can be taken to eddy waters and emptied.

When this approach doesn't work, try the following technique, which I learned from a Maine Indian guide on the Allagash River:

1. Securely tie a rope to a 12- to 14-foot long pole. Lash the other end of the pole to the broached canoe's center thwart so that the long end of the pole is downstream. Make sure the pole is lashed gunwale to gunwale to put even pressure on the canoe.

2. Pull the other end of the rope upstream on the shore, and have several people pull. With the pole acting as a lever, the canoe will roll upstream. When it turns upside down, the water will empty out.

3. If the canoe stubbornly sticks or has fragile thwarts, use the same technique with two poles—one lashed to the front thwart and one to the back thwart. Use a rope on each pole.

Backcountry swimming. Campers feeling free and full of outdoor energy may be tempted to embark on deep-water, long-distance swimming during a canoe trip in the backcountry. However, such swimming—and diving from cliffs, limbs or canoes—should be forbidden to ensure maximum group safety.

Backcountry swimming contrasts sharply from swimming in a pool. In a pool everyone and all obstacles are always clearly visible, but they're often hidden in rivers and lakes. By not recognizing the differences, campers risk injury and even drowning. Remind campers intent on long-distance swimming that expert marathon swimmers don't attempt long distances

without the insurance of having nearby boats and crews.

Appropriate backcountry swimming is really water play. It should take place only in a shallow lake or river area. Designate a swimming area near your camp, and require campers to wear shoes to avoid cut feet. Campers should be allowed to venture into deeper waters only when wearing life jackets.

Neither can certified swimming instructors be responsible for swimming in the backcountry like they are in local pools. Whether or not campers are supervised by certified instructors, they need to follow the same guidelines. Acceptable swimming and water-play activities should be agreed to in writing before your trip.

River Techniques

In addition to basic paddling and safety techniques, campers need to know a variety of other skills. Some ensure safety; others protect the equipment; some make canoeing easier; and some provide variety and fun. Let's look at these:

River canoeing rules. To have a safe and enjoyable river canoe trip, paddlers need to know and observe basic rules and procedures. Camp Notebook 18, "River Canoeing Rules," outlines these guidelines. Before leaving on your trip, have a "dry" safety session to discuss these rules (see page 125). Give campers copies of the Camp Notebook to get acquainted with.

Riding in a canoe. Kneeling in a canoe is the most stable position, particularly until campers get comfortable being in a canoe. It's more restful on flat water to alternate sitting and kneeling. For white-water travel, kneeling is more stable. Long flat stretches or eddy spots provide sitting rest breaks on rivers.

Standing and changing places. In the past instructors have drilled canoeists

Camp Notebook 18

River Canoeing Rules

1. All canoes follow the designated lead canoe. Never pass the leader.

2. The designated drag canoe brings up the rear. No one can drop behind the drag canoe. Keep the group emergency kit in the drag canoe.

3. Always keep the paddlers behind you in sight. Drop back if necessary to maintain visual contact. Use the following visual signals to communicate with the paddlers behind you:

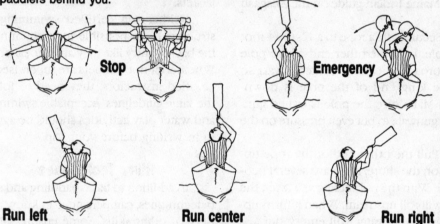

Stop   **Emergency**

Run left   **Run center**   **Run right**

4. Don't crowd the canoe ahead of you. Back-paddle and hold when you get too close. Wait until the canoe in front of you has cleared a rapid before entering it.

5. Don't use your paddle to stop yourself against a rock. (It could jab the paddle into your ribs or overturn the canoe.) Instead, use a draw or brace stroke on the upstream side and lean toward the rock to prevent swamping.

Correct technique   **Incorrect technique**

6. Never canoe alone. Always have at least three canoes—even when recon-noitering a river with experienced paddlers.

7. If a canoe swamps or capsizes, the swamped paddlers' first responsibility is to stay with the canoe *on the upstream side only*. Nearby paddlers' first responsibility is to help swimmers get to shore or shallow water. Then rescue the swamped canoe.

never to stand in a canoe. Instead they've taught a complex set of moves for exchanging places from bow to stern and vice versa.

Actually, both rules are incorrect. Seldom should campers need to change places in a canoe when they can't pull into shallow water or on shore. If changing places is necessary, it's safest to raft three canoes together to provide stability.

Second, the person in the stern must stand in a canoe if necessary while poling or to get a better view downstream to check for obstacles or for the best route through rapids.

The basic rule is to stand only when the canoe is headed downstream. Keep your feet apart and balanced. The bow person shouldn't paddle when the stern person is standing to check rapids.

Reading white water. With just a little practice, young campers can learn to "read white water" to discover the best approaches and techniques for negotiating a rapid. Even a small riffle contains whitewater dynamics in miniature (see Diagram 18, "Reading White Water").

Here are the basic signs to look for in the water:

Upstream V

● A submerged rock will deflect water to form an upstream V.

● Indicates water running over or around a rock.

● Steer clear.

Downstream V

● Two side-by-side upstream V's form a downstream V between them.

● Looks darker and smooth. Often ends in a series of standing waves.

● Indicates deeper, usually darker water running between rocks.

● Run the center, darkest water.

Standing wave

● Indicates deeper water.

Reconnoitering a river. The first time down a river for trip planners can be an adventure. The basic idea is to research the river ahead of time and to travel in a group—preferably with someone who's made the trip before. Use the same technique for reconnoitering a river to teach campers river skills. Here are some basic steps:

1. Gather topographic maps, printed river guides and as much information as possible about the river's history, geography and character. Find out about river gauge locations and safe running levels.

2. Talk with someone who's canoed the river before. If it's an intermediate or advanced stream, have a guide accompany you.

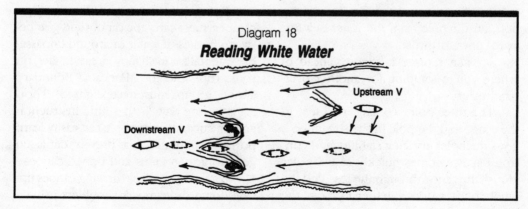

Diagram 18
Reading White Water

Upstream V

Downstream V

3. Once on the river, stay above major shoals, rapids or bends in the river where there's white water. Beach your canoes and scout from the bank. Sometimes you can get a better perspective from high rocks, cliffs or ridges.

4. Discuss different routes for running a section of white water. If there's a particularly challenging set of rapids, set up a throw-line rescue before anyone runs the rapids.

Poling. Poling is an almost lost art in the Western world, but it's been preserved by some canoe organizations and camps in Maine and Canada. Poling is possible whenever there are moderately shallow creeks or rivers. And it can be used for upstream travel even through minor rapids.

Just as artful paddling has many intricacies, so does poling. But the basic technique is easy and fun—even when you feel clumsy. The pole should be about 12 to 14 feet long and about 2 inches in diameter. Here's the basic technique:

1. Stand in front of the stern seat against the stern thwart. Spread your feet apart, with the onside (pole-side) foot angled slightly outward and the offside foot pointing straight ahead.

2. Place the pole on the bottom of the stream, and push forward with a hand-over-hand movement up the pole. As you push, the canoe will move forward.

3. When the canoe moves beyond the pole, lift the pole from the water in a forward, upward thrust.

4. Then replace it slightly ahead of where you're standing for another overhand thrust.

The three-point contact, two feet in the canoe and the pole in the stream bed, gives the poler amazing stability and control. Balance comes quickly as the poler "feels" the canoe through the feet, and the whole body works together to move the

canoe smoothly. It's a beautiful technique that's within the grasp of any group willing to experiment.

Canoe sailing. Ponchos don't help much during a rainstorm when you're canoeing. The wind blows the poncho up, and the rain comes in under it. But ponchos can be useful in a canoe—for sailing. If you're on flat water and the wind is right, a poncho can be a makeshift sail that makes it easy to sail for miles.

The bow person ties the long corners of a poncho to two sturdy sticks (or two canoe paddles). Then he or she holds the sticks up in the wind so the poncho catches the wind like a sail. The stern camper then steers the canoe using a paddle as a rudder. (See Diagram 19, "Canoe Sailing.")

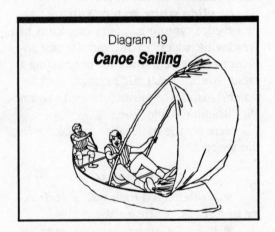

Diagram 19
Canoe Sailing

Portaging. Sometimes on canoe trips, campers must carry the canoes and gear between bodies of water or around impassable waterfalls and shallow areas. In fact, on some trips into the Minnesota Boundary Waters, groups must make eight to 10 portages in one day. With a little instruction and practice, young people can easily learn portage techniques that prevent damaged gear, forgotten items and tipped canoes.

Portaging involves carrying canoes upside down on campers shoulders using a canoe yoke or padded center thwart. Campers can help each other lift a canoe to carry. While this technique isn't the dramatic solo roll-and-flip technique of the professional Northwoods guide, it allows young, inexperienced campers to lift a canoe alone without undue stress or strain on the shoulder and back muscles. Here are the basic steps:

1. To prepare for portaging, unload each canoe when it's free-floating. Don't try to haul a canoe onshore with gear in it— or someone sitting in the stern. Lay ahead next to the trail any paddles or fishing rods you don't secure in the canoe. Lay packs nearby, leaving room for those portaging canoes to get on the trail without stepping on gear. The drag leader (who brings up the rear) should make sure everything has been portaged before setting out with the last load.

2. Have other campers help you lift the canoe's bow and turn the canoe upside down.

3. Crouch under the yoke and get comfortable.

4. When the canoe feels comfortable and balanced, lift it on your shoulders and stand upright.

5. When you need to rest while portaging, lean the canoe's bow between trees or on canoe rests along the trail.

Training Teenagers for Canoeing

Because of the many skills, safety concerns and techniques involved in canoeing, introduce campers to canoeing through a series of hands-on training sessions before you take an extended trip. Thorough training before your trip increases your chances of having a safe and successful trip down a backcountry river. It builds commitment in and relationships between campers. And it reassures parents and church leaders that you're leading a quality outdoor experience for your youth group.

A basic canoe training sequence includes the following progression:

1. Introduction to canoeing: basic safety, strokes and practice (three hours).

2. Paddling review: combination strokes and practice maneuvers (three hours).

3. Safety and gear: emergency gear and rescue techniques (three hours).

4. Tripping experience: one day canoeing on a class 1 or 2 river.

The exact timing and structure of these sessions are flexible. The first three sessions can be organized as an all-day event with plenty of time for breaks and a picnic. Some leaders conclude the first session with a rescue demonstration that includes all campers. Some hire a professional canoe instructor to lead the training workshops.

Whatever structure and methods you choose, find ways to get the teenagers involved as early as possible in hands-on canoeing. The questions that arise as they experiment and practice techniques provide teaching opportunities that you can't match through lectures, discussions, videos or demonstrations.

If you have access to a church or camp classroom during your training, you can take advantage of video canoe instruction in addition to hands-on practice. You can either introduce your training by showing a video or use it in sessions two and three as a review of what they've practiced.

Regardless of a trip's length or a group's previous experience, each canoe trip should include safety orientation or review and group practice. If you plan overnight or longer lake-country or flat-water canoe trips, you'll need a minimum of six hours of training. White-water river canoeing requires even more training—six hours plus a day trip before attempting overnight tripping. A series of progressive day trips is preferable before traveling intensifies with fully loaded canoes.

Session One: Introduction to Canoeing (three hours)

Several approaches can be effective introductions to canoeing. You can begin by showing a canoeing video followed by an on-the-water session at a lake or pond having campers practice as much as they can remember from the presentation. Or you can begin with free, unstructured on-the-water experience followed by a step-by-step review and practice.

Here's what you should cover in the first three-hour session:

Safety. Whatever specific training approach you take, safety should always be the central message. Campers should be admonished to wear a life preserver at all times. Preservers should be mandatory even when practicing in a calm lagoon. Review with campers the discussion of life preservers from earlier in this chapter (page 108). Discuss other safety matters in session three.

Basic equipment. Before you begin learning techniques, briefly discuss basic canoeing equipment—canoes, life preservers and paddles (see page 105). Have available canoes, life preservers and paddles, and let campers try them as you discuss how to use different equipment. Don't try to cover too much at once; save the details for when campers are secure in canoes and have specific questions. Here are some things to cover:

1. Paddles. Describe the different parts of paddles, how to hold a paddle properly and what a paddle can do. Assure campers that they'll quickly develop the skills to use paddles once they're in a canoe.

Explain to campers they'll need a paddle that's about as high as their chin or nose. Urge them to protect their paddle by resting it on their foot or placing it in a safe spot when they're not using it.

2. Canoes. Campers need to know a canoe's basic parts for giving directions. A good way to introduce the different parts is to begin by asking campers how many canoe parts they can name. Ask simple questions, such as: "What's this end of the canoe?" "Is the bow the front or back?" "What determines where the bow and stern are located?" "How is the seat location different in each end?" After you've exhausted their knowledge, review the different parts listed in Diagram 15 (page 108), "Canoe Parts," using a canoe to demonstrate.

One group made learning the canoe parts easier by stenciling "bow" on the front of its T-shirts and "stern" on the back. The left shoulder was labeled "port" and the right "starboard."

3. Life preservers. If the church supplies life preservers, show canoeists the jackets and how to put them on. Stress, once again, their importance. If campers are expected to supply their own jackets, discuss the differences between the different kinds. Have samples of each available for campers to try.

Basic demonstrations. Early in the demonstration process, you as leader should break the "staying dry" barrier by "wet footing"—wading into the water yourself. When campers try to stay dry all the time, they often upset and tip the canoe trying to get in it at the water's edge.

Don't try to cover too much during your basic demonstrations. Many techniques can be demonstrated on the river or lake when they're needed or when campers have specific questions. Here are basic techniques to cover during this introductory session:

1. Handling a canoe on land. Demonstrate how to take canoes off a vehicle or

trailer safely. Show campers how to carry a canoe properly, and give them opportunities to lift and carry a canoe.

2. Putting a canoe in water. Show campers how to put the canoe in water without dragging it on the beach. Emphasize that campers should never step in a canoe when it's not free-floating, since it could weaken or damage the keel. Again, have campers participate in the demonstration.

3. Boarding and deboarding. Demonstrate boarding a canoe with a camper, or have two campers demonstrate it together. Distribute copies of Camp Notebook 15, "Boarding a Canoe" (page 111). Once the campers are in a canoe, explain the advantages of kneeling in the canoe for stability.

4. Basic strokes. Once campers know how to board a canoe, it's time to teach the basic paddle strokes. Discuss with campers the basic tips for paddling such as handling a paddle, feathering strokes and varying basic forward strokes—the bow stroke and the J-stroke. Distribute Camp Notebook 19, "Basic Canoe Strokes," to campers. (See pages 110-113 for detailed instructions on the basic strokes.)

Campers need to get a paddle in hand and get on the water as soon as possible. Avoid lengthy discussions of different techniques; instead, let campers learn by experimenting and asking questions. Campers can practice basic strokes kneeling on a low dock, standing in midthigh-deep water, or sitting or kneeling in a canoe. Once they've tried on their own for 20 minutes or so, they'll eagerly learn proper techniques.

Be sure that paddlers always wear life preservers when they're in canoes—even when they're practicing. It's important to set safety patterns early.

The first time campers are in canoes, give them plenty of time to try their strokes, to experiment, and to get the feel of balancing themselves and working together. Watching and coaching them in conversational tones helps them—especially when they ask for assistance.

Once campers have tried their strokes, call them together to demonstrate fine points and additional basic strokes—bow sweeps, stern sweeps and the draws. Here are two common problems for beginners to focus on. Both movements slow the canoe's forward movement (see Diagram 17, "Paddle Angle"):

1. Bow strokes and J-strokes should always be straight down and parallel to the canoe's keel. (Paddling with the paddle at an outward angle is actually a turning stroke.)

2. Placing a paddle too far forward pulls down the canoe's bow or amidships. Likewise, pulling the paddle straight out of the water at the end of a stroke pulls down the stern or amidships—and makes water fly behind the paddle.

After the paddlers have practiced more, introduce additional basic turning strokes—bow sweeps, stern sweeps, draws and cross draws. Emphasize that these are basic and will come naturally to partners as they use them in combination.

When coaching, skilled paddlers should keep in mind these two cautions:

1. Pace campers, and don't push them to learn too much too quickly. Remember that being together is more important to them than learning canoe skills.

2. Avoid displaying your advanced techniques until campers have a lot to be proud of in their own abilities.

A practice course. After your demonstrations and some time for unstructured practice, instruct campers to practice again using the three-point route illustrated in Diagram 20, "Basic Practice Course." Use shore markers or buoys to designate your course.

Basic Canoe Strokes

Bow stroke (to give power)

 1.  2. 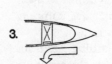 3.  4.

J-stroke (to steer and give power)

 1. 2.  3.  4.

Bow sweep (to turn and avoid obstacles)

 1.  2.

Stern sweep (to steer and correct course)

 1.

Draw and cross draw (to maneuver bow in white water or to move stern sideways)

 1.   2.

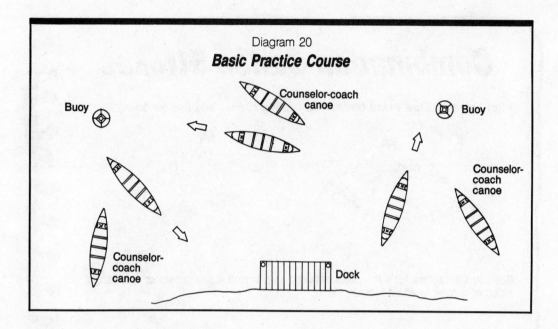

Diagram 20
Basic Practice Course

Counselor-coach canoe

Buoy

Buoy

Counselor-coach canoe

Counselor-coach canoe

Dock

Station two or more leaders along the route to coach and answer questions. Have campers alternate positions so everyone can practice both bow and stern strokes. As campers advance, they may want to test their skills by paddling solo.

Session Two: Paddling Review (three hours)

Session Two, which can follow Session One after a short break, builds on the campers' knowledge and provides the basic paddle skills they'll need on your canoe trip. Once again, be sure paddlers always wear life preservers while practicing.

Review. Begin the second session by reviewing what campers have learned. Give them opportunities to ask questions. You may choose to use a video, wall charts or handouts at this point to help campers conceptualize paddling dynamics.

Combination strokes. Once campers seem comfortable with the basic strokes, introduce the combination strokes. Distribute Camp Notebook 20, "Combina-

tion Canoe Strokes," as a handy reference for campers.

Practice maneuvers. Campers will develop their skills through demonstrations and on-the-water practice and coaching. A triangular course on a lake helps campers learn combination strokes and maneuvers. Mark the route with 15 or 20 plastic jugs or buoys. Each side should be about 100 yards long. Encourage campers to practice various combinations and maneuvers on the course to feel their ability to control the canoe. Rotate partners so each develops bow and stern skills.

After free practice and a review of combination strokes, set up a route with turns and specific maneuvers.

Session Three: Safety and Gear (three hours)

This third session prepares campers for their first canoeing experience. It covers basic canoe rules and what campers need on their trip. It concludes with a canoe-over-canoe rescue, which serves as a

Camp Notebook 20

Combination Canoe Strokes

High brace and low brace (to stabilize leaning canoes and to slow down)

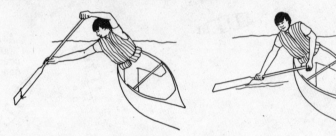

Spin or 90-degree turn (to cross between upper and lower rapids or to change sides of a river in white water)

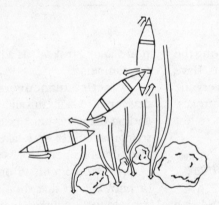

Side slip (to move to the side to avoid an upcoming obstacle)

teamwork-building time. The rescue is also a great climax event for a daylong training workshop.

Canoeing rules. Begin the session by reviewing basic canoe rules and etiquette. Distribute Camp Notebook 18, "River Canoeing Rules" (page 118), to campers. Discuss the rules and practice the signals.

Personal gear. Each trip requires a slightly different gear list. Have a fully packed duffel bag or canoe pack at your training session. Unpack it piece by piece. Laying out all the items then packing them in front of the group answers dozens of campers' questions. Demonstrate waterproofing methods and how conveniently to organize items in clear plastic bags. Answer any questions campers have about gear they'll need, how to use it and how to pack it.

Canoe-over-canoe rescue. The canoe-over-canoe rescue is a standard flatwater procedure that makes a great climax for your training event. A practice session builds your group since it requires teamwork and participation from everyone.

Select a warm day and make sure campers have dry clothes to change into after the exercise. Have two canoe teams volunteer to participate in the exercise. Have the other canoes circle around these two canoes.

Here's how the exercise works: Two campers overturn their canoe. The other canoe moves in for the rescue. Campers in the water should remain calm and help their "rescuers" keep the canoe upside down. The rescuers should talk through the whole process with the swamped paddlers. Then have the two canoes work together to complete the canoe-over-canoe rescue (see Camp Notebook 17, page 116).

After the first rescue, congratulate the volunteers and take time to discuss questions raised by the demonstration. Then re-peat the rescue maneuvers until all campers have been both the rescued and the rescuers.

A single demonstration isn't sufficient to teach rescue. Campers and leaders must experience the realities of cold water, physical struggle and teamwork themselves to learn what it really means to be swamped in a canoe. Impress on campers the importance of learning rescue techniques by reminding them that paddlers they find in trouble may not be from their group and may not know rescue techniques.

This activity is strenuous and should be scheduled when campers can have a dry-out time after the session. The campers need time to change clothes and congratulate themselves and each other. Lunch, dinner or snacks are good follow-ups for the rescue practice.

Session Four: Tripping Experience (one day)

The final preparation for a canoe trip is a one-day teaching river trip. The only way to teach many canoeing skills is for campers to experience them on a river. A day trip also diminishes apprehension and builds interest and enthusiasm for your group's longer canoe trips.

Preparation. Before taking your training trip, complete the following preparations:

1. Require everyone to wear a life preserver, wool socks, warm clothing, and wind and rain gear. Make sure everyone has extra dry clothing packed in a waterproof bag.

2. Select a river that's safe for canoeing and teaching canoe rescue. Limit a beginner trip to a class 1 or 2 river.

3. Reconnoiter the river before the event; then teach campers how to reconnoiter during your trip.

4. Know safe water levels and antici-

pate weather and river conditions. If the river isn't safe or the weather isn't good, postpone your training trip.

5. Make sure the instructors are familiar with the river and, preferably, have reconnoitered it recently as a team.

6. Carry a group emergency kit.

Review. Begin your training experience when you reach your put-in point by reviewing basic safety and basic strokes. If it doesn't conflict with other groups using the launch area, have time for some back-and-forth practice to warm up the group.

Teaching on the river. Concentrate on teaching during your training trip. The best teaching moments occur when campers celebrate their new-found skills, raise spontaneous questions or approach a new challenge on the river. By reconnoitering the river in advance, you will know when these teaching moments are likely to occur, so you can plan for them.

A good progression is to teach a little during the first half-hour. As you canoe down the river, use each new experience as a teaching opportunity. When you find the right places on the river, take time to help campers learn to read white water. Even a small set of riffles will have upstream and downstream V's and standing waves (see page 119).

Talk the group through the first couple of rapids by showing them how to read white water. Run them through rapids one canoe at a time to help them concentrate on teamwork. Raft the canoes together below each rapid to answer questions.

Then paddle without interruption for about an hour to let campers "feel" the river. Next take a snack break on shore to talk about what they've learned and to sharpen their skills in reading white water and using combination strokes.

Every white-water trip provides challenges that stretch and advance campers'

abilities to negotiate rapids. Take advantage of each unique challenge to teach safety, reconnoitering techniques and leadership. Even if you've personally run a particular rapid many times and know the perfect approach, stop the group before the rapid. Go ashore to check the rapid. Remind campers that some rapids always require a walking check to be sure they're free of limbs or tree trunks.

Then ask campers, "What's the best way to run this rapid?" Consider all answers. If campers suggest a route that's obviously unsafe, raise questions about the route rather than dismissing it outright: "What about that rock to the left?" "What strokes would you use?" "How many feet would you say there are between those rocks?" Thinking it through together is usually a better learning experience than approving or disapproving a particular choice.

When you've heard a number of suggestions, ask one team to volunteer to run the rapid its way. Set up a team with a floating throw line, and send the team through the rapids. Campers learn a lot from watching each other run the same rapid one at a time. The experience also provides a great time for taking pictures.

Celebration. Even a short training trip deserves a celebration and affirmation time. In the course of your day, plan a break to acknowledge God's presence and protection as you canoe together. Celebrate each other and the friendships and trust that have grown through your daylong adventure.

Planning Your Canoe Trip

Once group members have participated in a successful daylong canoeing trip, they're ready for a longer adventure. They feel comfortable with their basic skills, and they want to be challenged to refine techniques. Their fears of the river will have eased through the experience. And their parents will know that they've been properly prepared for a longer adventure.

Each area, each waterway, each season and each camping group create unique circumstances for a particular canoe trip. Thus numerous factors must be considered as you plan your trip.

Leadership. Qualified and experienced leaders are essential to group canoe trips. *Under no circumstances should a group set out on a river or lake without at least one leader who has firsthand knowledge of the entire route, the adjacent access points, and the risks and responsibilities of canoeing and camping along a particular waterway.* For most youth groups, this precaution means enlisting the help of a local professional guide.

In addition to ensuring safety, hiring a seasoned professional can have other benefits. One youth group asked its outfitter to find a Native American guide. The group's extra effort was rewarded by expert guiding, daily stories, and an introduction to Indian ways of living and cooking. At the end of the trip the friendships were strong, and the guide invited the group to visit his home for an afternoon cookout.

Another group hired a canoe instructor from a private camp as its guide. It could hardly believe it was spending a week with a national canoe medalist.

Participants. By its nature, canoe camping is a small group adventure. Teenagers accustomed to large youth group meetings will discover unique values in living and traveling in a group of eight to 10.

There's no physical reason to exclude particular teenagers from canoeing. I've taken a physically impaired junior higher canoeing. He had a successful experience—and our group felt something special in having him and his father on the trip. The best guarantee for safe, successful and rewarding canoe adventures is to plan your trip around the known skills and limitations of all potential participants.

If your group has no previous canoeing experience, prepare it to take longer trips through a series of progressive experiences. First, invite a few teenagers to go on a canoe outing where equipment is readily available. If you're inexperienced, contact an experienced canoeist to lead the trip. This short trip will give you a feel for whether your group is interested and ready to prepare for longer canoe adventures. These initial trips also help you develop a core of assistants who can speak firsthand when you plan trips for your youth group.

Then lead a series of training workshops followed by some day trips and overnight campouts. Gradually plan progressive experiences that stretch your group's previous skill levels. If your church has interested and capable adult leaders, plan short canoe experiences for older children and junior highers to lay a foundation for longer high school and family expeditions to distant lakes and rivers.

Distance. Groups near accessible waterways can avoid long travel times. They also can avoid some of the logistical limitations of longer trips. Some youth groups in Missouri and Arkansas, for example, use a support vehicle to carry camping gear from point to point on white-water rivers. This way the campers and leaders can run a stretch of rapids each day without the weight of camping gear on board. Thus they can use heavier gear and refrigerated food.

Groups that travel long distances enjoy the adventure of seeing another part of the country and the thrill of challenging waterways. However, it's often difficult for leaders to reconnoiter the river beforehand. Such groups generally rely on outfitted and guided trips. If this is your situation, contact several outfitters, compare services and check references. (See Chapter 3 for more on selecting support services.)

Water conditions. River levels, water conditions and weather are critical factors in your canoe trip's safety and success. And since each waterway is unique, each must be well-researched in advance. Lake travel requires less research on water conditions, but it still needs careful consideration of weather conditions and water temperatures.

Knowing acceptable levels for river travel is essential both for day tripping and camping. Groups should never attempt canoeing when conditions are beyond recommended parameters. Outfitters, guides, canoe organizations and guidebooks all provide information on rivers' minimum and maximum runnable levels and the usual water volume for a particular month. Most accessible rivers have river gauges at bridges that indicate water level.

Schedule. In planning your canoe camping event, you'll need to plan travel time to and from the waterway, orientation time on the water, time on the water and camping time. Thus a group planning a five-day event 300 miles from home will have only three days of actual canoeing.

Pacing. Like other forms of camping, canoe camping can be spoiled by focusing on conquering great distances. As you plan your canoeing itinerary, keep in mind the goals for your trip—fun, group-building and adventure. Pace your camp to allow time for rest, exploring and unstructured activities.

Some groups on long trips covenant together to put their watches and clocks in the packs and to live by the sun throughout the trip; the covenant is a challenging inner experiment.

See "Designing the Program" in Chapter 2 for more about creating an appropriate rhythm in your schedule.

Itinerary. Once you've decided on leaders, campers, length of camp, destination and type of canoe trip, develop a detailed trip plan. It should be written, evaluated and revised to be sure it is accurate, is feasible, meets the group's goals and covers any emergencies. Then distribute copies of your plan to parents, church leaders and a contact person near the point of river departure. Include the following information in your trip plan:

1. Departure date and time.

2. A marked map that shows and describes the route to your put-in point.

3. A map indicating overnight campsites, the nearest town to each camp, the access point for each site and the phone number of a local contact who knows the route to each camp.

4. A pastor's phone number in the area.

5. Return date, approximate return time and route home from take-out point.

First day on the water. The first day on the water sets the tone and pace for the entire trip. An easy day with only two or three hours of canoeing and plenty of time to set up camp helps the group get on "wilderness time." It's important to set up camp, have dinner and still have time to explore and fish before dark.

It's easy to underestimate the time it takes to load, unload, stop along the way, get used to group traveling and set the first camp. If you have a long drive and don't reach the waterway until midafternoon, spend the first night at a nearby state park, church, lodge or motel. A fresh start the next day will prevent trying to do too much in too little time, which would set an inappropriate pace and mood for the rest of your trip.

Setting camp. Setting the first camp is one of those teaching moments you don't need to cover until you have reached your first campsite or are looking for an appropriate spot. Again, plan an unhurried time to explore and choose the best place for your tents, woodcutting area, kitchen, latrines and canoe storage. See Chapter 22 for details on selecting a campsite.

Cooking. Canoe-trip meals can be fun and hassle-free. Diagram 21, "Sample Menus for Canoe Camping," lists several possible menus designed specifically for canoe camps. Also check Chapter 24 for general outdoor cooking techniques.

The challenge of meals on canoe trips is knowing how to carry them. Carrying food on your trip is much easier if you repackage it in advance. This can be done at church before you leave or en route if you have a long trip. Here are tips for repackaging and packing:

1. Repackage anything in glass containers (such as dried beef) in plastic containers or reclosable plastic bags. Many backcountry canoe areas now prohibit all cans and glass food containers. All food containers must be burnable. However, don't burn plastic or foil liners from packages. Instead, pack them in a double garbage bag.

2. Pack separate bags for beverages (tea bags, coffee, drink mixes and so forth), snacks and condiments so they'll be handy.

3. Pack bread in a pasteboard box wrapped in a large plastic bag and carried in a duffel bag or pack.

4. When setting out each day, put the lunch bag and the bag with beverage mixes, snacks and condiments on top for easy access during the day.

5. Canoeists in the northeast woods use "wanagans," or canoe boxes, to carry condiments, bread and fragile items (and sometimes kitchen utensils). Some wanagans are fitted with vertical and horizontal slots where you can insert wooden portage handles that double as table legs.

Celebration day. Don't wait until the final landing to celebrate. With canoes to load, other groups in the area loading and unloading, and the urge to go find a hamburger stand, celebration can be overlooked on the last day.

Choose a place along the river to stop, have fun and celebrate your time together.

Talking, singing and reading special scripture passages can set the mood for celebrating the meaning of friendship and community. Find a spot where campers can swim, practice self-rescue, float through rapids feet first and just sit together to share the day's meaning. Sometimes a long, level stretch of water near the end of your trip gives another good opportunity to raft all the canoes together (with each paddler holding onto another canoe).

Last day on the water. In a sense, the last day mirrors the first. The big difference is the group experience between the two days. Questions and excitement mark the first day. Ambivalence, eagerness to go home and reluctance to give up the group closeness and the outdoor freedom mark the last day.

No matter how far you are from home, the last day needs to be a time of unhurried reflection, evaluation and celebration. Campers should have informal and formal opportunities to express the meanings they found in journeying together on a wilderness waterway in Christian community.

The words of Major G.W. Browder, written in 1911, capture the ambivalence of the last day at camp:

To me it is rather a sad task folding up a tent and watching a camp-fire die; for you are all the time wondering if the same party will ever camp together again, or if, before another season comes, some one of you will have tak-

Diagram 21

Sample Menus for Canoe Camping

Breakfast

Pancakes and syrup	Oatmeal with raisins (QE)	Eggs a la Goldenrod (LD)	French toast
Bacon	Bagels	(see recipe, page 330)	Canadian bacon
Applesauce	Cream cheese and jam	Grapefruit sections	Dried fruit
Beverages	Beverages	Beverages	Beverages

Dinner

Hot dogs (QE, FN)	Beef stew (canned or	Fried ham (LD)	Spaghetti (QE, FN)
Lettuce and tomatoes	freeze-dried)	Macaroni and cheese	French bread
Chips	Fry bread	Walking salad	Salad
Individual cakes	Stuffed celery	(see recipe, page 329)	Gingersnaps and peaches
Beverages	S'mores	Snack cake (baked in	Beverages
	Beverages	reflector or Dutch oven)	
Split-pea and lentil soup		Beverages	
with ham hock (LD)			
Jerky or planked fish			
Bannock or biscuits			
Dried fruit and biscuit			
cobbler			
Beverages			

Lunch

Lunch menus can be	lunches for layover	peanut butter, raisins,	spreads, snack packs,
planned by individual	days. Here are some	jam or jelly, candy,	granola bars, fruit
meals or included in a	lunch possibilities:	cheese, jerky, salami,	leather, celery and
bulk pack. Plan hot	Bread, dried beef,	peanut bags, sandwich	carrot sticks
soup and sandwich			

Beverage bag	**Condiment bag**	**Snack bag**
Hot chocolate, coffee,	Margarine, salt and pep-	Dried fruit, candy
instant orange drink,	per, mustard, ketchup,	bars, gorp, hard can-
fruit drink mixes, pow-	cooking oil, matches,	dy, popcorn and
dered milk, powdered	hush puppy/fish breading	marshmallows
creamer, sugar and	mix, toilet tissue, soap	
bouillon cubes	pad, Wet Ones and pa-	
	per towels	

Key
FN: First night   QE: Quick 'n' easy   LD: Layover day

en the Long Trail where all the footprints point one way. But pack we must, and when we had loaded the wagon we climbed on and drove out across the ford and over the hills and far away to where the home lights were shining. The home road was long that night. And the Lord of the Temple had poured into our hearts the peace that passeth understanding; for we had found that pleasure which, like some wild flower, can be gathered only in a wooded valley beside a flowing stream.[3]

Canoe Camp Evaluation

Like other camps, canoe camps need proper evaluation and debriefing to allow campers to express their feelings about their experience together. Camp Notebook 21, "Canoe Camp Evaluation," is one method you can use.

Notes

[1]Sigurd Olson, *Open Horizons*, (New York: Alfred A. Knopf, 1969) pp. 105-106.

[2]Cliff Jacobson, "Leading the Pack: The Role of the Group Leader in Canoe Tripping," Canoe (March 1979) pp. 40-41.

[3]Major G.W. Browder, reprinted in "Some Camps of Yesterday," Sports Afield (November 1987) p. 103.

Camp Notebook 21

Canoe Camp Evaluation

1. Which of the following phrases describes your personal experience of our canoe trip? Make a few notes, and be ready to share your perceptions with the group.
    1. A mud hole.
    2. A lonely island.
    3. Niagara Falls.
    4. Trip down lazy river.
    5. "The land of beginning again."

2. If you could give the other group members a gift to take on their next canoe trip, what would you give? Think of one item per group member. Write it down with a brief reason. Be ready to share. Use the back of the page if necessary.

Person: _____ Item: _____ Reason: _____

Person: _____ Item: _____ Reason: _____

Person: _____ Item: _____ Reason: _____

Person: _____ Item: _____ Reason: _____

Person: _____ Item: _____ Reason: _____

Person: _____ Item: _____ Reason: _____

3. On the next trip, what should we plan, bring or do that would improve our experience together? Make notes, and be ready to share.

4. In what ways was our canoe camp a faith journey for you—new questions raised, insights, clarifications, affirmations, issues, struggles, concerns, decisions or celebrations? Make notes, and be ready to share.

Chapter 8

Snow and Winter Camping

The winter! the brightness that blinds you,
The white land locked tight as a drum,
The cold fear that follows and finds you,
The silence that bludgeons you dumb.
The snows that are older than history,
The woods where the weird shadows slant;
The stillness, the moonlight, the mystery,
I've bade 'em good-by—but I can't.

Robert Service
from *The Spell of the Yukon*[1]

Winter is, at once, mysterious and fun, ominous and calm, challenging and inviting. Surrounded by snowy trees just a few steps from the parking lot, you feel like you're miles into the wilderness. That's the magic of winter—magic that lures youth groups to high mountain places and snowy backcountry.

Few outdoor experiences provide the physical challenge, the spiritual contemplation and the just plain fun of winter camping. Whether rolling in the snow, building an igloo, dodging snowballs, skiing or crossing an unblemished blanket of snow, campers always discover new things about themselves, their relationships, their world and their God through a winter youth camp.

When some groups think of winter or snow camps, they consider only a downhill skiing retreat. However, the winter wilderness abounds with different opportunities for meaningful and challenging youth group experiences. Moreover, all snow camping isn't necessarily winter camping. In some places you can snow camp year-round. Anywhere with cold and snow has the possibility of enjoying a wide range of winter fun.

This chapter focuses on the unique opportunities, activities and challenges of winter and snow camping. It covers:

● Types of winter camps.
● Winter camping activities.
● Winter wilderness camping techniques.
● Preparing your group for a winter camp.
● Winter camp evaluation.

Types of Winter Camps

Just as summer camping has many

shapes, winter camping can take place in many different settings and include a variety of goals and activities. Let's discuss the different forms winter camps can take and what makes each form unique.

Winter Residential Camping

Many snow-zone residential camps stay as busy in winter as summer—especially on weekends. Winter residential camps can have formats similar to summer residential camps—workshops, activities, worship celebrations, adventures and special speakers (see Chapter 5 for more on residential camps). Later in this chapter (page 140) are activities that are appropriate for residential winter camps.

The primary differences from summer camps to keep in mind in planning winter camps include:

● Bring warm clothing to handle cold and wet conditions.

● Plan activities that take advantage of snow.

● Think snow, not sun.

In addition to these basic differences, there's a more significant and less obvious difference to consider when planning winter events for youth groups: Many winter activities are solo skills or solo experiences—sliding on an inner tube, downhill skiing or cross-country techniques. Campers can become so engrossed in building skills that they forget community. Also, theme and study times are reduced because of the time spent in winter activities and the shorter daylight hours.

In contrast, for example, canoeing or sailing involve a team challenge. They give a sense of unified achievement—something to celebrate as community. And summer residential camps that emphasize small group process team sports or backpacking trips have abundant daylight hours

for growing together. Thus community life is a primary focus.

How can winter camp leaders meet this challenge? It's particularly important to be conscious of group needs before individuals are so exhausted from their personal quests that they're too tired to participate in fellowship and group-development times. You can protect fellowship and group development times in at least three ways:

● Intersperse group experiences with solo challenges to create a more balanced experience of community life. For example, have campers build an igloo (page 146) one afternoon then go skiing the next day.

● Approach the camp theme, scheduling and pacing sensibly—especially if you plan a downhill skiing event. Know how much time campers will need for activities and how much energy the activities take, and then plan accordingly.

● Don't overlook theme times. Winter camp theme times are usually shorter than for other camping events. But these times are important to help your group develop and maintain its sense of purpose and mission. Even on an average weekend camp, you can schedule a day and a half of skiing and still have two evenings (no night skiing) and a morning for reflection and discipleship times. Scheduling a winter camp on a teachers workday weekend stretches the schedule by another day for more skiing and theme time. Drama, Bible study, concerts, creative arts and celebrations create an important focus for processing the winter event.

Because many residential winter camps are really downhill ski retreats, we'll discuss them more in the next section. However, many church camps near ski resort areas also include downhill skiing as an activity.

Downhill skiing during a residential

camp works best when everyone participates together. When offered as an option to tubing, cross-country skiing and other snow activities, downhill skiing takes campers away from the rest of the group for extended time periods. This separation sometimes infringes on meal and program times. Thus a group can have what becomes separate programs at the same camp. But when all campers participate in downhill skiing together, you can adjust the schedule accordingly and maintain the sense of group life.

Ski Retreats

The most popular winter residential camps are ski retreats. These may take place at church camps or in resort areas. Many last just a weekend, while other churches schedule weeklong trips during spring or Christmas breaks.

Basic tips. If you plan a downhill ski camp, here are a few tips to make the experience run more smoothly and safely:

1. Before your trip hold an orientation session. Cover what to bring, safety and group guidelines. Discuss clothing and equipment. Help campers understand the purpose of each article, how to layer clothing and how to care for the equipment. Mountain ski-resort weather can be very unpredictable. Thus it's important to prepare for both cold and warm days and cold nights. Camp Notebook 22, "Ski Preparation Checklist," which you can photocopy or adapt to distribute at your orientation session, describes what campers need to pack and practice for fun and safety on the slopes.

2. If you choose, show one of the many videos on basic and advanced techniques, which are available through ski shops. Some are highly entertaining and useful for orientation before leaving or for night sessions at camp.

3. Arrange ski rentals before your trip. Compare package prices, and determine if you'll rent at the ski resort or at a local shop before you leave home. Renting skis in advance saves time in being fitted at the slope—and often saves money. The process may vary slightly from shop to shop, but rental shops usually prefer one person to register the group with name, weight, shoe size and height of each ski renter. Then each skier visits the shop for proper fitting. The day before departure, pick up all the skis at once. Return them together after the trip as well.

4. One leader should purchase lift tickets in advance or while skiers are organizing their gear.

5. Require everyone to take instructions before skiing. All skiers need a basic review and a simple run at the beginning of each skiing event. This lets campers warm up and test equipment, and it allows leaders to check skiers' abilities if they don't know them.

6. Daytime introductory sessions generally work better with beginners than night sessions. Darkness, strangeness and feeling unsure of your skills aren't fun for young, inexperienced skiers.

7. Help beginning skiers get acclimated. Have one experienced young person help beginners put their lift tickets on properly. Leaders should answer questions, assist teenagers with maps of the ski area, and see that everyone is equipped and ready for ski class or practice runs.

8. Develop a "buddy system" for skiing all runs. Have campers team up in threes or fours, and let them change partners during the day. But insist that they always take lifts and runs with another group member.

9. After the last ski session, have skiers wash and buckle their boots and skis before returning them. Each person should

Camp Notebook 22

Ski Preparation Checklist

Clothing

Your clothing is important. The temperature at the resort could range from zero to 45 degrees—plus the windchill factor. Layer your clothing. The more layers you wear, the easier it is to adjust your body temperature to prevent overheating or getting too cold. Here's what to bring:

☐ 2 to 4 pairs of wool socks
☐ A wool cap that covers your ears
☐ A well-insulated jacket
☐ Ski bibs or wool pants*
☐ Goggles or sunglasses
☐ Boots (to wear to and from ski area)
☐ Long underwear (wool or wool-cotton-synthetic blend)
☐ Personal items
☐ _____

☐ A scarf
☐ Gloves and mittens
☐ Light and heavy shirts
☐ Sweater
☐ Skin lotion
☐ Chap Stick
☐ Your Bible
☐ _____

*Not blue jeans; they soak up water and keep you cold.

Safety and Health Tips

1. Walk slowly and watch your step on the ice and snow.
2. Take ski instructions before you get on chairlifts.
3. Don't try advanced slopes until you've mastered beginner and intermediate slopes.
4. Listen to your body. When *you* get tired take a break. Sit in the lodge and have something warm to drink.
5. Always ski in pairs 'or small groups.
6. If anyone in the group is sick or injured, the ski patrol will help. Don't try to ski down until you are checked out. Report to leaders as soon as possible.
7. Always check in with leaders at appointed times and places.

check in ski equipment with one adult leader when leaving for home. It's good to hear a ski shop operator comment that your church group brought all its equipment back—clean! Better still, you might even have the owner call you next season to lower your group rate because your group was such a good customer!

Build community. A youth group ski trip can exaggerate the emphasis on individual skills over group life. A question faces youth group leaders every time they plan a winter trip: Are we planning for a group of individuals or for a group? However, some creative approaches can help build community even while campers perfect their individual skills. Here are some ideas:

Use "secret friends" during the ski retreat. (See page 241 for an explanation.) Having someone buy you a cup of hot chocolate because your secret friend asked him or her to do it is a refreshing way to build a relationship.

Try a "buddy system." Counselors at an Atlanta church organize their teenagers by pairing up ski buddies based on skiing ability. Each beginner or first-time skier is paired with one of the most experienced skiers. After completing the basic ski class, the beginners stay with their advanced buddies, who spend a couple of hours helping the novices make their first chairlift ascents and downhill attempts.

After this initial time with their buddies, partners are encouraged to change throughout the day. But each skier and each pair of buddies also have a short list of information to gather during the day by interviewing other group members or people they meet on the slope. These get-acquainted questions focus on favorite, important or memorable experiences. Some questions include:

● What's the funniest thing that's happened this weekend?

● What's your favorite: movie, book, TV show, hair color, eye color and soft drink?

● What's the most important thing that's happened to you since you were born?

● What's the most memorable family story you've heard at home?

That evening the campers share their interview results from the day. Adult leaders give awards for different group members' skiing "abilities." Awards include "Most Fashionable," "Lucky-to-Be-Alive Award," "Fastest Forward," "Fastest Backward," "Most Falls in a Row," "Cutest Hat," "Heart Attack Award," "Coldest Nose Award," "Close Encounters Award," "Most Successful Wipeout," "Greatest Effort" and "Most Graceful." By the end of the weekend, almost every skier has been recognized for something he or she did or didn't do on the slope.

Use evening programs wisely. The key to maintaining group life on a ski trip is often the evening program. This should be a time of team-building and affirmation. Group members should be reminded that even if they didn't see each other much through the day, they're still members of a loving and caring community. And the activities should clearly say that the church's ski trip is different from a school- or club-sponsored trip. The church is providing a ministry based on mutual trust, care and support. Moreover, what happens in the lodge in the evenings is just as important as learning to snowplow or stem turn.

Don't try to do too much. Some youth groups try to pack so much skiing into their weekend that they miss opportunities for growth. A leisurely evening schedule sets the mood for your youth group's growth. Make sure campers stop skiing early enough to shower before supper. Then an evening of music, back rubs and sharing stories from the slopes adds meaning and growth to the experience.

Compare the above scenario to this one: A youth group spends the evening night-skiing then rushes to the soon-to-close restaurants before taking showers. After the late, rushed dinner, campers wait impatiently for showers. Then they sack out without taking time to celebrate the day. They need to get to bed early because they want to be up early on Sunday to beat everyone else to the ski lifts so they can ski half a day before their bus ride home. In their rush, none of the campers grew much closer, and they missed the real reasons for taking a church-sponsored trip.

Drive-In Winter Camping

Winter doesn't close all public drive-in campsites. Some National Forest and Bureau of Land Management campgrounds are open year-round. Some private campgrounds are also available to youth groups in the winter. And director-managers of many church camps will negotiate for groups to utilize their rustic summer campsites for winter drive-in camps, even if they don't publicize their facilities or programs for winter tent-camping.

Drive-in tent-camping is more adventurous than lodge and cabin camps, but it still provides a taste of comfort and security. Often groups can use the camping gear many church families already own. Groups can enjoy the winter outdoors and practice their outdoor skills in a snow setting without the equipment and skills needed for other winter backcountry adventures. It also gives more security to those wanting to practice their outdoor winter skills. If the weather gets worse, campers can always pack everything into their vehicles and head home—a luxury you don't have

when ski backpacking in the backcountry.

Drive-in winter camping allows groups to take advantage of all the winter activities listed later in this chapter (page 140). It also provides the challenge of learning many of the winter wilderness skills described in the section on "Winter Wilderness Camping Techniques" (page 148).

A precaution: The obvious security of a quick exit in case of bad weather can be undermined by the silent white stuff that can completely hide your vehicle's wheel covers between midnight and dawn. Since you have to get about five tons of equipment out of the parking area, you'll have to pay more attention to weather trends, elevation and weather forecasts than is necessary for skiers with just 40 pounds on their backs. And ventilating heated tents or camping vehicles is critical for safety, just as it is with snow caves.

Unless your vehicle has a restroom and a holding tank or restrooms are available in your camping area, campers should learn the proper way to dispose of human waste in the snow (see page 153).

Ski Backpacking

Just as summer backpacking challenges campers by taking them away from the amenities of modern life into the simple beauty of creation, ski backpacking lets campers enjoy the undefiled beauty of the winter snowscape while cross-country skiing.

A valuable step toward full-fledged ski backpacking is day hiking on skis. In some areas groups can arrange with neighboring camps or churches to ski-tour camp-to-camp or church-to-church. The primary considerations are leadership, adequate equipment and provisions for day tripping and overnighting.

Camp Notebook 26, "Cross-Country

Skiing" (page 147), illustrates the basic cross-country ski techniques you'll use.

Ski backpacking can take many forms depending on your group's abilities and goals. Here are three approaches to ski backpacking to consider:

Ski touring. Travel from camp to camp, and spend nights in cabins, lodges or churches. This touring is similar to Scandinavian touring and the resort touring that's becoming more popular in some Western states. The advantage for groups is that you don't have to carry as much on your backs; you carry only a sleeping bag, food and water, plus essential safety and emergency items.

Base camping. Base camping involves packing a heavy base camp on a pulka (see page 153) and setting up camp a mile or two into the backcountry. From there campers take daily ski treks in many directions. Using this approach, groups can set up a large group tent and stove for indoor cooking and Alpine tents for sleeping. Scandinavian skiers often pack all their gear on several pulki, and no one carries backpacks. American backpacking skiers often carry packs and a pulka for every three people.

Camp Notebook 23, "Group Equipment for Winter Base Camping," lists the basic equipment your group will need for this adventure.

Cross-country adventures. The final option for ski backpacking is much like a summer backpacking trip. The group has a long, one-way trek following a day-to-day itinerary. Campers carry Alpine tents, which they set up each night. Schedule layover days according to the trip's length and the route possibilities. Having a layover day at every campsite (two nights per campsite) permits alternate days of ski touring without full packs and without having to set up camp every night.

Winter Camping Activities

Whether having a weekend winter retreat or a weeklong backpacking ski tour, youth groups can enjoy numerous winter activities that combine fun, skill and group-building. The following pages list various low-energy, high-energy and indoor winter camp activities.

Low-Energy Winter Experiences

The following low-energy activities provide breaks from more strenuous winter activities, such as fast-paced downhill skiing or igloo-building. They also provide unique opportunities to experience nature and to build the group.

Snow hikes. Hiking through snowy woods or across a snowy field opens campers eyes to new aspects of creation. Organized snow rambles can add other dimensions to the hikes. Forms these hikes can take include:

1. Blindfold walk. Have campers pair up. Blindfold one person in each pair and let him or her lead the partner to experience the snow in some unique way. Then reverse the roles.

2. Patterns hike. Lead campers into nature after a new-fallen snow to find nature's unusual snow patterns. Check the volleyball net. Visit the camp dock. Walk along the creek or lake. Look for places where birds have landed and where snow has fallen from trees in patterns.

3. Guided nature walk. Invite a naturalist to introduce campers to the intricate and beautiful details of nature that aren't obvious to the untrained eye.

4. Photography hike. Have campers take slides on a hike. Then develop and use the slides for a camp slide show.

5. Tracking hike. Follow the tracks of a rabbit, squirrel or deer. Try to move quietly and see the animal.

6. Sense-of-wonder hike. Lead camp-

Camp Notebook 23

Group Equipment for Winter Base Camping

(For eight to ten campers)

Emergency Gear
- [ ] Group first aid kit
- [ ] Emergency kit: full arm and leg air splints; cervical collar, triangular bandage, wire splint, gauze
- [ ] Repair kit: spare ski tips, pack straps and waistbands; pliers; clevis pins; wire; tape

Trail Gear
- [ ] Plastic sleds or plastic stokes litter (used to transport an injured person over snow)
- [ ] Ropes and tubular webbing for sled harnesses
- [ ] Topographic maps

Shelter and In-Camp Gear
- [ ] 1 whitewall tent with asbestos stove ring or 8-foot-by-10-foot wall tent
- [ ] 1 sheepherders stove (if you use a whitewall tent)
- [ ] 1 plastic ground cover for community tent
- [ ] Tar paper to cover community tent floor
- [ ] 2 four-person mountain tents with flies, poles and ropes
- [ ] 2 ground covers for mountain tents
- [ ] Plastic lids to put under tent poles
- [ ] 1 Coleman lantern
- [ ] Spare lantern mantles
- [ ] 5 one-quart Coleman fuel bottles
- [ ] 1 filler cap
- [ ] 1 black plastic sheet for latrine walls
- [ ] 6 heavy-duty plastic bags for latrine
- [ ] 3 rolls of toilet tissue
- [ ] 1 or 2 aluminum grain scoops for digging snow caves
- [ ] 1 or 2 collapsible shovels
- [ ] 1 ice saw
- [ ] 1 folding saw
- [ ] 1 Hudson Bay ax
- [ ] 1 bag of assorted ropes and cords
- [ ] 1 #10 can with bail

Kitchen Gear
- [ ] 3 stoves (Coleman, Optimus)
- [ ] 3 stove bases (Ensolite or Masonite)
- [ ] 1 cooking pot
- [ ] 1 water pot
- [ ] 1 frying pan
- [ ] 1 wire mixing whisk
- [ ] 1 Teflon spatula
- [ ] 1 wooden spoon
- [ ] 1 long-handle water dipper
- [ ] 2 insulated gloves
- [ ] 2 nesting mixing bowls
- [ ] 1 pot scrubber
- [ ] Salt and pepper shakers
- [ ] 1 plastic bottle of cooking oil
- [ ] 1 plastic bottle with matches
- [ ] 1 collapsible water jug

Library and Documentation Equipment
- [ ] Books
- [ ] Cameras
- [ ] Film
- [ ] Group journal
- [ ] Pens and pencils
- [ ] Binoculars

Note: Be sure vehicles are filled with fuel and have a parking permit if required in the area.

ers on a contemplative hike, and give them time to write poetry or journal reflections on the snowy landscape. Then ask them to share their writing in a camp celebration.

Ice bubbles. When the temperature falls into the teens, blowing soap bubbles takes on a new dimension when the bubbles freeze. Use regular bubble mix with ring blowers, or mix your own in a large bucket using liquid dish detergent. Use different, large paraphernalia to blow multiple bubbles—try a strainer or slotted spatula. Blowing bubbles at night under an outdoor spotlight adds yet another dimension, since bubbles sparkle like diamonds when they freeze and burst in midair. Sometimes a frozen bubble will briefly hold its shape when it lands on soft powder snow.

Snow sculptures. Divide the group into small teams to make snow sculptures. Set a time limit and a designated area. Then let a panel of "judge nots" award prizes for tallest, shortest, most original, coolest, hottest or weirdest sculpture. Be sure to take pictures for a camp slide show.

Snowscapes. Give campers a piece of cardboard, three to five pieces of black construction paper and white chalk. Have them use the supplies to capture the drama of winter on the construction paper. Then hold a black-and-white art show at the camp lodge. (Use a spray fixative to keep the chalk from smudging.)

Extended High-Energy Winter Activities

The winter wilderness is full of opportunities for high-energy winter activities. These provide a day or afternoon of energetic fun and group-building during a winter camp.

Many winter activities are precise and require individual practice. No one learns to ski a telemark turn in one session. Young people need support from experienced leaders and companions as they learn and practice winter techniques.

Learning from mistakes, laughing at them and trying again are essential in winter camping. Kim, an athletic 11th-grader, describes his trial-and-error experience in a group journal from a winter camp:

Steve and Jim finished the skiing lessons with speedy runs. Then they told us to head on back to camp with map and compass. We finally made it back—after various wanderings. Once we overshot camp by a quarter-mile. Jim met us with a sly grin and a box of cake fresh from camp. Groan! We finally arrived to meet two grinning instructors who had dinner on the stoves. They informed us we were once 220 feet from the highway. Our wanderings made me realize that:
Good judgment comes from experience.
Experience comes from bad judgment.

Kim learned because two experienced leaders were patient and realized that solving their own dilemmas is an important experience for campers. Because the leaders knew the time available and the age and maturity of the group, they could let the group make a few mistakes for the sake of understanding and growing.

Tubing and sledding. If properly planned and supervised, tubing and sledding can be safe and fun winter youth group activities. Otherwise they're risky.

Before planning tubing or sledding, find out if these activities are permitted at the camp, ski area or resort you're using. Check if there are designated tubing and sledding areas. Some ski areas forbid tubing and restrict sledding to a small, isolated area. Where these activities are permitted—designated area or not—remember that tubing, sledding and skiing don't mix.

Once you know the regulations, evaluate the areas for safety. Each run should be free of trees and obstacles above and below the snow line. If you're concerned about hidden obstructions, probe the area with a piece of conduit. Designate a return route to the top of the run that does not cross the run.

Each activity area needs adult supervision—a counselor at the top of the run and another at the bottom. If the run has a bump for jumping in the middle, it should also be supervised by an adult. This counselor needs a shovel to keep the bump from icing over. (You can tell when to trim it down or to add more snow by the height and length of jumps.)

Only one tube or sled should be on a run at a time (unless you have a supervised tube chain). The bottom counselor signals the top counselor when the bottom is clear and ready for another run. Impress on campers that throwing anything or side-pushing sliders is never permitted.

Tube chains are safe under most circumstances since the chain slows down the slide. But it's unsafe for multiple campers to pile on a single tube or tube chains.

Snow caves. Digging snow caves can protect adventurers who take treks into the wilderness in cold winter months. But this survival technique is also a fun activity at a winter youth camp. Campers will be amazed at the warmth and creativity that are possible inside a snow cave. Here are some tips for digging your snow cave:

1. Conditions. Compacted snow is best. If there's a lot of powder, dig down to compacted snow. If there isn't enough snow, find the deepest place and shovel a huge mound on top. Then let it settle overnight. Or check the camp parking lot. If the camp uses a snowplow or snow blower to clear it, you'll probably find a deep area at the lowest adjacent point.

2. Supplies. You'll need waterproof gloves; warm, water-resistant clothing; a small plastic tarp or poncho to drag snow out of the cave; and short-handled shovels. (Aluminum grain scoops are ideal since they can move large amounts of snow.)

3. Digging. Have campers take turns digging to save energy and to prevent overheating—it's sweaty work! Once campers have tunneled inside, have them shovel snow on a plastic tarp or poncho. Then those outside can drag it out and dump it.

Round the ceiling like a dome to prevent dripping. Create an inner baffle or snow wall outside the entrance to block wind. Punch a hole in the ceiling for ventilation.

Camp Notebook 24, "Digging a Snow Cave," shows one way to design a simple snow cave. But campers can be creative when designing the cave's interior. Sculpture platforms for sleeping and sitting. Plan a snow cave kitchen. If there's time, you can even dig several rooms.

4. Sleeping. If they're equipped and eager, let as many campers as can fit in the snow cave sleep there. When sleeping in a cave, block the door with a backpack, and keep the ceiling vent cleared with a ski pole when it's snowing.

5. Showing off. If a small group of campers dug the cave during a camp workshop, hold an open house for visitors when the cave is ready. Have a camp stove inside and serve hot chocolate. Display inside and outside thermometers to let visitors see how warm the cave is even in the coldest weather. When people are inside or a small stove is in use, the inside temperature difference can be about 25 degrees at the entrance floor to as much as 60 degrees near the ceiling.

Igloos. Another backcountry survival technique is making igloos. You don't need huge snow piles to make igloos. You can make them any place with compacted snow that will support your weight—even

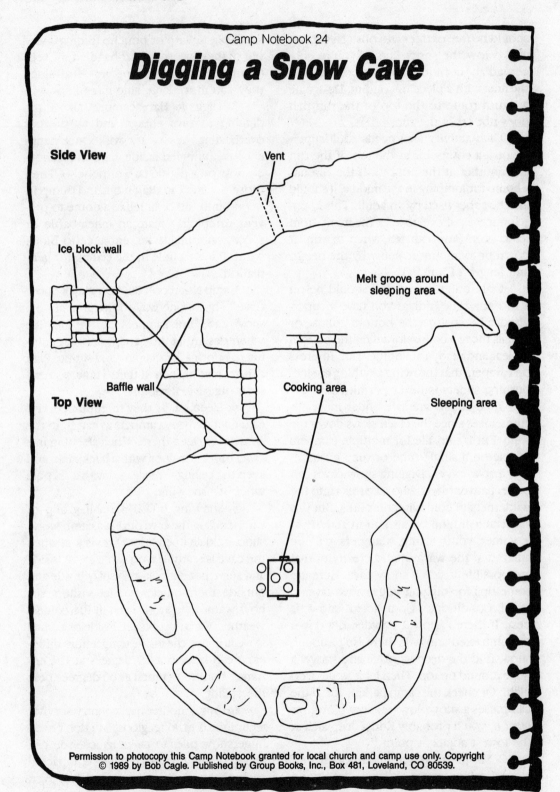

Camp Notebook 24

Digging a Snow Cave

Side View

Vent

Ice block wall

Melt groove around sleeping area

Baffle wall

Cooking area

Top View

Sleeping area

in the back yard or playing field. And you can tramp snow down to compact it.

In deep snow, make a half-igloo against a snowbank. Then dig a snow cave entrance on the downhill side, and carve down into the snow. Sculpture the bottom of the cave, and dig bedroom alcoves off the sides. If you're really creative, design a long, rectangular igloo with two or more entrances and multiple vents and sleeping platforms.

Camp Notebook 25, "Building an Igloo," shows the basic steps in constructing your igloo.

Downhill skiing. Downhill skiing is one of the most popular winter activities. It's discussed in detail on page 136.

Cross-country skiing. It's little wonder that cross-country skiing is popular. Almost anyone can do it with little practice, yet it's also a highly perfected competitive sport. One camp's local ski shop provides instructional films and occasional free on-site instruction because so many campers rent cross-country ski equipment.

When snow falls, familiar camp trails and public summer access areas become prime ski trails. Unplowed forest service roads, logging roads, camp boundary trails, stream-side and lake-side areas are also potential cross-country routes.

Telling campers how to cross-country ski is like teaching them to crochet without a needle and yarn. A video or film gets campers started, but demonstrations, practice and coaching fine-tune campers' abilities to shuffle and stride across the snow. Camp Notebook 26, "Cross-Country Skiing," shows the basic cross-country ski techniques.

Snowshoeing. If campers choose not to ski or if skiers want a different snow-travel technique, snowshoeing is a good alternative. Like shuffle-walking and striding on skis, it takes time to adjust. But basical-ly it involves just walking with your feet wider apart and learning to perfect your steps.

Indoor Winter Activities

Even the most dedicated winter camper enjoys indoor activities away from the cold. But you can keep the winter "feel" to your camp even during indoor programs. Here are a few ideas:

Ski festival or ski class. Develop an entertaining opening night at a residential winter camp using free promotional films from ski manufacturers. Invite a local ski expert to speak and demonstrate equipment. Ski shop operators can help you find films, speakers and printed resources.

Wind River sherbet. Top off a ski festival or ski backpacking trip with this special winter treat. For every 10 campers, carry a can of sweetened condensed milk (such as Eagle Brand) and a double package of your favorite gelatin dessert. (How about strawberry-banana?)

Fill a large, cold mixing bowl with about two quarts of fresh, clean snow. Sprinkle the gelatin powder on top, and slowly pour in condensed milk while gently mixing and folding in the snow with a large spatula or spoon. Add snow until you reach the right consistency and flavor.

The same ingredients carried backpacking in a summer snow zone produce equally refreshing results. Break out the spoons!

Drama. Reader theaters, drama and skits with winter settings or themes can brighten a tired bunch of campers. Groups can write their own mystery or drama to fit the camp setting and occasion. Or use ready-to-use scripts from drama books.

Slide developing and slide making. A warm winter camp activity is to develop slides using Kodak Ektachrome film and developing kits. Or have campers draw

Camp Notebook 25

Building an Igloo

1. Cut blocks of compacted snow with an old saw or machete. Blocks should be about six to eight inches thick, 12 to 18 inches high and 24 to 30 inches long.

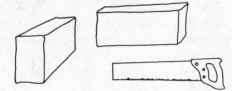

2. Draw a six- to eight-foot circle in the compacted snow. Place the first row of blocks level on compacted snow around the circle. Then spiral cut (angle) the blocks.

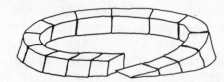

3. Continue laying layers of blocks like bricks. Overlap each block over the two lower blocks. Cut an angle or spiral in oversize blocks after they're in place. Tilt each block inward to create a dome.

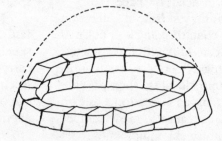

4. When the dome is complete, fill any cracks with snow. Make a ventilation hole in the ceiling.

5. "Design" the igloo's interior as you would for a snow cave.

Camp Notebook 26

Cross-Country Skiing

Shuffle-walking

Double-poling

Striding-gliding

Sidestepping

Herringboning

pictures and write thoughts on the Kodak Ektagraphic Write-On Slides, which are available in photography shops.

The closing celebration is a perfect time to use a winter slide show from the week set to taped theme music, scripture and camper comments. Remember close-up portraits and snow patterns!

Winter Wilderness Camping Techniques

Part of the mystique of backcountry winter camping is that it's so different from camping during other seasons. Not only do you have to contend with the cold, but you have to learn new techniques for everything from walking to cooking to sanitation. Diagram 22, " 'Snow Joke—There's a Difference," compares the realities of winter camping with camping in other seasons.

Winter camping requires rethinking outdoor living. And such rethinking can create an intriguing learning and growing experience for teenagers. Let's look at some of the skills and techniques you'll need when camping in the winter wilderness.

Campsites and Shelter

Much of winter camping's success depends on knowing how to shelter yourself at night. Let's discuss setting up your campsite and how to stay warm during winter nights.

Selecting winter campsites. Locate your winter campsite below the crown of a hill on the downwind side if the area has a prevailing wind direction. Situate the campsite near lines of trees for wind protection but not near leaning trees or under trees heavy with snow.

Choosing tents. A large whitewall tent with a sheepherders wood-burning stove is a comfortable wilderness mansion in winter. Barely 80 pounds, these large tents can be packed in the back of a car or truck. Then lash it on a pulka, a child's plastic sled or a sliding sheet, and a backpacking skier can pull it over the horizon for a million-dollar base camp.

These tents give you a big place where 10 to 15 campers can gather, cook and eat together in warmth and comfort. Then campers can disperse at bedtime to sleep in unheated mountain tents. The big tent also can serve as a base camp for two or three small groups of ski backpackers to practice their winter living skills as independent teams during the day. See Chapter 22, "Tents and Emergency Shelters," for more on choosing tents.

Setting up tents in snow. How do you set up a whitewall tent in snow when you don't have solid ground for it to rest on? Camp Notebook 27, "Setting Up a Tent in Snow," outlines a few tent tricks for snow country.

Sleeping dry and warm. Put a plastic or coated nylon ground sheet (or poncho) under or inside your tent. Lay down two Ensolite pads (not an air mattress) and spread out your sleeping bag to fluff it up as much as possible before you go to bed.

Dig a hole about 18 to 24 inches deep in the snow in front of your tent. This gives you a place to sit down to take off your boots and shake the snow from your pants before you get into the tent.

Once inside, wear insulated booties or wool duffel boot liners and pajamas or long johns. Don't sleep in the clothes, underwear or socks you wore during the day. They're damp. To dry them overnight, stuff them loosely in the foot of your bag or on either side of your legs. Your body heat will dry them before morning.

If you feel cold during the night, check whether the tent is ventilated. A tightly zipped tent will be colder because it retains all the body moisture you breathe. Also check for condensation on the tent wall.

If the tent fly touches the breathable inner tent wall, water will condense and drip at that spot.

If that's not the problem, put on your stocking cap. Pull it over your ears if necessary. If you're still cold, put on a sweater or insulated jacket. That should do it. The only thing left to do if you're still cold is to visit the latrine. Remember next time to listen to nature's call before you get in your

---

Diagram 22
'Snow Joke—There's a Difference

Summer Camping	Winter Camping
Travel	
Weather conditions are unpredictable—wet or dry; hot or cold.	Weather conditions are predictable—just cold or colder.
Trails are obvious and easy to follow.	Trails are covered by snow.
Campers can travel by foot, canoe or raft.	Campers can travel by skis, sled, snowshoes, horses or snowmobile.
Safety and Survival	
Campers must contend with bugs, bees and bears.	Most insects and animals are dormant or in hibernation.
Campers must know swimming safety.	Campers must know ski and cold safety.
You cook outdoors.	You cook outdoors and in tents.
Campers must have the "Essentials for Mountain Safety" (see page 288).	Campers must have the "Essentials for Mountain Safety" plus heavier clothing, insulation, more food, stoves and fuel.
Groups must find water sources to purify.	Clean water is abundant as melted snow.
Gear and Shelter	
Lightweight tents and tarps provide shelter.	Groups must have heavier tents.
Campers wear and carry fewer clothes.	Campers must wear and carry heavier clothing and have a heat source.
Food and Cooking	
Long days allow campers to cook outdoors by sunlight.	Short days and darkness limit cooking time.
Campers can use open fires.	Campers must use stoves.
A variety of menus are possible.	Simple, one-pot meals.
No refrigeration is available.	There's plenty of "refrigeration."
Campers use freeze-dried foods or cook from scratch.	Campers can use fresh foods or warm up precooked frozen meals.
Conservation and Wilderness Ethics	
Sanitation is below ground.	Sanitation is above ground.
Groups must beware of impact on the soil.	Groups must beware of littering in the snow.
Ropes, Knots and Hitches	
Campers tie knots with bare hands.	Campers tie knots while wearing gloves.

Camp Notebook 27

Setting Up a Tent in Snow

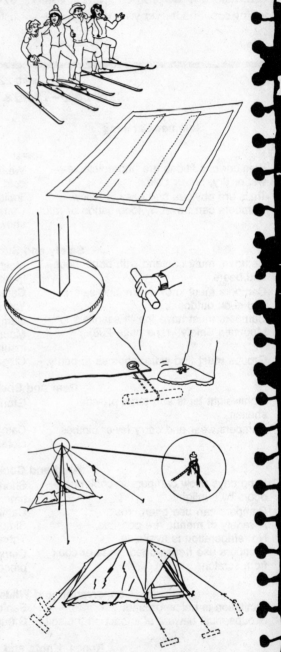

1. When you decide where you want to set up your whitewall tent, pack down the snow with skis or snowshoes. Make it a fun group project—the more the merrier!

2. Place a large, heavy-duty plastic tarp on the ground. Cover the plastic with overlapping strips of pre-cut tar paper (like builders use on roofs). This trick from mountain guides seals out the cold, reduces snow melt and provides a durable floor. You can walk on it, get it wet and dirty, and sweep it out and dry it off without worry.

3. Put vertical poles on large jar lids or thin wood blocks to prevent them from sinking in the snow. (Smaller tents with A-frame poles that fit into sewn-in pockets don't require a base.)

4. Secure the tent's bottom edges with a "deadman"—an anchor made by tying a cord on each grommet and then to the center of a 12- to 15-inch stick. With your heel, dig a hole near the edge of the tent. Drop in the deadman and pack snow on top of it with your foot. It will freeze in overnight.

5. Tie side ropes and guy ropes to trees, side-rig them on horizontal ropes or tie them down with a larger dead-man.

6. Double-roping and cross-roping all tents are good precautions against winter winds. This reduces the strain on stakes and seams when the wind lifts or billows the tent.

sleeping bag.

Keeping your boots warm. To keep your boots from freezing overnight, carry a plastic bag in your bag for your boots. When you take off your boots, knock the snow off and put them in the plastic bag. But don't seal the top. Then put the boots under your rolled up jacket for a pillow. If you really want to get the boots warm the next morning, put them—plastic bag and all—inside your sleeping bag for a few minutes in the morning.

Nutrition and Water

Winter living activities and living require lots of energy. Plan more calories per day—up to 1,000 more than for summer. Use extra margarine or butter in meals, and use cheeses and meats to provide a heavier fat (slow-energy) intake. Add extra peanut butter on pancakes and crackers for more energy. Serve cereals full of honey, butter and mixed dried fruits. Have a variety of snacks available for campers. These can include cookies, candy bars, hard candy, sausage sticks and nuts.

Diagram 23, "Sample Winter Camping Menus," lists several appropriate meal possibilities for winter camping. Directions for cooking most packaged or canned foods are on the package or label. Consult a cookbook for cooking from scratch, or use your own favorite recipes for similar dishes.

Frozen foods. Camping in winter gives you the option of using frozen foods during your camp. Before camp precook your favorite dish as you normally would at home. Then let it cool at room temperature. Place it in a plastic food storage container, and put it in the refrigerator until it's cold. Then freeze it.

When you're out in the winter weather, remember that your food will thaw when days warm up. Avoid letting food thaw in a warm tent. Hang food in bags in the shade outside your tent, or make a refrigerator by digging in the snow. A few hours before you plan to use the dish, place it in a warm tent or on the rear of the stove to thaw slowly.

Dehydration. Winter living requires more water intake. The body rapidly loses body fluid when cold air is humidified during inhaling, making dehydration a major threat for extended winter activities.

Winter campers need more beverages than they need in summer. Serve a variety of beverages through the day such as coffee, tea, hot Jell-O, instant orange drink and powdered milk. Leaders should insist that all group members drink at rest stops on outdoor trips.

Water. A safe and easy way to fetch water in the snow is to melt snow. On warmer days rig a piece of black plastic over four stakes. Let the plastic sag in the middle to form a funnel, punch a small hole in the center, and place a bucket or pot under the hole. You can melt snow even on an overcast day by spreading small amounts on the plastic. The plastic absorbs the sun's ultraviolet rays, melting the snow.

Fire-Building and Cooking

Winter fires provide warmth only when they're built in a sheltered spot away from the wind. But they always set the mood and warm campers' hands, face and knees! Here's how to build fires for cooking and warmth:

Fire-building in the snow. The first task in building a fire in the snow is gathering dry wood. This isn't difficult. Just look for leaning timber or standing dead trees (don't mistake a tamarack that's shed its needles for a dead tree).

If snow isn't too deep, scrape through the snow to the ground and build a traditional no-trace trench fire. If you must build the fire on the snow, lay a base of dead, wet logs on the snow first to keep heat from melting the snow and sinking your fire. Then add a layer of drier wood. Finally, build your fire on top. Use plenty of tinder and kindling.

A candle, fire ribbon, flattened milk carton or a few pieces of twine separated

and fluffed into a ball will keep a fire going until the large sticks catch and begin drying out damp wood.

Outdoor cooking. Cooking outside is easier with a wind screen. Use an Ensolite pad or a tarp to block the wind, or scoop out a cooking area at the base of a

---

Diagram 23
Sample Winter Camping Menus

Breakfast

Rolled wheat cereal with
 fruit (QE)
Zwieback toast (baby
 teething toast)
Butter, jelly and brown
 sugar
Beverages

Quick grits, chipped
 cheese and dried
 beef (QE)
Pop-Tarts
Fresh oranges
Beverages

Granola with honey (QE)
Bananas
Yogurt
Beverages

Scrambled eggs (LD)
Precooked bran muffins
Fresh fruit
Beverages

Pancakes with peanut
 butter or syrup (LD)
Applesauce
Canadian bacon
Beverages

Lunch

Pocket bread
Bagels
Swiss and Cheddar
 cheese
Cream cheese
Peanut butter
Honey
Fresh pineapple slices
Yogurt raisins
Gorp (raisins and peanuts)
Jerky soup
Sandwich spreads
Crackers

Dinner

Macaroni, cheese and
 Spam (or other
 precooked, canned ham)
 chunks
Stir-fried vegetables
Graham crackers and
 pudding
Beverages

Beef stroganoff with sour
 cream (QE/FN)
 (precooked and frozen)
Whole-wheat rolls
Fresh fruit
Beverages

Tuna-noodle casserole
 with peas (QE/FN)
 (precooked and frozen)
French bread and butter
Chocolate cake
Beverages

Taco salad with skillet chili
Tomatoes, cheese and
 lettuce
Frozen cheesecake
Beverages

Roast beef and gravy over
 rice (beef precooked and
 frozen)
Stuffed celery (pimento
 cheese and peanut
 butter)
Cookies
Canned peach halves
Beverages

Key
QE=quick 'n' easy
LD= layover day
FN= frozen

tree—providing the tree isn't loaded with snow, which will melt with the heat from the fire.

Indoor cooking. A whitewall tent with a stovepipe adapter is your best bet for indoor cooking. A wood-fired sheepherders stove is safe and provides winter comfort for several campers. However, cook inside a tent only if the tent is large and well-ventilated and you have a sturdy cabinet-style stove with legs.

Trail Etiquette

Even though your group may be one of the few groups out on ski trails, campers need to know how to respect the rights of other skiers they may encounter. Here are general etiquette guidelines to follow when skiing or snowshoeing:

● Avoid skiing or walking across cross-country ski tracks.

● Step out of ski tracks when taking breaks.

● Give downhill skiers right of way when skiing in a track.

● Avoid the downhill runs when cross-country skiing or snowshoeing through a developed Alpine ski area.

Pulling Supplies on Sleds

Plastic sleds or pulki make pulling supplies across snow easy. Whether commercially produced or improvised, these handy devices make it relatively easy for a cross-country skier to pull 40 to 50 pounds. You can buy pulki from ski specialty stores and catalogs. Or you can improvise by using plastic sleds bought in toy stores.

Homemade devices also work well. They can be as makeshift as an inexpensive 24-by-36-inch sheet of heavy plastic lashed to a large duffel bag containing three or four mountain tents. Or you can make them by attaching PVC tubing with clevis pins to a sled and attaching the fittings on a pad-

ded pack band. Make flexible harnesses using tubular webbing. Tie it with a Spanish bow-line knot to create loops for the shoulders.

When pulling a sled with a web or rope harness, you'll need a dragline for a tail skier to hold on downward slopes. Otherwise the slick plastic sled will run over the towing skier!

Snow Sanitation

As with summer camping, proper sanitation is essential in the winter. If you can dig through the snow to the forest floor, use a traditional trench latrine as you would in summer. If, however, the snow is too deep, dig a hole in the snow and line it with two plastic bags. Make a small drain hole in the bottom to drain water waste.

To make a more elaborate "restroom," lash a log to two close trees, knee-high from the ground. Tie a large plastic bag to the log and to two sticks so it's "open for use." Surround the trees with a black plastic tarp for privacy. Put toilet paper in a plastic bag nearby to keep it dry.

At the end of camp, seal the bags, pack them inside two more plastic bags and carry them out of the backcountry. (Draw straws to see who packs out the bag.)

Preparing Your Group for a Winter Camp

Preparing teenagers for living and traveling outdoors in winter is similar to any camp orientation process. Here's what to cover in writing and in a face-to-face orientation meeting for all participants:

Orientation letter. Send all campers a letter several weeks before your final orientation session before camp. Include the following information:

● When and where you'll have the orientation session.

● Ask campers to bring their clothing

and equipment to the orientation session packed as they plan to take it on the trip. Encourage campers to come full of enthusiasm and questions.

● An information sheet for families. Include names and phone numbers of local contacts where you're camping, directions to and from the campsite, departure and return times, and routes.

● An information form for parents to fill out that includes their phone number, health information, permission to participate and a medical release.

● Information about the camp theme, meals, cooking and money needed for eating en route.

● A packing list of personal gear and equipment and a list of emergency items campers should carry on day trips. (A personal gear list for backcountry winter camping is on page 300.)

● A Red Cross folder on hypothermia (and an avalanche folder if appropriate). Ask them to read the information before the orientation.

Orientation session. The orientation session can have the same elements and "feel" as the orientation session suggested in Chapter 20. Here are items to be sure to include:

● Cover the personal gear list. Discuss why you'll need each item, how to layer clothing and how to control body temperature. Have several people help check everyone's equipment and clothing. Answer questions and recommend changes if what campers have is insufficient or inadequate.

● Discuss the equipment rental process (page 136).

● Outline winter trail etiquette (page 151).

● Talk about how to keep liquids and boots from freezing overnight (page 151).

● Outline your plans for transportation, departure and return times.

● If your group plans and purchases food, discuss the process and set times.

Winter Camp Evaluation

Your winter camp deserves the same careful evaluation and debriefing you use with other camping experiences. Use or adapt Camp Notebook 28, "Winter Camp Evaluation," to help campers think through their experience. Then at the end of camp, give campers an opportunity to discuss their feelings together. This process not only gives you valuable information for planning your next camp or ski trip, but it also lets campers express and accept their joys, struggles and growth during their experience together.

Notes

[1]Robert Service, *The Spell of the Yukon* (New York: Dodd, Mead and Company, 1916) p. 17.

Camp Notebook 28

Winter Camp Evaluation

Complete all the following questions, and be ready to use them to guide your sharing as we talk about our experiences as a group.

1. How would you describe the mood of winter camp?

2. What "aha!" or first-time experiences or discoveries did you have during the camp?

3. Did winter camp change your feelings toward others and toward yourself? If so, how?

4. What was the camp's highlight for you?

5. Describe times during camp when you were most aware of being in a Christian community.

6. What new outdoor skills do you have now that you didn't have before camp?

Chapter 9

Specialty Camps and Adventures

Once you push youth group camping beyond traditional boundaries, you discover dozens of different camps your group could try. In his valuable book, *Accepted Peer Practices in Adventure Programming*, Karl M. Johanson lists 22 land-based adventures and 10 aquatic activities that would be appropriate for youth groups. These include bicycle touring, caving, rock climbing, service projects, tubing, sailing, swimming and lake touring.[1]

It would take several volumes to cover the broad range of possible camping experiences for youth groups in any depth. Previous chapters in this section have discussed the most common types of youth group camps. This chapter offers a brief introduction to several other specialty camps and adventures you might try. These are:

● Bicycle camps.
● Foxfire camps.
● Sailing camps.
● Workcamps.
● A winter wilderness survival adventure.

None of the descriptions of these camps is intended to be exhaustive. Instead, I've recommended the best resources to turn to for guidance if you plan such a camp experience.

Bicycle Camps

Bicycle camping involves all the characteristics of a major backcountry expedition—personal fitness, group safety, teamwork, precision planning, specialized equipment and outdoor skills. And it gives campers the chance to see more of the country, since they can travel longer distances on wheels than on feet. As a result, bike touring challenges youth groups and gives opportunities to build Christian community through a sport that requires concentration and teamwork.

Bike touring along scenic routes and through historic areas provides untold possibilities for groups seeking adventures on wheels. Camp routes can be put together by carefully researching general areas of interest in your state or in a state that intrigues your planning group. Pinpointing state and national parks, natural areas, historic sites, recreation locations, youth hostels and church camps in any given area multiplies the possibilities of linking a few pleasant day trips into a two- to six-day itinerary. As a general rule, the longer the trip, the smaller the group.

If your youth group wants to "test its pedals" with bicycle touring and camping, begin by sponsoring a series of programs and short outings. Invite guest leaders from local bicycle shops and touring groups. Have demonstrations, parking lot practice and video instruction to introduce young people to what's involved.

Equipment and Gear

What do group members know about the bikes they own? If they don't have bikes, can they borrow or rent them? Just because someone owns a bike doesn't mean he or she knows its performance value or limitations.

Ask a bicycle shop owner who's an avid touring cyclist to meet with your group. He or she can help members understand their own bikes' performance possibilities. Experienced leaders can also talk about different types of bikes for touring and camping.

A word of caution: When your group members see the latest, ultimate equipment, they can lose their enthusiasm quickly if they see the equipment as the group standard. A few teenagers may want to equip themselves completely with finely tuned road bikes or mountain bikes, panniers (bicycle saddlebags) and ultralight camping equipment, but a youth group can have lots of fun with their old bikes and with camping gear borrowed from church families.

However, you'll need to provide a backup system in case the older equipment fails. Equip a "sagwagon"—a van or other vehicle used to transport community gear and food—to pick up bikers and to repair bikes. Have "camp keepers" or an "entourage" (loving parents and friends) drive the sagwagon. Not only does this provide a safety net for broken equipment, but it also lets non-cycling parents and youth workers participate in long-distance trips. Moreover, it increases the margin of safety should someone become ill or have travel-ing difficulty.

Carefully chosen and packed personal gear is important for bicycle trips and camping. Camp Notebook 29, "Bicycle Gear List," is a checklist for personal and group gear for bicycle touring.

Bicycle Safety

Bikers are exposed to many potential dangers on the road. Thus they must exercise proper safe riding and camping practices under the watchful supervision of adult leaders who are experienced in group bicycle travel. As you prepare a group for cycling, you should state and rehearse frequently basic rules for group safety. These include:

● Always know and observe the travel laws and regulations in your state and area.

● Travel only in daylight with youth groups. Never travel at night, at dusk or in heavy fog.

● Adult point and drag riders must always pace the group so bikers can see each other at all times.

● Develop touring skills progressively by riding with partially loaded bikes at first and increasing the weight as experience and confidence increase.

Bicycle Maintenance

Proper bicycle maintenance is a key to a successful bike trip—regardless of camping style. Moreover, learning bike maintenance is a fun learning experience for group members. A pre-camp maintenance session should give campers a demonstration and some hands-on experience with the following simple maintenance requirements:

● Checking tires for pressure and wear.

● Inflating tires.

● Lubricating chains.

Camp Notebook 29

Bicycle Gear List

Personal Gear

☐ Bike flag

☐ Bike reflectors

☐ Bike markers

☐ Shoes and socks (comfortable and "broken in")

☐ Layered clothing for the season

☐ Bike poncho

☐ Rain chaps

☐ Gaiters

☐ Gloves

☐ Sunglasses and cap for sun protection

Group Equipment

☐ Tools and lubricants for bicycles

☐ Spare bicycle parts

☐ Emergency shelter (if staying in homes, hostels or motels)

☐ Tents (if camping)

☐ Protective sun cream

☐ Personal first aid kit

☐ Extra bike parts and tools

☐ Snacks and water

☐ Bible and journal

☐ Personal items

If camping:

☐ Extra clothing

☐ Sleeping bag

☐ Tent

☐ Food (or money to purchase food)

☐ Cooking utensils

☐ Stoves

☐ Fuel

☐ Group first aid kit

☐ Miscellaneous equipment

- Replacing brake pads.
- Adjusting cables.
- Tightening bolt and nut connections.
- Changing a flat tire.
- Adjusting spokes and rim alignment.
- Organizing a tool kit.
- Organizing a spare-parts kit.

Bicycle Training

Just as the bicycle must be prepared for a long trip, so must potential bikers. Physical preparation before the trip cuts down on the injuries and sore muscles on the trip. Here are some exercise steps to prepare campers for a bike trip:

1. Start with a calisthenics routine.
2. Ride the bike regularly and keep a written record.
3. Swim or walk to develop other muscle groups and to improve respiration.
4. Take short-distance rides.
5. Move to intermediate-distance riding.
6. Increase loaded weight gradually.
7. Graduate to long-distance riding.
8. You're ready to go!

Getting Started

Once your group is excited about the prospect of a bike trip, design short outings to increase the group's knowledge, skills and enjoyment for touring.

Being able to cycle on a fully loaded bike is essential for a safe and successful bicycle camp. And bikers can travel safely as a group only if they've practiced in parking lots and on side roads enough to know what to do without being told.

Prepare campers by building on their skills and knowledge with progressive training events. Begin practicing with unloaded bikes. Then advance to practice maneuvers and day trips with fully loaded

front and rear panniers. Practice on-off-on road-shoulder maneuvers with loaded bikes to help bikers get a feel for day-after-day touring. Finally, take an overnight shakedown trip with two days on the road to confirm a group's ability to plan and set out for longer ventures.

Researching a Route

Numerous factors must be considered when choosing a bicycling route. Elevation gain or loss, directness, scenery, historic enrichment, overnight accommodations, campsite availability, distance between campsites and food sources should all play important roles in your selection. Because of the variables, negotiating a route can be a great group-building event.

When you plan your tour, consult with an experienced adult cyclist in the community who knows how to choose safe and appropriate routes for groups. However, don't let the expert plan the whole trip. It's important for campers to share in decision-making—even if the leaders are highly experienced and have traveled a route dozens of times.

Leaders don't need to play games or withhold information, but they should be open to planning a route that's a learning experience, not a guided tour with a leader and some followers. The group-planned event allows everyone to learn from community choices. Talking about "our mistake" or "our great idea that worked" feels good to teenagers.

Discover possible routes from bicycle club newsletters, touring groups and local bicyclists. More than a dozen bike touring organizations provide leadership for bicycle camping. Several will even custom design trips and provide guides for groups. They also have maps describing bicycle routes throughout the United States. Suggested tour routes are rated according to distance and difficulty.

By joining these bicycling organizations, you're usually entitled to special magazines, newsletters, tour schedules, and rates for overnight accommodations in hostels or homes. These overnight stays give bikers a chance to share in cooking and cleanup and to meet other bikers and groups. The fellowship and information-sharing are great growing experiences.

Eugene Sloane lists these tour groups in his book, *The All New Complete Book of Bicycling*.[2] Two particularly good organizations to contact for information:

American Youth Hostels
Box 37613
Washington, D.C. 20013-7613

League of American Wheelmen
Ste. 209
6707 Whitestone Rd.
Baltimore, MD 21207

Up-to-date state road maps, bicycling regulations, city maps and topographic maps in mountainous areas are all useful guides for your choices. Many motel chains also provide current maps of various areas.

Bicycle Camping Tips

Camping styles for bicycle tours can be as boundaryless as for any other trip, so develop a style that fits your group. Here are some factors to consider:

Meals. A relatively simple and light-weight approach to meals involves preparing prepackaged breakfasts at camp, eating lunch at a country store, and picking up supplies in the afternoon to cook dinner at camp.

But if you take longer treks into more remote areas or if you want to get away from traffic, you'd probably choose to prepackage more meals, cook more of your own food and spend more time afield and less time on the road. Whatever your choice, keep it simple!

Carrying equipment. The weight of tents, sleeping gear and other camp equipment isn't a major issue when you travel with a sagwagon. However, weight becomes significant if you take an extended, self-contained trip. Every item—indeed, every ounce—becomes critical on extended cross-country trips.

Etiquette. Backcountry techniques and trail etiquette are as essential in bicycle camps as they are in backpacking or canoe camps. Just because you camp in more commercial camps or other developed properties is no reason to abandon concern for the environment, equipment and the courtesies everyone enjoys while traveling.

Protection. Bicycles and other gear are valuable, and unscrupulous passers-by could ruin your trip by stealing or damaging equipment. Remember to cable bikes in public places and to watch them even when they're cabled. Don't leave gear for long without someone who's responsible to watch it.

Foxfire Camps

The Foxfire experience began in 1966 when Eliot Wigginton's high school English students in Rabun County, Georgia, began listening to and writing down mountain folks' stories about the "olden days." Then what began as a unique school magazine project turned into a series of best-selling books that has sold seven million copies from coast to coast.[3]

The story of "Wig" and his creative ventures with high schoolers is unparalleled. Viewed theologically, the Foxfire experience embodies what youth workers call "ministry *with* teenagers." Teenagers' discoveries during a Foxfire experience can be summed up in one word:

appreciation. Whenever Foxfire classes have gone to interview, photograph and write these stories, they've come away with an incredible respect and love for the people they've met. They've left behind a trail of appreciation too—"Them young'uns really listen!"

Camp leaders have been aware of Foxfire through workshops led by Wigginton and his students. And some camps include some camper-community experiences with older generations and some hands-on exposure to pioneer American living. But only a few camps thus far have focused their primary program on the Foxfire experience.

How can a high school magazine staff, after listening to mountain folks tell stories, shape the values of teenagers in a church camp? And what would make a Foxfire camp different from other youth camps?

I asked Eliot Wigginton these questions, and he sent me to James Turpen, a pastor in the Rabun County area for 30 years. Turpen, pastor of his home church, is a man of the mountains who lives in the house where he was born. He supervises the work of several other pastors and churches and is an avid camper and leader for his area YMCA camp. I asked Turpen to help me visualize a scenario of a week of church camp totally built on a Foxfire approach to programming. What would it be like?

A Day in the Life of a Foxfire Camp

To give a feeling for the Foxfire camp experience, Turpen told how the Foxfire experience could be woven into a typical day at a Foxfire camp. This overview can guide your thinking as you design this type of "appreciation event" with your youth group. The activities may not appear to be much different from activities during many other camps; however, they gain their sig-

nificance through their focus on inquiry, honor and appreciation.

Waking up. Foxfire campers wake up experiencing the nature around them. "Being out in nature, you have the possibility for an appreciation of the world around you—beauty, good air and interaction with other people," Turpen says. "By the same process you're aware of creation and the world that's no accident. You wake up aware of the night you have spent and aware that somebody has prepared food." Campers confirm these awarenesses by giving thanks at breakfast.

Getting-up exercises. "Focus on the mind, spirit and body," Turpen says. He suggests that camper interactions after breakfast are used to "wake up the mind, soul and body early in the morning. Use vigorous experiences on a playing field."

Food and meals. Campers relive pioneer days with everyone participating in meal preparation. "In pioneer settlements," Turpen explains, "everyone had a role in mealtimes—either gathering, washing, peeling, breaking, cutting or cooking." Campers can gather vegetables for meals if you can work it out with a farmer, Turpen suggests. Or they can help snap beans, slice tomatoes or wash potatoes. Wigginton suggests adding cooking on a wood stove to Foxfire camp activities.

When possible, Foxfire campers serve food family-style to focus on family structure. Indeed, one goal is to live as families at camp any and every way possible. To make the family feeling more real, an intergenerational camp is appropriate, including teenagers, children, young adults, parents and senior citizens.

Tidying up. Campers always clean up after meals at a Foxfire camp. "They get appreciation and gain self-discipline by cleaning up where they are and taking responsibility for their cabins or tents and the campsite," Turpen says. He adds that "young people need that experience of cleaning up. Growing, harvesting, preparing and cleaning up are all part of the family mealtime process."

Morning activities. Foxfire campers spend the morning engaged in various mountain crafts and activities (see next section on this page). These activities take advantage of the available resources and facilities, and they require creativity and ingenuity.

Noon rest hour. "Old timers said they worked from 'sun to sun,'" Turpen recalls. "But in reality they rested in the heat of the day . . . The rest let their souls and their bodies catch up with each other." Turpen believes campers need that rest too. "It doesn't have to be sleeping rest, but quiet time, conversation time, a time for swapping ideas and not being rowdy," he says.

Afternoon activities. Many of the activities available in the morning also fill the afternoon. The flow of craft times, recreation and Foxfire activities is very flexible. Leaders can repeat activities so campers get a chance to do the things they missed in the morning. Or if an activity catches everyone's interest, then everyone can do the same thing—provided enough tools and supplies are available.

Evening activities. After supper, have more free time for campers to relax and have some one-to-one time together, Turpen suggests. Evening programs can feature a guest who recounts the area's olden times or who demonstrates an indigenous craft or skill. Square dancers, cloggers and other folk games also give campers good opportunities to experience celebrations from the past.

Evening campfire. Foxfire camp leaders should involve many campers in the evening campfire preparation and program—not just one person who leads all week. Use songs, scripture talks, meditations, Bible stories and authentic mountain stories with deep truths. Leaders should help campers share stories and swap ideas. Richard Chase's *Jack Tales* and *Grandfather Tales* are excellent sources of authentic mountain tales preserved as they were told to the author.[4]

Cabin devotions. Before campers go to bed, they can focus again on the Bible as they talk about their day's experience with a few friends and counselors. This family time around the Bible with sharing and prayer creates a valuable faith experience that some campers may not practice regularly with their families at home.

Foxfire Activities

Foxfire camp activities introduce campers to the crafts, games, skills, arts and recreation of another way of life in previous centuries. Each camp will be different as it relies on the people, resources and facilities available.

Discovering these available elements can give campers once-in-a-lifetime experiences. One summer Foxfire camp took place in an area where pine beetles had destroyed many trees. A neighboring farmer who had a sawmill was dragging out the salvage logs with an old-time logging horse. So the problem became an opportunity for campers to experience an almost-forgotten logging technique.

Another camp in West Virginia maintains the pioneer spirit by preserving an 1850 log cabin and by moving another hand-hewn cabin to the site. Each week of the summer the camp director's 83-year-old father visits. Sitting under an apple tree, he tells campers the life stories of the olden days. His cagey humor—"Well, I'd tell you about the time that . . . No, I guess I better not, you wouldn't believe me"—works magic for city kids who want to hear more stories.

Wigginton points out that the basic tools for every Foxfire camper should be a loose-leaf notebook (or journal) and a pencil to keep track of their experiences—stories, game rules, recipes and sketches of Foxfire skills. Wherever Foxfire students have gone, they've created a lasting memory with a notebook, tape recorder or camera. So prepare each Foxfire camper to document the camp experience Foxfire-style!

Let's briefly look at pioneer and mountain activities that enhance the Foxfire experience:

Woodcraft. Woodcrafting is a basic Foxfire skill campers can discover at camp. If you camp in the open and cook over fires you can focus on learning what types of wood are good for cooking and what types aren't. "You don't burn green wood with vines on it," Turpen illustrates. Why? "You could end up with the 'blamedest' case of poison ivy you've ever had!"

Campers can learn woodworking and woodcarving at many different levels. Turpen says teenage campers can do "everything from carving simple animals from soft woods to making white-oak splits for bottoming a chair or making a three-legged stool."

Working with clay. The traditional pottery-making workshops at summer camps take a new dimension when Foxfire campers gather clay themselves at the campsite. The quality of the finished products will depend on the clay that's available. Turpen notes that "working with clay has lots of scripture connections that shouldn't be overlooked."

Weaving. If skilled leaders are available, a workshop can teach the old art of hand weaving. Campers can easily learn simple weaving. If leaders have a loom,

they also can introduce campers to other techniques.

Corn crafts. "Corn shucks, stalks and cobs are all useful in mountain crafts," Turpen says. Campers love to whittle, and corn crafts provide that experience. The inner stalks are soft, making them easy to cut and shape into airplanes, doll faces and miniature tools. Corn shucks can be cut and twisted into a variety of creations—from doll dresses and bonnets to creatively woven coasters and place mats. Having campers gather leftovers in nearby cornfields is ideal, but corn can also be gathered ahead of time and stored for camp.

Basket weaving. Campers can make baskets "as simple or complex as you want," Turpen says. They can be simple twig-and-pine-needle baskets or intricate baskets woven from white-oak splits—or anything in between.

Camp newspaper. Having a camp newspaper re-creates the original Foxfire experience when the high school students gathered mountain stories for their magazine. While campers may not have time to tape interviews, photograph local people, type the interview and develop pictures for a newspaper, they can do most of the work. And with pre-planning and leader support, they can complete a respectable project—even if the final newspaper is mailed to campers later.

Local storytellers and resource leaders. Many local people near the camp can be valuable bridges to understanding the area's lifestyle and history. At their best, these settings are informal sharing times. The goal isn't classroom learning, but a time to appreciate families in the community.

If your camp is near a Native American population, ask local people to lead informal sessions on their crafts, customs and stories. Or contact nearby farmers ahead of time, Turpen says. Many are willing to explain to small groups of campers how crops are grown. In some places they can demonstrate tending livestock or plowing with a horse or mule. Even better, arrange to pick home-grown tomatoes or beans.

Swimming holes. Some campsites may have a clean creek nearby that can be dammed to make an old-fashioned swimming hole. "That's the way it used to be," Turpen says. "People made a place to swim, and by winter high water would wash it away." He adds that groups who make swimming holes at camp shouldn't wait for rain to wash the dam away. Instead, they should tear it down before they leave and restore the creek to its original appearance.

Informal nature walks. Have an outdoors enthusiast lead small groups on informal nature walks around camp. "Help campers develop an appreciation for simple things—water coming out of the ground, fish, beauty, the fullness of the earth," Turpen urges. "Small groups together out in nature can begin to see we're totally dependent on nature for our well-being."

Games and sports. Foxfire games are backyard family games—the kind of games people used to play at a family gathering or that kids would invent with simple equipment. Many are played with no equipment at all—circle and chase games, mind teasers and singing games.

Turpen suggests providing a mixture of familiar and Foxfire games. "Have enough of each to be a good contrast," he says. "We need vigorous, strenuous games for young bodies to burn up their superenergy as well as games that require mental concentration." Diagram 24, "Traditional and Foxfire Games," lists several high- and low-energy games that work well at youth camps.[5]

Sailing Camps

Unless you know nautical terminology, you may be surprised to learn that "unforgiving boats" can be just as appropriate as "forgiving boats" in a church sailing camp. Why? Forgiving boats are hard to tip, and they cover your mistakes. Unforgiving boats are sensitive to errors, making them

---

Diagram 24
Traditional and Foxfire Games

High-Energy Games

Traditional Games		Foxfire Games	
Broom hockey	Softball	Buck	Fox and hounds
Flag football	Volleyball	Buckety buck	Potato sack race
Soccer	Water polo	Fox and geese	Three-legged race

Low-Energy Games

Traditional Games		Foxfire Games	
Circle soccer	Parachute games	Horseshoes	Old Granny Wiggins is dead
Group juggling	Relays and races	Jump rope	Please and displease
Old plug	Spud	Lemon relay	Thimble

tip over easily if your technique isn't skill-ful and precise. Both types of boats provide great avenues for an unusual youth camp.

Sailing and seagoing camps offer many benefits for teenagers. They build personal skills, community, teamwork and safety consciousness. They also introduce young people to the history and lifestyles of shrimpers, lobster people and boating people.

The challenge of teamwork and the shared celebration of achievement provide an avenue to discuss life, faith and God out of the daily experiences. Like the rivers and mountains, the wind provides a challenge that can become a parable of life, giving new meaning to other parables. As John Farmer, director of a sailing camp in North Carolina, says, "You become a Christian community pretty quickly when you must depend on each other all day long." He has experienced this truth for years. "When we first started sailing," he told me in an inter-view, "I planned a few community activi-ties and devotional times for each evening. But I soon saw there was more to process than we could deal with—just from our daily interaction. The curriculum was in the group, and it was easy to process."

The Don-Lee Camp Model

Farmer's Camp Don-Lee in Arapahoe, North Carolina, runs a model sailing camp program for all ages of young people— from third grade through college. An over-view of the camp's programs suggests the possibilities for a youth group sailing camp. Let's look at the sailing camp options the camp offers:

Recreational sailing. The camp offers a simple recreational sailing program in which all sailing is "out-front"—in sight of the camp's waterfront. Recreational sail-ing involves no competition but focuses on providing fun recreation and teaching bas-

ic skills for "living groups," which spend the week together growing in Christian community. Drills include windward sail-ing, tacking, jibbing, turning over boats and righting overturned craft.

Interested young people can learn specific sailing skills during free-time elec-tives. Campers may also sail a buoyed course under the supervision of two staff members in a motorized "chase boat." An-other option for small groups is to take an "over-lunch" or "over-supper" sail on a 19-foot day sailor (a forgiving boat).

Special program sailing. The camp sponsors a two-week camp designed to pre-pare young people for "sail tripping." While the focus is still small group Christian programming, the program is more than recreational. Camp includes sailing theory classes as well as out-front and trip sailing experience. The camp doesn't emphasize competition, but it does teach racing rules, right-of-way rules and sailing nomenclature.

Classes begin with tacking drills and progress through weather awareness, storm procedures and course plotting. The two weeks include three sailing trips. First is an overnight tent camping trip with three or four miles of staff-led sailing. The second trip is a two-night trip in which groups sail 10 miles the first day, 10 miles the second day and return the entire distance on the third. The third trip is an up-river historic trip.

Advanced camp. The most advanced camp is a three-week experience in which campers learn to sail a variety of water-craft—from the Sunfish to a 30-foot sloop. Campers also race in a local regatta and spend nine to 13 days camping in historic areas. In addition to emphasis on Christian community and sailing skills, the program deals with North Carolina's early whaling history.

Another historic sea camp directed by

church camp consultant Richard Chamberlain takes place on an island five miles off Maine's coast. During this camp young people learn to crew a 40-foot wooden schooner and to row a dory—the solo boat of the early lobster trade.

Planning Your Own Sailing Camp

Because of the expensive, specialized equipment involved and the skills needed, youth groups interested in an open sea sailing camp will need the guidance of experienced professionals. And you'll probably have to rely on established sailing camps for equipment and facilities.

Before making a major commitment, though, you can plan some out-front time for sailing at summer events, church camp or family camp with sailing facilities. Or the youth group can spend a day at a nearby lake with small sailing craft and instructors. Another option is to find church members who sail and have their own craft. They're usually eager to help a group get a taste of sailing adventures. One youth group on a summer choir tour arranged in advance to crew a 40-foot sloop under the guidance of a licensed pilot in the Miami area.

The Sunfish is one of the most popular sailing boats for beginners. Camp and resort rental groups have relied on the Sunfish since the early '60s as an ideal, easy-to-learn sailing craft for children, teenagers and adults. The shallow V-bottom of the hull—together with its generous beam (width)—makes it comparatively stable and forgiving.

Sailing camps and public leasing opportunities vary widely from area to area. If you don't know someone who's familiar with sailing and sailing facilities, search the ads in sailing magazines. Also check for camps with sailing programs listed in Christian Camping International's *Official Guide to Christian Camps and Conference*

Centers[6] and the American Camping Association's *Parents' Guide to Accredited Camps.*[7] Two good, basic resources for sailing are Will White's *The Sunfish Book* and M.B. George's *Basic Sailing.*[8]

Workcamps

Some people erroneously describe today's teenagers as self-centered, passive and uninvolved. The hidden but steady growth of youth workcamps since the '70s challenges that stereotype. Each year thousands of young people participate in denominational, interdenominational or locally organized workcamps where teenagers give a week of hard work to those in need.

How does workcamping help people? How does it affect youth who participate? Are the results lasting? The following excerpt from a college-entrance essay by a high schooler who served a week in Jonesville, Virginia, helps answer these questions:

. . . Our mission was to repair, as much as possible, two homes of families who could not otherwise afford the renovations . . . Our group went through a number of workshops to prepare for this undertaking. We talked to former participants, studied the culture and history of the region, explored our theology of mission and servanthood, and sampled a typical meal of the area. Finally, to complete our training, we spent a weekend building a storage shed for a local youth camp. Yet, we weren't prepared for what we would experience on the trip.

When our group arrived, we were met by four other groups who'd be living at the campsite with us. Two groups were from churches in Minnesota, one from Michigan and another from Pennsylvania. The local project leader briefed us on our assignments, and goals were established for the week. Then teams of two from each group, a youth and an adult, went to see the work sites, meet the families and assess the condition of the homes. Their reports of the poverty the people lived in were almost unbelievable . . .

The next morning our group was split to go to separate sites. My crew included three boys, a girl and a young married couple. The two adults were home builders, but the rest of us had no experience. We'd have to do our best. Upon arriving at our destination, jaws dropped in amazement. We couldn't believe what we were seeing: Three people were using a tiny hay shack as a home.

Our hopes of making this house livable faded. Where to begin? What to fix first? . . . Our shock turned to pity when we saw the interior, which was in worse shape than the outside. The walls were made of newspapers, and the floor and ceiling were patched with cardboard—not much protection against a harsh Virginia winter.

Over the week, my work crew got to know the Jones family rather well. Bob, Rosie and their baby, Annie, didn't complain about their home. Bob had lost his job at the local sawmill and now worked on his father-in-law's farm . . .

After a surprisingly fast week, we finished the ceiling, floor and walls in the kitchen, painted the tin roof and built a new front stoop and door. One of Rosie's sisters even said it looked like a new house! . . .

This trip was filled with physical and emotional stress for me. In fact I got sick from working in the extreme heat, and on the last day I couldn't go to the work site. But the week showed me that a group of kids, perceived by some as spoiled, could give up their comfortable lifestyle and do good in a remote Virginia town for a nice young family.

A Day at Workcamp

A workcamp doesn't look like much on a schedule. That's because it's a *work*camp, and young people spend most of the day just doing one thing: work. A typical schedule looks like this:

6:30 a.m.	Rise 'n' shine/breakfast
8:00 a.m.	Load supplies and head for sites
8:30 a.m.	Work hard all day (interrupted by periodic refreshments and a lunch break)
5:30 p.m.	Supper
6:30 p.m.	Fellowship, reflection, group sharing or a special program
10:30 p.m.	Quiet time
11:00 p.m.	Lights out

However, this bare-bones schedule comes to life with new skills, funny stories and new friends when you read excerpts from group workcamp journals:

Today Scott and Jim came down before breakfast and loaded Sheetrock. We leveled the Sheetrock in the truck with two buckets of paint. Proposed new workcamp law: Don't level Sheetrock with full paint cans. They turn over and become roller skates as you drive off!

●

It's always hard getting to know new people—especially when you're with a group of old friends. Today we broke the ice with some people from Minnesota. It's interesting to see how much we have in common.

●

Nancy and Melissa, "Big 'un" and "Little 'un" as Mr. Carter calls them, painted the ceiling then the walls. Our pastor trimmed ahead of them, and Bob framed the window. Scott and Jim just kept on Sheetrockin'.

●

Today Mr. Carter told us more about himself. "They tried to get me in that mine," he said. "I told 'em 'No! I'll help skin the world but no way I'm gonna gut it.'"

Organizing for Workcamping

Organizing a workcamp requires juggling dozens of logistical pieces. In his book, *The Workcamp Experience: Involving Youth in Outreach to the Needy*, veteran Group Workcamp organizer John C. Shaw outlines the necessary arrangements and how to complete them successfully.[9] Instead of organizing their own camps, many youth groups take advantage of nationally organized workcamp programs sponsored by denominations or interdenominational groups.[10]

Even when you participate in a national workcamp program, your group must still prepare itself for the project. Working with the youth group in the following three areas will help your group have a more successful and meaningful workcamp experience:

Understanding the mission. Understanding the workcamp's mission is imperative to creating appropriate motivations and attitudes in group members. Sponsoring organizations often supply printed and audio-visual resources (usually a manual and a slide show or videotape) to facilitate this process. It's often effective to have an introductory workshop led by an experienced workcamper who explains the mission's principles.

It's important to spend time before camp helping the young people understand the local culture, poverty, how people feel about such projects, and what workers can do to affirm residents and build strong relationships. Use Bible study, discussions about faith, cultural awareness activities and simulation games to help workcampers think through their own motives and theology of mission.

A challenging, soul-searching way to discern motivations and attitudes about an upcoming workcamp is to have your group develop its own mission statement for the experience. Re-examine it several times in preparation, and revisit it daily during the workcamp. Add to it, revise it—grow together!

The week before you depart for a workcamp, have congregational worship events to dedicate and bless the work team. Such a service re-enforces the mission and undergirds it with the congregation's prayers and love.

Fund-raising. Different workcamp agencies require youth groups to contribute to the program in different ways. Some ask groups to pay their own room and board as well as a building-materials fee. Others cover the youth group's room and board but ask for a gift of money or materials.

In each case, youth groups must raise funds for the trip. You can use any of the conventional fund-raising methods youth groups employ for mission projects. Or your group can solicit building-material gifts from local hardware and construction supply dealers. Remember, though, that you need to plan transportation for these material contributions unless the sponsoring organization can pick them up. Plywood, Sheetrock and cases of paint can quickly overload the average pickup or van!

Skills practice. Learning building skills completes your workcamp team's preparation. If you plan well, you can actually do a smaller project at home before the workcamp where young people have on-the-job training. Some national organizations also offer workdays when young people can spend a Saturday learning the skills they'll need for their workcamp.

If you have builders or contractors in your congregation, ask them to help train your group and to be sponsors on the workcamp, if possible. Their expertise will give genuine skill practice before your trip. One youth group spent an all-day work session at a builder's construction site and then completed a building project for a local camp.

One idea that combines basic skills-building with group-building is to have the group make toolboxes together. Each camper can build and decorate a box to use on the trip. Or introduce a special dynamic for a celebration and dedication by having each workcamper build and decorate a toolbox for another team member.

A Winter Wilderness Survival Adventure

After training and gear checks, small groups of campers and leaders trek into the snow for an 18-hour winter survival experience (4 p.m. to 9 a.m.). The wilderness area isn't far—a wooded hollow over a small ridge only 200 yards from the lodge. The security of nearby safety and an easy exit in case of emergency reassures the novice campers about their ability to survive outdoors.

Once in the woods, the 12-person group breaks into three teams of four. Each team works separately but within sight of the others. In their packs the teams discover they have just enough materials to build a comfortable shelter with a dry, plastic bottom. Once the fire starts, they're warmed.

But they have to make some hard-nosed decisions about responsibilities and rationing food and water (which has been intentionally limited). Each team resolves in its own way the questions of how to construct the shelter, rotating sleeping or sitting up, gathering wood and keeping the fire going.

The weather is just as cold, the snow just as real as if they were 25 miles from civilization. The cold weather and the limited food create enough challenge to foster real learning. But campers don't worry or panic since they know they can walk to warmth and safety in five minutes if needed.

As the above scenario illustrates, a wilderness survival camp can be a safe, challenging and fun adventure for a small youth group. While most literature concentrates on solo survival, a group survival experience adds the important dimensions of group decision-making and caring for others under survival circumstances—another rich parable for exploring the Christian faith. The keys to a successful survival experience are being properly equipped and using an appropriate setting. Here's how to plan and prepare for a survival experience:

Learn basic survival techniques. Get acquainted with survival literature and the techniques. While most survival manuals deal with solo survival (someone who's lost or who has survived a disaster), the literature discusses the important survival issues and dynamics. This knowledge will help you adapt techniques to a group experience.

Get the group ready. Spend unhurried time doing group-building activities such as "Subarctic Survival Situation."[11] Then talk about each item in the campers' day packs (for a packing list, see Camp Notebook 30, "Wilderness Survival Gear"). While most items may be self-explanatory, discuss each one so group members are conscious of what resources they have on their backs. (The small piece of Ensolite, for example, is used to sit on. It's waterproof and equivalent to two inches of foam rubber—without the bulk.) Practice fire-building basics. If there's lots of snow, build a snow cave as a training and group-building event.

Arrange a location. Get permission from the camp director-manager or owner before scheduling your survival event. Then select a sheltered site that's close to a lodge or vehicles and that has abundant wood, undergrowth, downed trees and small breakable limbs.

Schedule the event to include the afternoon light through the morning light. Summer survival events can start later in the day and end earlier if desired. You'll also need to schedule a large block of time the next day for rest and sleep. Some leaders plan survival events to end midmorning and set aside several hours for rest. Whenever you begin and end, it's still important to group dynamics to have enough time in the woods to experience really being "out there."

Once you've chosen the site, think through the experience in light of its particular characteristics. Many variations can be effective. For instance, simulate having a sick or injured person in each group. This can supply another dynamic for group interaction and leadership. Your inventiveness and knowledge of your group can guide you into a fun-filled and challenging time.

Camp Notebook 30

Wilderness Survival Gear

Each camper should dress warmly and comfortably for the season and carry a day pack with the following:

☐ Extra clothing

☐ Rain gear

☐ 10-foot-by-12-foot plastic sheet

☐ Lighter and fire starter

☐ Flashlight

☐ 12-inch-by-12-inch Ensolite pad

☐ Water bottle and cup

☐ Extra food and snacks

☐ Map and compass

☐ Pocketknife (no sheath knife)

☐ 30 feet of 3/8-inch nylon rope

☐ Personal first aid kit

Two or more adult leaders should carry the above essentials plus the following group equipment:

☐ Group first aid kit

☐ Sleeping bag

☐ Sleeping pad

☐ Small stove

☐ Extra fuel with pouring spout

☐ Cooking pot or #10 can with bail

☐ One small folding saw for every four campers

Emphasize group technique.
Recognize and emphasize that group survival is more effective in groups of three or four than in groups of 10 or 12. Smaller groups let everyone actively share in leadership and decision-making. They also keep everyone involved and communicating. Finally, smaller groups are more efficient: Four people can huddle around a fire easier than a dozen can, and campers won't have to use as much physical energy to gather wood for a small fire.

Plan minimum food and water. For the survival experience to be effective, the group must face hunger, thirst and decisions about using their resources wisely. Otherwise the survival experience becomes an all-night stay-awake party with no real simulated stress. One way to add realism is to have each small group shop at a nearby grocery store using a set amount of money to buy the supplies. This experience more realistically simulates the snacks a wise wilderness traveler would have in a day pack.

During the night. Keep tabs on the groups throughout the night. Adult leaders should stay awake to ensure a safe and meaningful experience. Use the leaders' extra equipment only if requested by a group or agreed upon by the leaders. Plan a celebration time before leaving the survival site, even though you'll have a debriefing at camp.

Debrief the event. After you've returned to camp for showers and breakfast, take time to debrief before resting or disbanding. This important time allows campers and leaders fully to internalize the experience and its value.

Take plenty of time to recall feelings, learnings about leadership and personal insights. What would group members do differently if they were doing it again? How would they feel about their personal abilities to handle emergencies? Affirm each person—regardless of what was experienced.

Notes

[1]Karl M. Johanson (compiler), *Accepted Peer Practices in Adventure Programming* (Boulder, CO: Association for Experiential Education, 1984). (Available from AEE, Box 249, Boulder, CO 80309.)

[2]Eugene A. Sloane, *The All New Complete Book of Bicycling* (New York, NY: Simon and Schuster, 1983).

[3]The Foxfire story is vividly recounted in Eliot Wigginton, *Sometimes a Shining Moment: The Foxfire Experience* (New York, NY: Anchor Press/Doubleday, 1986).

[4]Richard Chase, *Jack Tales* and *Grandfather Tales* (Boston, MA: Houghton Mifflin, 1943, 1948).

[5]An excellent collection of Foxfire games is Linda Garland Page and Hilton Smith (editors), *The Foxfire Book of Toys and Games* (New York, NY: E.P. Dutton, 1985).

[6]Published annually by Christian Camping International, Box 646, Wheaton, IL 60189.

[7]Published annually by the American Camping Association, Bradford Woods, 5000 State Road 67 North, Martinsville, IN 46151.

[8]Will White, *The Sunfish Book* (Boston, MA: Sail Publications, 1983); and M.B. George, *Basic Sailing* (New York, NY: Morrow, 1984).

[9]John C. Shaw, *The Workcamp Experience: Involving Youth in Outreach to the Needy* (Loveland, CO: Group Books, 1987).

[10]For a detailed listing of 30 organizations that sponsor workcamps for youth groups across the country and overseas, see Eugene C. Roehlkepartain (editor), *The Youth Ministry Resource Book* (Loveland, CO: Group Books, 1988), pp. 276-284.

[11]This and other good group simulations are available from Human Synergistics, 39819 Plymouth Road, Plymouth, MI 48170. Telephone (313) 459-1030 Other available simulation experiences include: "Cascades Survival Situation," "Desert Survival Situation," "Desert Survival Problem II" and "Jungle Survival Situation."

Part Three
Camp Leadership

Chapter 10

Recruiting and Training Camp Leaders

Larry was a leader long before he became a counselor. As a camper he was best known for his early-morning rally cry: "Nothin' to it but to do it! Let's get rollin'!" For four summers Larry went on camps and trips with his youth group, and his leadership grew out of those experiences.

How did those trips contribute to Larry's leadership? Each event was designed to build leadership in the young people. The group developed each trip through consensus decision-making. Small teams of campers led each day's activities—cooking, cleanup, and morning and evening celebrations. Everyone worked on navigating, planning menus, shopping, washing clothes and setting up camp.

Larry would never describe himself as a "trained" leader. Yet when he became a camp counselor during college, his skills overshadowed those of many other college-age counselors. For him, leadership came naturally. His experience in his local church had been a training time for him.

Larry's story illustrates the primary goal of good camp staff training: to help leaders-in-training discover within themselves natural ways of being with campers as capable leaders and companions. People lead the way they're led. Thus leadership recruitment and training should be a priority in developing a camping ministry.

Recruiting Counselors and Leaders

What characteristics should you look for in a camp counselor or leader? Whom should you ask? What should you avoid? What should you ask adults to do? Let's look at these issues.

Important Characteristics of Camp Leaders

There's no precise checklist or profile for the perfect camp leader or counselor. Some individuals who seem like perfect leaders can fail dismally, and some people who seem unqualified may have just the right personality.

Counselors don't have to play guitars, look like movie stars, have theological training and be stand-up comedians. Instead, they should be growing in their faith, able to listen and able to relate well to teenagers. As you consider whether to invite a person to be a counselor or leader, ask yourself the following questions. If you can answer with an enthusiastic "Yes!" then that person could be a great camp leader.

1. Is he comfortable with teenagers?

2. Does she already have a good relationship with young people?

3. Can he listen with understanding?

4. Does she share her faith story in a natural manner?

5. Do youth group members see him in worship, teaching or serving roles in the congregation?

Potential Leaders

You'll notice that none of the above characteristics focuses on a particular age group, particular talents or particular looks. That's because a variety of people in the congregation—young adults, parents, senior citizens and middle-age adults—can contribute to youth camps as leaders.

Sometimes youth leaders choose counselors just because they're available and willing. While discretionary time is an asset (and it keeps you from having to ask people to use their vacation time), it doesn't qualify a person to support campers as they shape their faith journey.

Here are people to consider when recruiting camp leaders and counselors:

Parents. Parents of teenagers (and parents of former group members) are potential camp counselors. Sometimes youth workers don't include parents because they erroneously believe that "kids don't want their parents tagging along." However, current research on parents and teenagers reveals that there's probably greater openness to parent counselors now than in the past three decades.

While teenagers probably won't want their own parents as their cabin counselor, they're usually proud and feel more secure when their parents are on a trip. Moreover,

having parents at camp shows that they're interested in youth and supportive of the camp, making them good role models for growing disciples.

Actually, having parents at camp adds another important dimension: All campers need "mothers" and "fathers" at camp. A five-year study of campers' parents at a private camp in Tennessee confirmed this need by showing the mother's significant influence over a teenager's camp participation. In fact, after the study, camp director Ward Akers began training camp counselors to do what he called "mother functions." These included a variety of caring roles that counselors could do for mothers—everything from encouraging campers to write home to checking campers for cuts and scrapes. Moreover, the camp added a "volunteer mother" who was a dining host and a confidant for campers.

A good way to find appropriate parents to include is to ask the young people who are planning the camp. They already know the parents they're comfortable with and the parents who young people look to as mentors.

While being a camp leader is a valuable experience for parents, don't ask parents who are having personal struggles or family problems, hoping that being a counselor will help them understand or solve some problem. Parents who are leaders need to be able to focus on the group and the kids during camp—not their own needs.

Young adults. Many camps and youth groups rely on college-age and post-college young adults for camp counselors. And for good reason: Many young adults in their early to mid-20s take pride in modeling adult behavior; they're tolerant of teenagers' feelings, music and changing ways; and most young adults are close enough to their own teenage experience to remember clearly their own struggles, needs and accomplishments. All these characteristics add up to counselors who care—with a profound ability to empathize with young campers' feelings.

In choosing young adult leaders, however, avoid choosing young adults who've grown up but haven't found a place among their peers. Teenagers need adults who are fairly secure in their identities, not adults who are escaping adulthood by working in the youth group.

Other congregation members. Every congregation is rich with untapped resources. And many people with much experience and expertise are glad to give their time for young campers—a geology professor, a U.S. Forest Service employee, women who've developed special mission programs for their circle groups, farmers, school teachers, recreation leaders, and experts from a wide variety of professions.

Many church members also have cultivated their hobbies to a high level of knowledge and expertise. In one church, for example, there were three instructor-level downhill skiers, an executive banker who was also a scoutmaster, a high school coach who liked camping, an executive who arranged sports car road rallies, and four accomplished canoeists.

A good way to find good adult leaders is to create places where adults and teenagers can discover each other. These opportunities include service projects, community events and intergenerational church events where you can see adults and teenagers interact.

Camp Leadership Responsibilities

When you recruit adults as camp counselors and leaders, be clear on your expectations and their responsibilities. It's also important to ask them where they could see themselves best fitting at the youth camp. Use Camp Notebook 31, "Responsibilities for Volunteer Camp Leaders," to think about all the ways adults can help lead your upcoming camp—and which adults can fill different roles. (Some of the responsibilities also can be filled by responsible teenagers if you choose.)

Training Counselors and Leaders

Every type and size of camp needs a cohesive, trained team for quality growth experiences. And every camp needs leadership training and staff team-building. Trainers can include church volunteers with camping experience, youth ministers, pastors, year-round camp professionals or invited guest leaders.

Beginning a Training Program

Plan your first camp event as a training event. Limit participation to camp leaders and a few older youth who want to help lead your new camp program. Train more leaders than you need for your first camp to increase the training's value and to ensure program continuity. Otherwise the new program is vulnerable when trained leaders move away or shift their commitments to other places and programs.

Planning leadership training is much like planning a youth camp. The difference is that training involves consciously experiencing and reflecting on each element of the training event. The best way to ensure that the training experience transfers to the youth camp is to make training a fun-filled adventure. In this way, the training will have the sense of surprise, mystery, wonder and joy you want to foster at camp—and you hope will linger when campers arrive. Moreover, if counselors are encouraged to lead during training, they're more likely to encourage campers to lead

Camp Notebook 31

Responsibilities for Volunteer Camp Leaders

Responsibility	Possible Leaders	Confirmed
☐ Lead camp music (guitarist, accompanist)	_____	☐
☐ Lead workshops (one primary leader and one assistant per workshop)	_____	☐
☐ Lead recreation (one primary and one secondary leader)	_____	☐
☐ Lead evening activities	_____	☐
	_____	☐
☐ Supervise evening service setup	_____	☐
	_____	☐
☐ Lead morning watches	_____	☐
	_____	☐
☐ Coordinate camp promotion	_____	☐
	_____	☐
☐ Coordinate registration	_____	☐
	_____	☐
☐ Oversee first aid	_____	☐
	_____	☐
☐ Supervise bus loading	_____	☐
	_____	☐
☐ Prepare name tags	_____	☐
	_____	☐
☐ Coordinate cabin assignments	_____	☐
	_____	☐
☐ Coordinate class assignments	_____	☐
	_____	☐
☐ Coordinate sharing groups	_____	☐
	_____	☐
☐ Supervise camp cleanup	_____	☐
	_____	☐
☐ Solicit prayer support from Sunday school classes	_____	☐
☐ Lead or assign devotions	_____	☐
	_____	☐
☐ Coordinate and design homecoming service	_____	☐
	_____	☐
☐ Coordinate mealtime blessing assignments	_____	☐
	_____	☐
☐ Make and monitor question box	_____	☐
	_____	☐
☐ Prepare class materials	_____	☐
	_____	☐
☐ Drive vehicles to and from camp	_____	☐
	_____	☐
☐ Lead overnight campouts	_____	☐
	_____	☐
☐ Supervise meal preparation	_____	☐
	_____	☐
☐ Other: _____	_____	☐
	_____	☐

during camp.

The camp trainer's primary objective is to design ways to help leaders learn how to plan and lead outdoor ministry events. To do this, the trainer can't just tell counselors information or demonstrate various activities. Rather, training should be action-based and experiential—a chance for leaders to grow through creating, testing and openly evaluating their own experiments.

If you train counselors by holding a round-table seminar—with lots of up-front, director-centered time—they'll probably lead camp as if it were a seminar. Then the counselors will later wonder why fifth- or ninth-graders won't listen longer and talk more seriously. And campers will wonder why counselors talk so much and expect them to do the same.

Leaders at one outdoor leadership event asked counselors to analyze the first hour of training using these questions:

● How much time did the leader spend talking to the group?

● How much time did the leader spend demonstrating for the group?

● How much time did you spend interacting with other counselors?

● How much time did you spend demonstrating or practicing a camp activity?

After the hour, the group stopped and dissected the experience. Counselors quickly discovered that the leader had purposely limited verbal time and maximized group interaction and practice. Then counselors were invited to work in small groups to develop an hour-long plan to use with campers—a plan the group would analyze later.

Training Time

Training events involve a wide range of time frames, depending on the specific camp. Here are examples of the differences:

Residential camps. If your leaders are all from the same church or town, an afternoon or a few evenings at home plus an all-day training visit to the campsite should suffice as adequate training. Of course, subgroups that are responsible for leading specific areas will have to meet other times for planning.

Weekend campouts. If you plan a weekend campout, plan an overnight campout training event on the actual trail. This experience gives leaders a genuine feel for the upcoming event. The rhythm of travel, theme times, group relationships, skills training, leadership sharing and equipment management will provide a base for realistic planning.

Longer camps. Leaders for longer camps or people who spend a summer as camp counselors will need more training—three to five days or more.

Training Locations

Whenever possible, hold your training events at the camp itself. If on-site training isn't possible at a residential camp, at least visit for a few hours or a day. The visit helps leaders realize the site's programming potential. The visit should include as many of the leaders as possible as well as some teenagers who'll be leaders and participants. On-site training at the camp facility or on the trail helps leaders develop a sense of safety judgment, security needs and program possibilities. These can be achieved no other way.

However, distance sometimes makes on-site training or visits by all leaders difficult. In this case, find a closer location with similar facilities where you can train. Several churches in the Southeast that sponsor cross-country trip camping in places as far away as Idaho, Maine or Canada have a weekend "shakedown trip" at a nearby area that's as realistic as possible before the summer backpacking, rafting or mountaineering trip. The short excursions are designed to test camping gear, teach backcountry living skills, develop planning teams and give leaders a time of personal testing and group covenant-making.

Flexibility: The Training Watchword

"Leave that garter snake alone and go to the lodge for nature study!" To make a point, camp trainers often repeat variations of this timeworn statement. It reminds leaders that one of camping's greatest assets is the unplanned-for moment of discovery. No one can guarantee that fish will bite or that a particular sunrise or sunset will be extraordinary. You can't schedule an appearance by a doe and her fawn or a soaring eagle. And they won't wait until later—even if the dinner bell has rung. The leader's role is to see the potential, then, when the moment arrives, adjust the program to experience fully the new discovery.

There's no magic formula for knowing when to change plans to experience a new discovery. When campers began catching trout at camp during free time, one outdoor school director canceled the daily field trips to a nearby fish hatchery. Campers spent the time fishing instead. By the week's end almost all the campers had caught fish—for many, their first.

Another camp director decided to let a lone six-year-old spend the afternoon at a family camp helping the camp manager install new bunks in a cabin. The director felt the one-to-one time with the camp manager would be more valuable to the child than the church's planned program, since the boy lived with his mother and had few opportunities to work on projects with a male companion.

Trainers should model and emphasize this openness and flexibility during leadership training. Here are some ways:

● Establish a precedent for flexibility by discussing openly and evaluating the training design.

● Help leaders learn to distinguish between "expected" practice and "permissible" practice. The six-year-old in the story was expected to participate in the camp program. However, it was permissible for the director to ask the camp manager if the boy could tag along for a couple of hours. This flexibility is marked by the spirit of "grace," which contrasts sharply with the legalistic, law-centered approach that says everyone always does what's expected. Leaders should understand the difference between expected and permissible practice when camping with teenagers.

● Schedule a time (one to three hours) in staff training when the staff makes a group decision on "how best to use this block of time." The decision-making process is more dynamic if the trainer doesn't even suggest options, leaving the decision totally to the group. After the time block have a reflection and evaluation time. Ask the leaders to identify valuable insights about how they make decisions. This exercise provides a foundation for determining how to involve campers in decision-making and program-planning.

Areas of Training

The best way to ensure a balanced training design is to plan experiential camp training in a typical camp schedule. The flow of camp life for an overnight training event or a five-day event will present opportunities to include the seven major training areas. Here are some suggestions:

Outdoor skills. Include an overnight campout as part of training. Have counselors cook a meal that they'll later cook with campers during camp. Have teams of counselors plan and demonstrate the outdoor skill areas they'll be teaching campers.

Counseling. Use group-building experiences with counselors that they can later use with campers. Have counselors process simulated problems or case studies (see page 187 for examples). If you wish, ask a guest leader to cover basic interpersonal communication skills with a presentation and exercises.

Planning camp. Have counselors plan theme time activities to experience and evaluate as a counseling staff. Ask teams to plan a full 24-hour period of camp with each team planning a different day with different subthemes. Then have the different teams present their ideas.

Leading workshops and recreation. Include workshop and recreation leaders in staff training to permit counselors to experience some of the activities campers will experience during camp. Help counselors understand your philosophy of recreation and workshops. Brainstorm ways counselors can support workshop and recreation leaders and vice versa.

Leading Bible study. Lead the counselors in the same Bible study themes you'll be using with campers. If you use one main Bible study leader for your camp, ask him or her to participate in counselor training.

Leading worship. Ask teams of counselors to plan and lead worship times with the staff. Again, use the same theme, schedule and time block you'd use with campers.

Safety and emergency procedures. Simulate and role play accident management, using counselor teams to process a variety of typical situations. Review potential hazards and emergency guidelines with staff, and provide all staff with printed emergency guidelines (that will fit in their pockets), including all emergency numbers they might need.

Designing Training Episodes

Imagine the elements of your training event as parts of a large tarp or rain fly that you can pitch many different ways (see Diagram 25, "Rain Fly Training Image"). Each side is essential, and each is complete only with the other three sides. Moreover, each side changes its relationship to the other sides depending on how you pitch the fly.

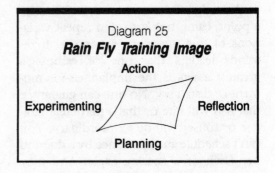

Diagram 25
Rain Fly Training Image
Action
Experimenting
Reflection
Planning

The same changing interrelationship holds true with the four sides of training—action, reflection, planning and experimenting. They're never exactly the same, and each affects the others. And the process changes shape depending on your needs. Let's look briefly at each element:

Action. Creating experiential involvement in a training area provides a base from which counselors can gain clues for inventing their own approaches. New games, for example, are most fun when counselors have played together enough to feel free to improvise their own games or to create new ground rules for making play more interesting.

Reflection. Set the stage for meaningful inventing and constructive critique by inviting counselor teams to reflect on what they would adapt for other situations to make an activity a better experience for campers. Having adequate time to question and think through their experiences in an activity is essential if counselors are to plan and experiment together with their own activities.

Planning. Counselors who plan together during staff training are more likely to involve their campers in planning during camp. Have small teams of counselors outline a day, plan an activity in detail or create a series of activities to use day after day.

Experimenting. Camp leaders need to lead what they've planned in order to grow and increase their knowledge of possible approaches to camp activities. The staffers who take charge during staff training will not only feel more secure leading campers, but they'll also be more open to critique and suggestions.

In training camp leaders, strive for balance between each element. However, each training event calls for concentrating more on one or two areas. For example, some training areas dealing with information are covered best in leader notebooks, correspondence, camp policies and other resources. These may not require planning or experiential involvement but will take place primarily in discussion or reflection times. Thus balance isn't giving equal time to each element; rather, it's making sure each element is part of the overall training design and is addressed in each training episode.

Leader Training Episodes

The remainder of this chapter consists of training episodes you can use with your leaders. Or use the rain fly image to design your own episodes in different skill-development areas. Use the various training ideas as you plan and prepare leaders for your youth camp.

Training Episode One:
Developing Planning Skills

This episode is designed to help you analyze the training process itself. You can analyze all the other episodes in the chapter using similar questions for reflection.

Preparation. Photocopy the "Camp Trainers Notebook" (Camp Notebook 32) for each leader. (Note: All activities listed in the training schedule are explained in this book.)

Training. Distribute the "Camp Trainers Notebook" (Camp Notebook 32) to each participant. Have individuals or small groups critique the training design using the following questions and activities as guides:

1. Identify and mark the four design elements in the leaders notes:

  Action
  Reflection
  Planning
  Experimenting

2. How is each element achieved?

3. Which design elements dominate the total design? Why?

4. What would you add, modify or omit to improve the design?

Training Episode Two:
A Group-Building Hike

This training episode is designed to heighten leaders' awareness of nature, to help them learn to work together and to show them how to design their own nature-awareness activities.

Action. Ask a naturalist to lead camp counselors on a half-mile hike around a lake or natural area. Have the naturalist lead a series of nature awareness activities—listening, seeing, touching and tasting—that develop the leaders' senses and curiosity.

Reflection. During a midhike break, invite the leaders-in-training to reflect on their feelings and discoveries. Ask: "As you experience this place are you reminded of other times in your life? Can you describe some sense of spiritual discovery you have

Camp Notebook 32

Camp Trainers Notebook

WEDNESDAY NIGHT

Camping catalog game – share – introduce partners
Share favorite memory of "being outdoors"
Slide show – WITHOUT A TRACE : A WILDERNESS CHALLENGE

REMEMBER:
1. Fall flower guide
2. Magnifying glass
3. Pack for Kim
4. Extra maps

Trip Overview – show route on topographical map
Distribute personal gear list
Demonstrate organizing personal gear and
                                    packing pack

Explain how community gear is distributed
Distribute rental and borrowed gear

FOOD – give out food criteria list / repackaging
                                    demonstration
        Volunteer by twos to plan, purchase,
         package and prepare food on the trail –
        sign up

CLOSING – readings from the Psalms and
            MAN WHO WALKED THROUGH TIME (pp. 209-215)
         Prayer – Circle of hopes

SATURDAY (meet at church)
        Check gear (rain gear, sleeping bag, pad)
            Weigh packs
        Breakfast at Danny's Restaurant
        NORTH GROUP – Bob / Jenny – drop at
                        Woody's Gap
        SOUTH GROUP – Kim / Rodney – drop at
                        Winfield
        Scott – park at ranger's house

continued

SOUTH GROUP (3.3 miles)	NORTH GROUP (3.1 miles)
—Drop group at trail head & park at headquarters	— Break at Big Cedar Mountain/ Read Olson's reflections
— Lunch at Gerrard Gap (team 1)	— Lunch at Granny Top Mountain (team 3)
— Rest stop—Burnette Fields	— Rotate leadership
— Rotate leadership	— Map-compass-orient map
— Rhythmic breathing technique	— Alternate water source?

BOTH GROUPS RENDEZVOUS AT BAKER MOUNTAIN CAMPSITE

★★EXCHANGE VAN KEYS   Long break-snacks-rest
Locate water source/sanitation-cat method
Demonstrations: Site selection
                How to pitch E-rope shelter
                Tent-pitching — set up all tents
Exploring Time: Gather wood/bring water (team 1)
                Basic no-trace technique
                Demonstrate—use of stove/safety
                    Knife, ax and saw
Teams: Cook in for supper (teams 2 + 4)
                Wood/water (team 1)
                Plan celebration (team 3)

Supper
Dish washing—soapless technique
Campfire (team 3)

SUNDAY

Breakfast (teams 1 + 3)
Share—wilderness emergencies & first aid kit
Gear management—evaluation— communion

SOUTH GROUP	NORTH GROUP
— Lunch at Granny Top Mountain Or the spring on ridge beyond	—Note chestnut logs on Baker Mountain—tell story
— Long stop at Big Cedar Mountain	— Pick up van at Winfield
— Rendezvous at Woody's Gap	— Scott—Treats at store; meets South group at Woody's Gap

in this place? Share either response in your own way—a memory you are reminded of or a spiritual quality you sense." Give the leaders an opportunity to reflect and share.

Planning. After the hike, ask counselors to pair up to rethink the hike and to "invent" a nature-awareness activity for a specific spot on the trail. Give each pair of counselors a few examples of nature-awareness activities (see Chapter 16) along with a trail map designating their specific spot on the trail. Allow each pair 30 minutes to plan, and tell them they'll lead the exercise with their fellow counselors on the return hike after lunch.

Experimenting. Hike the trail again after lunch. Have pairs of counselors each lead the awareness activity they planned. After the hike allow time for group reflection on the experiments. Ask the leaders to describe any positive, new awarenesses they experienced on the second trip that didn't happen on the first. Then ask pairs of leaders each to evaluate their own awareness episode and to talk about any changes or adaptations they might make when leading the activity with campers.

This evaluation process is carefully designed so that each person can share positive awarenesses, but no one is to suggest changes in awareness activities except the one he or she personally led. Use this approach the first few times a group reflects or evaluates together. Later, when the group has developed a sense of group trust, allow leaders to suggest improvements in each other's designs.

Training Episode Three: SAFEtalk

This episode introduces leaders to a listening technique and helps them prepare to use the technique with campers.

Action. Invite leaders to sit together where they're comfortable enough to car-

ry on a face-to-face conversation with a partner. Then introduce the listening exercise. Say: "SAFEtalk is a way to listen and communicate warmly and affirmingly. Using the letters of the word 'safe,' you have four guidelines for talking and listening to your partner:

Seek information.
Accept what you hear.
Feel what you hear.
Explore what you hear."

Continue: "Talking within these guidelines may seem a little stiff to you at first. But it comes easy after one or two statements, so stick with the four steps."

Then ask each leader to interview his or her partner on one of the two subjects, which you should write on newsprint or posterboard:

1. The first day of camp is the most important day.

2. The last day of camp is the most important day.

Have each leader choose which subject he or she wants to be interviewed about.

Conclude your introduction by saying: "Remember: Seek . . . accept . . . feel . . . explore . . . as much as you can in five minutes. Then your partner will interview you."

Reflection. After the interviews, lead an open discussion guided by the following questions:

● How was "SAFEtalk" easy or difficult?

● What did you discover about your partner?

● What did you discover about yourself?

● What did you discover about the importance of the first and last day of camp?

Planning. Then ask each pair to plan an easy and non-threatening way to facilitate a conversation or sharing time with campers. Remind leaders to focus on ways in which everyone can share something. Have them imagine any place or time in camp to use their conversation technique. Give each pair 15 minutes to plan.

Experimenting. When the planning time is completed, ask pairs each to find two other pairs and share the conversation-starters they created. As they share each technique, have them:

1. Identify the idea's strengths.

2. Explore ways to adapt the idea for another time and place.

3. Suggest ways to improve the technique.

4. Choose one technique or learning to share with the whole group.

Training Episode Four: Your Stop Is Coming Up

This episode helps leaders learn to share their ideas openly and elicit ideas from campers.

Action. Have leaders pair up and sit knee-to-knee with their partner to have a warm conversation even though many others are talking around them. Have each pair decide who is partner A and who is partner B. Say to the leaders: "I'm going to give you an imaginary situation, and I'd like your immediate response.

"Partner A: You're riding on a bus beside a seventh-grader. The young person tells you things aren't going well at home, and he or she needs some advice on getting parents to listen. Your stop is coming up in three minutes, so you have just three minutes to tell your partner what you'd tell the young person beside you on the bus."

Give the A's time to respond. Then say: "Partner B: You're also riding on a bus, but you're sitting by a tenth-grader. The young person asks what you'd do if you felt there was just nothing left to live for. You have

three minutes to tell your partner what you'd say."

Reflection. In an open discussion (or in subgroups, if you're training more than 12 to 15 leaders), have the A's share what they said to the seventh-grader. List each idea on newsprint. Also ask the A's to talk about insights they gained by imagining themselves in this particular situation and what they gained from hearing others' ideas.

Then ask the B's similar questions about their experience. Finally invite all the leaders to comment on the experience and what they learned.

Planning. Divide the group of leaders into small groups of four to six. Have groups each develop some imaginary situations they could use with the campers. Ask each group to outline their ideas on newsprint to share with the whole group. Allow 15 to 20 minutes for this planning.

Experimenting. After leaders have developed their ideas, have each subgroup choose two situations developed by another group to try. In pairs, have A's respond to one and B's to the other. Then call the whole group together to discuss the rest of the ideas. Encourage leaders to keep a counselor notebook for ideas, or have someone compile all the imaginary situations and photocopy the list for everyone.

Training Episode Five: Filling in the Blanks

Sooner or later every group encounters conflict. Conflict among leaders may come as a natural outgrowth of becoming a team. Sometimes it involves scheduling, site-use, dealing with a problem camper or the timing of a particular activity. Campers may get into a conflict for a variety of reasons as well—loneliness, homesickness, competition, peer conflicts, opposite sex relationships or unresolved conflicts back home.

Whatever the impetus for the conflict, the first step in handling the conflict effectively is to face it immediately and openly. As a counselor trainer once said: "Never pass up a good crisis. It will help you grow."

This training episode is designed to equip adult leaders to deal with conflict. It has several purposes:

● To overcome the idea that conflict is bad, unusual or destructive.

● To prevent denial and avoidance of issues.

● To deepen communication.

● To enable an openness for identifying issues that would become destructive if ignored.

● To practice conflict resolution as a shared ministry instead of deferring to a camp authority.

● To consider personal and group dimensions of familiar and unfamiliar conflicts.

Action. Divide the group of leaders-in-training into small groups of three. Then introduce the topic by saying: "Conflict crops up unexpectedly. It happens in any camp. Sometimes our greatest opportunity for ministry is in the midst of conflict. Our purpose in this session is to sharpen our skills in dealing with conflict. At the end of our time you won't be able to give specific solutions to every conflict. But you will be able to work with campers and other staffers in developing appropriate solutions."

Now ask the small groups to spend two to three minutes listing conflicts they think could arise at camp. Have them share their ideas with the whole group, and list the conflicts on newsprint.

Next ask the small groups to choose who in the group is A, B and C. Then say: "A, you have the hardest task, because you're first to face conflict in this exercise.

You'll also be working with some new rules. We'll support you, so hang in there!"

Then explain the exercise: "I'll read a brief case confrontation to you. Then you'll have two minutes to respond verbally, using the following five points to guide your thoughts:

1. Your immediate response as the person involved.

2. Other people's immediate response to you.

3. Your behavior.

4. Other people's response to your behavior.

5. The overall outcome for everyone involved."

Post the points on newsprint or posterboard so everyone can see them. Continue: "Use your imagination to visualize your response and other people's responses to the situation. Describe the total outcome with a succinct statement to your small group.

"After your response, I'll stop you and give you another bit of information. Again, you will have two minutes to complete the five steps. You may want to alter your original response based on the new information, or you may choose to keep the same response. Then I'll interrupt you the last time with one more bit of new information. Again you'll have two minutes to use the five-step response. When A is finished, B and C will have an opportunity to work through scenarios too."

When everyone understands the exercise, begin by reading the scenarios in Diagram 26, "Case Confrontations." Or write your own scenarios that relate specifically to your camp.

Reflection. Bring the whole group together to reflect on the three case studies. Ask the leaders to share their feelings about each case in order. List their thoughts on newsprint:

A. The camp counselor with Bill and

Pete's fight.

    B. The youth leader with Cindy and friends.

    C. The canoe trip leader with David, Lisa and the four campers.

    Then ask the leaders to share any discoveries and insights they gained from confronting the conflicts.

    When everyone has responded to the three case studies, prepare the group for another round of conflict resolution by spending six or seven minutes talking about conflict resolution (see Diagram 27). Add your own illustrations and elaboration as appropriate.

    Planning. Let your group size and

Diagram 26

Case Confrontations

Read the following case studies to the leaders-in-training.

Case A

    You're a camp counselor. As you return to your cabin one night, you hear loud voices: "Fight him, kick him!" You walk in and find Bill, the biggest boy in the cabin, fighting Pete, the smallest boy.

    Give two minutes to respond.

    New information: Unanimous voices shout, "Bill started it!"

    Give two minutes to respond.

    New information: After you speak to the group, you walk outside and Randy, another counselor, says: "I saw that. It started out here. Pete hit Bill from behind without warning."

    Give two minutes to respond. Then say: "We'll discuss all our cases. But now we'll move to B in each group."

Case B

    You're the church's youth leader. It's the third night of camp, and you see lights on in an unoccupied cabin. You walk in and find three counselors. It's almost midnight, but they don't seem to be making any move to leave.

    Give two minutes to respond.

    New information: Cindy's been crying, and the group is silent.

    Give two minutes to respond.

    New information: Cindy, the youth group president, lost her temper in a small group. She was openly corrected by Marie, an adult counselor who's new in your church. Cindy says she wants to call her parents to come pick her up.

    Give two minutes to respond. Then move to Case C.

Case C

    You're leading a canoe trip. The group is camped at Big Bay Landing. It's late, and everyone's asleep. Then a car drives up. It's the pastor from a nearby town with a message that David's grandfather has died. His father asked that you talk with David and make arrangements for him to return home. You're now at the tent where David and two other campers are sleeping.

    Give two minutes to respond.

    New information: After trying to wake up David, you discover he's the only camper in the tent. His two tentmates are gone—plus two other campers and Lisa, a college-age counselor from your church.

    Give two minutes to respond.

    New information: After a short search you and another counselor find Lisa and the four campers down by the shore.

    Give two minutes to respond. Then begin the whole group discussion.

Diagram 27
Basic Steps for Camp Conflict Resolution

1. Listen carefully to the other person's perceptions. Ask yourself:
- How does the other person see the situation?
- What appears to be his or her assumptions?

2. Open yourself to as many alternative responses as possible. Ask yourself:
- How can I avoid oversimplifying the situation into right and wrong?
- What are my assumptions?
- What are the implications of my assumptions?

3. Seek ways to set things right rather than assessing blame. Ask yourself:
- What must be done immediately?
- What can wait until later?
- How does my response minister to the group?
- How can we make a faith connection without moralizing?
- How can I avoid blaming or intensifying feelings?
- How can I help the group take responsibility?

---

time guide how you plan and process the next part of the session. Here are two options:

1. Ask pairs or triads of leaders-in-training each to write three conflict cases to give another small group. They don't need to write "new information" statements; they simply identify the characters and describe the confrontation.

2. Before the session, photocopy the six case studies in Diagram 28 (or create your own) and tape them to construction paper or index cards. Make multiple copies of each card and ask everyone to think about how to respond. Then share responses in a brief closing reflection time.

Turn the cards with cases upside down (or put them in an envelope), and have each person draw one card, read it and respond.

Experimenting. As each person responds to a case study in his or her small group, have group members respond immediately by suggesting alternative approaches to the same situation. Remind the leaders that they're not debating which is the "best" or "right" approach; rather, they're trying to discover in a brief time two or three good ways to minister as they try to resolve the conflict. Then when other members have proposed responses, move to the next case. Give each group time to talk through the cases.

If you work in subgroups, you may wish to close the experimenting time with some total group sharing. Or you may wish to see how many possible conflicts listed during the "Action" time have and haven't been covered in the session.

Diagram 28
Alternative Ministries Case Studies

1. You're a counselor with seven campers. It's very late, and the whispering and laughing doesn't stop—even after repeated requests from you and two campers. You try to strike a serious note. "Why did you come to camp?" you ask. One camper answers in a false voice, "Just to raise a little hell." Laughter and moans erupt.

Think of one or two ways you might turn this situation into a positive group time. Tell the members of your training group how you'd respond and how you hope the conversation would develop.

2. You're a counselor. One of the campers idolizes you. The camper's crush is getting out of hand, and you feel embarrassed by the camper's forthright remarks and physical contact.

Pick a member of your training group to be another counselor. Share your concern and decide together how best to deal with this situation.

3. You're a new youth minister on your first camping trip with your youth group. Three adult counselors have been on this campout many times. One of them continually uses the phrase, "Well, we've always done it this way." It's beginning to bother you.

How will you deal with the situation?

4. You're an adult youth adviser with your church. During the annual fall camp, you hear that a camper has brought alcohol to camp. How will you respond?

5. You're a counselor. You discover initials carved deep into a large tree. The initials lead you to believe they belong to two campers from your church.

What will you do? Role play your response with two members of your training group acting as the "suspected campers." Or role play with everyone in the group acting as youth group members (depending on how you feel you could best handle the matter).

6. You're a volunteer camp director. During the Wednesday night barn dance you noticed two things happening. First, four or five counselors sat on the side and didn't participate. Then campers began to drop out and talk to them. The barn dance organizers were very frustrated because they had to shout instructions and the group seemed very disorganized.

Today you've asked the counselors to meet briefly after lunch. You want the group to deal with the situation, since tonight's campfire might turn out the same way. How will you handle the meeting? (You can role play your response if you choose.)

Chapter 11

Developing a Group Spirit at Camp

"How do you create a new group spirit when you already know each other?" "How do you strengthen bonds in a group like ours? We see each other every week—sometimes every day."

Familiar questions? Like youth workers and Sunday school teachers, camp leaders face the challenge of helping groups grow closer during their time together.

It's important to understand from the beginning that camp leaders can't magically make campers grow closer to each other. Indeed, trying to predict group growth or trying to force it to happen are guaranteed to kill it. Campers can sense when the leaders are trying too hard to help them get close to each other. While leaders can create circumstances that make openness and honesty possible, they can't make a group grow closer.

Instead, group growth emerges in response to what's going on—or despite it. Most often, a camper's or leader's personal choice to be open and accepting is what allows a group to grow closer. It's a risk and gift—a "kairos" moment in the biblical sense. When one camper or leader feels free enough to be open, others are more likely to make themselves vulnerable too.

Molly gave her fellow camp leaders her risky gift of openness on the second night of staff training. She was a new lifeguard, while the other staffers were longtime campers or camp staffers. Molly was a college junior, 2,000 miles from home in a strange place among new people.

The second day included an overnight trip training event. The leaders spent the morning packing and organizing group equipment and food. Then they ate lunch at the trail head and set out on a three-mile trail to Trillium Lake. Each staffer took turns being "head" and "foot" for the group. Trail technique, map reading and safety procedures took the rest of the afternoon.

When darkness claimed the peaks and the lake view disappeared, Molly felt lonely and cold. The campfire and spirited storytelling did little to warm her up.

During the campfire conversation, Steven, the camp activities coordinator, changed the subject. "I want to introduce you to an activity you can use this summer with campers," he began. "It's called the 'Group Life Diagram.' It's a sort of life map of 'where we are' as a staff."

He passed each person a blank index card. "Write 'last night' on one side and 'tonight' on the other," he explained.

"Then, diagram our journey as a staff. Symbolize our relationships however you choose. Be sure to symbolize yourself and every staff member on both sides. When you're ready, we'll talk about our diagrams. Then after we've all shared our diagrams, we'll discuss the changes in our staff since yesterday."

Molly was last to share. As she talked she began to cry. Nancy put her arm around Molly. The group waited in silence. Steven gently said: "It's okay. Take your time."

Molly's diagram illustrated her story of feeling alone among friendly people in a strange place. "All of you seem so sure of what you're doing," she said. "And you're having so much fun. But it's strange to me. I didn't know we'd be camping in the wilderness."

Molly's description was like a personal map being drawn contour by contour, mountain by mountain, stream by stream. Other staffers didn't just hear, they understood Molly's feelings. And, one by one, staffers openly shared their own expectations, apprehensions and stories of life back home.

Other participants said Molly's honesty and openness were the inspiration they needed. It was a growing time for the staff. Each person sensed an unusual and unexpected closeness as Nancy invited everyone to gather around the campfire. Together they stood around the campfire, arms around each other, and prayed.

Leadership That Enables Growth

While growth is often spontaneous, rarely is it happenstance. Molly probably never would have taken her risk unless Steven had created the opportunity. Thus the atmosphere for group growth ultimately begins with the camp leader. While his or her attitudes can't force growth, they can stifle it. Let's look at some leadership behaviors that enable campers and staff to risk—and therefore grow.

Creativity. Camp leaders constantly struggle to find or invent new group-building activities. For this and other reasons, keep a personal journal or notebook that includes a catalog of ways to help groups develop. In reviewing my notes, trip outlines and journals from the past 20 years, I've discovered that they gain deeper and richer meaning with time. Indeed, some of the ideas I wrote down on my first training trip still inspire my sense of adventure. I've also discovered that ideas grow with us and serve many purposes.

Unconditional acceptance. The foundation to all growth is camper security and acceptance. Without these, campers will never feel free to express authentic feelings or be themselves. Campers need your unconditional acceptance—or what psychologist G. Keith Olson calls non-possessive warmth. Olson writes in *Counseling Teenagers*: "Non-possessive warmth is a freeing kind of love. It frees the teenager from the tyranny of pleasing the counselor in order not to feel guilty. It frees the teenager to be his or her own person, rather than the person someone else wishes."[1]

Of course, you don't become warm and caring simply by deciding to be accepting. Instead, you're nurtured into it, and you nurture behaviors that support this attitude.

Participation. Camp leaders should be group members too. Involve campers in activities you feel comfortable experiencing yourself. Invest yourself in the group's spontaneous direction. Follow their lead (they usually follow yours). Minimize doing things just to fill time.

Flexibility. Another common characteristic of effective camp leaders is an ability intuitively to change their plans depending upon the group's response. In leading campers, be open to the emerging group life. Sense campers' feelings and attitudes. Listen to their asides, sighs and struggles with each other. Then help them visualize possibilities for group experience.

One outstanding leader plans alternate and "squeeze time" activities. Alternate experiences fit the "either-or" category, replacing planned activities as needed. Squeeze time experiences are included "if there's time," and they continue "as long as the group's interested and committed to the process."

Describing how to keep a laid-back or easygoing style is difficult. On one hand, experienced leaders know lots of information—some of it very technical. On the other hand, their sense of time and timing overrides the "push to learn." A veteran camp instructor explains:

> We've worked together enough to take our cues from the kids and from each other. Sometimes we stop and check signals with each other; other times we just know—one changes direction and the other follows without question.
>
> On several occasions we've tested our initial plans with the campers to see how they feel and if they have suggestions. We don't feel we have to come off perfectly, and we try hard not to blame the group if things don't go the way we hoped they would.

Gentleness. Leaders have their own needs—to do a good job and be recognized. While high personal expectations can be helpful, they also can produce tension that confuses campers. Why are you so up-tight about a little Bible study session or cleaning the recreation room or writing your best friend who hasn't written you?

Don't assume campers understand you and your responsibilities. Instead, assume that they accept you—and like you—just as you are. Let yourself relax when it's appropriate so you convey the warmness and gentleness that are sometimes hidden behind high personal expectations.

Openness. Assume that you can't see the whole picture. There's more to each camper than you can understand. And getting to know each camper will take time—like reading a good story. So avoid closing out campers based on your first impressions. Instead, be open to hearing and watching their stories unfold during camp.

Calculating interpersonal risks. No two groups are ever the same. Even a church or scouting group that meets weekly seldom includes the same people on different camping trips. But even if it did, new places, different time frames, new activities and changing life-experiences will even make a group with the same people "new" and "different."

These differences pose a particular challenge for leaders, since each group has its unique and invisible dynamics. They're difficult fully to anticipate or calculate—especially early in camp.

Multiple dynamics are always present in the web of interpersonal relationships: person-to-person, person-to-group, group-to-individual and groups-within-groups. Author William Schutz believes interpersonal group dynamics center around individuals' needs for inclusion, control and openness. In his book *The Truth Option: A Practical Technology for Human Affairs*, Schutz writes: "One of the most obvious and yet the most neglected keys to improved relationships and to self-awareness is the concept of truth. 'The truth shall make you free' is a phrase I have heard all my life but only recently have I understood how fundamental it is. I find that at every level—body, individual, couple, group, organization, nation—the more truth, the more success."[2]

Youth leaders can see the behaviors—inclusion, control and openness—in any church parking lot before camp when junior highers are leaving parents and meeting other junior highers. (They're also present—but more subtle—in older people.) Kids intuitively know when they're included and when they're still trying to get in. They know if they're giving and receiving warm feelings or cold feelings. And they know if their opinion moves the group or if they're always following.

Camp leaders must learn to sense and respond appropriately to those levels of inclusion, control and openness. Sensitivity and flexibility go a long way in helping the camp staffer hear the stories of campers accurately.

More than being aware of the interpersonal dynamics, though, leaders must also take risks themselves in selecting a route for group life. They must carefully weigh alternatives and choose activities that minimize campers being left out, opposing each other or taking over. Sometimes leaders are deeply hurt when campers are shunned. Other times the pain is the pain of joy at watching a camper leave who blossomed through the camp experience.

The Group Development Process

In the same way that camp leaders can't magically make campers grow during camp, there aren't any foolproof activities that will make your group instantly become close. Instead, group development is a gradual, ongoing process that develops slowly through the camp experience. By nurturing the process, though, camp leaders can enhance the possibility for group development during camp.

To understand this development process, picture group development as though it were a bicycle trip. Campers begin by climbing a long, gradual hill, then

they cross a wide plateau, and, finally, they coast down a steep descent on the other side (see Diagram 29, "The Group Development Journey").

These three stages—up, across and down—symbolize how group life develops during any camping event—a daylong hike, a weekend canoe trip, a weeklong residential camp or a monthlong cross-country tour. Let's look at each stage in more detail, examining campers' needs, leaders' tasks and leaders' stance during each stage.

The Definition Stage

When campers arrive at camp, they need to resolve some basic definition issues as they become part of the new group. Each camper must find his or her place in and relationship to the group.

Teenagers who are all from the same church are no exception. The group of campers hasn't defined itself when it leaves for camp. To see the difference, imagine comparing a video of the first 30 minutes en route to camp and the first 30 minutes on the bus after camp.

One youth director described his youth group leaving the church this way: "Silence and low talk; 35 kids scattered on 48 seats eating sack lunches and looking out the windows." Then he described the return trip: "Campers were clustered on half a dozen seats, talking, singing and seeing who could get the most people on one seat." That's the difference between a group that has and hasn't defined itself!

Campers' Needs

Campers arrive at camp not knowing what to expect. While thoughts of new and different experiences may be exciting for some, they can be threatening and risky for others. Because of a fear of the unknown, many young people arrive at camp sad,

Diagram 29
The Group Development Journey

The Definition Stage ⇨

(The uphill climb.) Campers begin to identify themselves as a group. The leaders' main concerns are keeping everyone together, setting a comfortable pace for growth and helping campers become comfortable with each other.

Campers' Needs
1. To be recognized as individuals.
2. To be included.
3. To gain common ground with other campers.
4. To know about the camp program.

Leaders' Tasks
1. To reach out to campers.
2. To help campers feel at home.
3. To orient campers to the camp "way of life."

Leaders' Stance
1. To be outgoing in making contact with the group.
2. To accept the role of authority as the "one who knows."

The Discovery Stage ⇨

(Across a wide plateau.) Once on top, the campers no longer need to consume energy pedaling uphill, so they can discover each other with greater ease. They can stop, rest, explore, picnic and take side trips now.

Campers' Needs
1. To know and trust each other.
2. To be free to be themselves.
3. To become a covenant community.

Leaders' Tasks
1. To provide non-possessive warmth.
2. To support and encourage camper leadership.
3. To balance the group process.

Leaders' Stance
1. To teach from group interaction.
2. To involve campers in sharing and directing the group.
3. To shift dependence and authority from leader to group.

The Direction Stage

(Down a steep descent.) When the group reaches the end of the plateau and starts down, it enters a new dimension. Campers must seek direction. Using their momentum wisely, knowing the thrill of descent and recognizing the danger of losing control become critical.

Campers' Needs
1. To ponder the future and to plan for ways to share back home.
2. To identify learnings and growth.
3. To claim feelings about individuals.
4. To make a declaration of faith or commitment.

Leaders' Tasks
1. To help campers evaluate the camp experience.
2. To enable campers to think out loud about life back home.
3. To support campers in sharing faith and feelings.
4. To help campers celebrate their life together.

Leaders' Stance
1. To claim personal feelings toward individuals and the group.
2. To affirm ambivalent feelings as normal and acceptable.
3. To help campers assume personal responsibility for feelings and commitments.

scared or self-conscious—and smiling to cover up their apprehension. Let's look at their needs as camp begins:

To be recognized as individuals. Each camper wants to be seen, known and named by others. Have name tags for every camper and staff to add security to the definition process. Increase the recognition factor in name tags a couple of ways:

1. Have campers create their own name tags to express their individuality.

2. Make name tags out of puzzle pieces so that each person's name tag fits with three other campers' name tags.

To be included. Campers may feel alone—even in a crowd. Invite the first few who arrive to help load luggage or to fill water coolers or ice chests. In fact, many of the details of departing for camp that adults normally do can be turned over to young people. They'll feel included in camp from the beginning. And they'll feel a certain ownership that will encourage them to include other campers as well.

To gain common ground with other campers. Until campers have done something together that gives them something mutual to talk about, they'll have difficulty getting acquainted. Talking about common interests is easier after campers have experienced some fun times together. Early in the camp experience, teach an unfamiliar theme song or have campers fill out simple get-acquainted interview sheets about each other. By sharing these learning experiences, they'll develop a new basis for commonality as they discover that people around them have similar feelings and interests.

To know about the camp program. Young people either ask dozens of questions or no questions. Either response can show discomfort, uncertainty and uneasiness—a cry to be included and to know what's going on.

Each camp leader should be thoroughly familiar with all camp plans—even if part of the program is a surprise. Have a few extra schedules or brochures about camp activities handy even before camp orientation to get campers talking about the event. Even on the trip to camp, have leaders available to involve campers in activities and conversation. And don't ignore campers' questions. Even seemingly absurd questions—"When do we go swimming?" (it's now 40 degrees) or "When do we eat?" (it's now 2:00 p.m.)—are usually subtle requests to talk more, to know more and to feel more secure as camp unfolds.

Leaders' Tasks

The leaders' tasks during the Definition Stage correspond to the needs expressed verbally or non-verbally by campers. Here are the major tasks:

To reach out to campers. Face-to-face contact between campers and leaders is essential during the definition stage. The trip to camp or the first hour at camp sets the tone for the whole event. Youth workers who sleep en route or spend the time with other adults send a subtle message to the young people that this isn't "their" camp, but the leaders'. Teenagers certainly don't need to be smothered by adults. But they do need support and contact that communicate "we" to the campers.

Full-time camp counselors, guest leaders and all camp staff share in creating the right camp spirit. An enthusiastic greeting—"Hi, my name's Bob. What's yours?"—resonates with campers' needs to define themselves and the camp.

To help campers feel at home. There are dozens of ways to make campers feel at home at camp. One youth worker overlooks all the inadequacies of one camp facility simply because the manager remembers all his campers by name.

"That's what keeps us going back," he says. Another camp director always eats one meal each day with campers in the off-site pioneer camping area, sending a clear "reaching out" message to campers at the table.

To orient campers to the camp "way of life." Introducing young people to the camp way is another way of making them feel at home. Even before camp begins, you can create a base of information about camp life through a series of creative introductions, involvements and interactions. Orient campers by introducing the theme, the program and camp rules in creative ways. Here are some ideas:

1. Identify the camp theme with a sequence of subtle messages beginning with the acceptance letter or the special items on a "what to bring" list. Continue sending messages about theme and program as campers make the trip to camp, when they arrive and during the orientation.

2. Include an exciting theme description and a "group covenant" form for campers to sign along with the registration and permission/medical release form.

3. Include a paragraph in the acceptance/information letter about the camp theme and how campers will be involved in program and leadership. Also include clear-cut statements about acceptable behavior at camp.

4. Be creative and positive in writing camp rules. Use headings such as "Guidelines for Camp Life," "Ways We Live Together at Camp" or "Questions and Answers About Camp." Use humor and the names of individual leaders within the rules list. For an example, see Camp Notebook 33, "Ten Divine Camp Commandments."

5. In a large camp with multiple groups, minimize rules discussion during orientation. Instead, sing, welcome people, creatively introduce the theme and staff, and use humor and skits. Help campers have fun and get acquainted. Make only positive, brief statements about camp life. Be clear, concise and firm—with a smile.

6. Put copies of the camp guidelines in each cabin, then have cabin counselors clarify guidelines during cabin time or in a get-acquainted time.

Leaders' Stance

Leaders set the tone of their relationship with campers during the Definition Stage. Their stance should be characterized by at least two attitudes:

To be outgoing in making contact with the group. During the Definition Stage, leaders' spirit and attitude should reflect the fact that they're at camp for the campers. Even leaders who are with their own youth groups need to be outgoing at this stage to make campers feel welcome and to show that it's "our" camp.

To accept the role of authority as the "one who knows." Leaders should take the role of authority (not authoritarian) during this stage of group development. The authority is "one who knows," and leaders are "in authority" because they know what's going on and are committed to the program. This knowledge gives campers security and assurance.

Campers gain a deeper sense of the meaning of commitment and Christian community when they're supported by adults who use inner authority (warmth, commitment, enthusiasm and participation) rather than authoritarianism (distance, demands, self-interests, power, control and intolerance of varied viewpoints). To be properly in authority, leaders must be with campers—not in a separate, privileged space. Leaders must be seen as supportive while also affirming the camp leadership team's ideas and rules.

Camp Notebook 33

Ten Divine Camp Commandments

1. Thou shalt be on time. Show up for all scheduled events. They'll begin when everyone's there! Follow the schedule.

2. Thou shalt participate. Do it with all your heart! Avoid side conversations and other interruptions that slow down the fun. Participate in conversations during free time, meals and when leaders say "talk."

3. Thou shalt remain in camp. Leaders will announce scheduled, supervised activities outside the immediate camp. Otherwise, remain in the program areas marked on your map.

4. Thou shalt be safety-minded. Practice safety at the waterfront. Wear life jackets in canoes. Swim in the swimming area, and canoe in the canoeing area. Have a buddy, be a buddy.

5. Thou shalt respect. Keep your cabin neat—it deserves your respect.

6. Thou shalt know others. Practice eating meals and having conversations with people you don't know very well. People appreciate surprise snacks.

7. Thou shalt report problems. If anyone gets stung, bruised, splintered, attacked or sick of camp, send them to the "Last Aid Station."

8. Thou shalt assist. At some point everyone will be involved in the theme and program leadership. Be ready to help the leadership team make camp run smoothly.

9. Thou shalt remain at the table. At mealtimes we'll sing, have a table grace, make announcements and recognize some fantastic campers. Stick around!

10. Thou shalt be in the dark and silent after "lights out." Continued talking, being out of your cabins and destructive acts toward other group members will be handled long-distance. (If that's unclear, ask for details.)

The Discovery Stage

As a group develops, it moves onto the plateau where campers don't have to spend as much energy defining themselves. Campers and leaders begin to feel settled and comfortable with each other.

A clear signal that a group has reached the plateau comes when new themes and subthemes surface within the group. Sometimes the signal emerges in argument or debate. Sometimes it happens without warning.

I remember the nightly cabin discussions I had with 14 senior high boys at a camp during the Vietnam War. Each night after lights out, the boys and counselors from the other side of our cabin would join us on bunks or the floor. Usually we talked for an hour. Sometimes the talk continued when the other boys went back to their side of the cabin. It was a time of deep wondering and deep reverence, all of us aware that two group members were leaving for boot camp at the end of the summer.

Sometimes campers don't recognize the Discovery Stage until the last day or night of camp when they realize that something's been happening that suddenly makes them sad to leave. Yet even late in camp the discovery gives the camp a lasting impact on participants.

Campers' Needs

Once the group has defined itself, other needs and issues surface among campers. Here are some of them:

To know and trust each other. Young people want to get to know people—really know them. Camp is an ideal setting for young people to build deep relationships. Working and playing together, being challenged to think out loud on a new subject, or being forced to take a stand during a game, simulation or activity creates an atmosphere of mutual, supportive risking. By risking together, campers grow together.

The longing to have true friends is more likely fulfilled in the camp environment than in other settings that aren't as theme-centered or time-intensive. Because campers don't leave at the end of an hour-long youth group meeting, they're more likely to resolve misunderstandings or miscommunication. They don't have homework, meetings or friends to run away to or hide in. They must stay together, focus on the issue and resolve the problem—and grow from it!

To be free to be themselves. Campers who were shy or uncertain during the Definition Stage often discover that other campers are "just like me. I must be normal!" Thus campers relax and start to be themselves. Sharing in creating skits, devotional times, cooking, cleanup or work generates opportunities for self-expression and personal contributions to group life.

To become a covenant community. No camper will say, "I have a great need to be in a covenant community." But a camper will say: "I want to make friends" and "I want to have fun"—which translate to "covenant community."

Giving campers a voice in camp life, providing self-expression opportunities and letting campers make contributions through group tasks enhance the possibility for developing a covenant community among campers. Guidance, recognition and affirmation from caring counselors give a new dimension to the "hoped for" friends and fun.

Leaders' Tasks

The leaders' primary tasks during the Discovery Stage may sound simple: to clarify the group task and maintain the schedule and process.

Leaders who believe "teaching is telling" may find this approach confusing. At this point camp leaders should see themselves as guardians of a process that focuses on group life, community, group interaction and support. This focus doesn't negate the value of information, but it does make "information giving" secondary to working and being with campers on their journey of faith and discovery.

The leaders' three primary concerns or tasks during the Discovery Stage are:

To provide non-possessive warmth. Leaders must accept young people "where they are" and "as they are." The only goal should be to be together "on the journey" during camp. Leaders must value and cherish the person of each camper without judging or asking for change to please or be like someone else—even the counselor.

This focus doesn't mean leaders have nothing to communicate, bear witness to or teach, or that camping skills don't matter. Learning new skills and making personal changes are often appropriate, but they shouldn't be a condition for being accepted or cared for by camp leaders.

To support and encourage camper leadership. Many young people have their first leadership experience through their church youth group or during a summer camp. Hearing their own voice direct a group and sharing their opinions or expressions of the faith are important steps toward adulthood. By intentionally involving a few campers at a time so that all campers share in leadership by the end of camp, program leaders uniquely contribute to the personal growth and discovery of each camper.

To balance the group process. Building group life, sharing personal concerns and experiencing the camp theme are all important camp elements. But none

of these elements should be emphasized so much that the others are overlooked. Camp leaders must rely on their experience to keep each element in balance.

Unless leaders consciously keep the balance in mind, serious problems can develop. I once heard a backpacking leader tell about "his" backpacking ventures with junior highers. It seemed that every night he had to deal with a major crisis at campfire—some campers had hiked too far ahead or too far behind and thought they were lost; or the hike was much longer than he had remembered from previous trips, and he had "saved" the campers by cooking supper for them after dark.

Whatever the specifics, the issues were the same: First, campers were ignorant, vulnerable, scared or emotionally out of control. Second, someone must care for the campers and teach them how to be in control. Third, that "someone" was "him," the leader (not "her," his co-leader). Finally, each time, the group stayed up until one, two or three in the morning to put the campers on the right track.

Church camp leaders must understand the danger of such "leadership" for campers as individuals and as a group. And they need to think through carefully how they'll handle camp problems or issues. ("Someone took $5 from my suitcase" or "Some boys have been going in the girls cabins.") The goal always should be to provide a healthy, stable model of "home life" for the campers.

One way to help balance group sharing is to consider three sources of group discovery: "I"—the camper or counselor; "We"—the group; and "It"—the theme (see Diagram 30). By seeing these three points in the context of the total camp experience, the leader can focus on the individual, group or theme. If an individual seems carried away with his or her own experience, displacing or dominating the group's focus, the counselor may ask: "How do we relate that concern to our theme? Let's see if anyone can connect what Leslie is saying with something we've experienced as a group this week." In either case the balancing is a non-threatening way to help the group focus and refocus on the theme and group experience.

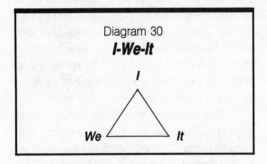

Diagram 30
I-We-It

Balancing the three elements doesn't mean they'll all be in balance at all times. Ruth C. Cohn, who developed the I/We/It model, uses a different cycling image to describe a leader's role in "dynamic balancing":

> *The balancing between I, We and It is never perfect but must shift in a dynamic forward direction. The group process results from shifting balances like a bicycle rolls because of the rider's shifting his weight from pedal to pedal. If perfect balance were ever achieved, the process would come to an end. The group leader's job is to employ his weight toward the "unused pedal," that is from "I" to "We", from "theme" to "I", from "We" to "theme," etc. He has to be sensitive to appropriate timing. Intervening too early or too late has an equally stifling effect on the group process—whether he negates or over-protects an individual, goes along with unrelated group interaction, or remains with a theme while group cohesion gets lost.*[3]

Dr. Cohn's primary maxim in working with individuals who risk or reveal themselves in group settings is "never harm the patient." This motto can be appropriately adapted for camp leaders: "never harm the camper." Self-revelation is a risky part of the group process, and camp leaders participate in a special calling when they listen and guide the process of personal and community discovery at camp.

Leaders' Stance

During the Discovery Stage, the leader's primary aim is to teach from the structured and informal group interaction. The leader maintains a stance that enhances group interaction; relates the interaction to the theme; and identifies behaviors and raises questions that permit and encourage campers to share leadership. Involving campers in sharing values and creating directions requires a conscious effort from leaders who could otherwise tell the group what to believe and do all week long.

The ultimate goal of the Discovery Stage is to depend on the group and the group process for discovering. But the goal is most often achieved only for brief time spans and is sometimes unknown or almost imperceptible to the group. Often the leader must help the campers name and describe their discoveries, growth, development and trust in the group.

How does authority express itself in the Discovery Stage? The leader, who consciously provides the group with knowledge and support during the Definition Stage, now shifts the dependence to the group and the group decision-making process. When campers first arrive, they depend on the leader. But as the group develops and the campers discover more about each other and the camp way of life, they should be able to trust the group, giving and receiving information, acceptance, affirmation and direction as a shared group experience.

The Direction Stage

As any camping event nears an end, campers begin seeking an unnamed direction for living beyond the life of camp—courage to say goodbye and to go home and act differently because of the camp experience. It's both a matter of grief—saying goodbye to a group that will never be the same again—and of assessing personal growth—expressed primarily in gratitude to others at camp for making them see what people can be in true community.

Campers' Needs

Campers' emotions and abilities to express themselves accurately at the end of camp are many and varied. Each expression points to particular camper needs as the camp concludes. Here are some of the needs:

To ponder the future and to plan for ways to share back home. Remember riding your bicycle downhill, full-speed? The wind in your face feels so good, and you're freer than ever. But you must put on the brakes and slow your momentum, or you'll wind up off the road or over a fence.

The same is true for campers during the downhill Direction Stage. Excessive talking and extreme silence are both clues that campers are struggling to come to grips with their experience of coming down the mountain. Providing time for personal space and structured ways to ritualize what the future means is important in the last hours of camp.

To identify learnings and growth. Most campers will first be baffled to name specific learnings beyond the new physical skills they've gained. But with a little assistance they can articulate ways they've learned to be better group members or to be in relationship with other people. And they'll share insights they've gained into the meaning of Christian community as well as new biblical and theological understandings.

To claim feelings about individuals. Most campers are aware of this need, but many have difficulty fulfilling it. Affirming and being affirmed by others are important rituals for campers—regardless of their form. Showing affection, resolving differences and expressing sadness are all important experiences for campers that need to be affirmed and supported.

To make a declaration of faith or commitment. Symbolizing or verbalizing new understandings of faith and commitment are essential ingredients of the Direction Stage. Campers want to do more and be more than they've been before. Their goals to go home and make a difference in their home, church or community will never be higher than during the last hours of camp.

Leaders' Tasks

The Direction Stage focuses on re-entry—returning home to be rerooted in more significant ways than before. Like our bicycling image, this re-entry requires that you manage momentum and slow down without falling down. Leaders have an important task in this process. Here are some ways to help campers prepare for the new directions they'll take:

To help campers evaluate the camp experience. Campers feel they've "made peace" with camp and camp life if they have an arena for evaluating camp and sharing their evaluations. Written evaluations need to be shared openly in a supportive setting. If campers have negative feelings, those feelings need public expression in a living group or cabin group before the camper goes home.

Consider one camper who marked zero or one on all the items on a 10-point scale—with 10 being most positive. She commented that the camp was a "dump" and was "dirty." She hoped "never to come again." It would help her to hear the other 46 campers who all marked their scales from six to 10, with most being eight to 10. They wrote comments like "beautiful," "inspiring" and "the best we've ever gone to."

The experience of publicly naming and claiming their own perceptions and experiences is valuable for campers. It's like a pre-briefing for the debriefing they have when they get home. Learning to be open and to identify their learnings and growth with their peers helps them delineate themselves as individuals—another step toward self-esteem and identity.

To enable campers to think out loud about life back home. Youth workers are sometimes surprised by how quickly significant camp experiences are diminished when campers aren't prepared for re-entry. Raising campers' awareness of going home will re-enforce their ability to hold onto a valuable experience. This issue is particularly important for weekend camping during the school year when experiences are often quickly diluted by the hustle and bustle of family schedules and unfinished homework.

One excellent way to evaluate the camp experience and to become aware of family relationships is to role play conversations with parents about camp. While young people tend to caricature parents (and themselves) at first, they soon settle into sharing the real reception and dialogue they expect at home.

To support campers in sharing their faith and feelings. The end of camp is filled with both joy and sadness, fulfillment and incompleteness. Campers need to hear—and if possible express—this reality. They need to know that camp, like life, involves each of these feelings.

Symbolic moments of closure for expressing feelings for each other and for affirming faith are also important in establishing direction. Campfire times, candle-lighting services, theme-centered activities, making a camp banner for the church or creating a skit to perform at a church family night are ways to begin sharing faith and feelings. Another way to create testimony in celebrating and telling about camp is to pass out an evaluation page or to have a group journal page marked "What Winter Retreat Meant to Me" or "What I'll Remember Most From Camp."

To help campers celebrate their life together. Celebrating camp experiences can be integrated into each group setting of camp—all-group events, discussion groups, camp workshops and interest groups.

In planning camp celebrations, the most important factor to consider is allowing each camper to communicate by word, activity or symbol his or her interpretation of Christian community and commitment to discipleship.

Whether campfire, communion, musical festival, memory hike or other symbolic event, the camp closure should emphasize that each camper is personally responsible. Each camper needs a reference point that establishes a memory—his or her own words spoken or written and shared with another camper, in a small group or with the whole group. This memory can take the form of a letter of reflection to be mailed to the writer six months after camp.

Young people from a single congregation can connect the closing camp celebration with a celebration back home. "Air time" or announcement time in worship services, bulletin boards with camper pictures and family night events are all places to give continued expression to the celebration of the camping experience.

Leaders' Stance

Sometimes the variety of feelings that come at the end of camp is as confusing to leaders as it is to campers. Dealing with your own faith and feelings and helping campers do the same can be overwhelming—especially if you're in charge of cabin-check or sweeping the lodge right before the bus loads. It's important to recognize and deal with this ambivalence during staff training.

Claiming personal feelings toward individuals and the group and expressing personal growth and faith are as important for leaders as for campers. In truth, we never come to the end of camp feeling equally close to every camper. The same is true for campers. People who are aware that these differences are natural need to help others be at peace with fluctuating feelings. More often, though, leaders only inwardly acknowledge their love and closeness for some campers and their lack of acquaintance or distance from others.

However you bring closure to camp, the activities should focus on helping each camper assume personal responsibility for his or her own learning. The authority shifts again, this time from the group to the individual. Each camper must assume responsibility for knowing and doing beyond camp.

In the great mystery of God's presence and human interactions, we can trust that the little steps toward personal authority will someday enable today's junior highers to be the church camp leaders when today's infants become adolescents.

Questions for Discussion and Reflection

Use the following questions for personal and group reflection with camp leaders:

1. What have been the key elements in groups growing closer in your experience as a camper or leader?

2. If you had been the camp director in Molly's staff training group, how would you have responded to the situation at the campfire?

3. Look at the campers' needs under the Definition Stage (page 193). Recall the first hour of your first or most recent camp experience. Did you have any of these needs? Did you have other needs that aren't listed? How were your needs met during the first hour of camp? Make a few notes and share them with another person.

4. Imagine some first-time meetings with campers or some early times of being together on the way to a camp. Write down some hypothetical conversation-starters based on the immediate, sensory and personal elements of the moment. Share your ideas with another leader, and reflect on ways campers feel supported by adults in your church or camp.

5. What are some times you'd like to live over again in order to help groups grow closer? What would you do—or not do—differently?

6. What do you understand about being a camp leader now that you didn't understand a year ago? What does that imply for your own leadership style during your next camping event?

Notes

[1]G. Keith Olson, *Counseling Teenagers* (Loveland, CO: Group Books, 1985), p. 5.

[2]William Schutz, *The Truth Option: A Practical Technology for Human Affairs* (Berkeley, CA: Ten Speed Press, 1984), p. 9. (In his chapter on "Behavior: Inclusion, Control, Openness," Dr. Schutz provides a series of five behavior activities with scoring and interpretation pages. They are easy to adapt for staff training events, and can be readily coupled with camp theological statements.)

[3]Ruth C. Cohn, "The Theme-Centered International Method," an unpublished paper, n.d. Used with her permission.

Chapter 12

Leading Campers

"Start where the learners are, not where the leaders are. It is not show and tell, but share and do." Steve Van Matre

"Learning by doing is a whole lot better than a bunch of theories presented to you by scholars." A Montana rancher

"**N**ow that we're here what do we do?" "Where's the action?" These questions dominate campers' minds when they arrive at camp. The leader's first task is to answer that question with action and words—preferably in that order. Yet the reverse often occurs as adult leaders let "being in charge with words" take precedence over "being with kids" and "doing things together."

Here's a quick self-test: Take a 3 × 5 card. On one side write an activity you like to lead or want to lead at camp. Then write on the other side the actual word-for-word statements you'd use to get campers who've never done the activity before involved.

Did the words fit on one side? How small did you write? More important, what did the exercise tell you about your leadership style?

This chapter focuses on experiential leadership styles that involve young people and adults in active learning. Since they're difficult to define in traditional terminology, I've chosen an umbrella term for all of them: Action-Based Leadership (ABL). In this chapter we'll consider:

● The dynamics of action-based leadership.
● Styles of action-based leadership.
● Using action-based leadership skills.

Then we'll conclude the chapter by discussing the unique dynamics and issues involved in leading campers with special needs or physical limitations.

The Dynamics of Action-Based Leadership

What is it about action-based leadership that makes it effective? What makes it different? What are its dynamics? Let's examine some of the characteristics:

It takes campers seriously. Once when I used this 3 × 5 card activity at a leader training camp, a longtime director commented: "He really means write our actual words! He takes us seriously!" No one could have stated more clearly the central theme of action-based leadership: It takes campers seriously. Such an experience is a refreshing and releasing change for young people who are usually held at arm's length and controlled by words.

It's action-oriented. Action-based

leadership begins where campers begin: with action. Being a young camper means being in action. Energetic young campers are on a voyage of self-discovery. They don't ask the question "Who am I?" with words but symbolize it with impulsive action. Words come later—just a few at first (especially if they don't really know you), then a few more and then, at some point, a conversation. When your friendship is safe, teenagers will be willing to risk talking more—to think out loud. That's the kind of conversation that means the most. It's the way they clarify who they are and what they believe—or want to believe.

But to reach this conversation level, you have to begin with action. And that's the appeal of action-based leadership.

How do you end—or at least minimize—the adult tendency to talk too much? Here are some ideas:

1. Put talk in perspective. Campers don't want to hear instructions and directions; their lives are filled with too much of these already.

2. Consider the talk teenagers thrive on: symbolic code words, jesting, and commercialized and searching conversations. Learn to communicate on their terms, not yours.

3. Ask yourself, "When do I have serious conversations?" Usually they follow times of doing things with other people and warming up to each other. It's no different for teenagers.

It doesn't focus attention on the leader. Action-based leaders seldom announce that they're the leaders or that they're going to lead. Most move into a group or meet an individual at a low, easy level. They're easy to be with, and their leadership is marked by openness, flexibility, a gentle pace and a high tolerance for different viewpoints.

It creates healthy interaction and relationships. Action-based leadership is more than a collection of leadership tips. It fosters an environment of acceptance and mutuality—essential ingredients for personal growth and community life. Through ABL, leaders create a "way of being together" that minimizes self-doubt, peer pressure and competition. They help set a tone for dynamic group growth through a progression of active camper interactions in the midst of almost any activity. Here are the elements of this progression:

1. Helping campers feel able and knowledgeable. Leaders can either call forth or overshadow campers' abilities. When leaders give campers opportunities to demonstrate their knowledge and awareness *before* the leaders give their input, campers feel 10 feet tall. Of course, other campers initially will poke fun when another camper is "sucked in" to telling or showing what he or she knows. But beneath the fun-poking is affirmation and respect.

Eric's an example. He raised his hand when the leader asked if anyone had ever shot a bow. Eric had, though the leader didn't know it before she asked. But because Eric volunteered, she asked him to demonstrate the proper technique. He did—perfectly. The counselor later learned that Eric's entire family participated in statewide archery tournaments. Imagine the difference in the learning experience if the leader had assumed no one in the class knew anything about archery.

2. Making campers feel appreciated. Open appreciation and approval are essential to reinforcing self-esteem. By appreciating and valuing individual campers' efforts, leaders give the whole group a source and precedent for valuing and appreciating each other.

Campers often compare their good

feelings about camp with negative experiences of being criticized or embarrassed by adults and peers—school teachers, parents, church leaders, work supervisors and even so-called good friends. Yet campers won't experience the affirmation at camp if camp leaders fall into similar traps. What are some things camp leaders should avoid that embarrass campers or hurt their self-esteem? _____

_____

_____

3. Helping campers feel successful. Campers who feel successful in small things are on their way to feeling successful in larger tasks. Early successes build a camper's confidence to undertake more difficult or advanced skills or to risk sharing openly in community times. By generating feelings of success in the face of a particular problem, campers become confident that they can overcome greater challenges and resolve interpersonal issues.

Picture Greg, a seventh-grader, in intense conversation with the camp director. "That's right," the director's saying. "Put in your quarter first, then dial zero and your home phone number. When you hear the tone, push zero again. And tell the operator . . ." Greg still looks a little puzzled as he heads for the lodge to make his first long-distance call.

Becky, a counselor, overhears the conversation. A mother of two boys, she picks up on Greg's bewilderment. "I'll do it for him," she tells the camp director as she turns to follow Greg.

"He can do it," the director responds.

Becky stops short and turns around. "You're right, he can," she admits. "I don't know why I always do that. I do it at home with the boys—I guess it's easier."

She's right, too. It's easier for adults to do things for campers. It takes less ener-

gy and empathy. But it cuts short the personal satisfaction campers get from doing something new. It short-circuits their sense of success and accomplishment.

If you could help campers feel successful about three things, what would they be? _____

_____

_____

_____

4. Helping campers feel responsible. Empathy and caring emerge quickly in tasks where campers and leaders help each other in maintaining the group, meeting living needs and learning new skills. Accepting responsibility grows out of group caring.

Campers take responsibility when they value themselves as part of a group—not to keep rules or "pull their own weight" at the leader's command. I've often seen campers volunteer spontaneously to take care of a camp job or help a leader or another camper. Such acts of responsibility are also acts of Christian caring and love.

Write down the times you feel most responsible. What helped you feel that way? _____

_____

_____

_____

Styles of Action-Based Leadership

In describing leadership styles, many people use a continuum of autocratic, laissez faire and democratic, noting that effective leadership utilizes all three styles at appropriate times. However, action-based leadership doesn't fit well on this continuum. Action-based leaders are primarily concerned with self-esteem and learning, not productivity. Thus this leadership style focuses on two basic areas: affirmation and instruction.

Because traditional categories don't fit well, we need new, more descriptive terms. I've chosen the following four ways to describe action-based leadership styles:

- Fill-in-the-blanks leadership.
- Direct leadership.
- Each-one-teach-one leadership.
- Blended leadership.

As we look at these leadership styles, remember that they're not exclusive of each other. Each is appropriate in a given situation, and they can be combined in a single leadership sequence.

Fill-in-the-Blanks Leadership

Picture a canoe instructor talking to junior highers for 20 or 30 minutes before they get into the canoes or the water. Then picture the opposite—a leader who gives no instruction but lets the kids figure it out for themselves.

Neither picture is pretty. In both cases, patience wears thin and the frustration weighs heavy. Oh, the latter style will appeal to kids—at first. But once they're struggling to paddle successfully on a river or from lake to lake, campers will be "shut-mouthed," wishing the day would end or asking counselors how to make their "bathtubs" go straight.

The fill-in-the-blanks leadership approach bridges these two extremes. Picture the canoeing group again. As you read this example, remember that we're not examining canoeing techniques here. Rather, we're examining a leadership style that both affirms young campers when they may feel unsure and awkward and instructs them on correct technique in incremental steps.

You're the leader. You assume some campers have canoed or boated before (remember Eric?). So you talk with the group in an unhurried manner:

"How much do you already know about canoeing?"

Campers shuffle their feet, joke and act silly. They jab each other in the ribs and push one camper toward the water while looking you straight in the eye. No answers from anyone. Everyone laughs. You laugh too and rephrase your question:

"Who can demonstrate how to board a canoe safely from the bank or dock?"

One hand goes up, then six more. Only three campers aren't ready to demonstrate their knowledge for the group.

As campers demonstrate, you "fill in the blanks," adding to campers' information and misinformation. You ask questions to sharpen camper leadership:

"Before we all get into the canoes, let's review what Susan just showed us. Who boards the canoe first—the bow person or the stern person? Who gets out first? Are there any exceptions to that rule?"

"Here's another thing for the stern person to keep in mind . . ."

Direct Leadership

Action-based leadership doesn't always begin with a camper demonstration—that's not always the best place to begin. What's important is to begin with activities that involve campers immediately—"active-early-easy" activities that are easy for everyone to accomplish in a short time. Such activities respond to campers' anticipation, lowering their anxiety and helping them experience success early in their camp experience.

Another active leadership style is direct leadership. Here's an example:

"Everyone select a life jacket. Sizes are marked in the back . . . Now choose a paddle that's about as tall as your chin or nose . . . Circle up down by the lake . . . No, how 'bout in the lake? Brrrrrrr . . .! Let's wade out to knee-deep . . .

"Choose the side that feels best to you for paddling . . . If you're paddling on the left, put your right hand down the shaft near the blade [You demonstrate and give directions for paddling on opposite side.] . . . Try a few strokes . . .

"Now change sides . . . Which feels best? Rich, that's a beautiful stroke! Do it for the group . . . [You give group unhurried time to practice before the next step.]

"Sandra, I want to invite you to be my partner, and we'll demonstrate how to board the canoe parallel to the shore—which is how we'll do it most of the time in the backcountry . . ."

Each-One-Teach-One Leadership

The basic idea of each-one-teach-one leadership grows out of the one-room school approach to education. Older, more advanced students helped younger students with the teacher overseeing the whole process, giving input where needed. Everyone's a learner and leader.

This style works well in larger groups, groups with wide-ranging skill levels or groups with large age spans. The basic idea of this approach is to have one coordinator or lead instructor who is supported by several assistants. These people are directly involved in leading smaller groups, while the coordinator watches, asks questions and gives support.

I've successfully used this approach with groups of up to 160 young people doing environmental awareness and day hikes at the National Christian Youth Congress. Eight adults worked with me, each taking smaller groups of 18 to 22 on the trail. I directed the process, giving initial instructions, asking groups questions and supporting groups when needed. In the process, an otherwise unmanageable group was easily dispersed throughout the area and led in meaningful hands-on outdoor ex-

periences that I could never have led alone.

Blended Leadership

Let's look at another group experience to see how to integrate the three styles mentioned:

This example begins with direct leading. You begin: "A horse is always mounted from the left side, by putting your left foot in the stirrup and swinging your right leg over the saddle like this. [You demonstrate and get off the horse.] Notice how I place my hands and use my weight so I don't pull the saddle off on the left or dump myself off on the right." [Demonstrate mounting again, and get off.]

Now you shift to fill-in-the-blanks leadership. "Who would like to demonstrate while I hold the reins? [A camper demonstrates.] Now someone else—Bill, how about you? [Another demonstration.]

"Have we left out anything?

"Do you have any questions? [A camper asks for clarification.]

"Who can answer that question?"

Now you move to each-one-teach-one leadership. "Choose a partner about the same height as you, and join one of our leaders by the fence . . . The leaders will hold the horses while you practice mounting and dismounting."

You watch and listen as campers practice. Sometimes you give fill-in-the-blanks, fine-tuning pointers—but only if it's something important the assistant has forgotten or a safety concern.

As you look at this example of each-one-teach-one leadership, note that campers have already experienced mounting and dismounting a horse in a gentle and supportive manner *before* they learn new terminology or refined techniques. The initial step of mounting and dismounting is simplified and easy, but it's essential in laying the groundwork for more advanced steps. It's also essential for reducing or identifying fears or initial resistance to learning a new skill. Moreover, the leadership technique allows the leader consciously to focus on each camper's abilities and needs without focusing the group's attention on an individual who's having trouble.

Using Action-Based Leadership Skills

How do you use these action-based leadership styles effectively at camp? Let's look at some of the practical considerations to keep in mind as you lead campers. As you read, think of specific instances from your experiences when you've seen the dynamics described and when you've used action-based leadership—even if you didn't call it that.

Alternating Leadership Styles

As previously mentioned, the most effective action-based leadership combines each of the three leadership styles appropriately for the skill being taught or the task to be completed by campers. Shifts in styles relate to five important factors:

Readiness to learn. The leader's ability to sense campers' readiness may be the most important guide for deciding how to lead. Spontaneous questions from campers are definite clues that the young people are ready to do more and know more.

Readiness to learn often surfaces when campers have been involved and need physical rest or a timeout. After an unhurried rest, a midmorning snack or a group pit stop, leaders have a natural opportunity to test the group's readiness. An open-ended question about how the group's feeling or asking "How are we doing?" will often call forth clear verbal or non-verbal clues about campers' energy level, readiness and motivation.

In group interactions that take all

morning or a full day (such as low-ropes or high-ropes initiatives), leaders simply "test" the steps ahead with the group, seeking a group consensus on energy level and readiness to move to another level.

Overall camp flow. Leadership approaches that offer immediate, hands-on experience are best suited to activities early in a camping event or for introducing a new activity or skill. Early in a camp, a single activity may serve several purposes: building the group, introducing a new skill and developing the camp theme. Hands-on action must be brief, but it needs to come when campers feel the tension of wanting to do something together but aren't quite sure how to go about it.

Time and teaching progression. How much time does an activity need, and how much time is available in each session? What style best fits the first session's activity? How much practice do campers need for this skill? These are the questions to ask yourself to help you blend and fine-tune your teaching progression. You may also identify optional plans or choose a couple of natural points where you could interrupt the activity if it needs to continue in another session.

The goal is to choose active leadership styles that fit naturally in the given time frame. Covering more material by teaching faster or demonstrating techniques without giving campers a chance to practice isn't teaching. Indeed, it actually hurts the group process. Campers become frustrated because they feel pushed too hard on the one hand or left out on the other.

This do-more-in-less-time panic was evident in one camp when the camp director watched two counselors lead their campers in four trust games in less than 30 minutes. The counselors' morning plan said all the activities had to be done before the lunch bell, so the dedicated counselors didn't give campers time to process the games' meaning and relationship to the camp theme or group communication. In the lunch line the director casually asked the counselors how the morning went. "Great!" one replied. "The kids love the trust games!"

Sometimes groups rally to a particular activity or have a prolonged discussion to process an activity. As a leader, you may feel that the activity or discussion should continue because of its significance to the group. Under such circumstances, you must adjust learning progressions and time frames. Sometimes you need to save an activity for another day—maybe next year's camp!

Group age and energy level. It's easy to plan too much and overestimate a group's energy level. In planning camp activities, develop an ebb-and-flow approach. Follow high-energy activities with rest times, sit-in-a-circle debriefings, further instructions or refreshments. The key to balancing energy flow is to plan for ebb-and-flow experiences. Then let the *whole* group's outward, non-verbal energy guide you.

Everyone needs a rest time—downtime—after lunch. Following the rest, you may plan high-energy activities. However, they should taper off as the afternoon progresses with intermittent breaks, free time or electives. The same pattern holds for after-dinner activities. For example, follow a high-energy square dance with snacks, a campfire and a quiet devotional before retiring for the evening, thus allowing campers to unwind and prepare themselves for rest.

Younger campers often need more breaks, and you need to break progressive steps into shorter steps for them.

Sequence of activities. In camps where leadership or elective activities ro-

tate, it's critical to consider what precedes and follows a single activity in determining what leadership style fits best. The overall flow of activities and leadership styles must be carefully monitored to match campers' changing needs.

Usually it's easier to "read" a self-contained "living group" because these campers spend many hours together as a single unit. The longer a group lives and learns together, the more it will naturally call forth the leadership style that fits its needs. Leaders in these groups also have greater freedom and flexibility to change focus or to give a group more intensive involvement or rest, since being with the group constantly gives them a deeper awareness of the group's needs.

Aims of Action-Based Leadership

There's no standard set of goals for action-based leadership. Indeed, such a list would straightjacket a leadership style that's designed to be adaptable and responsive to new and changing situations. Action oriented leaders constantly test and refine their aims. When it's time to lead they have their goals clearly in mind—accompanied by a variety of possible ways to get campers involved, depending on the unique dynamics of the particular group.

Here are several aims that may help you identify and refine your action-based goals for a specific camping event. These aims intersect whatever skill or task the group undertakes. Caring, warm and sensitive leadership puts these aims into action:

1. In the first hour, make sure each young person hears his or her voice in the total group. It helps kids feel at ease talking and being with other group members, and it sets a precedent for openness in the group. Regardless of the subject or activity, every leader can achieve this goal in the

first hour of any event. I picked up this goal 20 years ago, and it has stuck with me ever since. Though I often change the method or the timing during that hour, the aim remains the same.

2. As leader, make a personal verbal and physical contact with each camper every morning of camp.

3. Observe each camper's verbal and non-verbal communication during each rest stop or activity break.

4. Include each camper in planning and leading camp program activities— worship and celebration, game times, skits, presentations, campfire programs and activity setups.

5. Have a hiking, paddling or down-by-the-lake talk with three campers each day. Consider subjects such as home, feelings, caring, learnings, hopes, "after camp," successes, commitment, self-direction or life goals.

6. Watch the group each day for signs of trust, caring, hurting, responsibility and self-direction.

Bridges and Barriers to Action-Based Leadership

While there aren't any set rules or formulas for action-based leadership, there are some bridges and barriers that either enhance or detract from your ability to lead a group. Here are some of them. You can probably think of others that are just as important.

Bridges. Some leadership techniques and processes to follow that enhance action-based leadership include:

1. Prepare yourself adequately, thoughtfully and prayerfully whenever you lead. Regularly roll ideas around in your head and sound them out with friends or co-leaders. Ask some youth group members for their ideas on a specific approach you're considering. Keep notes in a note-book, and revisit your notes between camps. Think through what you wrote, and add new ideas that represent your growing edge.

2. Know your subject. Use correct terminology. If you need to fine-tune your knowledge or skills, practice or review beforehand.

3. Creatively focus campers' attention on the subject at hand. Arrange them in a circle by holding hands, forming a circle with a rope, putting paddle tips together in a circle, or lying on the ground facing the sky with their heads together like spokes in a wheel. Use a piece of equipment from the activity to focus campers' attention, or lead warm-up exercises related to the new skill they'll be learning.

4. Focus campers spiritually with a story, poem, litany or scripture spoken rhythmically, antiphonally or in echo.

5. Include every camper and leader in each activity. If you lead several activities at once, include everyone in the immediate group.

6. In introducing a new skill or experience, the first activity should be simple and safe enough to require only brief instruction. And it should be easy enough for every camper to accomplish on the first attempt.

7. Introduce one element at a time, and let the group practice to become comfortable before introducing another step.

8. Organize activities in progressive steps. Begin with brief, easy-to-accomplish, total-group steps with no options. Move progressively toward longer, more difficult, individual steps with options.

9. Give clear, concise instructions, and ask if anyone has questions.

10. Schedule breaks when campers need rest. Provide a snack if possible. Have a spontaneous break or rest time if an activity bogs down or if campers have dif-

ficulty.

11. Be gentle with campers who have difficulty. Use encouragement to support their efforts.

12. Make sure you touch or assist every camper during a given session. A pat on the shoulder or double-checking equipment suffices. Also enable the group to touch—have a group back rub.

13. In using demonstrations for sports, dances and other skills, remember right and left are opposite as you face the group. If the group needs to see both front and back views, use two demonstration teams in a circle. Or have demonstrators show front and back views while in front of a sitting group.

14. Take a joke. Laugh with the group. Be vulnerable.

Barriers. In contrast to the bridges, here are some barriers to avoid that detract from effective action-based leadership:

1. Asking questions such as:"How many have ever sung 'Kum Ba Yah' before?" or "How many know how to use a map and compass?" Such questions don't change the leader's intention to teach or lead the subject in question. Instead, they focus attention on first-time or inexperienced campers, making them, as junior highers say, "feel dumb" or "look stupid."

2. Giving detailed explanations before the group is focused or active in the first step.

3. Making statements or saying words that rush the campers—"Let me do this quickly, then we'll . . ." or "Let's hurry and finish so we can . . . before supper."

4. Telling campers they're doing something the wrong way.

5. Showcasing adult, practiced skills in a way that makes campers feel "shown up" or inadequate.

6. Setting a standard that makes campers feel they must measure up to the leader's skill or expertise level.

7. Pitting adults against young people, boys against girls, cabin against cabin, or ages and grades against each other. Competitive sports must be carefully planned and developed within the community.

8. Using scripture or camp activities to moralize or prove a particular viewpoint.

9. Using inside jokes, clichés, secrets or pet words that create distance and leave out some campers.

10. Joking about a camper's attempts to succeed.

11. Labeling campers or using slang and profanity when individuals or groups don't stay on track.

12. Mimicking or criticizing campers or staff members—publicly or privately.

Introducing Safety and Rules

A common question from camp leaders who've never tried action-based leadership is: "How do you make campers follow hard-and-fast rules without 'telling' them what to do?" The answer to the question is simple: The same way you introduce other activities, skills and new information—in a low-key manner that's marked by deep commitment to campers and their personal authority.

Hard-and-fast rules encompass health and safety, equipment care, group limits, group covenants, and interpersonal and public responsibility. Most of the time, introduce these rules gradually—a section at a time—when group members are already comfortable with and enthusiastic about camp life.

This action-based approach to rule-setting won't guarantee that your group will always operate smoothly, appropriately or perfectly. (Of course, no approach can do that.) Rather, it emphasizes that appropriateness, responsibility, group understanding and personal authority should take precedence over authoritarian, leader-centered rules and consequences.

Here are some guidelines for introducing hard-and-fast rules:

1. Wait until you sense campers feel comfortable doing what you're leading before you introduce the rules.

2. Ask campers, "What are the most important things for us to keep in mind for the whole group's well-being?"

3. Introduce rules and guidelines in relationship to specific activities. Be as concise and simple as possible, and give reasons for the rules.

4. Use a typed handout or notebook page headed "Questions and Answers About Group Life" or "Guidelines for Group Living" (see page 197 for an example).

5. On trip camping events, make a general statement about emergency procedures. Indicate evacuation routes on maps. Remind campers that the people who need help may not be in your group.

6. Avoid statements that intimate mistrust or expected rule-breaking—"I won't tolerate . . ." or "I better not see anyone . . ." Don't refer to previous negative experiences of the (few) campers who broke rules.

Sharpening Your Action-Based Leadership

Developing action-based leadership skills takes experience, practice and reflection. Individuals and groups can use the following skill-practice exercise for reflection and interaction about action-based leadership:

1. Make a list of all the things you can personally lead in a small group of campers (such as crafts, circle games, music and volleyball). If you're in a group, make a group list on newsprint to include everyone's skills. When two people share a skill, list everyone who named that skill beside the activity.

2. Make a second list. What else could you lead with some preparation and practice? You could include activities such as canoeing, Bible study and building campfires. Push yourself. Share lists with other people in the group.

3. Choose an activity from either list that seems easy for you, and write your introductory statement to campers. Don't write a description of what you'd do; just write word-for-word the actual instructions you'd give. For example: "Everyone hold hands in a large circle and spread as far back as possible. The game doesn't really have a name, so before it's over I want you to help me name it with the most creative name possible. Now take one step toward the center of the circle . . ."

4. When you finish your instructions, label the action-based leadership style or styles you're using. Use your own words to describe your style if the ones suggested in this chapter don't fit you.

5. Share your leader statements with others in the group. Don't comment on each other's leader statements yet. Hear them and think about them.

6. Rewrite your original statement or another statement introducing a new subject. This time try to reduce the statement to one sentence that introduces and moves the group into the first activity. For example, "Grab hands in a straight line across the field and run with me to the other end without getting ahead or dropping behind the group."

7. In group sharing time, help each other by rephrasing and sharpening your one-sentence statements until you believe they'd be clear to the campers you have in mind.

Leading Campers With Special Needs

Increasing numbers of churches are aware of the need to include teenagers with disabilities in their youth activities. Many churches have made their facilities accessible to people with special needs, and youth groups have begun reaching out to young people with disabilities.

But including young people with disabilities doesn't have to stop at the church wheelchair ramp. Recreation and camp leaders across the country are discovering that any camper with special needs can participate in youth group camping programs and events. Because of the recent emphasis on "adaptive recreation," people with disabilities can enjoy wheelchair fishing, canoeing, kayaking and sit skiing—to name a few of the challenging outdoor activities.

Outdoor specialist George Holland, former recreation director for Atlanta's Shepherd Spinal Center, illustrates the value of including people with disabilities in activities by telling about a scoutmaster he knows who, after a disabling injury, returned to his role as a scout leader:

Initially he had a number of worries whether he'd be accepted by his troop because he could no longer walk. What I stressed was that he had a lot to share about his disability in making scouts more aware that individuals with disabilities are still persons and could be a very active part of their outdoor experience—even though physically they might not do the same things . . .

That man got to the point where he was very active and satisfied in his scout work. [His involvement] didn't repair the injury, but he had a very meaningful role with his troop. He could still push around camp, and he gave individual attention to campers, which other leaders could not give. Sometimes he'd sleep out with them, sometimes he'd go back home because of his limitations. But he had a very special niche and was very fulfilled in scouting.

Holland's interest and involvement in helping people with disabilities to enjoy outdoor recreation grew from his experience of having a spinal injury from a climbing accident when he was an outdoor leader. Now recovered from his injury, Holland helps others who have experienced injuries enjoy the outdoors. In an interview he told me that being outdoors helps heal the spirits of people with disabilities. "Being out in the environment . . . people feel a sense of being back to where they were before their injury," he explains.

How to Include Disabled Youth

How can youth groups involve teenagers with disabilities in camping ministry events? What's possible, and what isn't? What special provisions need to be made? Holland outlines several major considerations for parents and churches that want to include handicapped teenagers in church camping events. Here are some of his suggestions:

● Help the young person with a disability feel like part of the group. This must be done in non-threatening, natural ways. A young person who's first invited to Sunday school, worship and then a short outing will be more open to attending a camping trip or a canoe outing than someone who's invited out-of-the-blue to "come on a camping trip." It takes time to build relationships and establish trust. Friendships between young people and adults create the natural climate for any teenager to become enthusiastic about an outdoor adventure. Disabled teenagers are no different!

● At first plan short events close to home—30 minutes away instead of three hours. Gradually increase distance and work up to longer experiences.

● Give more time and flexibility for activities. Highly structured activities in which everyone does the same thing within a certain time are impossible if you include disabled campers. It may take some disabled campers an hour and a half to set up a tent. Take away the pressure of time and competition. Give disabled campers the challenge they need, but don't set it so high that they feel in competition or like they're holding up the group.

● Have several activities taking place at once. This allows people to break into small groups and pursue their interests. Some youth groups can subgroup and keep several things going, thus circumventing the unspoken pressure of "waiting on that person who's handicapped."

● Be aware of disabled campers' privacy and physical needs. Sometimes kids feel "on stage." They need breaks from constant exposure. Such privacy can make the difference in whether some participate or don't participate. It takes more time for disabled campers to take care of their personal hygiene needs. If possible, explore alternative sleeping arrangements. The discomfort of sleeping in a sleeping bag can be intimidating to a young person who isn't agile. A nearby motel with privacy gives handicapped campers a breather and an out from the group when they're needed.

● Adapt the recreation you already know to make it work with the disabled young people involved. You can adapt almost every camp activity for different levels of camper abilities; it just takes time, imagination and willingness to do it.

Take the variation of a familiar game such as "Rock, Paper, Scissors" as it's described in the *New Games Book* (played by lines of people rather than two individuals). You can easily translate that game for a mixed group of able and disabled young people. Form two teams. The first team consists of disabled people in wheelchairs. The second, able-bodied team is handicapped by having each person hop on one

leg. The able-bodied are slowed down, giving the disabled a chance to escape if they show the wrong symbol. Thus neither team loses, because everyone plays for the fun of meeting a challenge together.

● Work with other organizations. If your church doesn't include any young people with disabilities, use your outdoor skills (as well as group members') to minister to disabled young people through specialized organizations. Learning outdoor recreation and skills requires the patient assistance and skill of those who know the sport. By checking with agencies and rehabilitation groups, you can open a door to a significant ministry.

Preparing Parents

The other major challenge of including young people with disabilities is to convince their parents that their child will be safe and well cared for during camp. Parents can be the greatest asset or the greatest limitation in including disabled campers.

Some parents are reluctant to pass responsibility for their disabled child to someone else. They don't want to see their kids in pain or discomfort, so, too often, they provide an easy out by overprotecting the child. While this tendency is natural, it shouldn't discourage those willing to work with the disabled young people from challenging families to let disabled young people experience the joy and healing of outdoor adventure.

Here are some suggestions for easing parents' fears and gaining their enthusiasm:

● Talk with parents about the program. Listen to their concerns and fears, answering their questions openly and honestly.

● Focus on abilities, not disabilities. A parent needs assurance that the new environment won't be too threatening to their teenager. Even when parents welcome the occasion for their teenager to camp out, it's still difficult for them to see their child suffer and struggle to try something new—especially if their child is scared. Focusing on their teenager's abilities and possibilities helps them let the young person attempt new challenges.

● Suggest parents be distant observers. Parents know they need to allow their children the freedom to be on their own with the caring church group where relationships are strong. Support them as they let go—even though it hurts inside.

● Go slowly. Even though the young person may want to go camping and the parents may see value in it, the experience involves a leap of faith into new and uncomfortable territory.

Chapter 13

Leading Camp Worship and Bible Study

In the fading light of a New England sunset, 40 young people and their leaders amble along a beach, sweat shirts warming them from the cool evening breeze. At a stream strewn with polished glacial stones the group pauses. "Pair up with another person," a leader instructs. "Be silent, but be aware. Follow me."

The group crosses the stream on a footbridge to the back side of a small island—a three-acre remnant of ragged rock. The surf crashes on three sides as the teenagers walk silently, single file toward the crest. Everyone stops again. "We've talked this week about friendship and faith," the leader continues. "We've sung about Christ and caring—about living our lives in remembrance of his life."

A group member reads a call to worship from the Psalms. Then an invitation: "Find a place with your friend somewhere on the rocks. Close your eyes and listen. Take time to listen. After a while, open your eyes and look around. Feel . . . Remember . . . Think . . . Take time to have a conversation together. Talk about two things: what you see and feel and the most important memory you'll take home with you."

As the sky changes from red to rose and yellow, the group leader stands on the highest rock—a sign for everyone to gather. A simple worship center with a goblet of juice and a loaf of freshly baked bread has been set in a natural amphitheater among broken rock.

Participants are invited to continue their conversation with the total group. Almost everyone briefly recounts stories from camp—friendships, loving acts, hard times, funny moments and special wishes for graduating seniors. A young person reads scripture, and the pastor speaks:

Once there were some teenagers playing on a beach—running, splashing, throwing Frisbees, kicking foot bags and chasing a big black dog. As the afternoon ended they gathered to finish the picnic leftovers. As they ate, an old sailboat appeared from out of nowhere—a fishing boat with a throw net draped over the bow. It eased toward shore and touched the sand.

The fisherman threw out an anchor and waded ashore toward the picnicking young people. "Come have some lunch—or what's left of it." The group's leader couldn't believe she said that. The leathery man of the sea smiled and joined the group, gladly drinking the last soft drink and rummaging in the potato chip bag with his calloused hand. His T-shirt was faded and tattered. He talked easily and joked about fishing.

A wind kicked up, swinging the fishing boat around, and the man in the tattered T-shirt rose to one knee—almost as if called by the wind. Silence . . . Listening . . . Only the wind. Then he took a piece of bread from the picnic basket and looked into the young people's eyes: "This is my body broken for you. Wherever you go, remember me. Whatever you do, remember me—and the God who sent me."

Each person took bread and ate reverently. The man in the tattered T-shirt smiled again and walked toward his boat. Just before he reached the lapping waves, a group member called out: "Mister! Hey mister! Take this!" She ran after him, holding out a bright T-shirt. The fisherman's smile broadened as he slipped the new T-shirt over his shoulders. Gently he kissed the teenager and pressed his tattered T-shirt in her hand.

As he sailed away everyone could read across his back: "Grace Church Summer Youth Camp."

Then the pastor invited the young people gathered around the rock to partake of the bread and the cup. "Ye that do truly and earnestly repent, draw near with faith and take this holy sacrament . . ." They came in twos—silently, reverently. The sun had gone down, and tomorrow they'd go home.

The next day on the bus the group journal passed from hand to hand. Young people recalled the previous night's worship:

● "Being on the island last night made me realize what life is all about. I also realized that's what I'm most afraid of. I realized we are all together and here for each other. It feels good to know when you feel the most pain and have given up, someone's there with a loving hand."

● "Up on the rocks I felt as if there was a sense of magic in the air. I think I have never felt so close to Jesus as that. When it was almost over I looked up at the moon, then the ocean. The moon had a ray

on one part of the ocean. To me it looked like a light from heaven."

● "I closed my eyes and I felt close. I looked around at the sea and the rocks and the ocean horizon. I thought about the people of the past who had stood here looking out across the ocean watching for ships to come in carrying loved ones home. They too probably were alone with the scenery. But we're not alone with the Lord as our friend . . ."

● "Last night on the rocks I felt so close to the Lord . . . I felt that no matter what we all go through—or if we go out on our own—there's always someone there to understand, to listen, to love, to share with, to care—the Lord. I thank everyone for helping me realize the things I have . . ."

The Importance of Worship and Bible Study

Listening to young people's camp testimonies and reading their camp journals confirms the potential impact of camp worship and Bible study. The challenge for camp leaders is to plan and lead camp worship and Bible studies that encourage young people to grow in their Christian faith and commitment.

Just as they are central to church life, worship and Bible study should be central elements of Christian youth camps. Through times of study and worship, young people gain a new perspective on themselves and their faith. They begin to see their own connections to the larger body of Christ.

Perhaps the most significant element of camp worship and Bible study is the bridge they build between beliefs and living. As we've emphasized throughout this book, each element of daily camp life—planning together, resolving differences and group activities—is a parable of Christian faith. Through camp, young people experience what it means to live in Christian community and to relate to other Christians as brothers and sisters.

Camp worship and Bible study highlight the camp parable, building a bridge between daily life and Christian faith. The significance of this bridge cannot be overemphasized. As theologian Robert McAfee Brown writes in *Creative Dislocation—The Movement of Grace*:

> *What we do determines who we are . . . On the one hand there is* orthodoxy, *which means "right belief" and on the other hand there is* orthopraxis *which means "right action." Orthodoxy is what goes on in our heads, which may or may not get translated into our lives. Orthopraxis is what goes on in our lives, and it lays right out for everybody just who we are . . . Our self-definitions are not constructed in our heads; they are forged by our deeds. The payoff is not a consistent theory, but a committed life.*[1]

At camp the entire community is especially conscious of the relationship between beliefs and practices. Thus the camp experience becomes an important laboratory where campers tie together their beliefs (orthodoxy) and their lives (orthopraxis). Through worship, study and discussions, campers struggle to find consistency between word and deeds—not only in themselves but in their parents, families, friends and church.

In each of these—and other—ways, their faith becomes more real and alive through camp. While such growth can result from many elements of camp, it becomes particularly evident through times that are set aside to focus on Bible study, devotion, worship or celebration.

In this chapter we'll examine the unique opportunities and challenges of camp worship and Bible study. We'll begin by focusing on camp worship; then we'll examine two effective approaches to camp Bible study.

Uniqueness of Camp Worship

In Chapter 1 we discussed how camping allows us to "uproot in order to reroot"—how camp takes us away from familiar settings to see ourselves and our lives in a new light. Nowhere is this truth more evident than in camp worship. Camp worship stands in sharp contrast to the forms and features of worship back home. Glistening sunrises and golden sunsets replace stained-glass windows; fallen logs and wave-hewn rocks replace cushioned pews; tall pines replace church steeples; and crashing waves and singing birds replace organ music. Away from the structures of traditional worship, camp can breathe fresh air into Christian celebrations.

At the same time, camp worship connects the outdoor experience with life back home and the larger body of Christ. A story retold and explained, a Psalm sung or a passage read responsively reminds the campers of who they are and connects them to the faithful at home and in history.

Sometimes people of different beliefs share in a camp or camp training event. When we have worked, worshiped, studied and broken bread together we discover kinship and connectedness with other Christians. We often discover that we have more in common with others than we have differences.

We can see the uniqueness of camp celebrations by examining three theological assumptions about living in Christian community:

- It's a corporate rebirth experience.
- It's a reconciliation experience.
- It's a faith-sharing experience.

Corporate rebirth. Camp's natural emphasis on community-building opens a door for considering the camp experience as a process of becoming part of Christ's body. Through worship experiences, campers are challenged both individually and as a group to make new commitments to Christ and the church. One church emphasized this corporate dimension in its summer camp theme: "Body-Building—Spiritual That Is!"

Celebrating a group's rebirth and new commitment involves affirming the pain of groaning and struggling to become a Christian community. It also involves realizing that we're being born anew as a community—to God, to one another and to ourselves.

Many local church groups are, in reality, two or three groups with a few core members who bridge the gaps. Camp can bring the different groups together. One youth group was "created anew" when the fall camp weekend included both the youth choir and the youth fellowship. The distance between the group closed during the weekend as the young people created a closing worship celebration together. In workshop times, the choir rehearsed music for the celebration, while youth fellowship members created a liturgy.

On the final night, 40 young people and their leaders processed through camp with hand bells tolling in a candlelight prelude. Then in the light of two long lines of candles in the open-air recreation building, the young people sang antiphonally, dramatized scripture passages, and received the bread and juice two by two. It was a new beginning for the church group—a milestone of unity, spiritual sensitivity and personal awareness about each person's value to the group.

Reconciliation. Reconciliation takes a new dimension at camp. At home when worship is a set-aside time each week, the need for reconciliation during worship is often less apparent. However, at camp worship takes place in the immediate context of extended, person-to-person living.

The meaning of reconciliation comes alive when campers realize that, even during worship and celebration, they're with the people to whom they must be reconciled. It's difficult to avoid or deny the reality of alienation or broken relationships. And because campers can't escape these relationships during camp, they're more likely to face problems and offer forgiveness through group discussions, person-to-person counseling, or corporate worship and celebration.

If you want to test this assumption, ask a junior higher who's been at odds with another camper if the evening campfire or morning watch helped rebuild the two campers' friendship.

Sharing personal faith. Camp is a faith-sharing place. Few other church settings provide camp's extended hours and contact with other Christians that give campers non-threatening opportunities to verbalize—and to hear others verbalize—their faith.

Hearing other people's faith stories is as important to sharing faith as articulating one's own faith. Often teenagers hear another camper or counselor say words that make their own experience suddenly become real and meaningful. Thus that other person's expression of faith becomes a touchstone—a memorable moment—from which the campers can express their own faith story in the future.

Some teenagers come to camp without experience in a faith community, giving them little Christian identity of their own. For these campers, camp becomes a faith laboratory to discover firsthand the connection between what people of God believe and what they do. For them, the celebrating moment may be the best time to raise questions and seek clarification for their own Christian pilgrimage.

Camp celebrations are also marked by hope. Camp celebrations are focusing events that tie campers' hopes together and provide the context in which young people can give public testimony—either symbolically or literally—of their hopes. These hopes include:

● Hope that the campers' faith experience will continue to have meaning beyond the camp.

● Hope that in making covenants for the week, campers are laying foundations for lifelong covenant-making.

● Hope that living and learning in small groups will give some clues to family living and an appreciation for the worldwide family of God.

● Hope that in exploring God's world of wonder we're sowing the seeds of reverence and gratitude.

● And hope that, in accepting others, we demonstrate God's love for all creation.

Elements of Camp Worship

All worship has a structure. And while the different elements of worship may vary from setting to setting, church to church, and denomination to denomination, worship leaders from most perspectives include the basic elements of worship found in Isaiah's temple vision (Isaiah 6:1-9) and in the Emmaus road experience (Luke 24:13-35). These basic elements are like ascending steps that take worshipers to new levels of relating with God (see Diagram 31, "Elements of Worship").

These same elements can guide camp worship. One camp uses a rugged back-country day trip to teach campers about worship. Leaders briefly describe the hike's destination without giving details—just enough to help campers see how the celebration fits into the outdoor experience.

Every camper takes part in pre-trip preparation. Leaders use the Isaiah vision passage and worship bulletins from their home churches to explain the biblical movements of worship. Each subgroup is given written instructions for preparing one movement of the hiking celebration. The instructions are brief and allow flexibility:

Adoration and praise. Select a familiar song of praise, and write an act of praise or choose a Psalm of praise to read.

Confession. Write a prayer of confession or a litany of confession with verses

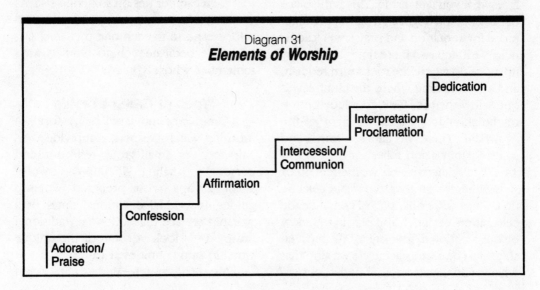

Diagram 31
Elements of Worship

Adoration/Praise → Confession → Affirmation → Intercession/Communion → Interpretation/Proclamation → Dedication

for a group member to read and refrains or responses for everyone to repeat between verses.

Affirmation. Write a statement of affirmation, or use an affirmation that each person can use with one other person. Choose a song of assurance for the group or one person to sing.

Thanksgiving and dedication. Write a prayer of thanksgiving and create an act of dedication to use after communion.

The next morning after planning is complete, the group drives to the trail head and sets out over a dense pine ridge. The descent leads to a meadow filled with wild grasses and flowers, divided by a cold, rushing stream. Ahead, the valley narrows into a steep talus slope. Above are snowfields and a craggy peak with three rocky spires.

On the last grassy rise before the rocky ascent, the leaders unload a backpack and pass out the morning snack. When the hikers are rested, the leader invites them to be silent and listen: "Be aware of the wind and all you see. Be aware of your own senses—your tired legs, the perspiration on your face, what you feel inside. This is the place our celebration begins. The group that prepared for adoration and praise will lead us here. We'll stop two more times on our way up: once up where the rocks turn reddish; and a second time where the climb levels out below the top. We'll conclude on top of the shoulder just to the right of the snowfield. There we can see north and south for miles and miles.

"Each time we stop we'll circle up or sit together for another step in our celebration. Once we're on top we'll conclude the celebration, eat lunch and play in the snow on our way down. It's okay to talk between stops; just be aware each time we stop that what we do then is another part of our en-

tire worship celebration."

Then the first planners lead a song of praise and read a Psalm. And the group hikes toward the mountain.

At the peak's base by a lake, each camper takes a small stone to symbolize his or her sins and trespasses. The planners had printed the prayer of confession on a large piece of paper that they now unfold and hold up for everyone to pray together. Then, while a soloist sings a song of assurance, each person throws his or her stone into the water. Finally, campers share a litany of affirmation (written by another group) and hugs of affirmation (with each person hugging everyone else).

Higher up on the level spot, a rounded amphitheater of stones encircles the group as the camp's director-manager leads a reflection on "God's Resting Places." He concludes by leading communion, using grape juice in a Sierra cup and bread from the camp kitchen.

Atop the rocky saddle, a breathtaking view greets the campers. Their thanksgiving prayer is almost blown away by the wind. The last worship group surprises everyone with hand-twisted string bracelets that each camper ties on someone else. As each bracelet is tied, campers and counselors respond to each one by name, saying: "We dedicate you to God. Always remember whose you are!"

Types of Camp Worship

Camp worship takes many forms—morning watch, vespers, campwide worship services, small group reflection and personal journaling. Worship can involve small groups with prepared worship guides, individual devotional times or a worship service that follows a traditional liturgy. Let's look at some of the unique worship opportunities at camp:

Morning watch. Many camps begin

with a morning worship celebration called "morning watch." It usually takes place before breakfast and lasts about 30 minutes. It can be a solitary time for personal prayer and devotion. In these cases, a printed guide with scripture, reflection, a prayer of self-examination and a thought for the day sometimes helps guide each camper into the new day.

In addition to personal devotion time, morning watch can be a time of group celebration with a song, prayer, scripture and a brief message or sharing time.

Having morning watches at special places at camp that catch the morning light—a lake, dock, porch or hilltop—enhances the experience. Good places to begin planning morning watches are 1 Thessalonians 5:5-6, Luke 12:37 and other Bible passages listed in a concordance under "watch," "watchfulness" or "watchmen."

Mealtime celebrations. Table grace is the most regular camp celebration. Using a variety of table graces led by campers and staff can develop a deeper awareness of God's presence in all of life. Here are some variations:

1. Pray in an all-camp thanksgiving circle, holding hands or putting arms around each other.

2. Print a blessing on table tents (cards folded in half so they stand) with instructions for someone to lead the table group.

3. Print directions on a table tent for group-sharing at each table. For example, "The person wearing the brightest shirt invite everyone at the table to share his or her most important moment of the day so far."

4. Sing thanksgiving songs, hymns or choruses as table blessings. Use different tunes to "Doxology."

5. Use thanksgiving scripture passages or theme-related passages to introduce the table grace.

6. Make three-panel table displays for "Thoughts for Today." Make them by bending construction paper or Manila folders in three panels (about 5 × 11 inches) and stapling along the edges to create an upright, triangular display. Use one panel each for morning, noon and evening. Decorate them with quotes, poetry, proverbs, wisdom and art related to the day's theme.

7. Break bread together. Invite one person to take bread, break a piece for the camper to the left and say, "Scott, Jesus is the Bread of Life" or "Rosa, may God's grace sustain you." The camper who receives the bread then takes the same piece of bread, gives bread and repeats the "words of assurance" to the next camper, and so on around the table.

Closing worship. Perhaps the most significant worship experience in camp is the closing worship service on the last night. The service culminates the camp experience and becomes the setting for campers to express the feelings and commitments that have developed during the time together. Thus camp planners usually focus a great deal of attention and effort in preparing a particularly meaningful celebration.

James Thompson, a pastor in Georgia, tells a story that typifies the emotion and impact of closing worship experiences. His group was at an island camp off the Georgia coast. One camper who was from a group home was particularly uncooperative and hostile. He broke every rule and created as much turmoil as possible. The counselors and several campers talked together about how to respond. They decided to love the boy—to affirm him whenever possible.

By the week's end, he had totally changed. No camp task was too big for him. The pastor remembered the significance of the closing communion celebration for that boy. "I gave each person a piece of bread and had them share their bread with every person in the group," Thompson recalled. He continued:

As they shared with others, each [camper] was to tell what they had found good in the other person—what was special about that individual. When [this boy] and I shared bread, he threw his arms around me and cried. Later we spent some time at the dock and he sobbed. He said he didn't want to go home. But that summer he ended up getting to go back to his family.

Each camp will have a unique conclusion shaped by the particular leaders, counselors, teenagers and experiences. The closing worship celebration should culminate the whole week's theme and experiences. Such a climax can be evoked in many ways.

At the beginning of a weeklong ocean-side camp, one pastor asked each camper to "find something for every other person in their group during the week." During the closing celebration, group members presented each other the collected gifts from the woods or beach—shells, driftwood, butterfly wings and mosses. For his gifts, the pastor wrote personal notes to each camper and placed them in bottles he gathered that had washed ashore.

The closing worship celebration should also help campers and leaders clarify, channel and symbolize the faith commitments that grow out of their camp experience. Celebrations that include communion have built-in steps to commitment: invitation, confession, response and thanksgiving. But there are many ways to invite campers to share their experiences. Here are some ideas:

1. Give campers opportunities to share their thoughts and intentions openly, giving them a chance to verbalize their faith to the whole group.

2. Lead a sharing time within small groups that have been together all week for intense study, discussion and interaction.

3. Invite campers to write their commitments on paper and to burn the papers in the campfire as an offering to God. Or have them tack their commitment to a cross as a symbol of their commitment.

4. Let campers and leaders put their faith into words by praying, verbalizing hopes or commitments, or sharing their commitment with one other person.

5. Ask campers to write letters to themselves. Then mail each camper his or her letter at Christmas or the new year as a reminder of the camp commitment.

6. Have campers form small group circles and give each person a candle. Then light one person's candle, and have him or her share anything he or she chooses. This person then lights a neighbor's candle, and the neighbor shares. Continue around the circle until everyone's candle has been lit and everyone has shared something.

Because of the closing event's importance, a lot of thought and preparation should go into planning it. Indeed, planning for the closing celebration can become an important ritual in itself. The youth group from a Georgia congregation concludes its weeklong Love Week camp with a Cross Service.

As the tradition has grown, preparing for the service has become more significant. It's now an honor to serve on the Cross Service committee. Each year the group carefully builds a new cross and buys candles. When the committee arrives at the campsite, it spends hours finding the perfect place for its Cross Service. On the closing night, the cross glows with candles—usually reflected in nearby water. Then in the cross's light, the campers sing, and the camp minister invites them to share their experiences and decisions that have grown out of their week at camp.

Another multiethnic camp shaped its closing celebration around the stories a Native American leader told. He told how his grandfather was taught from childhood that our shadows leave us at night and run around and play till they're brought back home by a song. He recounted the morning ritual of going to the water to begin the new day as a day of prayer. And he told how "giving away" was a sacred act of affirmation in which eagle feathers or special symbolic gifts were shared in the tribe and how the day's prayer ended only in sleep.

The celebration planning group decided to use these stories to create the closing celebration. Planners framed the elements of songs, scripture, prayer and testimony in the Native American motif—singing our shadows home, meeting the morning, going to the water, and touching and giving away.

On the last morning of camp in the light of a Northwest coastal dawn, the campers quietly followed the storyteller to the lake. With soft guitar music providing a reflective background, the storyteller waded into the silvery pink waters. He cupped his hands and with long, reaching strokes swept the water into showers of diamonds around his shoulders. His breath hung in the cold air. Again he swept the cold water. And again . . . And again.

Then a reader on shore read from the famous Santee Dakota Indian physician Ohiyesa:

In the life of the Indian there was only one inevitable duty—the duty of prayer—the daily recognition of the Unseen and Eternal. His daily devotions were more necessary to him than daily food. He wakes at daybreak, puts on his moccasins and steps down to the water's edge. Here he throws handfuls of clear, cold water into his face, and plunges in bodily. After the bath, he stands erect before the advancing dawn, facing the sun as it dances upon the horizon, or offers his unspoken orison. His mate

may precede or follow him in his devotions, but never accompanies him. Each soul must meet the morning sun, the new sweet earth and the Great Silence alone!

Whenever, in the course of the daily hunt the red hunter comes upon a scene that is strikingly beautiful or sublime—a black thundercloud with the rainbow's glowing arch above the mountain, a white waterfall in the heart of a green gorge; a vast prairie tinged with the blood-red of sunset—he pauses for an instant in the attitude of worship. He sees no need for setting apart one day in seven as a holy day, since to him all days are God's.[2]

The celebration continued. The campers stood on the grassy shore and followed a printed celebration guide that blended the ancient American drama with the biblical drama. We must not equate traditional Native American worship with Christian worship. However, through music, scripture readings, reflections and actions that used American Indian imagery to elicit biblical truths, the campers experienced a new dimension of their faith and camp experience.

In planning your closing celebrations, keep in mind the following points:

1. The closing worship service is no time to invite a guest speaker who hasn't been with the group all week—no matter how well he or she communicates. To elicit appropriate expressions of both personal and corporate commitments, the leader must understand where the group is as a faith community.

2. Young people know when they're being pressured to do or say something that isn't a natural expression for them. All teenagers express themselves differently. Thus invitations during your closing celebration should provide opportunities for a variety of responses. These might include outward rituals; praying alone or together; open sharing; speaking personally to close friends; holding hands; or placing arms

around one another in a circle to share or sing.

Planning Camp Celebrations

Camp worship and celebration forms can vary dramatically, depending on the camp's creativity, theme and freedom to adapt the worship style within the campers' denominational tradition. Yet each worship form contains threads that tie the experience to worshiping congregations everywhere. In planning camp worship, it's important to help campers identify these threads. What connects camp celebrations with worship traditions at home? How do our camp worship experiences relate to other forms of Christian worship? Helping campers make these connections equips them more fully to understand worship at camp and in their home churches.

Arbitrary, innovative or novel ideas led without interpretation undermine campers' ability to make connections with other worship experiences. Thus it's critical to involve campers in camp celebration preparation and leadership. When campers have themselves gone through the process of imaging, interpreting and creating an element of worship, they become involved in the praise and proclamation even before the actual event. Their investment in creating and leading confirms those unseen threads of tradition.

While worship generally involves common threads and the six elements highlighted in Diagram 31 ("Elements of Worship"), camp celebrations need not be limited to traditional elements and orders of worship. Sometimes camp celebration can focus on a particular element of worship—praise, thanksgiving or interpretation.

For example, the "Worship Walk" in Camp Notebook 34 focuses on experiential interpretations of Bible passages. Each camper leads a brief step in the celebration. A letter of the word "S E R V E" designates each camper's part and ties the celebration to the camp theme. Leaders distribute the Worship Walk instructions to groups of five campers who lead the celebration together.

Neither do elements of worship require specific expressions. Confession may be a song, litany, antiphonal reading or silent confession interpreted by a mime or dancer. Proclamation may be a sermon, sermonette, dramatic reading, slide show, video or movie clip, or a dialogue sermon involving other leaders—or the whole camping group.

Some camps have campwide celebrations that closely follow the movements of traditional liturgical worship. The primary difference is that they use more antiphonal readings, interpretive movement, dramatic monologues, drama and contemporary musical presentations.

In addition to their knowledge about worship, camp leaders should draw on the resources of the Spirit, the church's tradition, and the campers' creativity and inner experience. For example, campers can lead prayers from a prayer book or a book of worship or they can write prayers. By asking three campers to use a prayer book as a model for writing their own prayer for this particular time and place, leaders nurture campers' concern for prayer and their capacity to talk openly about prayer with each other.

To make your camp worship meaningful, keep the following guidelines in mind as you plan and prepare:

1. Describe daily camp celebrations in camp brochures, camper orientations and letters. Discuss the value of prayer, Bible study and sharing at camp.

2. Include all campers in some way in worship planning and leadership. Model the celebration style and provide the pri-

Camp Notebook 34

Worship Walk

Good morning! Form groups of five with other campers. Stand in a circle. Tell your names and why today is a great day. While you're in a circle, spell the word "serve" by assigning each person one letter of the word. The letter will designate the leader for each section of this Bible study. "S" will begin the celebration.

S: Read Philippians 2:5-6. "Your attitude should be the same as that of Christ Jesus: Who, being in very nature God, did not consider equality with God something to be grasped."
Have each person look around and think of a camp experience that reminds him or her of the "nature of God."

E: Read Philippians 2:7. "But made himself nothing, taking the very nature of a servant, being made in human likeness."
Have each person find something to do for the other group members or for the camp. For example, pick up gum wrappers, give someone a back rub or loan someone your jacket. Then ask each person to describe what it means to take on the "nature of a servant."

R: Read Philippians 2:8. "And being found in appearance as a man, he humbled himself and became obedient to death—even death on a cross!"
Lead the group, single file, in a brief walk. As the leader, "R" can make the group do and say whatever he or she does and says. After a few moments, ask each camper to tell how it felt to follow a path of obedience. Compare these feelings to how Jesus must have felt.

V: Read Philippians 2:9. "Therefore God exalted him to the highest place and gave him the name that is above every name."
Have the group sit down and face the mountains. Ask each camper, "What do you think it means for a servant to be 'exalted to the highest place'?" Read Matthew 19:30 and Mark 9:35 for additional insights.

E: Read Philippians 2:10-11. "That at the name of Jesus every knee should bow, in heaven and on earth and under the earth, and every tongue confess that Jesus Christ is Lord, to the glory of God the Father."
Ask members each to tell how they see God using them as servants like he used Jesus. Have everyone kneel and offer a prayer of praise.

mary leadership the first couple of times, but include campers from the outset with invitations to lead specific parts of a celebration. Shift leadership more to campers as camp progresses. Give younger campers structure. Challenge experienced campers to conceptualize and create their own celebrations.

3. Provide a variety of resources and supplies for campers to use in planning. Many are listed in the resource list on page 343.

4. Simplify tasks, use subgroups, give clear instructions and help small groups as they prepare.

5. Whenever possible, avoid setting time limits. Help campers focus on what is to be celebrated and how that can be done rather than trying to fill space. At first, celebrations will tend to be short; later, campers will generate enough ideas in one planning time to lead three celebrations!

6. Plan an entry movement that focuses the group and develops a group spirit. A processional, silent walk, reflective mime or song, camp theme song, circle and rhythm movements, echo scripture, dramatic readings, film clips, darkness, candlelight and light shows are all useful as the entry movement when shaped appropriately.

7. Plan an exit movement that unifies the group and permits person-to-person celebration. Such movements could include theme songs or popular unifying songs, circles, holding hands, passing the peace, hugs, candy showers and general invitations to affirmation.

8. Involve campers in visualizing and deciding on the setting for celebration and the symbols needed.

9. On the day of the event, talk through the celebration event with youth leaders. If you have a printed guide, read through it to understand the movements.

Answer questions. Ask questions that help campers connect camp celebration to worship in their home congregation. Encourage them to reflect on their own worship experiences and to consider how worship at camp will enrich their ongoing worship life. Pray together for God's guidance, other campers and staff, families back home and being able to share the faith back home.

10. For celebrations that involve a lot of group movement, print important responses, prayers and words of songs in large letters on four sheets of newsprint. Place one sheet on each wall so campers can see the words no matter where they stand or sit during the celebration.

Camp Celebration Ideas

As I've emphasized throughout this chapter, camp worship should be creative enough to capture campers' attention while at the same time helping them make connections between this worship experience and their worship experiences back home. Here are some different celebration ideas particularly suited for youth camps:

Fantasy-sharing. Carefully crafted fantasies capture young people's imaginations. They also can be natural invitations to campers to celebrate their time together and what God is doing in their midst. Diagram 32, "Camp Fantasy Story," illustrates this approach to camp celebration.

Create a fantasy in which campers actively participate. Use it as a parable to invite campers to share personal feelings and faith experiences. When creating and using fantasy stories, keep the following guidelines in mind:

1. Carefully plan your fantasy story. Keep it brief (three to six minutes).

2. Create a setting and experience that campers can easily identify with. If possible tell the fantasy at the same time of day

Diagram 32
Camp Fantasy Story

Center the group by saying: "I'm going to tell you a story about a camper. Make yourself comfortable. Close your eyes if you wish, or focus on a visual point. As I tell the story, put yourself in the camper's shoes. Let yourself become the camper. Feel what the camper feels. Be aware of every detail of the camper's experience. Now, the story:"

Once in the late afternoon a group of campers stopped to rest on a high, flowering meadow overlooking a river. Above the meadow were little fringes of tall trees that merged with the forested shoulders of a long ridge. Beyond were higher peaks.

While other campers rested and talked, one camper decided to explore higher up where the trees touched the meadow. Soon the lone camper was beyond the group's voices—then, at the edge of the trees.

There—where the spring flowers ended—was a faint trail . . . a mysterious, inviting trail. The camper followed it. It took some time to adjust to the deep woods' darkness down the trail. There were long, blue shadows, brown needles on the ground and only occasional glimpses of light overhead.

The camper decided to return to the meadow. Just then the faint smell of smoke drifted on the wind. Fright seized the teenager. Fire? Where? But for some reason the camper ran toward the smell of smoke, not down the mountain. A hundred yards further panic turned to fear . . . then to mystery.

There against an overhanging rock was an old man by a tiny fire, sipping from an ancient cup. "Come," he said. "Sit." His hand beckoned the teenager to the fire.

The old man's eyes looked new inside his weathered face. It was easy to talk with him. And it was easy to be there when neither spoke. But suddenly the camper looked up through the trees. Darkness was coming on fast. "I must go; they'll be looking for me."

"Wait!" The old man shuffled through a faded rucksack. "Here, take this." He pressed the camper's hand around an unseen object. "Go. Go find your friends."

The darkness of the woods behind, the camper descended the flowered slope. Far below friends waved, but their words weren't clear. What was the object? Hand open, the camper gazed in disbelief. How would he tell the others? Would they believe this story?

When you finish the fantasy story, pause. Be silent and restful. Then invite the campers to open their eyes. Choose one of the following two approaches to help campers process the fantasy story.

● Here's how to process the story using the sharing approach:
1. Talk about how you felt as you became part of the fantasy.
2. Did any memory from your past come to you during the story? Describe what that memory was like.
3. Describe the conversation you fantasized with the old man.
4. What was the object in your hand?
5. Was there any overarching truth or learning in the fantasy for you?

● Here's how to process the story using the parable or allegory approach:
1. Invite the group to think of the fantasy story as a parable or allegory and ask, "How would you relate the story to life?"
2. Ask the group to relate the parable to their life as a group or seek clarification if someone has already made the association.
3. Ask campers what images were significant and what the images mean to them. Introduce significant images for you as leader. Identify any images that are overlooked: the flowering meadow and the dark woods, the hidden trail, the campfire, the campsite, the ancient cup, the conversation, the faded rucksack, the old man's gift or the question of telling friends.

described in the story.

3. Choose a comfortable place—outdoors if possible. Center the group before beginning the story itself.

4. Keep the story simple, vague and mysterious. Use images that are strong and easy to visualize.

5. Use inclusive language so guys and girls can both identify with the central character.

6. Take time to process the fantasy (20 to 40 minutes). Campers can process the story by sharing feelings, images and memories or by exploring the fantasy as a parable or allegory. Guide the sharing so that everyone shares something about the fantasy.

7. Don't press the story to prove a point. Help campers avoid heavy moralizing from fantasy stories.

8. Don't insist on a "correct" interpretation. The interpretation belongs to the group members because it's their personal response to the story.

9. Follow the fantasy with a faith connection, Bible reading, prayer, selected song or related activity.

Balloons. When people think of balloons in celebration, the image usually consists of a grand finale event when hundreds of helium-filled balloons are sent skyward amidst music, laughter, tears and hugs—symbolic praise on the wind. But there are also many other ways to use these popular symbols of hope in celebration at camp:

1. Sharing groups. Use different balloon colors (or balloons with numbers or symbols) to group campers for times of intergroup sharing, praise or prayer. Simply direct each to find other campers with balloons with his or her color, symbol or number.

2. Symbolize breaking barriers. Have campers pair off, and give each pair a balloon. Direct each pair to put the balloon between them face-to-face and then to hug until the balloon bursts. Then talk about how holding onto each other breaks barriers between us.

3. Hopes and dreams. Ask campers to write or symbolize on their balloons their hopes, prayers and dreams using a felt-tip pen. Have campers share with each other what they wrote. Then have campers exchange balloons to symbolize letting others support and pray for their concerns and hopes.

Bread-baking. Teach campers to bake bread from scratch. Bake fresh bread for the celebration, and use selected Bible passages about bread (there are dozens) and songs about bread in your communion, community or mission themes. If your group is small, the bread-baking can even be part of the celebration.

Bread and fish. Re-enact with campers the scene of Jesus cooking breakfast for his disciples in an early morning Galilean celebration (John 21:1-14). Cook fish on a charcoal or wood fire, and serve camperbaked bread. If possible have the cooking area by a lake where it can be seen from a great distance.

Pass the pages. Find some small books of inspirational thoughts, poetry and full-color photographs (one per page). Carefully remove the cover and trim the pages with scissors, giving you a set of loose pages. Protect the pages in a selfclosing plastic bag.

Have campers form a circle and invite them to pass around the pages. Ask campers to let the pictures and the written selections speak to them. When a camper finds a page he or she would like to share, the camper simply keeps the page and passes others along.

When everyone has a page, begin sharing. Keep the sharing open, inviting campers to offer individual perceptions and interpretations.

Use the same pages over and over, since they elicit different thoughts for different individuals as the group grows together. Selections can relate to the camp theme. And pages can be laminated for backcountry trips.

Story-making. Blend the camp experience with an excerpt from Jesus' life into a contemporary story (such as the story that introduced this chapter, page 217). Almost every camp event has the place and experience that everyone can visualize. That framework becomes the key to blending a biblical event with imagery that connects directly with campers' experience.

Jesus' parables, his wilderness experience, his person-to-person experiences and his appearances after the Resurrection are all easily adaptable. In creating your story, take great care to keep it simple and clearly focused.

Circle of prayers. Use this continual praying activity gradually to encourage campers to pray openly within the group. It also works as part of a morning watch, devotional time or time of thanksgiving.

Begin by distributing paper and a pencil to each person. Then introduce the subject of prayer by saying: "Take a few minutes to describe something you'd most like to change in yourself or your family. Think about it for a few minutes. Be specific in what you write. Put it in your own words for the rest of us."

When all campers have completed their writings, have them tell what they've written. Give them the option of passing if they don't want to speak.

Then say: "Now think over what you've just said and heard from others. Prayer is like what we've just done—it's sharing openly with God, just as if we were talking with an intimate friend. It's telling God what we want to change, accept or

celebrate as his people. As we learn to pray together this week, let's seek new ways of praying that feel natural and fit our feelings."

Begin the prayer process by making available Bibles, devotional guides and books of prayer. Have groups of three use the resources to write a short prayer. Then have each individual write a short prayer. When kids are finished, gather the whole group together in a circle. First have the trios read their prayers, then have individuals read theirs.

Having a piece of paper to read from gives campers security, especially those who haven't had experience praying at home. Repeat this exercise periodically throughout the week. As kids become comfortable with the structured experience, invite them to pray spontaneously within the large group. When you gather as a large group, here are ideas to stimulate teenagers to pray individually:

1. Say: "Think about what you're thankful for at camp and in our group. As you express thanks to God in your mind, choose what you feel most thankful for and say a couple of brief prayers. Start with 'God, I'm thankful for . . .' and end with 'because . . .' I'll begin."

2. Say: "Pray silently for someone back home in your family, church or school. Feel the importance of praying for the individual you have in mind. Then identify aloud the person you're praying for by briefly describing him or her to the group and giving his or her name if you choose to. I'll start."

3. Say: "Let's hold hands in a circle. We're going to say three different prayers. We'll go around the circle three times. The first round will be prayers of gratitude and praise. The second round will be prayers for our families and world concerns. The third round will be prayers for each other.

I'll begin and then introduce each new round of prayer as the circle's completed. If you want to pass, squeeze the next person's hand."

Leading Camp Bible Studies

Camp Bible studies require an innovative and involving approach. Effective camp Bible studies help campers build bridges between their experiences of living together in Christian community and their faith. By turning to the Bible and letting it illuminate camp's daily struggles, joys, conflicts and new learnings, leaders bring the Bible alive to campers.

During recent years two Christian educators—Walter Wink and Thomas Groome—have developed profound and innovative approaches to experiential Bible study that fit the camp environment perfectly. These Bible exploration methods actively involve campers, and they're easy for volunteer youth workers to grasp during training events. Indeed, both of these educators have been involved in camp leadership training for many denominations.

While each approach is different in several respects, they both have the following characteristics:

1. They help campers "get inside" the biblical events through art, drama, role play, skits, film, music and creative group activities.

2. They call for campers' personal faith responses to biblical events.

3. Both are refreshing to camp leaders because they can be led "naturally" as conversation connected to a real camp activity.

On the following pages we'll briefly outline these two approaches, suggesting ways youth workers can plan their own Bible explorations based on these models. The resource listing on page 343 suggests additional resources for planning and preparing camp Bible studies.

Transforming Bible Study

Wink's approach to experiential Bible study blends personal imagination, biblical scholarship and psychology into a step-by-step process that bridges the gap between human life issues and Bible study.[3] He asserts that "a well-phrased question will last a lifetime, with 10, 20 or 30 different answers—all of them true!"

Thus the educator advocates focusing experiential Bible study on "questions that count." At the heart of each Bible exploration is a series of questions that grow out of careful study of each text. The progression of questions opens doors for campers to explore passages and identify personally with God's action in their lives.

For example, consider the counselors who ask campers during a study of the Psalms, "What's the song of your heart?" An apparently simple question raised in a small group by a stream or on a mountaintop grows in significance at home as campers ask themselves: "What is my song today? How is the music of my life changing? How do I sing God's song in a strange land?" (Diagram 33, "Exploring the Parable of the Sower (Mark 4:1-9)," is one example of more than 25 studies in Wink's book, *Transforming Bible Study: A Leader's Guide*.)

Wink's style of gentle, probing reflection places a new emphasis on a personal devotional life, opening the Bible as a fresh resource for campers to explore everyday issues.

Of course, being able to form sensitive and open questions is no substitute for thorough Bible study. In reality, the leaders often prepare even more thoroughly, equipping themselves to be able to introduce small bits of word study and historical background during the dialogue.

Perhaps the most different aspect of preparation is the leader's reading between the lines of scripture and commentaries to raise a series of questions from which the first questions will come. Sometimes the most important question is the one searching to answer the unwritten elements of a story—the question that seeks to visualize the biblical event.

For example, a person preparing to involve campers experientially with the story of Jesus as a youth (Luke 2:41-52) might ask:

● What was it like to stay behind?

● Was Jesus alone? Were there other 12-year-olds with him? Was this unusual?

● Was Mary a supermother or a normal human being?

● What would we do if our child disobeyed? Was what Jesus did disobedient?

● Was Jesus a normal kid? Were the teachers amazed because of Jesus' wisdom? Would most adults be amazed if they really listened to 12-year-olds?

● How are we like Jesus? Mary? the teachers?

Wink admits that this questioning approach may seem threatening and difficult at first. However, he suggests several guidelines for leading a Bible study using his approach.[4] Here are some of them:

1. Begin with a time for centering. Encourage campers to relax, breathe deeply and begin focusing on the task of understanding the Bible and what it means for them.

2. Ask a volunteer to read aloud the passage you're studying. Throughout the study, participation should be voluntary.

3. Trust your questions. Discussion usually begins slowly, but overcome the temptation to answer the question in face of the group's silence. If silence persists, restate or rephrase the question, but never answer it.

4. If someone asks a question you plan to deal with later, either deal with it now or—if it interrupts another issue inade-

---

Diagram 33

Exploring the Parable of the Sower (Mark 4:1-9)

1. Look first at the refrains in Mark 4:9, 23, 24; and Matthew 13:19, 43. What does this warning lead you to expect about Jesus' teaching about the kingdom . . .? What were the current Jewish expectations about the kingdom? With what colors would you describe it? What gestures?

2. Identify with the sower. What then would the parable say to you? (Ask people to be specific and make "I" statements.)

3. Identify with the soil. Where is this beaten-down path in you? What is it that keeps us from hearing the new word that we need to hear?

4. Can you locate the rocky soil in yourself?

5. What are your thorns?

6. This good soil that produces an abundant harvest—do you know this soil in yourself? Are you in touch with the reality of this fruitfulness?

7. Meditate for a few minutes: At which point does this parable find you out—as sower or as one of the soils? Where does it resonate most in you? What does it say to you?

8. What does this parable suggest about the nature of the kingdom? How does it contrast with current expectations of its coming? What does it imply about the nature of God?

quately discussed—ask the person to hold it until the group can come back to it.

5. Be aware of your progress through your series of questions, but focus your full attention on what people are saying.

6. When one camper or a few people dominate (as often happens), widen involvement as tactfully as possible.

7. If people begin debating, encourage them simply to let their differences stand without trying to "correct" one another.

8. If the exploration doesn't appear to be going well and you feel yourself pressing to make things happen, stop internally, relax your body, breathe deeply several times and establish eye contact with whoever is speaking. By letting go of your need to control you may be able to flow with the process better.

9. When you have difficulty with a question, don't be afraid to acknowledge your difficulty.

10. Don't approve or disapprove of what participants say unless they involve factual errors.

Conversations With Scripture

A second approach to Bible study that's particularly suited to camp was developed by Catholic educator Thomas Groome. He calls his approach "Experience/Story/Vision." It seeks to bring together in dialogue participants' experience and knowledge with the Christian "Story/Vision" so that participants come to "a new knowing and decision-making about how to live their Christian faith."[5]

Groome suggests an opening focusing activity and five teaching movements to make the connections between experience, story and vision. Groome emphasizes, however, that his approach shouldn't be rigidly followed. Indeed he admonishes leaders to adapt it to different situations, au-

diences and time frames. He's used the approach with all ages in various settings and for different time frames. In fact, he has used the five-step approach to teach college classes and has even consciously used all five steps in a ten-minute conversation!

While the original approach is couched in adult language, it translates easily into language appropriate to leading teenagers. Let's look briefly at the elements of Groome's process, which are preceded by a focusing activity:

Focusing activity. The focusing activity can involve music, skits, role plays, films or any other activity that helps participants focus on the topic at hand. The focusing activity makes Groome's approach exciting for camp, since camp is filled with experiences that in their own right create a setting that invites campers into a faith conversation.

Naming our knowing. This first teaching movement involves making participants aware of what they already know. For junior highers the question is: "What's happening now?"

Reflection on personal story and vision. A junior higher would ask, "What's my story?" In this movement participants share their experiences and personal stories that give perspective to the issue at hand.

Christian community's story and vision. "What is the faith story?" would be the question for junior highers. During this movement participants discover the Christian church's "story" by studying the Bible and by examining church tradition, history or faith practice—things which enrich the Christian experience and vision.

Dialogue—my story and the Story. Once participants have shared their stories and have heard the church's story, they begin a dialogue between the two stories. For teenagers the questions become: "How is what I do like what happened in the Bible? How does my story connect with God's story?"

Faith response. When participants have connected their lives with the Christian story, the questions become: "What will I do? How will I respond?" This final teaching movement allows young people to respond to the dialogue with personal life changes. It helps participants decide how they'll live their lives differently because of the time they've spent sharing, reflecting, supporting and growing as partners in faith.

Because of its emphasis on both inner and outer dialogue, this learning process is both an educational vehicle and a personal journey of discovery for campers and counselors. The approach moves beyond a "message" that adults give teenagers to a message that both adults and teenagers discover in the dialogue itself. And it's a process that's incomplete unless campers decide how they'll live their faith as a result of the shared experience.

The following Bible studies illustrate how Groome's approach can be effectively used in a youth camp setting, building naturally on the events and opportunities of camping.

On Friendship

Focusing activity. Play "Friends" by Michael W. Smith. Have campers write on a 3×5 card what friendship means to them right now.

Naming our knowing. Have campers share what they heard and thought as they listened to the song and wrote about friendship.

Reflection on personal story and vision. Ask campers to illustrate what they shared with a brief story about a friend, a family member or themselves.

Christian community's story and

vision. Have three campers read and act out Luke 11:1-13.

Dialogue—my story and the Story. Ask: "How is Jesus' story like our stories of friendship? How is your relationship to your friends like a prayer?"

Faith response. If you're leading staff, ask, "How would you pray for the friendships of your campers?" Have groups of two or three leaders write prayers. Pray the prayers in the total group.

If you're leading campers, ask, "How would you pray for your friends or friendships in our group this week?" Have groups of two or three campers write their prayer together. Pray the prayers as a closing time or evening devotion.

At Mealtime

Focusing activity. A camp cookout when all campers are involved in preparing and cooking the meal.

Naming our knowing. Ask: "What are you thinking and feeling about our cookout? How did cooking as a group affect you?"

Reflection on personal story and vision. Ask, "What are some other meals you remember at home or other places?"

Christian community's story and vision. Read (or have group members recall) the story of the Last Supper (Mark 14:12-26) or the story of Jesus cooking fish for his disciples (John 21:1-14).

Dialogue—my story and the Story. Ask, "How is the meal we cooked together like the Last Supper or the meal Jesus cooked?"

Faith response. Ask, "What would you like mealtimes to be like in your home?" If campers ask, "My home now or my home when I'm grown up?" say, "Either one you want to describe." Then ask, "What can we do to make our mealtimes times of communion, servanthood and celebration while we're at camp?"

On Building Each Other Up

Focusing activity. Building a rope bridge outdoors (or an indoor bridge-building exercise in which you build a bridge between two tables, using drinking straws, tape, paper clips, rubber bands, Tinkertoys and other assorted small items).

Naming our knowing. Ask participants to share their feelings and thoughts about building the bridge.

Reflection on personal story and vision. Say to participants: "Build a bridge to your past. Tell about someone who has provided a bridge in your life—someone who has built you up or given you courage."

Christian community's story and vision. Read Ephesians 4:29. Ask campers to comment briefly on Paul's words about building each other up in faith according to need.

Dialogue—my story and the Story. Have participants build a bridge to the present. Ask, "What's happened in our group to build you up?"

Faith response. Have campers build a bridge to the future. Ask them to make a choice: "What would you choose to give our group this week to build people up? Or what do you want from our group to build you up this week?"

The Song of Your Heart

Focusing activity. Listen to the recording "It's Not a Song" by Amy Grant.

Naming our knowing and **Reflection on personal story and vision.** Ask participants to remember lines from their favorite songs that inspire or guide them. Then ask them to remember when they heard the songs first and how the songs have helped them. Encourage participants to relate their favorite songs to the lines in

"It's Not a Song."

Christian community's story and vision. Read selected Psalms that express a variety of feelings. Consider the psalmist's feelings in the following Psalms:

1. Psalms 19 and 29—Awe and wonder of nature

2. Psalm 34—Joy and fulfillment

3. Psalm 40—Rejoicing and singing out

4. Psalm 102—A troubled heart

5. Psalm 104—The wonder of creation

Dialogue—my story and the Story. Ask: "Can you relate some of the psalmist's feelings to your feelings? What connections do you see between the psalmist's 'songs' and the songs that are meaningful to you? Describe the similarities."

Faith response. Have participants write the "song of your heart" that expresses how they want to respond to God. Have them write the words to a tune they know or as a poem, prayer or declaration of faith. Encourage them to focus on expressing their faith, not on perfecting the words.

Questions for Discussion and Reflection

1. What are your experiences of worship? Use Camp Notebook 35, "Camp Worship" to discuss and reflect on the place of worship at camp.

2. Here's a training episode like those in Chapter 10 for camp leaders to use to process the Bible study approaches of Wink and Groome.

Action. Lead the camp staff in a biblical exploration, such as Diagram 33, "Exploring the Parable of the Sower (Mark 4:1-9)." If possible lead an exploration that correlates with the upcoming camp theme.

Reflection. Reflect on the steps used to develop the biblical exploration as they're explained in this chapter. As leader, be able clearly to outline the steps in-

Camp Notebook 35

Camp Worship

1. Begin your reflection by reading and discussing John 4:19-24. What does this passage say to you about worship?

2. Think about your own experiences of worship at camp. For each of the six elements of worship, write one way you've seen that worship element being interpreted creatively at camp.

Adoration/Praise: _____
_____

Confession: _____
_____

Affirmation: _____
_____

Intercession/Communion: _____
_____

Interpretation/Proclamation: _____
_____

Dedication: _____
_____

3. Which elements does your own worship tradition emphasize? Think of some ways to integrate your tradition into the camp experience.

volved and to share one or two other examples from either Wink or Groome.

Planning. Have Bibles, reference works, concordances, paper, pencils, and creative art supplies available. Divide the group of camp leaders into planning teams of three or four leaders to design their own Bible explorations for different times during camp (such as morning watch, morning Bible study or a campfire).

Be sure to give sufficient guidance to each group. As needed, help groups with the theme, scripture passages, supplies and resources. Tell planners that when they lead this biblical exploration during the training event, they'll need to talk through their purpose and outline in an open group discussion after the exploration experience.

Experimenting. Have each planning group lead its Bible exploration for the other leaders-in-training (not role-playing campers but involving other leaders as participants in the exploration to experience it as a group).

After the exploration, reflect on the experience. Here are some suggestions to guide the reflection:

1. Ask planning teams to share their outline and to comment on how they felt the Bible exploration went, changes they'd make if they were leading it again, how they might change it with campers of a specific age or things that happened that they hadn't planned on.

2. Ask participants to share how they experienced the exploration—its personal meaning, new awarenesses they developed and how they'd adapt it to their own leadership with campers.

3. As a total group, reflect and brainstorm ways to adapt the activity or optional directions that might become possible when used with campers.

Notes

[1]Robert McAfee Brown, *Creative Dislocation—The Movement of Grace* (Nashville, TN: Abingdon Press, 1980), pp. 108-109.

[2]Quoted in T.C. McLuhan, *Touch the Earth: A Self-Portrait of Indian Existence* (New York: Simon and Schuster, 1976), p. 36.

[3]Discussed in Walter Wink, *Transforming Bible Study: A Leader's Guide* (Nashville, TN: Abingdon, 1980) and Walter Wink, *The Bible in Human Transformation: Towards a New Paradigm for Biblical Study,* (Philadelphia, PA: Fortress Press, 1980).

[4]Adapted from Wink, *Transforming Bible Study: A Leader's Guide,* pp. 68-77.

[5]Thomas Groome, "Model C: Experience/Story/Vision," in D. Campbell Wyckoff and Henrietta T. Wilkinson (editors), *Beautiful Upon The Mountains: A Handbook for Church Education in Appalachia* (Memphis, TN: Board of Christian Education of the Cumberland Presbyterian Church, 1984), p. 108.

Part Four

Camp Programming Ideas

Chapter 14

Group-Building Activities

Campers find their own ways for being in the center of things or on the edge of things. Camp staffers who include campers through games and other group interactions with a friendly presence or warm word will eventually be entrusted with some campers' innermost feelings. Campers take risks when they feel secure. Besides, the activities are lots of fun!

There are several positive ways to help individuals and subgroups grow closer through activities that minimize interpersonal risks. Here are three types:

1. Activities that randomly incorporate campers in a common task, such as the "Camp Catalog Game" (this page) or games from the books *Playfair* or *New Games* (see resource listing, page 343).

2. Activities that put each camper in contact with every other camper and leader in the group, such as "Group Life Diagram" (page 242) and "Family Fact-Finding Mission" (page 241).

3. Activities designed to put campers in one-to-one relationships for brief times, such as "Secret Friends" (page 241) and "Care Cards" (page 244).

The following group experiences are designed specifically to help campers grow in their awareness and appreciation of other group members. Most require minimal preparation and materials, and each is adaptable to various camp settings.

Camp Catalog Game

Use this activity to help campers get acquainted and to form small groups.

Time. Five to 10 minutes.

Materials. Pages from camping equipment catalogs and scissors.

Directions. Cut out pages that have camping equipment photos on both sides. Cut each page diagonally to form two pieces. Make sure you have the same number of pieces as there are participants. (If there's an odd number of people, cut one page into three pieces.) Distribute one piece to each person.

Say: "Look at your piece of the page and decide which piece of equipment you'd most like to have and why. Then find the person in the group who has the other part of your page. Introduce yourself and tell why you chose the piece of equipment you chose. Then with your partner decide which single item on your two catalog pages you'd like to buy that's the best buy for the money. Be ready to tell two other people why you think it's the best buy."

Give five minutes for young people to find each other and talk. Then say: "Find another couple and sit down together in a tight circle. Introduce your partner and share in fours. Then as a group of four, consider all your catalog page pieces, and choose the one item most needed in a survival situation. Have someone from your group be ready to describe the item to the whole group."

If you want to form small groups of larger than four teenagers, have three or more pairs get together to introduce each other and share their decisions.

Family Fact-Finding Mission

Use this activity for young people who don't know each other to learn more about each other. You can also use it midway in an event to help campers rediscover each other. Participants will practice telling about themselves, learn to appreciate other group members and focus on each camper in a non-threatening way.

Time. Thirty to 40 minutes.

Materials. A pencil and piece of paper for each camper and counselor.

Directions. Sit in a circle. Distribute a pencil and piece of paper to each person. Go around the circle and have each group member call out his or her name while the others write it on their paper.

Say: "Now let's move about freely to give and receive facts from every person in the group. Tell something about yourself or your family back home. Learn as many facts as you can about each other. Next to each name write one fact about that person. Remember that as you give information about yourself you can't give the same fact twice. When you've gathered one fact from every group member, sit down in the circle again. Let's begin!"

When everyone is seated, have campers each share what they have written. Focus on one camper at a time, sharing all facts about him or her in succession. Then ask that person to add a new fact about

himself or herself.

Secret Friends

Use this activity to build community. Participants will learn to appreciate and pay attention to others, practice being confidential, and create a spirit of caring and giving.

Time. The entire event.

Materials. None.

Directions. Assign each leader and camper a secret friend. Invite campers to do something special for their secret friend every day of the camping event. (See the "Friendship Lanyard" activity for additional ideas.)

Say: "You may give gifts or ask someone else to help you arrange some special deed for your secret friend. Be creative. Don't let your secret friend know who you are. If you know who someone else's secret friend is, keep it confidential. At the end of camp we'll identify ourselves to our secret friends."

Friendship Lanyard

Use this creative activity in conjunction with the "Secret Friends" activity. Participants will create a special gift that expresses friendship and show appreciation for their secret friends.

Time. The entire event.

Materials. Thirty feet of variegated yarn per person; beads, shells, feathers and any symbolic articles that can be tied on; tape; and scissors.

Directions. Cut each strand of yarn into 10-foot lengths. Tape each set of three together. Give a set of yarn pieces to each person. Then have group members divide into pairs. Demonstrate and give the following directions on how to start a lanyard:

1. Hold one end of the three strands between your thumbs and forefingers while your partner does the same. Keep the

yarn stretched between you. Then each person twists to the right until there's a moderately tight twist.

2. One person in each pair should double the twisted yarn by grasping its middle and giving the end of the yarn to the partner. Then each partner holds the doubled yarn lightly in his or her hands and lets the yarn twist itself. Now pairs should have a six-strand lanyard, five feet long.

3. Secure the lanyard with a simple overhand knot four to five inches from the end of the loose ends. (Now the partners can make a second lanyard.)

When the pairs have finished, say: "The loose ends form a tassel that can be used to string beads or to tie on shells, feathers or other articles that help demonstrate friendship and your appreciation for your secret friend. At the end of camp you'll present your lanyard to your secret friend.

In a closing celebration or on the last day of camp, secret friends reveal themselves by hanging their lanyards around their friends' necks and offering words of appreciation: "John, we're bound together as friends; we're bound to God." "Laura, we're bound together . . ."

Rhythmic Speaking

Use this activity as a crowdbreaker warm-up to an exercise requiring concentration. It helps focus campers' attention and allows them to practice cooperation.

Time. Five to 8 minutes.

Materials. Bibles.

Directions. Divide into small groups and have each group huddle like a football team, with arms over each other's shoulders. Ask each team to pick a short Bible verse. Or select a single verse that links the group's focus with the camp theme.

Say: "Repeat the verse over and over with one person saying the first word, the next person saying the next word, and so on around the group. Try to make the verse flow as if a single person were saying it. Vary the cadence and inflection of your voices to gain different emphases as the verse goes around the circle."

Group Life Diagram

Use this activity on the last day of camp or staff training. Or use it as part of a celebration time. Participants will draw diagrams showing how the group has changed and reflect on their camping experience.

Time. Thirty to 60 minutes, depending on group size.

Materials. Pencils and blank pieces of paper.

Directions. Say, "Let's look at our time together up to this point by examining the differences and similarities in our experiences."

Distribute a sheet of paper and pencil to each person, and ask group members to write "first day" on one side and "last day" on the other side.

Next have campers sketch figures, symbols, words or ideas that show how the group's views, thoughts and feelings have changed from the first day until the last day of camp. Ask them to include themselves and different group members in their diagrams.

When young people are finished, have them volunteer to interpret their diagrams to the whole group. Hearing from various participants will reveal the common threads of the group experience as well as unique insights. The activity also will help campers see the different ways people have changed. And teenagers will be able to think about how they themselves have changed.

Group Journal

Use this activity throughout the camping event for campers to think about and communicate different aspects of their time spent together. The journaling provides a record of the camping event, and it stimulates personal expression and reflection.

Time. Five to 30 minutes after meals, while traveling, during free time or before bedtime.

Materials. A spiral notebook, a felt-tip pen and a brightly colored drawstring bag to protect the notebook from dampness.

Directions. Place the journal in a place that's accessible to all group members. Always keep the journal with the group. Explain to campers that the journal's purpose is to share and discover insights as they use their inner eyes and ears to interpret what's happening in the group.

Invite campers to write something every day in the journal about their camping experience and to read what others have communicated. Encourage free expression—poetry, quotations of other campers, fond memories, new friendships, philosophizing and recording of events.

No Questions Asked

This activity cultivates self-reliance, cooperation and sensitivity. You can also use it during outdoor skills-training sessions. Participants will become aware of their abilities to figure things out, act independently and focus on other people's needs.

Time. All day.

Materials. None.

Directions. After breakfast say: "Today's a no-questions-asked day. You're not allowed to ask a single question; this goes for counselors too. We'll go about our normal business today, but we can't ask any questions."

Then explain that each camper must figure out how to communicate without questions and how to obtain the information he or she needs without questioning. Then say: "All of us are in this together. So from now through dinner no questions! Any questions? Just kidding. Immediately after dinner we'll talk about what we learned. Then we can ask questions—if we need to."

Picture Framing

Use this activity to reflect on events throughout the day and build trust. Participants will reveal the most memorable part of the day and listen to each other's perceptions.

Time. Ten to 15 minutes plus two to 10 minutes per person during the sharing time.

Materials. None.

Directions. This activity should follow low-energy activities such as reading, singing or silence. Make sure group members are comfortably seated in a circle or lying in a circle with their heads together like the spokes of a wheel. Other ways to help the visualization process are to sit around a campfire, sit on a boat dock or lie on sleeping bags while staring at the sky during a moonlit night.

Say: "As we come to the end of the day, let's participate in a photographer's expedition. First make yourself comfortable with your hands by your side or in your lap. Then listen to the little sounds around you . . . Be aware of your body . . . your breathing . . . your tensions. Listen to the sounds far away from you . . . close to you. Can you hear your heart beat? Relax . . . just let everything be."

Then say: "Now let your mind take a photographic trip through today—from the time you woke up until right now. In your mind photograph all the day's events . . .

(long pause). Take a few more shots . . . Now pretend all the photographs of the day are lying before you. Select one to enlarge, frame and hang on your wall. Give yourself time. Look them over and pick one. Why did you choose that one? When you're ready, open your eyes."

Ask campers to describe their picture and tell why it's important to them. Then ask: "What do our pictures have in common? What picture would you like to have in your mind tomorrow night?"

Some campers will choose difficult experiences to photograph. As they tell about their picture without getting judgmental comments from others, the group members' trust level will deepen.

Close with a prayer of thanksgiving.

Care Cards

Use this activity to warm the atmosphere among campers. Participants will show their appreciation of one another and receive affirmation through note-giving.

Time. The entire event.

Materials. Several felt-tip markers, tape, a bunch of 3×5 cards, pencils and a 5×7 envelope for each person.

Directions. Find a blank wall that's accessible to everyone, and set a table nearby with the 3×5 cards and pencils on it. On the first morning of camp, distribute a 5×7 envelope to each person. Make available several felt-tip markers and tape. Ask each person to write his or her name across the back of the envelope. Then have campers tape their envelopes to the wall so others can drop their care cards in them.

Tell campers to use the 3×5 cards and pencils on the table to write messages of affirmation to different people every day. Encourage them to show their appreciation to at least one different person each day. Let campers peek in their care-card envelope after supper each day.

Swamp Ladder

Use this fun activity to teach kids how to climb trees safely without exerting a lot of energy. Participants will be able to increase their height temporarily to see further.

Time. 30 minutes.

Materials. A large tree with big limbs that are about 12 feet from the ground. Five sturdy poles that are two, four, six, eight and 10 feet long and three to four inches in diameter.

Directions. Lean the two-foot pole against the tree. Then lean the four-foot pole about one foot beside and above the two-foot pole. Continue in this way with the six-, eight- and 10-foot poles (see Diagram 34, "Swamp Ladder"). Make sure all poles are secure against the ground and the tree—not wobbly. Then have people take turns stepping up the poles while they hold on to the tree for balance. Place spotters to catch anyone who slips.

Diagram 34
Swamp Ladder

Morning in a Tree

This activity builds community as campers spend a morning in a tree together then talk about their experience.

Time. All morning.

Materials. A large tree with strong branches that reach out and can support all members of a group. The tree should be easy to climb so everyone can participate without embarrassment. You can use a swamp ladder (see previous activity) if you choose.

Directions. Prepare the campers the night before by saying: "We'll spend tomorrow morning in a tree. It'll be fun at first, but it might get a little uncomfortable before we come down for lunch. So be prepared. Decide what you want to take up the tree with you so you'll have it ready at the appointed time. It might rain. You might get hungry or thirsty. But we won't come down unless there's lightning or heavy wind."

Give the group precautions before leading campers up the tree the next morning. After you've come down and eaten lunch, examine the experience by asking: "What do you wish you'd taken up that you didn't take? Did you take anything you didn't use?"

Then ask: "What went through your mind while you were in the tree? Use examples from your interactions with other people in the tree as a parallel to living together as the body of Christ. What did you learn about yourself? Did you learn anything that could help you back home?"

Detaining Stone

Use this activity to teach kids how to make a unique "do not disturb" sign that will keep private and devotional times from being interrupted.

Time. Five minutes.

Materials. A softball-size round stone or river rock and a yard of bulky yarn.

Directions. Say: "It's easy during a busy camp to walk into a cabin or tent and suddenly realize you're interrupting a personal devotional time, private conversation or counseling time. A Japanese tradition has a remedy to this: It calls for a stone

wrapped with yarn with a bow tied at the top. The Japanese would place this 'detaining stone' in the walkway of their dwelling as a sign for visitors to come back later."

Then say: "We can do the same thing here—make a detaining stone for each cabin, tent or meeting place to protect groups' privacy. And we won't offend our unsuspecting friends." Demonstrate how to make a detaining stone, and encourage campers to make them for their cabins or tents.

Powwow Blanket

Use this activity as a ritual to gather kids' concentration. Participants will have a symbol that means it's time to listen.

Time. A few moments at the beginning of any meeting.

Materials. A large bedspread, blanket or canvas.

Directions. Campers usually respond well to a symbolic way of saying "Let's listen" or "Let's get serious." A powwow blanket eliminates the need to say, "Let's settle down and listen." During the first meal or first devotional time at your camp, show how to use the powwow blanket.

Say: "Whoever's leading a group initiates the time by spreading the powwow blanket on the floor or ground. Any group leader can use the blanket for cabin devotions, reflection times, special meals and to announce non-verbally that it's 'group time.'" Encourage campers to decorate the blanket with fringe, beads, hand-stitched designs, drawings and other items.

Breakfast in Bed

Use this activity to show servanthood to other group members. Participants will serve others a meal and show their appreciation.

Time. Forty-five minutes before breakfast.

Materials. Orange juice, cinnamon rolls, paper cups and napkins.

Directions. Keep this activity a secret to the campers. Arrange with the camp kitchen to make cinnamon rolls. Forty-five minutes before the normal wake-up time, you and the staff gather in the camp kitchen. Then split up and carry the rolls and orange juice to campers' cabins. Campers will get a big surprise. "Breakfast in Bed" can work the other way around too—have campers surprise counselors the same way!

Feather In Your Hat

This activity builds on a Native American tradition of gift-giving. It gives campers a chance to give each other symbolic gifts, and it facilitates community and appreciation among campers.

This activity is particularly meaningful to teenagers who have backpacked or canoed together. A gift of a sweaty bandanna, a dented Sierra cup or suspenders is priceless when it's given in the context of a group nearing the end of its journey. Your own variations to make it fit your group will add even more significance.

Time. Varies.

Materials. Used personal gifts.

Directions. Introduce this activity by saying: "Native Americans have a tradition of honoring each other by giving feathers on significant occasions. Each feather has two special stories. First is the story of how the feather was found or received. Second is the story of how the feather was given away.

"When they found a feather, they never kept it for themselves. Instead they treasured the feather until the right moment came to give it to the right person. Thus feathers given as gifts were much more valuable than feathers earned.

"So it is with all we possess. We have been given much of what we own. And even though we work for some things we own, the opportunity to work and the health and energy we have are gifts. God is the source of all we possess, and we live by God's gifts—God's grace."

Then ask: "What would you give this group out of love and appreciation? Think of two or three things you already have in your duffel bag or pack that you'd like to give to our group. What feather would you like to give someone as a memory of our life together?"

Asking campers to think of what they'd give to the whole group focuses on the camping community, not on an individual. Asking them to think of two or three things helps them sense what they're open to giving away. And the actual experience of giving to a specific person helps them choose the right gift.

As part of a closing celebration or a special place during camp, invite campers and counselors to bring their gifts. Once the group is together sitting in a circle, lead songs, readings or whatever ritual seems appropriate. Make it clear at the beginning that each person gives and receives only one gift.

Then invite the camper facing most directly west (or use your own method) to be first. Have that camper choose another camper to affirm and to tell the two stories of his or her gift—the story of where the gift comes from and the story of why he or she chose to give it away. Ritualize the point of giving away with a hug, group response or something that's particularly meaningful to your campers.

After the first gift is given, the recipient chooses the next person and continues the process until everyone has received a gift.

Chapter 15
Trust-Building Activities

Building trust in a camp staff or a group of campers is a fundamental goal of Christian camping. Letters from campers who feel camp has changed their whole value system are gratifying. The following excerpt from a staff evaluation by an 18-year-old kitchen assistant highlights the impact a trusting atmosphere at camp can have on campers and staff:

Being on staff this summer has shown me how to be a minister through duties such as cooking and dish-washing. Having time to get acquainted and to go hiking and canoeing together before we started our jobs helped us form a family group. The easiness everyone felt with each other from the start was a great beginning. I felt as if I had known these people for a long time!

I really appreciated and enjoyed the acceptance of everyone on staff. I have grown to accept myself more. This growing experience has come in a perfect place in my life, as I'm becoming more independent and really forming ideas about myself. I think being with older leaders helped me mature more fully into being a young adult rather than a teenager.

The activities in this chapter provide experiences where you can foster trust through play, discussion and shared problem-solving. The activities are designed to build on each other and may be used during a camp or training event in the sequence they appear. Or you can combine individual activities with others that seem more appropriate to your situation.

Stretching and Balancing

Use this physical activity to prepare for community-building activities.

Time. Twenty minutes.

Materials. None.

Directions. Have campers stand in a circle. (If your group is large, divide into groups of 10. Assign a counselor to lead each group.) Go at an easy pace and speak softly while giving the following directions (or others that seem more appropriate for your group):

1. "Let your hands drop loosely by your side. Breathe deeply."

2. "Bend from the waist and let your hands dangle just above your toes."

3. "Reach above your head and act like you're climbing in the air."

4. "Bend from the waist and touch your toes. Then repeat step #3. Do this several times."

5. "Spread your feet apart, put one hand on your waist and put the other hand on your ankle. Then go back and forth, switching places with your hands."

6. "Fold your arms over your chest. Close your eyes, drop your head and exhale."

7. "Spread your arms apart and rotate at the waist from right to left, then left to

right. Repeat several times."

8. "Spread your arms apart and stand on one foot."

9. "With arms spread apart and one foot in the air, close your eyes. If you lose your balance, open your eyes, check your surroundings and try again. Keep trying until you can stand there without losing your balance."

10. After the exercise, move on to other trust-building activities. Or have campers stand in a circle, and use a brief quotation or prayer of self-giving to make a transition to another activity.

Push, Pull, Lean and Fall

This activity illustrates harmony and partnership. Campers will learn how to balance their strength and energy with a partner.

Time. Thirty minutes.

Materials. None.

Directions. Have campers find a partner about their same height. Give the following directions to partners:

"Stand face-to-face and toe-to-toe. Relax, and put your hands palm-to-palm. Push gently . . . Still palm-to-palm, slowly move your hands up then down, continuing to push and relax. Don't push each other off balance. Just lead and follow each other.

"Now turn around and stand back-to-back. With your hands by your side, place them palm-to-palm with your partner. Push gently. Then raise your arms a few degrees and push again. Go up again until your arms are straight out. Then rotate your hands so they're back-to-back, and continue raising and pushing your arms until they're straight over your heads.

"Next, stand back-to-back, heel-to-heel. Fold your hands across your chest. Lean against each other's back until you're balanced. Move your feet forward a few inches, and lean back against each other

again. Keep each other balanced as you continue creeping forward as far as it's comfortable."

Continue the exercise by asking campers to sit on the ground face-to-face with their knees bent and their feet together. Then continue with these directions:

"Raise your toes to rest against your partner's toes. Clasp your hands, and pull each other until you can stand up. Experiment with pulling against each other so you don't overbalance each other but balance your strength and energy. Invent your own balancing techniques.

"When you're up, stand facing each other and lay your head on your partner's shoulder, neck-to-neck. Face outward. Move your feet backward until you balance each other."

Before moving to the next exercise, explain and demonstrate it. Emphasize safety and falling only as far as is comfortable. Say: "Choose one partner to be the faller and the other a spotter. The faller clasps his or her hands together in front of his or her chest and stands rigid. The faller should trust the spotter." Then explain the following rappelling signals to campers, and have them use the signals to prevent falling when the spotter isn't ready:

● Faller: "Spotter ready?"
● Spotter: "Ready."
● Faller: "Falling."
● Spotter: "Fall."

Then have campers call their parts in unison as they begin the exercise. The spotter stands in front of the faller and catches the faller as he or she leans forward. The spotter shouldn't wait too long to catch the faller—or catch the faller too soon. Then have everyone switch roles. Increase the trust level by increasing the distance between the spotters and fallers.

Another way to increase the level of trust is for the faller to clasp his or her hands as follows: "With your arms hanging straight down in front of you, cross your wrists and clasp your own fingers together palm-to-palm. Then raise your clasped hands straight up, rotating your wrists close to your chest where you let them rest. This method secures your hands so that the partner does the work and you do the trusting!"

One-Legged Balancing

These activities let campers practice working together to balance each other. The activities are very physical. Variations make it lively and entertaining. Each activity is illustrated in Diagram 35, "One-Legged Balancing."

Time. Five minutes each.

Materials. A tape player or record player and music.

Directions. Begin with stretching or relaxation exercises. Then have campers choose a partner who's about their own height. If you wish, play music during these activities. Then let campers try the following balancing activities:

1. One-legged dancing. Say: "Stand facing your partner. Put your left hand on your partner's right shoulder. Then raise your left foot and put it in your partner's right hand. Now hop around." Use music to turn the hopping into a dance!

2. Quad balance. Have each pair get together with another pair of about the same height. Have the four campers stand in a circle facing inward with their arms on each other's shoulders like a huddle. Then one person raises his or her right leg and places it on the right-hand neighbor's right thigh. That person then raises his or her right foot

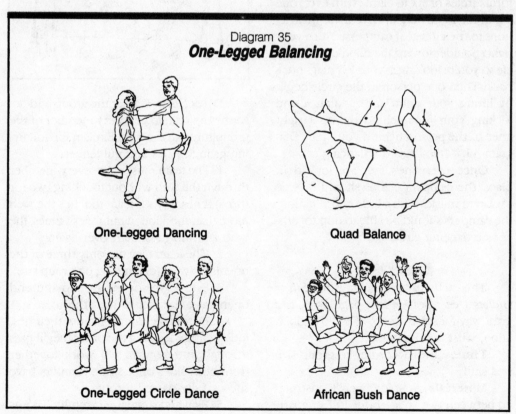

Diagram 35
One-Legged Balancing

One-Legged Dancing

Quad Balance

One-Legged Circle Dance

African Bush Dance

on the neighbor's right thigh until the circle is complete. Once everyone's in place, the circle will keep everyone balanced.

Sometimes it takes a while to get the hang of this activity. A demonstration beforehand helps. Often groups can make it easier by switching around to make the legs fit better.

3. One-legged circle dance. Form groups of eight campers in circles with everyone standing in a counterclockwise circle facing each other's backs. Say: "Put your left hand on the shoulder of the person in front of you. Then bend your right knee back to raise your right foot so the person behind you can grab your ankle." Have all the circles get coordinated, then have them hop around in a circle to the beat of the music."

4. African bush dance. Have campers form circles of six to eight, with everyone about the same height. Give these instructions to the circles of campers: "Turn your right shoulder toward the middle of the circle so you're looking at your left neighbor's back. Then one person in the circle begin by lifting your right leg, bending it and locking your foot behind the bent right knee of the person behind you." (See Diagram 35, "One-Legged Balancing.")

Once everyone's feet are locked in place, the campers' hands should be free to clap to music. With a little coordination, the campers should be able to hop together as a dancing circle.

Spider Web

This activity, originally from *Silver Bullets* (see resource list, page 343), is a great way for small groups to build cooperation, trust and community.

Time. Varies according to group size and skill.

Materials. A "spider web" constructed between two trees about 10 feet apart.

Use heavy waxed linen thread or nylon cord. Design the web so that it has at least 12 openings of various sizes that campers can pass through without touching (see Diagram 36, "Spider Web"). Hang a toy rubber spider on the web that will move if someone touches the web.

Diagram 36
Spider Web

Directions. Gather the group and describe the task: to get every member of the group through the web. Explain the following ground rules and guidelines:

1. The team must move every member through the web without touching two (or three) times. If your team touches the web more than the allotted number of times, the whole group must start over again.

2. The team may use only three of the openings twice (depending on group size).

3. The lower openings and the end openings are easier to pass through.

4. Encourage campers to use their best judgment in deciding the order they'll pass through and how they'll work together from both sides once some campers have successfully passed through.

5. Plan and strategize carefully. Take as

much time as needed to be successful.

6. No one may dive through the web. Diving can result in serious neck injury, cord burn and web destruction.

7. When campers are doing the activity, use adult spotters for safety.

8. Here's an optional rule: One or two group members must be mute. They cannot speak to the group except with sign language. Others may talk.

Hand In

Use this activity as a quick icebreaker when campers don't know each other.

Time. Two minutes.

Materials. None.

Directions. Divide into groups of eight. Have each group stand in a circle. Begin with the camper whose birthday is nearest to January 1. This person places his or her hand in the middle of the circle (palm down) and tells his or her name. Then the group repeats the name in unison. This process continues around the circle, with campers each placing a hand on top of the others as they tell their name.

Sharing Circle

Use this activity to develop group sharing in an easy progression. Teenagers will feel more comfortable with each other as they participate in this ritual.

Time. Varies.

Materials. A foot bag, small beanbag or small ball.

Directions. It's always easier to talk with something in your hands. The object you choose (a foot bag, small beanbag or small ball) will symbolize permission for a camper to talk. Anyone not holding the object may not talk. Say: "This object means it's my time to talk. I'll go first and then I might pass it to you. Then you may tell us about yourself. When you want to stop, pass the object to someone else." Start by

talking about your family, your friends and where you live.

You can also use this activity when campers have questions after you've explained an event or game. Once campers get accustomed to the special object that gives them permission to talk, it will take on great significance at camp.

Use the following two guidelines for initiating sharing:

1. If the subject is easy to talk about, pass the ball around the circle or let campers throw it to the next person who wants to speak.

2. If the subject is difficult or risky for some campers, ask them to raise their hand when they're ready to share. This procedure eliminates the need to say "I pass" or the feeling of being put on the spot.

Lineups

These activities are creative ways for groups of campers to work together to arrange themselves in a specific order. They're great warm-ups for games that require cooperation and teamwork.

Time. Twenty minutes.

Materials. Blindfolds.

Directions. Divide into appropriate team sizes for your group and the next activity. Then have the teams race to see which one can line up specific ways. Make the games crazier by blindfolding everyone. After the game ask the winning team if a leader emerged and how he or she coordinated the effort. Try the following ways:

1. From the shortest to the tallest.

2. From the youngest to the oldest. Since teenagers' birthdays are close together, they'll have to communicate clearly and quickly.

3. Birthday circle. Have campers line up in the order they were born during a calendar year. For example, a camper born on January 4 would precede one born on

March 12 and so forth.

4. Number line. Before the activity, count the number of people in the group and write numbers on pieces of paper for each participant. If, for example, there are 12 people, take 12 pieces of paper and write a different number from 1 to 12 on each piece. Then give each camper a piece of paper and a blindfold. After participants look at their number, have them each put on a blindfold. Then the race is on to line up in sequence. The catch: no talking. If you have a large group, divide into teams of 12 or 15. Trying to complete the activity with more than 15 takes too long.

When it sounds like campers have stopped moving, ask if everyone is ready. Then let participants take off their blindfolds. Time the group and repeat the activity to try to break the record.

Sensory Meal

Use this activity to stimulate awareness of the senses while eating a healthy meal.

Time. Forty minutes.

Materials. Finger foods, including a variety of textures, aromas and tastes—oranges, grapes, peanuts, celery, crackers, peanut butter, freshly baked bread and boiled eggs.

Directions. Pack the finger foods and find a place to have a picnic. Ask the group to sit, be comfortable and stay silent for the first 15 minutes of the meal. Use a quotation or focusing thoughts to center the group. Invite campers to eat slowly while touching, smelling and tasting each bite. Say, "Be aware of anything out of the ordinary you experience so we can talk about it after we're finished eating." You may want to save one item as a dessert to eat as you talk together.

Don't announce when 15 minutes have passed; let the conversation begin from the group. And don't try to guide the discussion until you believe everyone has finished with the meal. When you're ready to begin the discussion, pass around your dessert and ask: "What kinds of awareness did you have as a result of focusing on food and silence? Were you more aware of your sense of touch, smell, taste or hearing? Explain. What new awareness did you have during the meal? Explain."

Web of Life

Use this activity to help kids discover ecological relationships within nature. They'll create a visual diagram for understanding relationships among plants and animals. Some camps use this activity as an introduction to basic ecology.

Time. Forty-five minutes.

Materials. A ball of yarn and peel-off labels.

Directions. On labels write the name of an insect, reptile, bird, mammal, amphibian, fish or plant. Invite campers to sit in a tight circle, and give each participant one of the labels that they can use as a name tag.

Give one camper a ball of yarn, and ask him or her to wrap the end around a finger. Then he or she must toss the ball of yarn to someone his or her creature relates to. For example, a raccoon may consume crawfish, bird eggs and blackberries. When that person receives the ball, he or she holds onto the yarn and tosses it to someone his or her creature relates to. One person may receive the yarn several times. A plant, for example, may be a producer for several consuming birds, animals and insects.

The process continues until the yarn makes a beautiful web in the circle center that illustrates the natural community and how it all works together. Then have campers discuss the interrelationships of different parts of nature. Use the producer-consumer-decomposer cycle to help campers understand ecological relationships. (See resource listing, page 343, for books about nature's ecological relationships.)

Death is also an important part of nature's economy. After the initial discussion, have one camper let go of his or her yarn, then another camper. Campers easily see what happens to the web of life when members are threatened or made extinct.

Here's a variation on "Web of Life" that you can use to help campers familiarize themselves with other campers' names:

Ask teenagers to sit in a tight circle. Be-

gin the activity by wrapping the end of the yarn around your finger. Toss the ball of yarn to someone and say his or her name. Ask the camper to hold onto the yarn also while he or she throws the ball of yarn to someone else and says his or her name. The object is to build a web without forgetting a name.

You also can use this activity at the end of camp as a closing celebration: Each person gives a statement of appreciation or affirmation and then tosses the ball of yarn. The web symbolizes the bonds built during camp.

Chapter 16

Nature Awareness Activities

Being aware of nature and at ease outdoors doesn't happen quickly—not in a week of camp, much less in a day or in one nature awareness activity. However, you can foster the process of being "at home" outdoors through continued nature awareness activities that focus campers' attention on the world around them. Hopefully unplanned, natural happenings will occur along the way that give meaning to the contrived or structured activities.

I remember a late afternoon on the edge of the Bridger-Teton National Forest east of Pinedale, Wyoming. After a long day of rock-climbing practice, our young people were taking it easy after supper. Just below camp we heard a ruffed grouse. A few of us went to investigate. Soon we located the fowl in a small stand of alders. To our surprise, it didn't fly away but continued to beat its chest with wing motions so rapid you could only see a blur of feathers. Every camper got close enough to look, and we even ran back to camp for the camera and telephoto lens.

Later that same evening as the sun laid its last glow on the high meadows, our group snuggled like puppies in the shadow of another clump of alders further down the creek. A lone cow elk broke out of the timber 200 yards beyond our mead-

ow. Then another and another and another. Finally, 53 elk of all sizes grazed together as their calves scampered from cow to cow. No one spoke as we silently passed binoculars from camper to camper. (You want to shout with joy when nature teaches its lessons, but you seldom do.) Then, as quickly as they came, the elk took to the timber again and were gone.

In all my years of camping, I'd never experienced these two events before. But there have been other surprises just as wonderful. So I continue to play nature awareness games and to talk about nature—waiting for the natural, transforming moment to arrive to make me and campers really aware of nature.

Here are a few nature awareness activities that are easy to use. Perhaps they'll help you invent some variations of your own.

Nature IQ Test

Use this activity to help campers get acquainted. Participants will test their concentration and memory skills. (This icebreaker works especially well while kids are waiting in line to check in to camp.)

Time. Ten minutes.

Materials. For each pair of campers: two 8½ ×11 inch pieces of cardboard and two sets of the same nine objects, such as peanuts, walnuts, acorns, pine needles, pine cones, rocks, leaves, sticks and feathers.

Directions. Draw a grid that has nine sections on each piece of cardboard. Divide the group into pairs, and distribute two pieces of cardboard and two sets of the same nine objects to each couple. Have one partner place an object in each section without the other partner seeing. Then let the other partner view the grid for 10 seconds and then try to duplicate the arrangement with his or her own cardboard piece and set of objects. Have partners switch roles.

Sense of Wonder

Use this activity to challenge teenagers' creativity. Participants will focus on their deep feelings during a time of solitude and later tell the group about their experience.

Time. One hour.

Materials. 3×5 cards and pencils.

Directions. Give each person a 3×5 card and pencil. (Variations of this activity are to use clay or watercolors.) Ask campers each to choose an isolated spot along a trail. Invite them to find a comfortable place away from everyone else so they can look, listen, rest and get in touch with their surroundings.

Say, "After you've settled down and thought for a while, disclose the wonder you're sensing by writing a poem, verse, song, letter or any other creative expression." Have participants return when they see you standing in a certain place (don't whistle or yell).

As people return, have them take off their shoes and sit in a tight circle. Ask campers if they'd like to read and explain what they've written. Then ask: "What's God saying to us today through our experiences? How is this experience together

like Moses taking off his shoes in front of the burning bush?" Affirm all answers. Don't push for a lengthy discussion.

If you're near a stream, invite group members to wade in and wash their feet.

The Wilderness Is a Sanctuary

Use this activity to sharpen young people's awareness of nature. Participants will use the thought you give them at the beginning of the day as a reference throughout the day.

Time. Five minutes to explain in the morning and 30 minutes in the evening for the sharing time.

Materials. Sunflower seeds.

Directions. After breakfast, give sunflower seeds to everyone. Say: "Now I'd like to give you a spiritual seed to hold in your mind and heart. It's this: 'The wilderness is a sanctuary.' Think about it throughout the day. Let it guide the way you see everything around you. Let it give you energy."

After supper ask: "Were you aware today of our spiritual seed—'The wilderness is a sanctuary'? What thoughts or feelings did your spiritual seed sprout in you?"

Use other spiritual seeds on subsequent days: Psalms, Proverbs, other Bible passages or poetry.

Listening Pictures

This activity tests campers' knowledge of small insects. Campers will have fun finding and describing their small creatures to others who can't see them.

Time. Forty-five minutes.

Materials. Cups, magnifying glasses, blank paper and charcoal.

Directions. Divide into trios. Give a cup, magnifying glass, paper and charcoal to each trio. Ask one person in each trio to find a tiny creature under leaves or along the edge of a stream or lake. The smaller the better. Say: "After you find your little critter, put it into the cup. Don't let the other two people see it. Using the magnifying glass, describe it without telling what it is. The other two people should sketch it with charcoal. Then see how accurately they sketched it. Change roles until everyone has had a turn finding a creature and describing it."

A variation is to use larger objects that require no magnification. Partners sit back to back while one partner describes and the other sketches.

Color Hike

Use this activity to explore the variety and beauty of nature's colors. Working with a small group is best.

Time. Forty-five minutes.

Materials. Different colors (preferably pastels) of construction paper.

Directions. Give a small piece of construction paper to each camper. Make sure everyone has a different color. Have young people each search the woods, fields or meadows until they find something that's as near to the color of their paper as possible. When they find it they should return to you but leave the discovery undisturbed. When everyone comes back, as a group go to each discovery and look at it together.

True North

Use this practical activity to sharpen kids' sense of direction. It's a fun break to take periodically while on hikes.

Time. Fifteen minutes.

Materials. Sticks and a compass.

Directions. Ask campers each to take a stick and point it to where they think true north is (they can't consult a map or compass). After they lay down their sticks, use a compass and allow for declination to locate true north. This game can be played over and over without losing its appeal.

Add some of your own hints on how

to find your way over the terrain. Or tell stories of how the old-timers did it. For example, frontier cooks always turned the tongue of their chuck wagons toward the North Star at night so the drivers would have bearings the next day if it was foggy or cloudy.

Animal Map

Use this activity to examine and discover animal habits. Campers will have a good time "tracking" an animal.

Time. Forty-five minutes per person.

Materials. Binoculars, a watch, a large rolled-up sheet of newsprint and a pencil.

Directions. Ask: "Have you ever wondered what kind of road map an animal leaves behind? Today we'll take turns tracking an animal." As a group choose an animal to observe such as a horse, cow, dog, cat, duck, squirrel, deer, turtle, snake or even a person. Each camper takes a 45-minute shift to draw the animal's travel on the same piece of newsprint designated as the "Animal Map." The camper should also record any interesting activity. It also helps to write how long the animal spent at each point on the map.

Discussing the map at the end of the day leads to many unique questions and insights into the animal's habits.

Talking Across the Water

Use this water activity as an unusual means of conversation and to stimulate communication.

Time. One hour.

Materials. None.

Directions. Henry David Thoreau wrote in *Walden* about the luxury of talking to a friend across the waters of Walden Pond. Your campers can experience the same "luxury."

Find a creek, river, pond or lake inlet and invite campers to each pair up with a friend. One partner stays on one side of the body of water while the other goes to the other side. Pairs should spread out so they're out of earshot of the other pairs. Then they can talk about anything for 20 minutes.

Gather back together and ask: "How loud did you have to talk to be heard? How quietly could you talk and still be heard clearly? How was talking across the water different from normal conversation? Was Thoreau right?" You can also split the group and have a group conversation across the water.

Balloon Voyages

Use this activity to relax on a lake and talk about life on the water.

Time. Ninety minutes.

Materials. Boats or rafts, life jackets and paddles.

Directions. Take boats or rafts, life jackets and paddles to a lake with clear water. Read Mark Twain's description of balloon voyages from his book *Roughing It*.[1] He writes about a special boat exercise he and his friends took each day while camping at Lake Tahoe. Use Twain's description as directions for this activity:

We usually pushed out a hundred yards or so from shore, and then lay down on the thwarts, in the sun, and let the boat drift by the hour whither it would. We seldom talked. It interrupted the Sabbath stillness, and marred the dreams the luxurious rest and indolence brought. The shore all along was indented with deep, curved bays and coves, bordered by narrow sand beaches; and where the sand ended, the steep mountainsides rose right up aloft into space—rose up like a vast wall a little out of the perpendicular, and thickly wooded with tall pines.

So singularly clear was the water that when it was only twenty or thirty feet deep the bottom was so perfectly distinct that the boat seemed floating in the air! Yes, where it was even eighty feet deep. Every little pebble was distinct, every speckled trout, every hand's-breadth of sand. Often as we lay on our faces, a granite boulder, as large as a village church, would start out of the bottom apparently, and seem climbing up rapidly to the surface, till presently it threatened to touch our faces, and we could not resist the impulse to seize an oar and avert the danger. But the boat would float on, and the boulder descend again, and then we could see that when we had been exactly above it, it must still have been twenty or thirty feet below the surface. Down through the transparency of these great depths, the water was not merely transparent, but dazzlingly, brilliantly so. All objects seen through it had a bright, strong vividness, not only of outline, but of every minute detail, which they would not have had when seen simply through the same depth of atmosphere. So empty and airy did all spaces seem below us, and so strong was the sense of floating high aloft in mid-nothingness, that we called these boat excursions "balloon voyages."

After groups have taken their balloon voyages, have them pull their boats or rafts together and explain what they saw and the sensations they felt. Then have them all lay back and discuss the different cloud formations they see.

Night Hike

Use this activity to explore nature at night in the country surrounding camp. Kids will observe what's around them, listen to the night sounds, learn about the stars and have a time of thanksgiving.

Time. Two hours.

Materials. Flashlights for leaders, a star guidebook, snacks, drinks and ponchos for everyone.

Directions. Select an area along a trail or old roadbed that provides overlooks, a view overlooking water if possible and open views of the sky. Familiarize yourself with the trail during the day. Ask participants to wear comfortable clothing and bring a poncho. Ask a naturalist to come along to help identify night sounds. Pack snacks and drinks to give as a surprise.

Begin the first 45 minutes of the hike as a time for talking, joking, standing around in the dark and answering questions to help the group have fun as everyone's eyes get adjusted to the dark. Encourage inquisitiveness and delight in the mystery of the night. Consult a star guidebook to identify some stars.

Ask everyone to whisper or be silent during the last 200 yards of the hike. Mention that it's amazing how much you can see once your eyes adjust to the dark. Ask if someone can explain the process of how rods and cones in the eye adjust to darkness.

As you walk together stop periodically, wait and listen for night creatures. See whether kids can identify sounds—owls hooting, ducks feeding, coyotes howling, foxes barking, bats squeaking or ranch animals calling. Sometimes you can see animals and birds at night if you move quietly, stopping at the edges of fields, marshes and water sources.

In an open space have kids spread out their ponchos and lie on their backs with their heads together, like spokes in a wheel. Watch for shooting stars.

Identifying stars and animals accurately isn't as important as enjoying the sense of discovery and adventure and participating in the group's spontaneous conversation.

Before you start back to camp, have a time of prayer and thanksgiving.

Viewing Party

Use this nighttime activity to sharpen campers' sense of smell and taste. It's especially effective during the spring when flowers are blooming or during late summer and fall when fields are full of newly cut hay. (You may want to combine it with the "Night Hike.")

Time. Twenty minutes.

Materials. Flashlights for leaders, individual communion cups, a small bottle of apple juice and a small tray.

Directions. Place enough communion cups on a tray for everyone (plus a few extra in case some are dropped or spilled). Fill each cup about half full of apple juice.

Following a relaxed time of watching stars, listening to night sounds and talking with each other, invite the group to get comfortable and be quiet. Give each person a cup of juice. A small taste of it is more effective than a large amount, because it focuses the sense of smell better. In the night air the group may be able to smell the juice as it's passed around. Ask campers to remain silent after they get their juice. Ask them to enjoy the aroma of the juice before tasting it.

Say, "Be aware of how many other senses are heightened as a result of smelling and tasting the apple juice." After a period of silence invite the group to talk about the experience. Close with a scripture, prayer, time of thanksgiving or reflection.

Stalking Circle

Use this fun activity to practice self-control. Do this activity just before lunch.

Time. Thirty minutes.

Materials. None.

Directions. Have group members spread out in a circle while you stand in the middle. The object is for everyone to creep up and touch you (the animal) without you seeing any movement. When campers see that the "animal" isn't looking, they sneak toward the center. If you point at moving stalkers, they must start over from where they started.

When all group members have touched you without you seeing them move, it's time for lunch. Note: Sometimes you must be lenient (or go hungry).

Thread Circle

Use this activity to develop patience while learning more about nature.

Time. Ninety minutes.

Materials. A spool of fine thread.

Directions. Have each person pick a comfortable place at the base of a tree near a game trail or likely spot for seeing wildlife. Campers should be out of sight of each other and downwind of the game trail so animals can't smell them and run. Have counselors tie each camper to his or her tree with the fine thread.

The object is for campers to remain still and quiet for one hour without breaking the thread. After an hour have counselors contact the kids and bring them back to the rest of the group.

During one "Thread Circle," a junior high girl who was deathly afraid of snakes had a snake crawl near her. But the thread helped her keep cool, and she's no longer afraid of snakes.

Spider Web Tour

Use this activity to promote trust, self-confidence and sensitivity to nature.

Time. One hour.

Materials. A blindfold for everyone and several spools of thread.

Directions. Choose a 50-yard-long trail. The trail can have a sunlit part, shady part, open area and dense area. It can go over logs, around boulders, under tree limbs and near water. String a piece of thread along the trail. End the tour at a spot where everyone can comfortably sit in a circle.

Explain: "In a few moments the counselors and I will blindfold you and lead you to a strand of a spider web. You must follow the strand and be careful not to break it because others will follow. Don't rush. If you bump into someone, pause and wait until he or she moves on. Follow carefully.

Be aware of what you touch, hear and smell. There are no tricks or scary parts. Just trust the string to lead you to the destination. When you're there we'll take off your blindfold." Give the group direction to provide security and to set the stage for discovery.

Use clean blindfolds that block out as much light as possible. Start campers at intervals to keep them from running into each other. When all have completed the tour, process their experience with questions such as "What were you aware of as you followed the spider web? Describe how trust played a part in what you experienced. How would you describe your own sense of trust? What was mysterious to you? What would you like to go back and see with your eyes open?"

Take the group back on the route to see the things they felt were mysterious.

Bark Weavings

This craft activity elicits campers' creative expression and concentration.

Time. Varies.

Materials. Large blocks of bark, scissors, small nails, assorted yarns and strings.

Directions. Most camps with fireplaces have wood piles with lots of tree bark that's fallen off the logs. Here's how it works:

1. On a piece of sturdy bark (pine, fir, poplar, oak and hickory work well), nail two rows of nails six to eight inches apart. Each row should be four inches long with nails about half an inch apart.

2. Once nails are secure, string a single fine-cotton string up and down until you form the warp (lengthwise threads to weave between). Secure, tie and cut off the string ends. Make the cross-weavings from fine bark shreds, grasses, pine needles, yarn, animal fur, feathers and shedding plants. Insert the materials over and under

the strings until they protrude from both sides.

3. After every few layers, use an old comb to pack them tight by pulling them toward one end. The completed weaving can be used as a wall hanging or desk art piece.

Caution campers not to put living flowers in a weaving. Picking wildflowers not only destroys a temporary natural beauty for other campers, but it removes the seeds from their natural home and soon destroys the flowers completely.

Shadow-Tracing

Use this activity to trace shadows using the sun as the light source. Campers will look at natural objects and other things around camp with a different perspective.

Time. One hour.

Materials. Newsprint, cardboard, charcoal and pencils.

Directions. Give a sheet of newsprint and a piece of cardboard to each person. Teenagers can draw either with charcoal or pencils. Say: "Find a shadow that appeals to you. Then place your newsprint (with the cardboard underneath) so the shadow falls on it, and trace the shadow with charcoal or a pencil. Before or after lunch is a good time because the sun is high and shadows are straight down."

Natural configurations of plants such as ferns, flowers and weeds are everywhere in the height of summer. Objects around camp work well too, such as cross-country skis, fishing tackle and tennis shoes.

Display large tracings in a prominent place. Include the smaller tracings in the camp journal or in a camp newsletter.

Rubbing Collage

Use this activity to create a close-up impression of the natural world.

Time. Forty-five minutes.

Materials. Rice paper, crayons, charcoal and pencils.

Directions. Give each person rice paper, and make available crayons, charcoal and pencils. Ask campers to find something with which to make a rubbing. They may choose an object such as tree bark, backs of leaves, grass, a shell of a turtle, a rock formation, a deer antler or a nutshell. Campers can make individual collages, or they can combine them in a big group collage.

Notes

[1]Mark Twain, *Roughing It*, (New York: New American Library, 1960), p. 138.

Chapter 17

Games and Fun Times

Good camp games are comfortable games—games we know and games we learn quickly. Inventing, improvising and adapting games are basic to the spirit of play. It's important, therefore, that staffers and campers catch the spirit of play that says, "There are many ways to play a game—not just a right way and a wrong way."

To draw kids into play, think through your first "inviting" words. How you invite kids to play sets the tone for the game. Here are some differences to consider:

● Use directions, not questions— "Everyone form a big circle," not "How many people have played . . . ?"

● Use imagination—"Lie down in the weeds like this, and imagine you're a tiny bug," not "How many know how to play 'Ants Eye View'?"

● Use invitations—"Let me invite you to find someone about as tall as you are, either boy or girl," not "I want all the short people over here and all the tall ones over here."

● And above all include campers in leadership—"I need two campers to help me plan and lead games tomorrow morning. Come tell me if you're interested right after the next song."

Here are some games you can use at your camp. Have fun!

How Many Ways?

Use this activity as a spontaneous game that will keep kids laughing and will stretch their creativity.

Time. Twenty minutes.

Materials. None.

Directions. Get the group together in a circle. Say: "Let's all walk in one big circle . . . Now mill around . . . Now walk like you're on a railroad track . . . in an airport and late for a plane . . . in a cow pasture . . . on ice . . . on hot coals . . . Now you name some ways to walk." Let campers call out different ways to walk, then have the group do each.

Then move to other variations. Say: "Now for 45 seconds we're going to see how many ways we can make three-point contact with the ground (so that three parts of our bodies touch the ground at once). Keep count. Ready, set, go!"

Another variation: "Now let's see how many ways we can talk. Get with two other people. First talk like you're from New York . . . Georgia . . . Chicago . . . Texas . . . New Jersey . . . Australia . . . Now you name some places."

Finally: "How many ways can you make four-point contact with another person? Find a partner. You have one minute! Keep count of the ways you discover. Ready, set, go!" After a minute find out who did the most. Have that pair demonstrate all those ways to the whole group.

Circle Soccer

Use this activity to encourage teamwork and self-control. Campers who've never played soccer often excel at "Circle Soccer" because it requires minimal energy but high concentration and deliberation.

Time. Thirty to 60 minutes.

Materials. Soccer ball.

Directions. Divide the group into two teams. Have the whole group form one large circle, with one team on one side of the circle and the other team on the other side. Campers should stand an arm's length apart.

Begin by saying: "This game requires teamwork and control of the ball. Stay alert and keep an eye on the ball. Always kick the ball at ground level for safety. Protect yourselves if someone kicks the ball too high." Demonstrate that long-range kicking is a disadvantage. Then place the ball in the circle, and let each team practice controlling the ball and kicking it back and forth.

Draw a line through the middle of the circle so that the line divides the teams. Have each team assign a center player who stands in the middle of the circle behind the line. He or she is the only team member who can score goals. The center player scores a goal by kicking the ball between any two members of the opposing team.

Team members work together to set up the ball for the center player to score. Everyone participates in the ball-control strategy. Team members may block the ball and set it up with their feet or knees for their center player to kick. Hands aren't allowed except to place the ball in the cen-

ter to resume play.

When a team scores a goal, both center players trade places with two other team players.

Meltdown Relay

Use this cool activity on a hot day. Have everyone dress in bathing suits and tennis shoes.

Time. Thirty to 45 minutes.

Materials. Same size blocks of ice for each team.

Directions. Freeze water in milk cartons or milk jugs for however many teams you choose to form. Divide into teams, and give each team a block of ice. Teams race to see who can completely melt the ice block first. Teams can use only their body heat to melt the ice. The ice can't touch the ground, and teams can't use water. Just imagine all the ways to speed the melting process!

Here's another ice activity: If you're near an old-fashioned ice plant, stage an ice-sculpture contest. Give each team one or two sculpturing tools (spoon, dull table knife or screwdriver). Set a time limit. Have a panel of volunteers judge the sculptures and present prizes.

Running Water Relay

Use this wet activity to teach cooperation.

Time. Thirty minutes.

Materials. For each team, a one-gallon container (such as a milk or bleach jug) with nail-size holes and two four-ounce cups.

Directions. Divide into however many teams you want, and have everyone stand 50 to 100 feet away from a water source such as a stream, lake or ocean. Give each team a one-gallon container with nail-size holes in it and two four-ounce cups. Make sure the containers are the same size and have the same number of holes.

Here's how the game works: One or two players on each team run with the cups to the water source and bring water back to pour into the hole-filled jug. Teammates must work together to keep the holes plugged with their finger tips (or whatever). Group members can switch roles or figure out more efficient ways to fill the container while the game is in progress. The first team to fill its container with water wins.

If you have extra-large teams, use discarded 55-gallon drums as containers and 5-gallon buckets to haul water.

Other variations are endless. Haul water in a canoe, swim with capped water bottles, have cyclists carry water in open or closed containers and so on.

Boot Shuffle

Use this wild mixer for campers to have a great time laughing and joking together.

Time. Twenty minutes.

Materials. Campers wear their hiking boots or shoes.

Directions. Have campers pile their boots or shoes in a heap in the middle of the room or field. Say: "Pick two shoes and put them on. They must not match, and they can't be your own. Stick your toes in them if they're too small. When you have both shoes on, shuffle around and find whoever has a matching shoe. Then hook ankles so the matching shoes are side-by-side. Put your arms around each other's waist to keep from falling. When you hook up with someone, chant 'Shoes! Shoes! Shuffle your shoes!' Remember: Two other people are looking for you too."

Pretty soon a line will form and everyone will be marching forward, with ankles hooked and arms around each other.

Coconut Tag

This energetic variation of hide-and-seek inspires teamwork in campers and releases lots of energy. The game illustrates the possibilities for creating your own games; my son, Hoke, invented it when he was five, and youth groups have perfected it. It's also a reminder that adult planners aren't the only ones who can invent games.

Time. Twenty to 30 minutes.

Materials. None.

Directions. Choose "seekers" (have two or three in large groups) in your group. Then have everyone else hide within designated boundaries while the seekers close their eyes.

When everyone has hidden, seekers then hunt "hiders." When they find someone, they chase the hider, tag him or her and yell, "Coconut Tag!" When tagged, a hider becomes a seeker and must tag someone else before returning to home. No one can get "home free" without being tagged and then tagging someone else. All players are chased till tagged, then they chase, tag and return home. If chasers need rest, they can return home and tag someone who's reached home who then goes chasing.

By using a confined hiding area, several people may run simultaneously—without anyone knowing exactly who's chasing and who's fleeing. Several seekers can chase one hider. The strategy is to gang up on those elusive, fleet-footed runners.

Spud

Use this activity as a different way of playing dodge ball.

Time. Thirty minutes.

Materials. Plastic or rubber ball.

Directions. Have the group stand in a circle and number off. Designate one person as "It." It throws the ball into the air and yells another camper's number. Group members run as far as they can before the camper whose number is called catches the ball and yells "Spud!"

Then the camper can take three long steps toward anyone and throw the ball to hit that person. A hit means the new person is It and must throw the ball up and call a number. A miss means the camper must throw the ball up again and call a number.

Circle Jump Rope

This variation of jump rope includes your whole group in a fun game that builds cooperation.

Time. Just a few minutes.

Materials. A medium-size, 20-foot-long rope.

Directions. Have campers stand in a circle facing the center. Put one person in the middle. He or she swings the rope low to the ground around the circle so that the other campers have to jump over it. Each person jumps the rope with turns getting faster and faster.

It takes a few turns for everyone to get the hang of jumping and for the rope swinger to be able to turn around as he or she swings the rope.

Line Jump

This variation of jump rope builds teamwork in campers.

Time. Fifteen minutes.

Materials. A long, heavyweight rope.

Directions. Have the group line up along a rope that someone holds at each end. Then the end people swing the rope back and forth (not over the heads) and the lined-up campers try to jump it simultaneously. They jump back and forth as many times as they can without missing.

In longer lines adjust the swinging rope so that its entire length is low enough for everyone in the group to jump.

Once campers "get the swing" of jumping together, try variations with everyone holding hands, holding shoulders or facing various directions. Or have campers individually call out particular jumps to try out their ideas for improving their teamwork.

Square Tug Standoff

Use this activity for a strenuous, fun variation of tug of war.

Time. Thirty to 45 minutes.

Materials. A long, strong rope with the ends securely tied together.

Directions. Draw a large plus sign (+) on the ground or floor to be the game boundary lines. Lay the rope around the plus.

Divide into four teams. Assign each team a section of the rope. Each team pulls the rope simultaneously until one team pulls another team across a boundary line.

The losing team gets one member from the team opposite it, thus increasing the losing team's strength for the next round. As the game continues this way, teams will become evenly matched and a standoff in equal strength will occur.

Give everyone blue ribbons. The sense of accomplishment and cooperation is exhaustingly wonderful. Presenting everyone with a blue ribbon magnifies the sense of community and achievement.

Quick-Change Artist

This unusual relay lets campers discover how fast they can dress and undress.

Time. Twenty minutes.

Materials. For each team, a large sleeping bag, large pair of shorts and extra-large T-shirt.

Directions. Have all the campers wear bathing suits. Divide into teams (as many as you need), and have each team line up single file at the starting line. Put a sleeping bag for each team 80 feet from the starting line. Give the first member of each team a large pair of shorts and an extra-large T-shirt.

On "go," the first person in each line runs to the sleeping bag, gets inside, zips it up and puts on the clothes over the bathing suit. Then he or she unzips the bag, runs to the next teammate and takes off the clothes. Then that next person repeats the process. The team that finishes first wins.

As a variation you could gather clothing and gear for a particular camping venture for campers to put on in the sleeping bag.

Clock Race

This activity challenges teams' ability to organize themselves and to work together.

Time. Thirty minutes.

Materials. None.

Directions. Divide into teams. Say: "I'll call out a time and your team must enact the correct time. The fastest team on the most times out of 12 wins. Assign some people to be the big hand of the clock and others to be the small hand. Having a pivot person makes it easier."

Don't give any instructions on how to move—let teams invent their own ways. First call out easy times (3:00, 9:00) then more difficult times (2:25, 10:40).

A variation is a compass race in which teams point in a particular direction. Use instructions similar to the "Clock Race." Teams don't need a pivot person. Each team should designate one person as the "magnetic end" that points in the direction called. Designate directions in the room or playing area (north, south, east, west). Start with simple directions, then move to more complicated ones (southwest, northeast).

Heavy Canoe Race

Use this activity to see who can trans-

port the heaviest canoe without spilling.

Time. Forty-five minutes.

Materials. Several canoes, paddles and life jackets.

Directions. Have several canoes tied to a dock. Distribute life jackets, and have campers pile in the canoes. Each canoe should be loaded to the point where it's almost submerged but not taking water. Assign a counselor to each canoe to help. Give paddles to the canoeists once they're loaded and ready to paddle. Have teams paddle 100 feet or so and then paddle back to the starting point. Tell teams that the object isn't to go fast but to stay afloat.

You may want to have a "weigh-in" in which campers weigh themselves on bathroom scales. Most canoes have a weight capacity stamped inside—usually from 800 to 1,200 pounds. Begin at this weight and move up. Establish a camp weight record for teams to try to break.

Rescue Relay

Use this activity as an introduction to a course on first aid and rescue. Asking teams to use their best judgment is one way to develop campers' knowledge and skills.

Time. One hour.

Materials. Paper, a canoe for each team, paddles, life jackets, splints, backboards or old doors, old sheets and old clothing.

Directions. Cut the old sheets and clothing into bandages. Divide into teams of 10. Seven members of each team are the "injured" and three are the "rescuers." Designate an "injury" to each of the injured—a broken back, neck, arm, wrist, leg or ankle. Give each of the injured a piece of paper describing his or her injury. Take the injured of each team to an island, a floating dock or the opposite side of a lake.

The three rescuers of each team are to

paddle their canoes to the injured, take care of their wounds (with splints, bandages and so on) and take each injured person back to shore one at a time using the backboard or old door as a stretcher. The injured may not speak to the rescuers. Assign a counselor to each team to rate the rescue procedure:

4=excellent in all respects.

3=good, but bandages or splints could be better.

2=fair, rescue manner is handled roughly.

1=poor, the rescuers hurt more than they helped!

Time each team and add the time to the rescue score. The team with the highest score wins. Thus it's better for a team to take longer, do a better job and get a higher score.

Each team must figure out how to manage its rescue. Make sure everyone wears a life jacket. Have a water-safety director in a separate canoe supervise the event.

Bag Drama

Use this activity to challenge campers' creativity as they create crazy skits based on miscellaneous items. "Bag Drama" works well on backpacking trips while sitting around the fire.

Time. One hour.

Materials. A bag for each group filled with assorted objects such as kitchen utensils, wigs, glasses, clothing, hats and toys.

Directions. Divide into groups, and give each group a bag with assorted items. Give groups 15 minutes to plan and practice a short skit that incorporates all the items in the bag. Group members participate as actors, props or special effects.

You can also assign the same punch line for all groups to give at the end of their skits. For example, "Guess who forgot the matches?" It's interesting to discover the range of creativity within the group.

Indoor Cross-Country Ski Relay

Use this activity to practice a ski relay indoors. Do this game in a gymnasium or large room with a tile floor.

Time. Thirty minutes.

Materials. Plenty of used stockings or panty hose. (Sometimes a hosiery factory will give undyed stocking rejects.)

Directions. Divide the group into two evenly numbered teams. Give each person two stockings or legs cut from panty hose. Say: "With your shoe on or off, place the top of the stocking or hose on each foot. It provides a slick way to slide across the floor. Grab the toe ends in hand and stand upright. As you slide each foot forward, stretch the stockings in your hands, simulating ski-pole action." Campers must slide their feet on the floor. No walking allowed.

Begin the game by having the first person on each team "ski" around the room and come back to tag the next player, who then skis. The first team to finish wins.

Gully Washer Day

Use the activity for indoor fun on a rainy day.

Time. Half a day.

Materials. Make a big carnival box filled with the following miscellaneous items (plus any other items you can think of): pingpong balls, old tennis balls, plastic balls, beanbags, balloons, newsprint, markers, pencils, empty boxes, milk crates, rubber bands, clothespins, string, straight pins, masking tape, cans, case of empty soft drink bottles, thread, sponges, tacks, shoes, hats, old clothes, and odds and ends. Also have newsprint, markers, folding chairs, stools and folding tables available for each team. You may choose to arrange the items on a table.

Directions. Divide into groups (cabin groups or living groups work best). Have each group devise and set up its own carnival game and booth using the supplies from the carnival box or supply table. Give each team 20 to 30 minutes to:

● Devise the game.

● Write the rules on newsprint so other teams can play the game.

● Write the scoring method on the newsprint.

At a set time groups go from booth to booth to play the carnival games as teams, recording team scores for each game. When groups are finished compare team scores.

Part Five
Backcountry Living Skills

Chapter 18

Teaching Backcountry Living Skills

Learning outdoor living skills isn't incidental to camp programs and group life. The challenge of learning new skills is often the key for unlocking hidden talents in campers. As author and adolescence researcher Sol Gordon writes, "There is hardly anything more energizing than learning something new."

Gordon suggests that teenagers who feel down, lonely and miserable should learn something new. "You'll start feeling better when you put a little effort into learning something new . . ."[1] Learning new skills at camp provides a sense of personal accomplishment equaled by few other educational experiences.

Mike's story illustrates how learning outdoor skills provides the framework for building campers' self-esteem. Mike's older brother was big, handsome and naturally athletic. He overshadowed all Mike's efforts in high school. Mike was small, wiry and soft-spoken. His eyes always seemed cast down. He was a kid on the fringes.

But his life began changing when he started camping with his church group. He had a knack for learning outdoor skills. The dramatic turning point was a two-day

mountaineering class in which Mike discovered he was a natural-born rock climber. Everything seemed to fall into place. He felt good about himself—and good about helping other campers learn his new-found skill. A dozen years later Mike is still a devoted camper and rock climber.

Campers are the first people to recognize that the new skills they learn at camp will impact other areas of life. Evaluation sheets from junior highers who've learned outdoor living skills at camp indicate the young people's hopes to camp out with their family or friends back home: "going camping more as a family" and "showing my family how to camp" are the most frequently mentioned "going home" hopes.

Parents often confirm the long-term impact when their teenagers learn new skills at camp. One mother said, "Our daughter came home and cooked supper for our family—the same meal she had cooked at camp." Another camper volunteered to organize a youth dinner committee to prepare a meal for a visiting youth group. Again, she chose a menu she'd helped plan, purchase and prepare at camp.

In this chapter, we'll look at four guiding principles for teaching outdoor living skills in ways that will maximize the camper's sense of personal satisfaction and achievement. They are:

- Create interest in outdoor skills.
- Introduce skills in small segments.
- Develop subgroups for personal support.
- Help campers visualize a system of outdoor skills.

Create Interest in Outdoor Skills

One camp director introduces outdoor skills in an intriguing way. Before the first campers arrive, the staff sets up a rope-making apparatus in front of the lodge. Leaders teach the first arriving campers to make ropes. Then the rope-making continues as the early arrivals introduce the craft to the next group. Within an hour, 20 campers and their parents fill the front yard, enjoying refreshments, talking and making ropes. The spirit is informal, yet structured learning takes place.

As the last campers arrive and begin making a rope, a counselor invites a few campers to help her build a fire for lunch. Another staffer invites three other campers to help set up a ropes practice area nearby. A third staffer asks some campers to help carry food from the kitchen to the outdoor fire circle. After lunch everyone gathers for an orientation session. Then parents leave.

By the time other get-acquainted games get underway and small groups are formed for the week, everyone feels comfortable. And everyone's interest in outdoor skills has already been increased, since camp began as soon as campers arrived. Campers didn't have to stand around and wait for things to begin. Everything was getting done. Everyone was involved—including parents. Interest was high.

It's best to teach backcountry living skills when interest is high. Building in-terest requires ingenuity and innovation. "How can I make learning fun for the campers?" is a key question—especially when introducing skills in the early stages of group formation.

Each backcountry skill area in this section contains suggestions for introducing skills through group-building activities.

Introduce Skills in Small Segments

Being well-versed in any subject or skill carries with it the temptation to talk too much—to ask and answer secondary questions before campers have experienced the primary answers. Introducing a new skill in a brief, simplified form usually communicates best.

Campers are motivated quickly, and most want to get on with the action. When introducing new skills, stick to one subject at a time. Campers will welcome second- and third-level applications once they've had hands-on time.

For example, when teaching fire-building, begin with basic principles and have the campers build the kind of fire they need for the immediate occasion. Don't explain three or four types of fires before demonstrating the first. After the group has experienced building a fire, then future instruction can take place when you need a different type of fire. And the cooking group can call a brief demonstration time when it uses a reflector oven.

One leader used this approach: "We're going to learn one important thing this evening: how to put out a fire—I mean really put out a fire! That means we have to build a fire and cook first. Here are the matches. There's the wood."

The campers didn't know the wood was especially selected before they arrived. It was powder dry, so it wouldn't take any special techniques to get a fire going. While the campers debated how to build a fire and who would strike the first match, the counselors were organizing a simple hot dog meal. As a result campers felt free to be in charge. They were proud of their roaring fire. And they were just as eager to prove they knew how to put one out. This apparently off-the-cuff approach was actually intentional and thoughtful. It built campers' interest in learning the basic steps involved in mastering a new skill.

Camping for several days gives young people a chance to practice and build on their new skills. Sometimes group leaders use a variety of gear and shelter during a single camping trip so campers experience a wide range of skills and equipment use. Instead of setting up the same tents every night, have campers build shelters with ropes, tarps and ponchos on different nights to build ingenuity and teamwork. Using soft packs and frame packs, two types of stoves, and two or three types of tents will broaden campers' abilities to apply their learnings beyond the immediate situation.

Teenagers get a great deal of satisfaction from improvising and learning outdoor skills. They also have an immense sense of humor that keeps leaders watching their words. "You said peel the potatoes. We peeled the potatoes. You didn't say how many. How were we to know?" This quote came from a teenage camper who with two friends peeled 25 pounds of baking potatoes in one sitting. Do you think they would've done that if their leaders couldn't take a joke?

Develop Subgroups for Personal Support

Many individual skills are often best introduced in groups of two or three. Having campers help each other lowers the feelings of awkwardness or being put on the spot. It also reinforces a model of group life in which people support each other. Campers who successfully build fires or tie knots with a partner will be eager to prove to themselves that they can do it alone.

Having small groups cook various parts of the first meal is a fun way to include everyone. When everyone is experimenting and learning together, no one feels on the spot. The same is true in learning to use a map and compass. Invest in enough maps and compasses for at least every two people. Campers want to "do it now," and subgroupings quench the desire to get into the action. They also free leaders to give individual attention to group members who need extra personal support. Leaders can also ask pairs who have grasped a particular task to help another group that's having more trouble.

Help Campers Visualize a System of Outdoor Skills

Paul Petzholdt, founder of the National Outdoor Leadership School, was once asked, "What is your main goal in training outdoor leaders?" The veteran outdoorsman's succinct answer: "To teach them how to keep their bodies at 98.6 degrees all the time. That's it. It's that simple." Petzholdt's answer is simple but not simplistic. It focuses all the tasks in backcountry living in a single sentence.

Leading groups outdoors includes teaching personal responsibility and judgment for living in a wide variety of conditions that change from day to day. Thus outdoor living involves learning a system of new skills step by step.

Backcountry living skills involve a variety of outdoor adventure activities. They are the how-to camp skills that keep groups warm, dry and well-fed. These skills areas include backcountry judgment and safety; personal gear and packing; ropes, knots and hitches; tents and emergency shelters; wood-cutting and fire-building; food and cooking; and map and compass navigation. (Successive chapters in Part Five deal with each of these skills areas in detail.)

Whether a group is touring, backpacking, canoeing, skiing, horse-packing or mountaineering, young people must know how to camp safely and responsibly. Camp leaders who teach outdoor skills must help campers see a larger picture—how skills relate to each other and build on each other.

For example, leaders can explain that when campers learn to build a fire outdoors, they can also build one in a fireplace. Fire-building also links to cooking and emergency skills, and using an ax, saw and knife safely. All the skills are interrelated and important. They fit into a larger bank of knowledge that doesn't just come automatically when we decide to camp. Rather, they're part of a web of skills—a system that supports campers' abilities to take care of themselves or someone else.

Campers also need to see what they hear and practice. Visual aids reinforce skills campers learn, and they help campers remember skills once they've gone home.

Here are some ways to help campers see what they're learning:

1. Photocopy outlines, steps or diagrams of different skills. As you teach skills, design handouts for campers to keep in their notebooks. Or photocopy and distribute the Camp Notebook pages in this book.

2. Use graphic displays and outlines with line drawings of different skills. Leaders at one wilderness school camp outlined each skill area on plastic window shades. Then they built a large, upright, plywood box with rows of shade brackets inside. This display sits in the corner of the dining tent. After breakfast or in the evening, leaders often present the day's skill by pulling down the appropriate window-shade outline as a visual guide.

3. Stock a camp "library" with half a dozen books for campers' self-directed skill development. Campers even enjoy looking at one or two selected resources while traveling to and from camp.

Notes

[1]Sol Gordon, *When Living Hurts* (New York, NY: Union of American Hebrew Congregations, 1985), pp. 32-33.

Chapter 19

Backcountry Judgment and Safety

It was the first supper at Cedar Crest Camp. The camp director welcomed campers and introduced summer staffers—from counselors to cooks. "This year two of our staff have returned in special counseling roles," she continued. "Jeff and Sally are our backcountry leaders. They'll direct our backcountry trips for overnight campouts. They're also orienting the two groups that will leave tomorrow for canoeing and backpacking."

The two groups were introduced too. One group was going on a camp-sponsored canoe trip; the other was a local church backpacking group using the camp as an overnight base. Sally and Jeff were helping the two groups' leaders prepare for six days of backcountry living.

Backcountry Living Demonstration

Both groups gathered in the main lodge after supper. Jeff and Sally had spread a poncho in front of the fireplace and had arranged various camping articles and equipment on it.

Sally began the session: "Jeff and I want to use this hour to help you think about having a safe and healthy trip. Turn to someone near you and in 60 seconds see how many camping safety tips you think

of together."

Then campers began calling out responses that Jeff wrote on newsprint: "Don't play with matches," "Wear your shoes at all times," "Be careful when you kiss!" "Don't eat yellow snow," "Always kneel when you cut wood," "Open and close your knife away from you," "Don't diet," "Put on your raincoat, carry an umbrella and walk on the water," "Don't use your hair dryer when your canoe has water in it" . . . The list continued as eager campers recalled quotes from the afternoon session, things mom and dad said, cute attention-getters and serious chiding.

"You've got the idea," Sally concluded. "Some of what you've said is funny and serious at the same time—you definitely have some backcountry smarts! Some of the funny things we joke about are also serious matters of health and safety—like going to the bathroom. It makes a difference when there's no bathroom!"

Jeff continued: "Each item on the poncho symbolizes some decision or judgment you need to make in the backcountry. We want briefly to cover each one and answer your questions." Sally added that much of what they'd be explaining is condensed on a handout that they'd distribute (Camp Notebook 36, "Backcountry Judgment").

Camp Notebook 36

Backcountry Judgment

The only real danger in the wilderness is your inability to calculate the risks. Most people who get into trouble are not being foolhardy; they simply haven't thought through the risks. On the other hand if you calculate the possible risks—based on location, season and group experience—and equip your group accordingly, you'll be prepared to avoid emergencies and to help others who aren't prepared.

Here are some dangers—and how to avoid them:

Exposure	Protection
Unplanned hiking or canoeing, or rambling away from camp without trail guides, maps or compasses.	Plan travel with trail guides, maps and compasses. Know how to use a map and compass.
No water at a campsite when it's needed.	Carry water, and consult trail guides and topographic maps for water sources.
Continuous, day-after-day travel. Long mileage days (more than eight to 10 miles per day).	Plan layover days (one per three days of travel). Plan reasonable mileage days (five to eight miles).
Depending on trail shelters or using ponchos for shelter.	Pack a tent or shelter.
Eating odds-and-ends meals. Eating late, skipping breakfast, dieting and carrying just enough food.	Plan three meals as well as snacks each day. Set up camp and eat before dark. Eat leisurely breakfasts, and eat all you want. Carry extra meals.
No spare clothing—thus no protection from rain. No source of heat. No first aid kit.	Carry extra clothing. Keep one set of clothes dry—even if you must hike or canoe in wet clothes. Carry rain gear and a source of body heat (food and fire-starting materials). Carry a first aid kit.
Day hiking, skiing, climbing, fishing and jaunts away from camp in light clothing with no day pack or emergency equipment. Traveling alone or with too few people.	Plan hiking, skiing, canoeing and climbing with at least three people (and three or more canoes). Carry a day pack with the "Essentials for Mountain Safety" (page 288). Distribute extra gear among group members—stove, tarp or tent fly, sleeping bag or insulated coveralls, and ground insulation or Ensolite pads.

Then Jeff and Sally took each item on the poncho and began talking about back-country safety and judgment.

Water bottle and cup. "We drink frequently to stay healthy—two to three quarts of liquid per day in the summer and three to four quarts each day in the winter. But drinking directly from a canteen or from someone else's water bottle spreads germs around. It's always best to drink from your own cup. That way you can share water from another bottle without sharing your saliva. 'Nuff said?"

Aluminum pot and long-handle dipper. "Much of the water you use in the backcountry will be from springs or streams. So you have to purify it either with a microfilter or by boiling it for three minutes. If it rains, you can catch water in pots or water bottles. It may taste like birch leaves, but it's good water you don't need to boil.

"There's a little 'critter' we hope you don't meet on the trail; its name is *Giardia lamblia*. Even the clearest streams may be infested with this invisible little creature that invades beautiful streams primarily through beaver droppings. The disease it leaves behind causes cramps, nausea, diarrhea and extreme weight loss. The only simple, sure-fire way to avoid the problem is to boil water.

"Also be careful with boiling water. When you fill your cup, set the cup down and use the dipper to fill it. Never pour from the pot. And never pour hot water into a cup you're holding or a friend is holding. You could badly scald someone's hand."

Scouring pad and bottle with "no soap" label. "You rarely need to use soap in the backcountry either for washing dishes or personal bathing. To wash your personal dishes, use 'duff'—pine needles, decaying leaves or ashes. Fill the dishes with water, and scour with a handful of duff or a small piece of moss. Then fill them again, and throw the residue out in the woods. When a dish is free of food particles, rinse it in running water and then pour-rinse with a dipper of boiling water. Let your dishes air-dry.

"The same process works for cooking utensils. Sometimes you need to use a scouring pad or plastic scrubber to cut away grease or burned food, but rarely do you need soap. Pour waste-water from cleaning cooking utensils into a hole by your fire. When the waste-water drains, burn the residue."

Towel. "For personal cleanliness rinse your clothing in streams and dry clothes in the sun. Even at small streams, take time to strip down and wash yourself with cold water. It's refreshing!

"If you use soap or shampoo, use it in the woods away from the water. Get wet first, then lather up or shampoo—not superlather. Then have a friend you trust splash off the soap with buckets of water. This way the soap leaches into the soil, not into streams."

Swimsuit. "Just as we can endanger backcountry water by polluting it, it can endanger us if we don't use good backcountry judgment. Most of the time back home we swim in clean pools under the watchful eye of a nearby lifeguard. In the backcountry, though, confine swimming to shallow areas. Don't try to swim across a river or lake that's over your head. Do deep-water activities in the backcountry only while wearing a life preserver. Have fun and enjoy the water—but don't put yourself or another group member at risk." (Diagram 37, "Backcountry Swimming," is from a public service advertisement from the Shepherd Spinal Center that describes what can happen when you're not careful when swimming in the backcountry.)

Diagram 37
Backcountry Swimming
Ending Up in a Wheelchair Is as Easy as Diving Off a Log
"Or, as it happened in my case, diving off a rubber raft. It started out to be a perfect day. Our senior prom had been the night before, and my friends and I were looking forward to a lazy afternoon, floating down the river. When the sun really started to beat down, I dove off our raft into the cool water. The next thing I knew, I was lying on the bottom of the river, unable to move.

"I'll be finishing college soon, but things are really different now. Because of that one time I didn't check the water level before making a dive, I'll be a quadriplegic for life." —Susan Nugent

Swimming and diving accidents that cause lifetime paralysis are avoidable. So don't take chances. Do follow these simple safety rules:
- Swim around in the area to check for hidden objects before you jump or dive.
- Before attempting a dive, jump in feet first to be sure the water is deep enough.
- Never assume an area is safe because other people are diving there, or because you have been swimming there before.
- Never attempt a jump or dive that's beyond your ability.
- Don't swim alone.
- Don't drink and swim.

Reprinted with permission of Shepherd Spinal Center, 2020 Peachtree Rd., Northwest, Atlanta, GA 30309.

Pocketknife, ax and saw. "You'll hear many of these statements again, but they deserve emphasis:

1. Supervise yourself and supervise each other when you're cutting.

2. Cut in a designated area only under a spotter's supervision. Counselors should have spotters too.

3. Use a knife only when you're sitting down and away from the group.

4. Open and close a knife away from you.

5. Don't walk around with a knife.

6. When cutting with an ax, kneel with your legs spread apart.

7. If you haven't been shown or don't know the appropriate technique for using cutting tools, ask for instruction before you use them in the backcountry." (See Chapter 23 for more on knife and ax safety.)

Sleeping bag. "Sleeping soundly and getting plenty of rest are as important as the food you eat. Keep your sleeping bag dry.

When you go to bed, take off damp clothes and sleep in pajamas or dry underwear.

"You can dry the body dampness from clothing and socks by putting them in the bottom of your sleeping bag. Open your sleeping bag and hang it out in the air on dry, sunny days."

Day pack. "When you leave camp for a day trip—hiking, fishing or exploring—take rain gear, extra food, matches and emergency supplies with you in a day pack. Pool your emergency gear into one or two backpacks, and take turns carrying."

Trowel and toilet tissue. "One other question you might have: Where do you go to the restroom when there is no restroom? The answer: Make your own.

"Always locate your toilet area at least 200 feet from a water source. You can dig a latrine for the group: Select a screened spot, and dig a trench about eight inches deep and three feet long. (To maximize decomposition, don't dig deeper than eight inches. The bacteria in the first few inches enhance the breakdown process.) Every time someone uses the latrine, burn the toilet paper and cover the waste with a little dirt. Cover and camouflage the entire area when you break camp.

"Another way to dispose of human waste is the 'cat method.' Each person digs a small six- to eight-inch-deep hole and completely covers it after one use. This works best along the trail during the day or for small groups that aren't camping for multiple nights."

"One note: Don't bury tampons; animals dig them up. Instead wrap them and burn them in a hot fire with other burnables. Or bag them and pack them out with other garbage—unless you're in grizzly bear country."

Large plastic jug. Sally picked up the final article on the poncho—a wide-mouth plastic jug. She opened it and explained: "This is your group first aid kit. The jug is waterproof. It contains articles you don't have in your personal first aid kit. Have the last canoe or foot-person in a hiking group carry the group first aid kit."

Sally opened the jug and took out the items for the group to see. A full arm-length and short leg air splint were rolled inside the jug with all the other items tucked down inside. Items included:

● Thermometer, tweezers and scissors.

● Topical ointment, alcohol pads, zinc oxide ointment and Percogesic (non-aspirin pain tablets that don't require a prescription).

● Gauze pads (2 × 2 inches and 4 × 4 inches), eye dressings, triangular bandages and gauze.

● Moleskin, tape, butterfly closures and Band-Aids.

● Small bar of antiseptic soap.

● Meat tenderizer (monosodium glu-

tamate)—used to treat bee stings.

● First aid chart (available from hospitals, doctors, insurance companies and other sources of safety information).

After explaining the different items, Sally concluded the demonstration by saying: "The main thing we want to emphasize is that everything we do outdoors involves making judgments about how our actions affect our group, the environment, individuals and other groups we meet along the way. We want you to make good judgments in the backcountry."

Backcountry Safety Guidelines

Backcountry camping is an exciting and safe adventure when you maintain certain safety and leadership standards whenever you head to the wilderness. The following guidelines for camping safety (adapted from the American Camping Association's "Tripping Standards") provide important standards to maintain in all your youth camping trips:[1]

● Is the main trip leader at least 19 years old? Does he or she have documented skills, endorsements of leadership and experience in leading similar trips?

● Is there at least one other leader at least 18 years old? Having just one 19-year-old leader is acceptable only when camping with six or fewer teenagers who've been selected and prepared to share leadership and respond to emergency situations.

● Do leaders have knowledge and skills about activities, geography, climate, and health and accident procedures to help them handle emergencies?

● Is at least one person on the trip certified in safety skills through one of the following programs?

1. American Red Cross Standard First Aid or the equivalent.

2. CPR from the American Red Cross or American Heart Association or the

equivalent.

● Is the person on the trip responsible for supervising water activities certified in American Red Cross Advanced Lifesaving or Lifeguard Training or the equivalent?

● Is the physical condition of each camper and leader screened within 12 hours of departure and return by a qualified doctor or nurse?

● Do trip leaders know how to obtain medical assistance on the trip? Do they have a record of the exact locations of assistance with them on the trip?

● Does the trip leader have copies of all campers' health histories, insurance information to obtain medical assistance if necessary and signed release forms for emergency treatment?

● Have leaders filed a written itinerary with the base camp (or responsible individual) and with local authorities?

● Is the group following written procedures for minimum environmental impact, including policies regarding the following?

1. Group size limits.
2. Refuse disposal.
3. Soap.
4. Human waste disposal sites.
5. Human waste.

● Have trip leaders obtained necessary permissions to use all trip sites?

● Is all drinking water obtained from tested and approved water supplies or purified by boiling or chemical treatment?

● Are all food utensils cleaned and sanitized after each use and protected between uses?

● Is food prepared and stored under safe and sanitary conditions, with particular care given to maintaining perishable foods at correct temperatures?

● Is everyone who uses camp stoves instructed in their proper use and care and supervised until he or she demonstrates

competence?

● Are water bottles clearly distinguishable from other bottles by shape and style? Are all non-consumable fluids clearly marked?

● Does pre-trip orientation for all campers include first aid procedures, emergency and rescue procedures, environmental awareness, and program experiences related to mode of travel, activities and geography?

● Are campers and staff adequately protected from the natural elements with shelter, clothing and sleeping gear appropriate to the season?

Backcountry First Aid

Most backcountry injuries for youth groups can be averted by using good judgment and being cautious. However, medical emergencies do occur, requiring a basic knowledge of first aid by at least one person in the camping group.

The most common minor injuries in the backcountry are bee, wasp and hornet stings. Chigger and tick bites are also common irritations.

To prevent chigger bites, fill a saltshaker (or a can with holes in the lid) with sublimated sulfur (available at drugstores). Shake the powder into sock tops and belt lines. It's odorless, and it will keep the pests away.

The best way to prevent stings is to choose campsites free from wasps nests or overhead hornets nests. If a camper is stung, use a paste of monosodium glutamate (meat tenderizer) on the sting.

Before your backcountry trip ask campers if they have allergic reactions to stings and if they normally carry a bee sting kit. If they do, be sure to carry it at all times in the backcountry.

Diagram 38, "Wilderness First Aid," outlines backcountry first aid basics, exposure problems and how to address the most common injuries. However, the article is only an outline of basic skills and should not be considered a substitute for professional first aid training. Distribute Camp Notebook 37, "Health and Safety Guidelines," to all campers to keep with them in case of emergencies.

Diagram 38

Wilderness First Aid

By Pat Stone

Anytime you get away from the trappings of civilization, you also leave behind its medical services. Hence, a knowledge of basic first aid is just as important a survival aid as those matches in your pocket or that knife on your hip. Probably more important—you don't have to be far from home for a serious injury to mean serious trouble.

This article will cover how to cope with the most common backcountry accidents and injuries. Remember, though, by far the best way to learn these skills is to take some of the widely available classes in first aid.

Three First-Aid Basics

1. Keep calm. Fear or panic will make any first-aid situation worse. They can lead to or increase shock. They can keep you from properly treating injury.

2. Do no harm. This is the golden rule of first aid. Don't risk a cure that may be worse than the injury. This rule is a standard for doctors in hospitals; it certainly applies to amateurs in the backwoods.

3. Get help. First aid must not delay first treatment. Get the victim to professional medical help, or vice versa, as soon as possible.

Exposure Problems

Shock: A side effect of almost any injury—from heat exhaustion to snakebite—may be shock. Symptoms are paleness, weakness and rapid but weak pulse. Breathing may be shallow. The skin may feel sweaty or clammy. Unconsciousness may result, even death.

First identify and treat the cause of shock—such as severe bleeding or burns. Then have the victim lie down, kept warm in a sleeping bag. Unless the person has a head injury or difficulty breathing, elevate the feet and legs to improve blood flow. Give warm water. Comfort to reduce panic.

Trench foot: Due to exposure to wet, cool (but often not freezing) conditions, the foot becomes cold, swollen and waxy. It may become numb. The foot is *not* frozen, but if untreated, the flesh may die and amputation will be necessary.

Treat by drying and warming the foot. Avoid trench foot by bringing extra dry socks and using them.

Frostbite: Parts of the body will freeze if exposed to excessive cold and wind. The hands, feet, ears, nose and cheeks are most likely to be affected. Flesh first becomes discolored, turning gray or chalky white, and then becomes numb. Eventually, the flesh can freeze and die. Gangrene can set in.

Treat by warming the affected area. Blankets, clothes and warm hands will help, but the best remedy is to immerse the area in warm, not hot, water. Keep the frostbitten area clean against infection. And don't let it refreeze—that could result in substantial tissue loss. Once a limb is thawed, it can't be used until healed, so if you have a frostbitten leg but must hike out, do it *before* thawing the limb.

Hypothermia: This is one of the leading killers of outdoorsmen and -women. It occurs when the body loses heat faster than it can replace it. Wind, moisture and cold all contribute to cause hypothermia.

continued

The warning sign is shivering. If untreated, the shivering will become intense and uncontrollable. The victim will then have trouble speaking. Thinking will become sluggish. When the shivering begins to stop (from muscle fatigue), the victim will become apathetic and helpless to save him- or herself. Unless the person is quickly helped, death will result.

The best treatment is always to be on the lookout for hypothermia, avoiding serious symptoms by quickly warming anyone who has a bad case of shivering. Failing that, strip the victim and one or two helpers and have all lie together in a sleeping bag. (The victim will not get warm if left alone in a sleeping bag.) Provide dry clothes, warm, non-alcoholic drinks, and candy or other high-energy food.

Snow blindness: Sunlight reflected off snow can cause serious eye damage. The eyes first burn or feel scratchy. They may tear readily and wince at light. Severe pain and headaches then lead to total blindness.

To treat, keep the eyes completely covered with cool compresses, take aspirin for the pain, and rest. Most people recover within a day. It's best, of course, to wear sunglasses with side covers in bright snow.

Heat exhaustion and stroke: Heat exhaustion is a form of shock caused by over-exertion in hot weather. So much blood is diverted to the skin to help cool the victim that the blood pressure of the whole system weakens. The person feels tired or faint and may sweat heavily. The face pales, breath becomes short and vision blurs.

Treat for shock—have the person lie down, and elevate the feet. If the victim is conscious, give him or her lots of drinking water and salt.

Heat stroke is more serious. Initial signs may be sweating, weakness, headache, cramps, confusion and irrational behavior. In the full stroke—a complete breakdown of the body's heat control process—the victim may lose *all* ability to sweat. He or she looks pallid and clammy and falls into a coma. Body temperature rises rapidly and leads to death if not promptly treated.

The best remedy is to totally immerse the victim in cold water. Do whatever you can to cool the victim. Massage the limbs to promote blood circulation. Then keep a close watch on the victim's temperature and get the person to a physician immediately.

Altitude sickness: If you're not acclimated to exercising at high altitudes (8,000 feet and higher), you can be struck with an array of serious symptoms: headache, nausea, vomiting, shortness of breath, weakness, coughing, rapid heart rate, chest congestion, mental confusion, vision and coordination loss, coma and even death.

The cure is obvious but essential: Get the victim back to a lower altitude. Other helpful steps are to replace fluid loss, restrict salt intake and administer oxygen.

Snakes

There are four poisonous snakes in America: the rattlesnake, copperhead, water moccasin and coral snake. The first three inject their venom through two fangs; the last chews its victim.

All treatment procedures are based on slowing the body flow of toxin-carrying lymph. Keeping the victim calm and still helps slow lymph circulation. Do not give coffee, tea or alcohol—which would increase lymph flow.

There is disagreement about what treatment procedure is best. Most experts say that if you're within two hours of a hospital, to splint the snakebite area with an elastic wrap like an Ace bandage and get the victim to a hospital.

Another method—favored by some, renounced by others—involves placing a constricting band close to the wound, between it and the heart. (Don't apply a tourniquet, which cuts off all circulation.) The risk here is that you can cut off blood flow and cause the person to lose a limb! So the band must allow blood flow—you should be able to see or feel pulse on both sides of it. It should also be released briefly every 15 minutes and refastened a bit closer to the heart.

At the same time, make short, shallow (skin-deep) incisions at the cut and suck out

continued

the venom for 15 to 30 minutes. If done within three minutes of the accident, you may be able to suck out 1/4 to 1/2 of the venom. Then cover the wound with a sterile dressing.

Be alert for signs of shock, and treat the victim if necessary.

Injuries

The standard first-aid sequence for treating injury is to 1) check airway, 2) re-establish breathing, 3) check circulation, 4) check cervical vertebrae for fracture, 5) stop bleeding and 6) treat shock. The first three steps—airway, breathing, circulation—are easy to remember by their initials: ABC.

Breathing: The best way to give artificial respiration is with the mouth-to-mouth technique. First clear any obstructing material out of the throat by scooping it out with your fingers. Tilt the victim's head backward by putting one hand under the neck and pressing down on the forehead with the other. (If you suspect a broken neck, don't tilt the head; use one hand to open the jaw.) This should open the air passage.

Pinch the nostrils shut with the same hand that is holding the forehead back. Place your mouth completely over the victim's, and give four quick, full breaths. (If the victim's chest does not rise, check the airway again for obstructions.) Remove your mouth, inhale, wait for air to come out of the victim, then give another full, strong breath. The victim's chest should visibly rise and fall from your efforts.

Apply breaths every five seconds to adults. With children, cover both the nose and mouth with your mouth, and breathe (not as forcefully) every three seconds. If necessary, hit the victim sharply on the back to free a lodged obstruction.

Choking: If someone is conscious but choking, apply the Heimlich maneuver. Grab the victim from behind by locking both arms around the person's waist. Then squeeze sharply, thrusting both fists into the upper abdomen and chest beneath the sternum. This should force air in the lungs to push the obstruction out like a cork from a bottle.

Bleeding: Serious bleeding can lead to death. Have the victim rest, and—if no injuries prohibit it—elevate the bleeding section above the level of the heart. To stop intense bleeding, apply firm pressure to the wound, preferably with a sterile pad but if necessary with the bare hand. Add another dressing and more pressure if necessary.

This should stop the bleeding in almost all cases. Do *not* use a tourniquet unless all else has failed and you're willing to sacrifice a limb to save a life. Once bleeding is controlled, do what you can to prevent infection, or else serious complications may ensue. Puncture wounds should be washed out as deeply as possible with sterile (boiled then cooled) water. The wound should be covered with a clean, sterile dressing. If there has been a large loss of blood, the victim will need to be immediately transported to a hospital to receive blood transfusions.

Fractures: The basic first-aid treatment for fractures, i.e., broken bones, is *immobilizing* the injured part. First, though, you need to identify that a fracture has occurred. Obvious signs are a severely bent limb or when the victim hears or feels a bone snap. A less obvious indication is severe localized pain or tenderness: When you press gently on the injured spot, it hurts, but pressing a few inches away does not. Early swelling may or may not be a sign of fracture. If you have any doubt, treat the injury as a fracture.

Stop the bleeding and clean and dress wounds before splinting. Be sure to—as first aiders say—"splint them where they lie," that is, immobilize the injured limb before moving the victim. Rig splints with bandages, clothes, wooden slats, ax handles, poles, etc., so that the joints above and below the fracture are fixed in place. Pad the splints where needed. Often, as with a broken collarbone, you can splint the injured part to the rest of the body.

Pelvis, neck and back fractures are very serious. The best course of action is to keep the victim completely still (cover with blankets, and treat for shock or breathing difficulties if need be). Don't move the victim. If it is absolutely necessary to evacuate

continued

the victim, be extremely careful—movement of the neck or back could cause permanent paralysis or death. Move the injured person onto a rigid stretcher while keeping the hips, neck and back stiff and straight. Pad the person well, and carry the stretcher very carefully.

Sprains: A sprain occurs when ligaments, tendons or other tissue surrounding a joint are stretched or damaged. Sometimes it's hard to tell a sprain from a fracture—in both cases, the area may swell and be tender to the touch. When in doubt, treat as a fracture. If you're sure it's a sprain, elevate the injured area and apply ice in cloth for 20 minutes at a time or cold rags for at least a half hour to reduce swelling. Keep the sprain immobilized if at all possible.

Burns: Treat the pain of a superficial burn by immersing the afflicted area in cold water. Then clean the burn with non-medicated soap and water and rinse thoroughly. Cover with a dry sterile dressing, and change that every 48 hours.

Serious burn victims are in danger of losing their lives. *Immediately* treat victims of deep or extensive burns for shock—even before you treat the burn itself. It's vitally important to replace lost fluids, giving the victim as much fluid as he or she will tolerate (five quarts or more in the first eight hours). It's even more important to evacuate the victim promptly to a hospital. To treat the wound, remove all clothing and jewelry from the burned area (but don't pull out any that is stuck in the burn). Cover the burned area with clean dressing—do not apply greasy ointments. Leave the dressing in place, and get the victim to medical help as soon as possible.

Heart attack: Symptoms of heart attack include chest heaviness or pain, shortness of breath, pale appearance, weakness, and pain radiating into the neck or arms. The main treatment is rest. Place the victim lying down or with the head and shoulders elevated. Keep the person calm (don't talk about "heart attacks"). Treat the person as a total invalid and get medical help—don't transport unless absolutely necessary.

Check the pulse at the wrist or near the voice box, or listen to the chest for a heartbeat. If the heart has stopped, use cardiopulmonary resuscitation, an advanced first-aid skill. You cannot really learn it from an article, but excellent first-aid classes in CPR are offered all over the country. Taking such classes is easy to do when you're in civilized country. Having such skills when you're not may save a life.

Discussion and Reflection

Here are three true safety scenarios you can use to help leaders or campers sharpen their backcountry judgment and group decision-making skills. Each scenario is the beginning of a true story. (The real-life conclusions to the stories are described in Diagram 39, "Safety Scenario Outcomes," on page 286.)

Read a scenario to your group. Have each group member write an immediate response on a 3×5 card to share with the group. Then form small groups and take 10 to 15 minutes to work out a group decision on the most effective response. Write it down. Next bring the whole group togeth-er to share and design a whole-group response. Then turn to the scenario conclusion and read the actual outcome.

Safety scenario one. It's February on a mountain lake where several camps are located. Late on a Saturday afternoon campers hear faint cries for help as they walk the lake trail. Finally one of them spots someone with a life jacket clinging to a submerged canoe 200 yards offshore. But the person appears not to be wearing the life jacket. The wind's blowing. Six boats are locked nearby without any paddles. A nearby marina is locked for the winter.

How would you respond individually? as a group?

Camp Notebook 37

Health and Safety Guidelines

Avoid Emergencies

When you leave camp for a hike or trip:

1. Tell the youth or camp director where you're going and when you plan to return.
2. Carry the essentials for mountain travel: compass, map, whistle, flashlight, plastic tarp, nylon rope, extra clothing, sunglasses, extra food and water, matches or lighter, knife and first aid kit.
3. Carry rain gear for every group member if you're hiking far from camp.
4. Keep your group together.
5. Always have at least two supervising adults on each hike or trip.

If an Emergency Arises

If a camper or counselor is injured:

1. Remain calm, and keep the group together.
2. Keep the injured person lying down and warm. Don't move the person until the extent of injuries has been determined.
3. Examine gently. Look for:
   - Hemorrhage.
   - Cessation of breathing.
   - Shock.
   - Lacerations.
   - Head, neck and spine injuries.
   - Fractures.
   - Dislocations.
4. Treat severe bleeding and cessation of breathing immediately. Have the most experienced person direct first aid.
5. If you must go for help, send a counselor and a camper. The second counselor should stay with the injured person and the rest of the group. Keep the group together.

Medical and Emergency Information

Area doctor:
Name:_____
Location: _____
_____
Phone: _____
   If no answer:_____

Area hospital:
Name:_____
Location: _____
_____
Phone: _____

Camp headquarters: _____
County sheriff: _____
State highway patrol: _____
Other: _____

Safety scenario two. It's late March on a river in northern Florida. Rain has swollen the rivers, so local canoe rentals aren't sending out canoes. A family of three, an adult couple, and two teenagers and a child are picnicking at a recreation site along the river. The child is wearing a life preserver. The two teenagers take the child and float downstream on air mattresses, kicking their way across the river. The child's mother arrives and floats across the stream on another air mattress. Then the grandfather arrives. He asks the others how they'll make it back across the river. They try to paddle back, but the current is too strong.

One bystander suggests they walk upstream through the dense undergrowth and enter the river there. Another onlooker suggests they tie themselves together (they have a rope) and float across as a group so no one gets separated. The couple suggests they contact the park ranger and rescue the four stranded people in a canoe.

How would you respond individually? as a group?

Safety scenario three. It's a cold and rainy early June evening in the Appalachian Mountains of northern Georgia. An outdoor store operator hears a knock at his door about 9 p.m. Three adults and several children tell their story. At 5 p.m. three family members had set out on the trail for an afternoon hike that the adults thought would take a couple of hours. But the actual distance was 11 miles over rolling ridges and a 4,000-foot mountain. The hikers range in age from seven to 11 years old. The adults have driven from road crossing to road crossing several times, expecting the children to return to their drop-off point or to come out at the outdoor store where the trail crosses the highway.

The store owner is an experienced trail hiker and knows the distance and the elevations. He also knows half a dozen access trails and roads in the area could be mistaken for the Appalachian Trail.

How would you respond individually? as a group?

Notes

[1]These standards represent a small portion of A.C.A. standards for accreditation. It must be clearly understood that these adapted guidelines provide a system for self-evaluation. Accreditation by the American Camping Association, Inc., is an entirely separate process, and A.C.A. assumes no responsibility for any group's satisfaction of these adapted guidelines or for any injury or other damage related to a group's failure to meet the guidelines.

Diagram 39

Safety Scenario Outcomes

Look at these real-life outcomes only *after* you've developed your scenarios.

Outcome of scenario one. The campers acted quickly. They ran to the camp manager's home. The manager and an adult group leader unlocked the recreation room, took out paddles and life jackets and raced to the dock. A boat was quickly unlocked, and—after several turns at the oars fighting the head wind—they reached the swamped canoe.

The boy in the water had taken an unlocked canoe from a nearby camp and had capsized in the wind. He had drifted more than half a mile in the wind, holding onto the canoe with one hand with his arm around the life jacket. He was so numb from hypothermia that they had to lift him aboard the boat. The manager put his jacket around the boy, hugged him for body heat, and shielded him from the wind as the other adult rowed back to safety. Wool blankets were ready at the dock.

The boy was wrapped in the blankets and carried to camp. There he was placed in a cool tub of water that was gradually warmed up to body temperature. He was dried off and wrapped in blankets. Several people massaged him through the blankets to restore additional circulation. They gave him warm Jell-O to drink.

In retrospect the leaders criticized the availability of an unlocked canoe in the middle of winter. They also wished they'd carried a blanket with them in the boat.

Outcome of scenario two. The four people across the river did push their way through the heavy undergrowth to a point farther upstream. One bystander discouraged them from tying themselves together for fear they would get tangled up—putting someone on the bottom in a dangerous situation. When the group started across the river, two men waded out as far as they could in the current and met the swimming foursome.

In retrospect, one person said the safest response would've been to wait for the park ranger's canoe or to walk downstream to a nearby bridge. The picnickers were in no immediate danger as long as they stayed on the other shore. The grandfather's panic and fear had encouraged an unnecessary and unwise quick crossing.

Outcome of scenario three. The store owner's experience paid off. He listened carefully to the scared family's story. He realized that no one had waited at the drop-off point to find out if the children turned back. "Before we call the civil defense team," he said, "what's your phone number?" He called the family's home. To his delight (but not his surprise) an 11-year-old answered: "It started raining and we thought, 'This is a bummer.' So we turned around and hitchhiked home."

It would be easy to improve the family's search-and-rescue strategy. But few could improve on the children's backcountry savvy!

Chapter 20

Personal Gear and Packing

"What do we need to take to camp?" "How will we carry it?" "How will we keep all our stuff together in a tent?" "How will we keep our clothes dry?" Whether you're backpacking, canoeing, or traveling by bike or bus, campers will want—and need—answers to these kinds of questions. They become particularly important for extended trips, when managing weight and volume are critical.

Personal gear is a camper's bedroom, closet, bathroom cabinet and dining table condensed and reduced so that he or she can carry it. The challenge of packing is to organize campers' clothing, bed and personal articles in the most transportable way.

This chapter discusses specifics on selecting, organizing and packing day bags, duffel bags, backpacks, Duluth packs and sleeping bags. The chapter concludes with suggested group-building activities centered around gear and packing, followed by personal gear lists for various types of camps.

Bags and Packs

Carrying the right bags and packs can make a tremendous difference in your comfort while camping. Here are the types of bags to consider.

Day Bags

A day bag carries the items you use first, last and throughout the day. It can be a small day pack, a fanny pack, or a stuff sack with a cord sling.

When backpacking, carry your day bag on top of your backpack. Or empty the day bag contents into a large pack pocket, and fold the day bag inside the pack for side trips. On longer trips or when you stay at a base camp and spend days side-tripping or mountaineering, a larger day pack can double as a bedroll bag and a day pack for side trips (see Diagram 40, "Essentials for Mountain Safety"). Diagram 41, "What to Pack in a Day Bag," shows what to pack in a day bag for easy access.

For canoeing or extended day trips, use a sturdy plastic bag as an inner liner. Be sure it's inside to keep it from tearing. Twist and tie the top, or fold it over tightly.

Duffel Bags

Campers can use duffel bags for residential camps, many canoe trips and carrying gear on long trips to a wilderness venture. Some duffel bags zip down the side; military types open on the end. On canoe trips duffel bags can carry both clothing and sleeping gear.

Most duffel bags aren't waterproof. It's

Diagram 40
Essentials for Mountain Safety

Always carry the following items in a day bag when you take day trips from base camp:

- ☐ Map and compass
- ☐ Extra food and water
- ☐ Whistle
- ☐ Lighter and fire-starter
- ☐ Plastic tarp and nylon rope

- ☐ Folding pocketknife
- ☐ Extra clothing
- ☐ Personal first aid kit
- ☐ Flashlight
- ☐ Sunglasses

Pack the extra food in a metal container that can double for heating water in an emergency.

Diagram 41
What to Pack in a Day Bag

- ☐ Toothbrush and toothpaste
- ☐ Toilet articles
- ☐ Insect repellent
- ☐ Sunglasses
- ☐ Drinking cup
- ☐ Canteen

- ☐ Poncho or rain suit
- ☐ Bible, journal and pen
- ☐ Camera and film
- ☐ Personal first aid kit
- ☐ Map
- ☐ Compass

---

simple to waterproof (and in the process organize) a duffel bag using three plastic bags with about the same diameter as the duffel bag. Pack pants and shirts in one bag; socks, underwear, towels and assorted articles in the second; and heavier clothing, moccasins and so forth in the third.

If you're backpacking you can use a stuff sack as a miniature duffel bag to pack essential clothing. Carry the bag in the bottom of the backpack. The articles are fairly lightweight, and you usually need them only at night or in the morning when the backpack is unpacked.

Backpacks

There are two basic types of backpacks: external-frame packs and internal-frame packs. Most hikers use external-frame packs, while internal-frame (or soft) packs are used more for mountain climbing or cross-country skiing. Some hikers prefer internal-frame packs because they're easier to load. However, they tend to be hotter

when backpacking in warm weather.

When leaders or campers are choosing backpacks to purchase, it's important to look for the best quality, not the latest gimmick—even if the better pack costs more. Any pack you purchase will be "outdated" when new models come out with better zipper pulls or neater logos. But those features won't make much difference in the pack's comfort and durability. (Camp Notebook 38 shows how to lift and carry a backpack.)

Packing a backpack. For most backpacking trips, pack lighter items low in the pack and heavier articles high. But for winter trips on skis or snowshoes or for trips involving lots of steep trails and rock climbing, pack heavier items near the center of the bag close to your back. Camp Notebook 40, "Overnight Backpacking Gear Checklist," shows how to arrange gear in a pack. Here are a few other tips:

● Compress essential clothing into a backpacker's miniature duffel bag (stuff

Camp Notebook 38

Carrying a Backpack

1. Grasp shoulder straps to lift pack.

2. Lift pack to rest position on knee.

3. Slip one arm under shoulder strap.

4. Slide pack over other arm.

5. Correct pack position (shoulder bar level with top of shoulders and straps leading straight back to it).

6. Side view (correct shoulder strap angle and waist strap location).

7. Hunch shoulders while connecting and tightening waist straps.

8. With your shoulders relaxed, the pack is now properly positioned.

sack). Place the bag in the bottom of the pack since it's light and since you rarely need it on the trail.

● Carry a parka or heavy jacket under the pack flap or in the end of the bedroll bag where it will be easily accessible when weather changes and for rest stops when your body cools off.

● Some packs have a lower zippered compartment where you can easily pack clothing using a plastic bag as water-proofing.

Making a pack cover. It's easy and inexpensive to keep your pack dry when hiking in the rain. Make a homemade pack cover with a heavyweight garbage bag (see Diagram 42, "Pack Cover"). Lay the bag flat, and make a big "T" on one side out of duct tape. Cut along the center of each tape strip. Then roll up the cover and store it in a pack pocket.

Diagram 42
Pack Cover
Large, heavy-duty garbage bag

Duct tape

Cut along center of duct tape

When you're hiking in the rain, fit the split side over your pack straps or harness. Tuck the bottom corners behind your waist—thus completely protecting your pack. If you need to store your pack overnight in the rain, stand the pack in another heavyweight plastic bag and place your pack cover over the top. You'll get complete rain protection.

Duluth Packs

On canoe trips without portages, you can carry personal gear in a duffel bag. However, on canoe trips with many portages between lakes or rivers, you'll need a large-volume Duluth pack. This pack will hold two sleeping bags and two sleeping pads, or two stuff sacks of clothing and personal articles.

The large pack rides lower on the shoulders than other backpacks, allowing campers with physical strength and endurance to portage a canoe and carry a pack at the same time. Again, waterproofing each bag with a plastic bag inside is the only guarantee against rain and water.

Sleeping Bags

Manufacturers have dozens of sleeping bags on the market, each touting different advantages and features. When purchasing a bag, compare insulations, temperature ranges, inside dimensions, zipper lengths and strength, and loft (height of insulation when fluffed up). In selecting your sleeping bag, here are some issues to keep in mind:

Temperature. Sleeping bags are designed for different comfort ranges based on the outside temperature (0, 20 or 40 degrees). Be sure to choose a bag that supplies the lowest comfort range you need for your camping area.

Construction. There are three basic types of sleeping bag construction: sewn through, layered and baffle. With the sewn through construction, the stitching holds the insulation in place. Layered construction blocks the cold spots at the stitching. Baffle construction reduces cold spots and shifting insulation.

Type of bag. Sleeping bags are designed several different ways. Let's look at the advantages of three basic styles:

1. Double-layered bag with collar. This

bag provides two layers of insulation with little heat loss through stitching. The collar eliminates draft and seals out heat and cold.

2. Wide-foot bag. This bag allows more room to move around and is more comfortable for long-term camping.

3. Mummy-type bag with oval foot. This bag provides freedom in the foot area plus the high loft and small packing advantages of a mummy bag.

Insulation. The basic question in insulation is down versus synthetic insulation. Down is the elite insulation—lightweight, warm, breathable, easy to pack . . . and expensive. Outside its cost, the biggest disadvantage of down is its inability to insulate if it gets wet. The feathers clump together, providing no insulation value.

Newer synthetic insulations provide warmth even when wet, and they retain their shape. They're comfortable, and they're generally less expensive than down. The greatest drawback, though, is their bulk. You can overcome this problem to some extent by using a stuff sack. With a little practice campers can learn to stuff their bag in a stuff sack. (A stuff sack with compression straps helps considerably.)

Keeping a sleeping bag clean. Outdoor schools and rental dealers usually use washable sleeping bags. Good ones will undergo 30 or more washings.

A practical, inexpensive way to keep a sleeping bag clean is to make a sheet liner that's slightly smaller than your bag. Hem the top edges, and sew down one side, across the bottom and halfway up the other side. Attach it inside the sleeping bag with Velcro tape. Then you just need to wash the liner—not the bag itself—after a camping trip. Moreover, in some climates the liner by itself is plenty of cover on hot summer nights.

Keeping a sleeping bag dry. Keeping a sleeping bag dry is critical to campers' safety and comfort. Here are the three steps to keeping a sleeping bag dry:

1. Waterproof your bedroll bag with a plastic bag inside the stuff sack. Always re-pack the plastic bag with the top twisted and tied.

2. On clear days hang your sleeping bag inside out in the open air before packing it and again before going to bed. This lets body moisture evaporate. Unpack your sleeping bag as soon as you set camp to give it more time to dry.

3. On rainy days pack your sleeping bag and gear inside the tent.

Using a bedroll bag. If you're carrying your bedroll in a large duffel bag or internal-frame backpack, use a small- to medium-size stuff sack that will compress the bag as much as possible. Then put the bag in the bottom of the pack. You can also get stuff sacks with compressor straps that let you compress the sleeping bag even more once it's packed. Pack your sleeping pad separately under the pack's flap. Or fold it and lay it flat in the bottom or side of the duffel bag.

If you're carrying the pack on a pack frame, use an oversize, coated nylon stuff sack. First roll your Ensolite sleeping pad inside the bag. Then stuff the sleeping bag into the pad's middle. Fill the extra space at the end of the bag with a sweater, jacket or parka. Use two nylon straps or strong cord to compress the stuff sack as you strap it to the pack frame.

Clothing

Dressing for outdoor living should be guided by what's comfortable, durable and warm. Usually these criteria translate into baggy legs and pant seats, loose shirts and good insulation—spelled W-O-O-L. Wool or wool-blend clothing is the watchword for fall, winter and spring—and in some areas even for summer nights.

Comfort. Comfort and utility are the most important factors to consider when choosing clothes for a backcountry adventure. (Fashion makes little difference in the backcountry!) Outdoor clothing should fit loosely.

Campers don't have to go buy all new clothes for your camp. Often they can borrow just what they need from family and friends. Otherwise thrift shops and garage sales often have great outdoor clothes at bargain prices.

Layering clothing. Dressing by layering works best for the active camper. Layering allows you to take off layers of clothes or to add more layers depending on the weather. The layers vary considerably with the changing season:

1. Spring and fall. Wearing a short-sleeve pullover shirt, a long-sleeve shirt and a down-filled vest will take you through the cool mornings until the day's heat calls for short sleeves. Add a water-resistant parka plus a hat over these other layers, and you're ready for frosty, windy or rainy days. A cap or hat is essential to shade you from direct sunlight and to prevent body-heat loss—20 percent or more of your body heat escapes off the top of your head.

2. Winter. Layering for cold begins with long underwear, wool-blend pants, one or two shirts, a vest or sweater, and a parka. In extremely cold temperatures, you may want an insulated parka. Add a warm wool cap or hat and gloves, and you're set to peel down until comfortable. Avoid blue jeans in snowy and wet winter areas.

3. Summer. Don't underestimate summer temperatures. In high mountains you still need a sweater or parka in the mornings. I've backpacked in Colorado on hot days that would blister your nose. But when the clouds blocked the sun, we had to pull out long pants and parkas to pro-

tect ourselves against the wind and lowering temperatures. Consider pants most carefully. Lightweight, quick-drying trousers are worth the money when canoeing or backpacking in wet areas where mosquitos are likely to buzz your legs if they're not covered.

In all seasons, carry rain gear on every trip and side trip. A combination of a long parka with rain pants or chaps works well. A poncho is good for backpacking, but it tends to be unruly for canoeing. Never let campers "just get wet, because it's warm rain." Even on an 80-degree summer day, your body must work to warm its environment to its own temperature, thus draining energy. Hypothermia isn't just a winter emergency; many emergencies occur in the southern Appalachians when hikers take too little clothing.

Marking clothes. With several campers out in the backcountry together, it's easy for them to get clothes mixed up. Avoid any conflicts or misunderstandings by having campers mark each item of their clothing and personal gear with their name, initials or personal, "Western" brand.

Using wool. Wool is synonymous with warmth in winter. Even when it's wet, wool insulates. In contrast, blue jeans, corduroy or other cotton clothes have no wicking action, so they carry wet and cold to your skin rather than away from it. Thus it's actually dangerous to wear cotton when it's cold, snowy and wet, because cotton steals so much body heat.

The best sources of wool clothing are your family attic or trunk, Salvation Army stores, garage sales, Goodwill Industries stores and Army-Navy surplus stores.

Taking care of your feet. Your feet are your most important asset when hiking. Boots should fit and be broken in to conform to the hiker's feet.

In choosing new boots, consider

several factors:

1. Look at different styles, all-leather or leather-and-fabric combinations with a sturdy sole and a steel shank for strength. Recently hikers have begun moving away from heavier boots and toward lighter weight models with softer soles and smoother lug patterns to prevent trail damage.

2. Before you decide to buy medium-weight or heavyweight boots, consider the seasons you'll be hiking, the roughness of the terrain and the distance of most of your trips.

3. Always wear boots that cover and protect your ankles.

4. When you're in the store, boots should fit comfortably over two pairs of socks (a lightweight inner-sock and a heavyweight wool over-sock).

When you buy boots, salespeople will tell you to break them in by casual walking around the house and neighborhood and—if you can stand the stares—to work or church. What most salespeople forget is that you're probably going hiking the day after tomorrow! So what do you do?

Here's a method to break in boots that makes your boots really fit you: Early one morning, submerge your new boots in a sink of lukewarm water for three to five minutes. Make sure the boots are completely under water, full of water and soaking wet through and through. (Traveling in the backcountry can soak your boots through anyway, so don't let a little water in your boots scare you at home.)

Then immediately pour out the water, drain the boots as much as possible and put them on over the two pairs of socks you'll be wearing. Wear them for an hour, then change socks while your first pair tumbles in the dryer. Walk around a lot, and carry some loads (maybe practice with your backpack). The more you use your boots

under heavy conditions during break-in, the better they'll conform to your feet. The creases that develop across your boots during break-in show that the boots are conforming to your feet, so they'll feel just right!

Keep changing socks and wearing the boots all day. By evening your socks will have soaked away all water from the boots. Now your new boots are ready for a good coat of snow seal (or another waterproofing product) and some oil around the stitching on the soles.

There's one other trick for foot comfort when camping: lock-lacing. The normal way to lace boots is to enter the string from inside the eyelet and pull to the outside. Reverse the process—enter the string from the outside eyelet and pull to the inside. This process creates friction on the lace, so it doesn't slip easily. If, however, your heel starts slipping or if your boot feels loose, tie a square knot in the laces right over the arch of your foot. If your boot has hooks, tie a square knot and take another turn around the hooks. Then lace more loosely from there to the top. By experimenting with different tying techniques and different tautnesses, you can create a comfortable and blister-free fit.

Leaders usually have a "foot check" during hikes to check for hot spots (red places where boots are too tight or rubbing). When hot spots occur on campers' feet, have them adjust boot lacings and socks. If hot spots persist, cover the spot with moleskin, stick-on skin padding.

Group-Building Activities for Packing

The best way for campers to learn how to organize and pack gear is through a first-hand demonstration and packing session. Seeing the "tricks of the trail" in action and then having a chance to reshuffle and organize their gear immediately answers dozens of campers' questions.

Include campers in the demonstration session before camp by sending them a personal gear list and asking them to prepare in advance. Also invite parents to the orientation session to answer their questions about securing personal gear for the backcountry event.

A packing demonstration is essential to the orientation session. Before the packing demonstration, organize and display in the demonstration area every item on the personal gear list for your camp. The demonstration should be relaxed, allowing plenty of time for questions and answers.

During the demonstration, don't spend too much time on the details of equipment construction and the advantages of equipment types. This information is best introduced after campers have their gear packed (or on the trail) when questions are asked—and they will be asked.

The one exception to this general rule involves campers who plan to buy new items and need guidance. As a general rule, though, encourage beginners not to buy new equipment for camping. Instead, urge them to borrow or rent equipment until they're sure what they want. One trip gives the first-timer a chance to ask questions and to see what others are using.

Begin the demonstration by spreading the gear you're demonstrating on a poncho, ground cloth or plastic sheet. As you present and describe each piece of gear, show how to pack it. Also show the group how to stuff a sleeping bag—don't just describe the technique verbally.

Introduce the demonstration by saying: "Our personal gear is our bedroom, clothing closet, bathroom cabinet and dining table all condensed and reduced so we can carry it. What we want to demonstrate is how to organize your clothes, bed and all the personal articles you'll need during camp. What we show you will be basic; you'll find your own creative ways to fine-tune this process.

"We begin by dividing our personal gear into three stacks for different bags:
1. Day Bag
2. Duffel Bag
3. Bedroll Bag."

Then start with the day bag stack. Explain what a day bag is and what campers will carry in it. If you wish, distribute appropriate Camp Notebook pages as you demonstrate. Answer any questions, then move on to the duffel bag and bedroll bag. Demonstrate how to stuff a sleeping bag into a stuff sack, and attach it to a backpack with straps.

Don't spend much time on the initial demonstration. After a few moments for questions and clarification, ask campers to spread out their own gear and begin organizing and packing. If you've already selected tentmates for camp, have them work together. This cooperation will help everyone to be conscious of the need to pack with care. Have experienced leaders circulate among the campers to answer questions and to help as needed during the packing process.

If you're using backpacks, have loaded packs available for campers to try. Ask a camping store or outfitter to loan you different types of sleeping bags and other gear for campers to see and test. Continue the demonstrations and camper experiments until campers understand what they need for camp and how to use their gear.

If you're also camping en route to a base camp for a wilderness venture, campers will probably have extra personal gear. Thus it's essential to repack at base camp. Give campers direction for packing for both the long trip and the wilderness venture.

Personal Gear Lists

Leaders need to make sure that all the campers are adequately equipped before going camping. Make sure their rain gear, clothing and sleeping gear are adequate. If they're not, help them get substitutes. Also help campers eliminate unneeded gear and clothing. (They won't want to carry them!)

Because every camping venture is different, review your personal gear checklists from previous trips or from camping books before you distribute them. Double-check the lists to make sure they have everything your group members need. (Gear lists in two reliable and widely used backpacking books don't list "pants" as a personal gear item!)

The personal gear checklists in Camp Notebooks 39-43 can be adapted for most camps. When finalizing your gear checklist, keep in mind climate differences in the camping area and home. Also anticipate the possible extremes in weather during the season when you're camping, and pack accordingly.

Camp Notebook 39 is a maximum gear list. It contains everything necessary for the extremes of spring, summer and fall in most rainy and mountainous areas. (It's not a winter gear list.) All articles on this list are necessary unless otherwise indicated. Campers may not need to take as many articles as are listed, but they shouldn't pack more than the stated number.

Camp Notebook 39

Maximum Gear Checklist

This gear list contains everything necessary for the extremes of spring, summer and fall in most rainy and mountainous areas.

Day Bag (to carry in the van or bus)

☐ Poncho or rain suit
☐ Small flashlight and batteries
☐ Bible, journal and pen
☐ Sunglasses
☐ Insect repellent
☐ Drinking cup, canteen and snacks
☐ Personal articles
☐ Comb or brush
☐ Toothbrush and toothpaste
☐ Camera and film
☐ Personal first aid kit
☐ Map and compass

Bedroll Bag (to pack in the trailer, van or bus)

☐ Sleeping bag
☐ Sleeping bag liner (made from a used sheet)
☐ Ensolite pad (3/8-by-21-by-56-inch or similar size)
☐ Small pillow (optional)

Duffel Bag (to pack in the trailer, van or bus)

☐ One hat or cap (for sun and rain protection)
☐ Two pairs of long pants (blue jeans, cotton or light wool)
☐ Two pairs of shorts (one pair to double for hiking and swimming)
☐ One heavy, long-sleeved shirt (preferably wool)
☐ One lightweight, long-sleeved shirt (knit, cotton or flannel)
☐ Four short-sleeved shirts (knit or cotton)
☐ Field jacket (polyester and cotton blend, Army surplus or hunting coat)
☐ One heavy sweater, down vest or field jacket liner
☐ One pair of wool gloves
☐ Underwear for five days
☐ One pair of long johns or thermal underwear
☐ One pair of heavy boots for hiking (or rough high-top shoes)
☐ One pair of everyday shoes (tennis shoes or running shoes—no sandals)
☐ Three pairs of heavy wool socks
☐ Three pairs of medium-weight cotton socks
☐ Two towels and two washcloths
☐ One swimsuit
☐ One or two bandannas
☐ One belt
☐ One folding pocketknife (no fixed-blade sheath knives)

Optional Items

☐ One or two books
☐ Musical instrument
☐ Shower robe and thongs
☐ Binoculars
☐ Gaiters
☐ Fishing gear

Note: This gear list includes the clothes you'll wear on the day you leave for camp. From this list you'll be able to select appropriate clothing for backpacking or canoeing. Mark each item of clothing and personal gear with your name.

Camp Notebook 40

Overnight Backpacking Gear Checklist

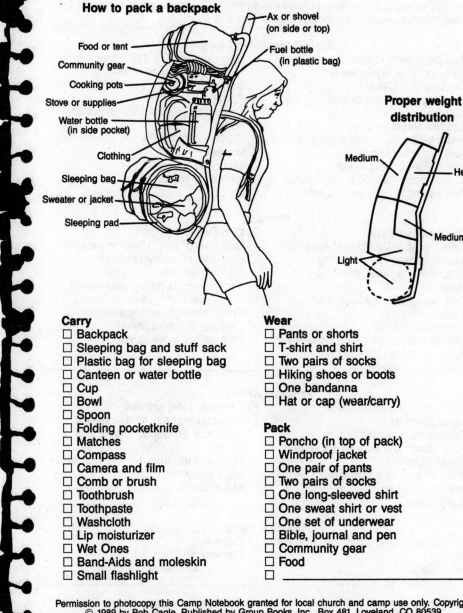

How to pack a backpack

- Ax or shovel (on side or top)
- Food or tent
- Fuel bottle (in plastic bag)
- Community gear
- Cooking pots
- Stove or supplies
- Water bottle (in side pocket)
- Clothing
- Sleeping bag
- Sweater or jacket
- Sleeping pad

Proper weight distribution

- Medium
- Heavy
- Medium
- Light

Carry
- ☐ Backpack
- ☐ Sleeping bag and stuff sack
- ☐ Plastic bag for sleeping bag
- ☐ Canteen or water bottle
- ☐ Cup
- ☐ Bowl
- ☐ Spoon
- ☐ Folding pocketknife
- ☐ Matches
- ☐ Compass
- ☐ Camera and film
- ☐ Comb or brush
- ☐ Toothbrush
- ☐ Toothpaste
- ☐ Washcloth
- ☐ Lip moisturizer
- ☐ Wet Ones
- ☐ Band-Aids and moleskin
- ☐ Small flashlight

Wear
- ☐ Pants or shorts
- ☐ T-shirt and shirt
- ☐ Two pairs of socks
- ☐ Hiking shoes or boots
- ☐ One bandanna
- ☐ Hat or cap (wear/carry)

Pack
- ☐ Poncho (in top of pack)
- ☐ Windproof jacket
- ☐ One pair of pants
- ☐ Two pairs of socks
- ☐ One long-sleeved shirt
- ☐ One sweat shirt or vest
- ☐ One set of underwear
- ☐ Bible, journal and pen
- ☐ Community gear
- ☐ Food
- ☐ _____

Camp Notebook 41

Extended Backpacking Gear Checklist

Here's the gear you'll need for an extended wilderness trip of five days or more. The clothing listed here includes what you'll be wearing when you start. The list doesn't include community equipment and food.

Basic Backpacking Gear

☐ Backpack (with straps or cords for tying on other equipment)
☐ Day bag (for side trips)
☐ Sleeping bag, liner, plastic bag and stuff sack
☐ Ensolite sleeping pad
☐ Two plastic bags large enough to cover your backpack
☐ 8-by-10-foot plastic sheet
☐ 30-foot small (3/8-inch) nylon rope
☐ One flashlight with extra batteries

☐ One drinking cup (with wire handle to hang on belt or pack)
☐ Bowl
☐ Spoon
☐ One quart-size canteen or water bottle
☐ Folding pocketknife (no sheath knives)
☐ Compass
☐ Lighter or matches
☐ _____

Clothing

☐ Poncho or rain suit
☐ Field jacket (60/40 blend, Army surplus or canvas hunting coat)
☐ One heavy sweater, down vest or jacket liner
☐ One heavy long-sleeved shirt (preferably wool)
☐ Two short-sleeved shirts
☐ One or two pairs of long pants (blue jeans, cotton or light wool)
☐ One pair of shorts

☐ One belt
☐ One pair of long johns or pajamas
☐ One pair of heavy boots (or rough high-top shoes)
☐ Three pairs of heavy wool socks
☐ Three pairs of lightweight socks
☐ Three changes of underwear
☐ One hat (to shed water)
☐ One pair of wool gloves
☐ _____
☐ _____

Personal Articles

☐ Washcloth and hand towel
☐ Lip moisturizer
☐ Toothpaste and toothbrush
☐ Face cream (for sun- or snow-burn)
☐ Insect repellent
☐ Bible or scripture portion
☐ Journal and pen
☐ Sunglasses

☐ Personal toilet articles
☐ Personal first aid kit (Band-Aids, moleskin, antiseptic cream, eye wash)
☐ For day trips from base camp, always carry the "Essentials for Mountain Safety" (Diagram 40)
☐ _____

Optional Items

☐ Fishing rod, reel, small lure box and license
☐ Binoculars
☐ Tennis shoes or moccasins

☐ Gaiters
☐ Camera and film
☐ Musical instrument or book
☐ _____

Camp Notebook 42

Extended Canoeing Gear Checklist

Here's the personal gear you'll need for an extended canoeing camp of five days or more. The list doesn't include community equipment.

Basic Canoeing Gear

- ☐ Duffel bag and several plastic bags with twist ties
- ☐ Paddle (if you bring your own)
- ☐ Life jacket (if you bring your own)
- ☐ One clean plastic milk jug for water
- ☐ One plastic bleach jug for bailer
- ☐ 30 feet of 3/8-inch nylon rope
- ☐ Sleeping bag, liner, plastic bag and stuff sack

- ☐ Ensolite sleeping pad
- ☐ One flashlight with extra batteries
- ☐ One drinking cup with handle
- ☐ Plate, fork and spoon
- ☐ Folding pocketknife (no sheath knives)
- ☐ Compass
- ☐ Lighter or matches
- ☐ _____

Clothing

- ☐ Wet shoes (tennis shoes or boots to wear in the canoe)
- ☐ Dry shoes (tennis shoes or moccasins to wear in camp)
- ☐ Poncho or rain jacket and pants
- ☐ Field jacket (60/40 blend, Army surplus or canvas hunting coat)
- ☐ One lightweight sweater or sweat shirt
- ☐ Two medium-weight, long-sleeved shirts

- ☐ Three short-sleeved shirts
- ☐ Two pairs of long pants
- ☐ Two pairs of shorts
- ☐ One belt
- ☐ One pair of pajamas
- ☐ Three pairs of medium-weight socks
- ☐ Three pairs of lightweight socks
- ☐ Four sets of underwear
- ☐ Swimsuit
- ☐ Two towels
- ☐ Hat (with brim) or rain hat

Personal Articles

- ☐ Washcloth and hand towel
- ☐ Lip moisturizer
- ☐ Toothpaste and toothbrush
- ☐ Face cream (for sunburn)
- ☐ Insect repellent
- ☐ Bible or scripture portion

- ☐ Journal and pen
- ☐ Sunglasses
- ☐ Personal toilet articles
- ☐ Personal first aid kit (Band-Aids, moleskin, antiseptic cream, eyewash)

Optional Items

- ☐ Fishing rod, reel, tackle box and license
- ☐ Binoculars

- ☐ Camera and film
- ☐ Musical instrument or book
- ☐ _____

Note: This gear list includes the clothes you'll wear the day you leave for camp. However, pack a separate set of "going home" clothes in a plastic bag to leave in the bus or van until the last day.

Camp Notebook 43

Winter Gear Checklist

The items on this checklist will equip you to enjoy the outdoors for long periods of time in snow, wind and rain. Your outdoor clothing should fit loosely and give you plenty of room inside to hold body heat. You can often borrow gear from family and friends.

Winter Gear

☐ Backpack
☐ Small day bag
☐ Sleeping bag (minimum 2 pounds down or 3 pounds Quallofil or other synthetic filler)
☐ Stuff sack and a plastic bag to fit inside the stuff sack
☐ Two Ensolite pads
☐ One 8-by-10-foot waterproof tarp
☐ 30-foot small (3/8-inch) nylon rope

☐ Plastic bowl
☐ Plastic cup
☐ Spoon
☐ Two quart-size water bottles
☐ Two large plastic trash bags your pack will fit inside
☐ Snowshoes or cross-country skis
☐ Ski boots
☐ Ski poles
☐_____

Clothing

☐ One set of wool or wool-blend long underwear
☐ Two T-shirts or fish net undershirts
☐ Two pairs of loose-fitting underwear
☐ Three pairs of heavy wool socks
☐ Three pairs of medium-weight wool socks
☐ One pair of wool pants
☐ One wool shirt
☐ One wool sweater
☐ Wool cap or balaclava that pulls down over face
☐ Two pairs of wool mittens (or a pair of mittens and a pair of gloves)

☐ Insulated parka (or a down vest, an extra wool shirt and an outer shell)
☐ Night clothes (flannel pajamas, thermal underwear, sweat suit, or comfortable pants and sweat shirt)
☐ One pair of waterproof hiking boots
☐ Rain and wind gear (waterproof pants and jacket)
☐ Bandannas
☐ The clothes you wear to camp and an extra set for the end of the campout
☐_____
☐_____

Personal Articles

☐ Bible or scripture portion
☐ Journal and pens
☐ Toothbrush and toothpaste
☐ Washcloth
☐ Wet Ones
☐ Snow seal for boots
☐ Lip salve
☐ Sun screen
☐ Sunglasses for snow

☐ Extra pieces of nylon cord
☐ "Essentials for Mountain Safety" for day trips (see page 288)
☐ On extended winter day trips, carry extra fire-starter, a stove with fuel and a sleeping bag for every four people.
☐_____

Optional

☐ Gaiters
☐ Space blanket

☐ Pillow
☐_____

Chapter 21

Ropes, Knots and Hitches

Knots are handy for all sorts of things—tying your shoes, wrapping birthday presents, lashing a canoe on top of a car . . . or catching a cookie thief.

That's right. A simple knot on a string caught one of the sliest cookie thieves of all time. Once a ship's chef discovered cookies were missing. He had no idea who could be the culprit, and while everyone knew cookies were missing, no one confessed. Cookies continued to disappear. Finally, on a hunch, the chef tied a string around the cookie box. The next morning at breakfast he announced that he'd discovered the cookie thief. He pointed to a young sailor—the newest crew member.

The sailor hung his head and then admitted his weakness for cookies and his night-watch thievery. "But," he asked, "how did you find out?"

"Well I suspected you, but I couldn't prove it," the chef replied. "I knew all the other sailors here were *real* sailors. But you? We all know your dad pulled strings to get you in the Navy. I figured you wouldn't know the difference between a square knot and a granny knot. Last night I tied the cookie box with a square knot, knowing any real sailor stealing cookies would recognize the knot and tie it back the same way. So when I discovered it was retied with a granny knot, I knew you had to be the culprit."

Basic Knots and Hitches

Knots are commonplace, and we use them all the time. But all knots aren't created equal to campers. Each rope, knot and hitch has a special purpose. Knowing just six or eight good knots will equip campers to handle almost any situation where they need a rope.

This chapter shows how to tie and use basic knots and hitches. Each knot and rope use is introduced through fun, group-building activities. Camp Notebook 44, "Basic Knots and Hitches," summarizes the techniques that are introduced in the activities.

Camp Notebook 44

Basic Knots and Hitches

Bowline knot topping off a fly pole

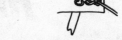

Bowline knot used for leverage

Bowline: A loop knot on the end of a rope—for topping off fly poles or getting leverage on tight lines.

Stopper knot: A securing knot that never slips—for tying canoes to a vehicle's bumper.

Taut-line hitch: A securing knot that slips—for using on tents and fly sheets to prevent ripping in rain and high winds.

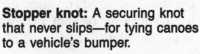

Figure-8 knot: A loop knot in the middle of a rope—for leverage on tight lines, attaching other ropes or tying in the middle person in mountain climbing.

Sheet bend knot: A joining knot—used to tie two ropes together.

Loop knot: Used to top off fly poles or for leverage on tight lines.

Permission to photocopy this Camp Notebook granted for local church and camp use only. Copyright © 1989 by Bob Cagle. Published by Group Books, Inc., Box 481, Loveland, CO 80539.

Rope Activities

The best and most enjoyable way to learn knots and hitches is through a series of group-building activities. Here are several, which build campers' knowledge.

Circle of Ropes

"Circle of Ropes" is a fun group-building activity to use at the beginning of camp. It allows you to identify knots campers can already tie and teach. Or you can use it as a parable for exploring what it means to be a group.

The activity requires an 18-inch length of 3/8-inch nylon rope for each camper. After you cut the rope, be sure to burn the ends with a candle to prevent unraveling.

Begin the activity by inviting group members to stand in a circle. Then ask campers each to tie the ends of their piece of rope to both of their neighbors' ropes. The object is to tie all ropes together to form one large circle.

When all the pieces are tied together, say: "Now we're going to test the strength of the rope circle you made. Hold on to your rope and step backward to pull on the rope. You may want to place one foot slightly forward to keep your balance. Pull evenly as you move slowly backward."

If the rope pieces come untied at any point (which they probably will), stop and wait for the campers to retie the knots. Have participants keep tying and testing the ropes until all the knots hold with firm pulling.

After the activity, spend some time talking about what everyone has learned. Here are three directions to take in the discussion:

1. Ask the group to identify the different knots that were tied during the activity.

2. Sit in a circle and pose a discussion question such as "What can tying the circle of ropes teach us about living together at camp?"

3. Develop your own analogy relating three elements of camp life to the three strands of an ordinary rope.

Ropes Practice Area

A ropes practice area at camp allows several campers to practice the same knots or different knots simultaneously with a leader nearby. It's easy to build a temporary or semipermanent ropes practice area for your camp (see Diagram 43, "Ropes Practice Area").

First, lash a long pole between two trees high enough for campers to reach comfortably. Secure another pole directly below the top pole at about knee level. Then drive two rows of large wooden stakes about eight feet on either side of the poles. The poles and stakes provide attaching and securing points for simulating tying tent ropes, securing a canoe to a car bumper or practicing any variety of knots where you tie both ends of a rope.

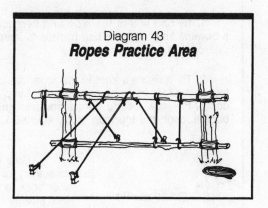

Diagram 43
Ropes Practice Area

Tightropes

Ropes strung tightly between two trees can serve many purposes during a camp. You can use them as clotheslines, a ridge line for a shelter, or a fixed rope for hand-walking or crossing a stream. Stretching a mountain-climbing rope across a deep creek or lake inlet adds a new dimension to tightrope games. Younger children enjoy a hand-walking rope—no matter where you put it. One note: Use only strong mountaineering ropes to support campers.

The first activity in this section teaches campers to make a tightrope. It's followed by several different relays that use tightropes.

Tightrope demonstration. Before camp, acquire small-diameter ropes for the activity (3/8- to 5/8-inch hemp or nylon, which are available in most hardware stores). Have at least one 20- to 30-foot rope for every two campers. (Some camps include a 30-foot length of 3/8-inch nylon rope on the camper's personal gear list.) Choose a demonstration area with lots of trees without lower limbs.

Begin the demonstration by having groups of 10 to 15 campers put up tightropes between trees. If you have lots of campers, divide into small groups and have simultaneous demonstrations. Use the step-by-step approach in Diagram 44, "Putting Up a Tightrope." As you complete each step, let each team of two campers do the same step. Then move on to the next one.

Gear ferry. Use a carabiner (a metal ring used in rock-climbing to reduce friction), two long cords, and buckets or milk crates to create a ferry for shuttling water, supplies or firewood into the campsite. Set up timed relays to see which team spills the least water on a round trip using an open bucket on the ferry. (See Diagram 45, "Gear Ferry.")

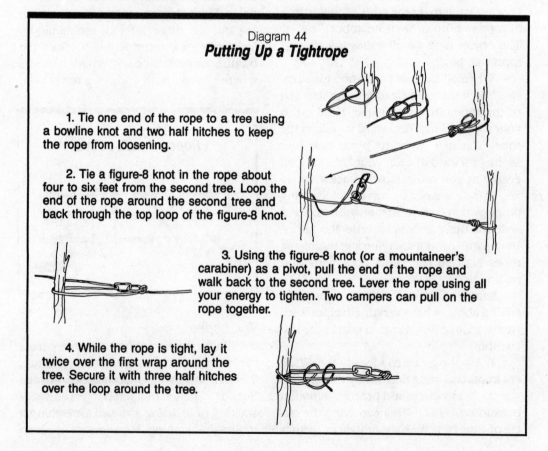

Diagram 44
Putting Up a Tightrope

1. Tie one end of the rope to a tree using a bowline knot and two half hitches to keep the rope from loosening.

2. Tie a figure-8 knot in the rope about four to six feet from the second tree. Loop the end of the rope around the second tree and back through the top loop of the figure-8 knot.

3. Using the figure-8 knot (or a mountaineer's carabiner) as a pivot, pull the end of the rope and walk back to the second tree. Lever the rope using all your energy to tighten. Two campers can pull on the rope together.

4. While the rope is tight, lay it twice over the first wrap around the tree. Secure it with three half hitches over the loop around the tree.

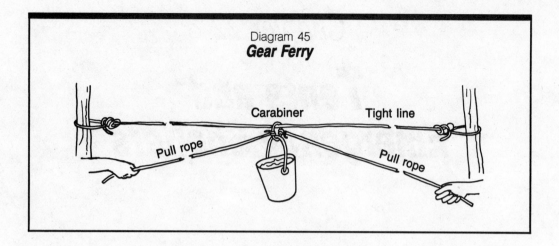

Diagram 45
Gear Ferry

Carabiner   Tight line

Pull rope   Pull rope

Hand-walking relay. Set up a tight-rope across a field, river, pond or pool, and have campers form teams to traverse a make-believe "oil spill" or "crocodile canal." Each camper crosses hand-over-hand on the tightrope without touching the ground or water. Some campers will prefer using hands and feet. If campers touch the ground or water, they must return and start over.

Base the distance on group members' abilities. If the tightrope crosses a river or lake inlet, have onshore spotters on both sides, a nearby spotting canoe and observers to check the knots after each crossing.

Rainy Day Ropes

Tying ropes, knots and hitches makes a great indoor activity for a rainy afternoon at camp. One group of junior high campers found refuge in a backcountry picnic shelter during a rainstorm. The sturdy structure had a myriad of poles and logs in a peaked ceiling. Once the fire was going in the cooking fireplace, out came the ropes. The highlight of the afternoon came when the group rigged a seat for the smallest camper and hoisted him to the highest pole rafters.

Another inventive rained-in day-camp group taught different knots by lashing together tables in the church basement. They turned the existing tables upside down to provide the upright posts for legs. Then they borrowed three bundles of quarter-round poles from the local lumberyard and lashed them together for the table top.

Chapter 22

Tents and
Emergency Shelters

"The sky's clear. Who needs a tent?" Experienced campers traveling in mild weather who are equipped with rain gear and emergency tarps may be able to defend such a statement. But group camping without shelter is out of the question. You can never assume that the weather won't change. In fact even on backcountry day trips you should carry personal rain gear and an 8-by-10-foot plastic emergency tarp for every four campers as insurance against foul weather or an emergency.

Even with adequate gear, setting up a tent in the rain requires skill and forethought. A good rule to follow in backcountry camping is to set up your shelter or tent at every campsite. If the weather is clear and you can sleep under the stars, great. But it's backcountry wisdom to sleep under the stars with a tent pitched nearby in case of an unexpected storm.

Choosing Tents

Selecting appropriate tents is an important consideration for camp leaders. In the long run it's often a good idea for a church to purchase a set of matched tents that all campers learn to use. But—at least for the first few trips—most camping groups and churches borrow or rent tents. This ap-

proach can help leaders decide what works best for most of the camping experiences they lead.

As a general rule, a good tent combination includes lightweight tents for sleeping and a larger wall tent for group meetings. The lightweight tents are useful both for backcountry trips and stationary base camps. Here are several items to consider in outfitting your group:

1. Weight, style, size and construction. These are the major factors to consider in any tent choice. Compare cost and value.

2. Tent style. Tent styles vary a great deal. Internal-frame tents are currently the most popular, since they're easy to set up and they're rigid in windy and rocky areas. Camp Notebook 45, "Common Tents," shows the most popular styles.

3. Camping season. Will you be camping in the winter or summer or both? Tents are classified as three-season or four-season. Four-season tents are more weather-resistant, have a heavier construction and are more expensive.

4. Number of people. How many campers do you want in each tent? Two-person tents give campers privacy and rest and increase the chance that everyone will be included in conversations.

Three- or four-person tents provide more height and sometimes less weight per person. However, three campers and their gear usually fill a four-person tent. Four people can use a four-person tent if they store their gear outside in plastic bags or under tarps.

5. Group tent. A large wall tent or base camp tent is the key to group life in winter or inclement weather. A western-style whitewall tent with an asbestos roof ring for a sheepherders wood stove provides comfort and space in any kind of weather. However, these big tents are heavier and harder to dry, and they take more time to set up and take down.

Tenting Tips

In addition to having appropriate equipment, a tenting camp's success also rests on using the tent in the best ways possible. Here are some tips to keep in mind in choosing your tent site, pitching your tent, protecting your tent and taking it down:

Choosing a tent site. In selecting a tent site for your camp, look for a place with the following characteristics:

1. A level site keeps campers from rolling downhill while they sleep. It also allows you to avoid trenching rainwater runoff.

2. Avoid having to cut and clear undergrowth. Also make sure it's free from poisonous plants, anthills and bee nests.

3. Find a place that's protected from wind. Pitch the tent with its back into the wind. Also make sure it's protected from overhead deadfall trees and limbs. Also check for overhead snow-loaded limbs. Don't choose a site in a canyon, ravine, gully or dry stream bed that might flash flood.

4. Set the tents upwind from the campfire to prevent possible fire hazards.

Pitching a tent. Once you've chosen a site, here's how to set up the tent for com-

fort and durability:

1. Remove fallen sticks, cones and rocks that are uncomfortable for sleeping. (Put them back later to restore the wilderness to its condition when you found it.)

2. In snow, pack down the snow with a shovel or skis—or shovel down to compacted snow. (See page 150 for more on setting up tents in snow.)

3. Stake out back corners. Then pull front center forward until the floor is taut and smooth. Next stake out the front corners so the floor is square.

4. Set up poles and stake out tent walls. Secure the tent to trees, rocks, stumps or roots if doing so doesn't create a camper hazard or harm vegetation.

5. Place tent fly over the tent and stake it out, leaving plenty of air space between fly and tent ceiling to prevent condensation.

Protecting a tent. Tents are a major camping investment, so it's important to take care of them. With proper care they'll give many years of service. Here are some pointers:

1. When entering or leaving a tent always unzip the entrance zipper completely—top to bottom and center to side. Otherwise you can tear zippers, screens and flaps—a deadly prospect in mosquito season!

2. Make a quick tent-repair kit by wrapping eight to 10 inches of silver duct tape around your tent poles. The tape is always handy to make a temporary repair over a small rip or hole.

3. Use a plastic ground sheet to prolong the tent floor's life. It also prevents water from coming into the tent during rain. However, a ground sheet keeps water out only if it's rolled under at the edges. This way the tent wall completely overhangs the ground sheet. Otherwise, the ground sheet catches water, sending even more under the

Camp Notebook 45
Common Tents

Backpacking Tent
A lightweight tent that sleeps two campers. Easy for one or two campers to set up. Also comes in a four-camper size.

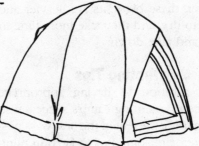

Dome Tent
Sleeps three campers and their gear—or four campers with gear stored outside. Easy for two campers to erect.

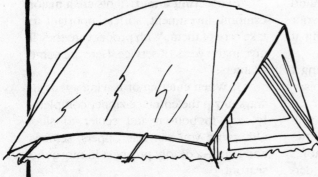

Base Camp Tent
A larger version of the backpacking tent. It provides a large meeting space for a group in cold or wet weather, and three or four campers can set it up. Maximize space by storing gear outside.

Western-Style Wall Tent
With an asbestos roof ring for a sheepherders wood stove, it provides comfort and space in any kind of weather.

tent.

4. Slip a few handfuls of leaves or pine needles under the edges of the rolled-under ground sheet to keep the edges slightly off the ground. This will help water run under the sheet where it's absorbed into the ground.

5. In high wind areas, cross-rope and double-rope tents. To cross-rope tie long cords diagonally, corner-to-corner over the fly. When a high wind blows, the cords distribute the stress evenly over the fly, preventing tugging at the corners and grommets. Double-rope the end poles or end frames by using an 18- to 20-foot cord rope. Tie a larks-head knot in the middle of the rope over the pole tip or frame. Tie both rope ends diagonally away from the center poles.

6. If you leave for a long time, slightly loosen all the ropes.

Packing up a tent. How you pack up and store your tent after camp has a major impact on how many times you'll be able to use the tent. Let's look at how to pack a tent quickly and effectively:

1. An easy way to clean a tent is to turn it inside out and shake it.

2. To protect zippers, close all zippers before rolling the tent.

3. Spread a tent flat. Then fold it side-to-side in thirds, and roll from back toward the front. This procedure puts the least pressure on zippers and netting. As you roll, brush away any leaves and dirt that cling to the tent.

4. Unroll wet tents as soon as possible, and hang them up for drying before storage. A good way to dry a tent at the end of a trip is to hang it upside down by the corners to nearby tree limbs or the garage ceiling.

Other Backcountry Shelters

You don't have to have a manufactured tent to have shelter in the backcountry. There are several inexpensive alternatives for warmer weather and for emergency situations. Let's look at some of these. They're also pictured in Camp Notebook 46, "Shelters."

E-rope shelters. You can make a practical and inexpensive E-rope shelter for warm summer climates out of builders plastic. Here's what you need for a shelter that will accommodate eight to 10 campers:

● One 10-by-16-foot sheet of 6-mil builders plastic.
● One 12-by-16-foot sheet of 6-mil builders plastic.
● Two 30-foot pieces of 3/8-inch nylon rope.
● Two 15-foot pieces of 3/8-inch nylon rope.
● 24 strong clamps. (Office paper clamps work well used over a durable plastic patch to protect the plastic sheeting.)

Choose a spot with a triangle of trees—two about 20 feet apart and a center tree about 12 to 15 feet off the line between the first two. The third tree should be downhill from the first two. (See Camp Notebook 46, "Shelters.")

String a tightrope (A) between the first two trees about four feet above the ground (see Chapter 21 for instructions on tying a tightrope). Before stretching the rope, tie a figure-8 knot midway between the trees.

Once tightrope A is in place, tie a center ridge rope (B) between the center of rope A and the center tree. You now have two ridge ropes in the form of a "T." Then tie two more ropes to rope A about seven feet to either side of center rope B. Later you'll secure these two ropes to the ground. The E-rope framework is now in place.

Next lay the 12-by-16-foot plastic sheet on the ground under the rope framework. Then clamp it to tightrope A with about six

Camp Notebook 46
Shelters

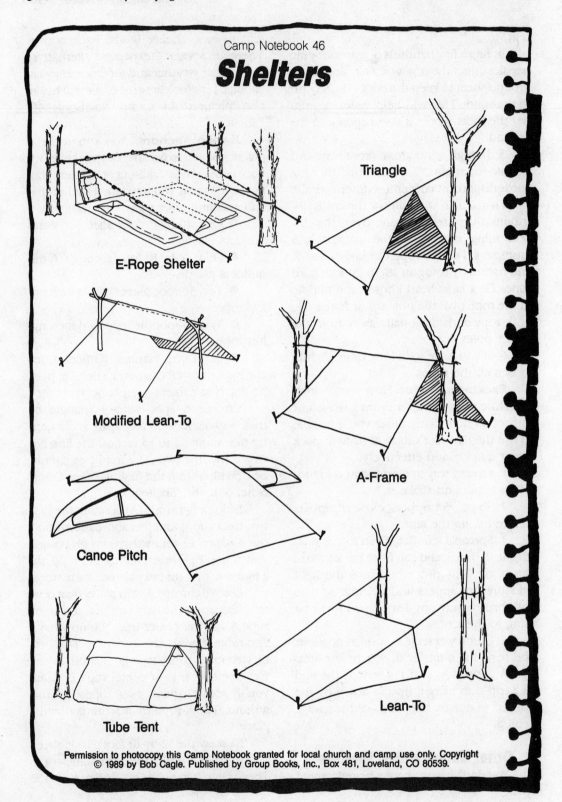

Triangle

E-Rope Shelter

Modified Lean-To

A-Frame

Canoe Pitch

Tube Tent

Lean-To

inches of overlap. It provides ground cover and the back wall of the shelter. Water running downhill from behind the shelter will pass beneath the plastic floor.

Now clamp the second plastic sheet over the edge of the first sheet and along the three ropes tied to the main rope A. This sheet forms the roof. Attach the two hanging ropes to the ground with stakes or rocks, or tie them to roots or tree trunks.

For further protection secure ponchos or pieces of plastic at either end of the shelter. Use the same clamps along the top edge and fasten at ground level with rocks or string.

The E-rope shelter provides enough snug space for as many as 10 campers and their gear. On a rainy day you can prepare a meal on a stove under the shelter's front peak. The shelter's total weight usually runs about 10 pounds—or one pound per person.

Tarp shelters and tube tents. It's easy to set up a version of the popular plastic emergency tube tent. All you need is a single tightrope between two trees. Use strong clamps to secure a plastic sheet or tarp to the rope. Then secure the edges to the ground using rocks or stakes or tying the ends to roots or tree trunks. To keep from getting wet in blowing rain, pull the ends inside and clamp them. This also prevents water from running into the tent from the bottom edge.

Nylon and plastic reinforced tarps with ropes and grommets in the edges are useful for rain flies, cooking shelters or tube tents. Outdoor warehouses and builder supply houses often have special sales on 8-by-10-foot and 9-by-12-foot sizes. Experimenting with several ways of pitching tube tents or tarps can help you decide which way they work best and how many people they will shelter. Camp Notebook 46, "Shelters," shows some of the many ways to make shelters out of tarps.

Tent-Pitching Activities

Pitching a tent at camp can be a great group-building time for your group. Not only do campers set up shelter for the night, but they work together and learn new skills. Here are some activities you can use to teach campers to set up different tents and shelters.

Emergency Shelter

Inventing an emergency shelter is a new experience for many campers. To do it without instruction adds another challenge. It's a good first-day activity for base camp. It's ideal for preparing backpackers, canoeists and day trippers for dealing with unexpected weather.

Materials. Each group of two to four campers will need the following items packed in a day pack:

1. An 8-by-10-foot plastic tarp or sheet.
2. Thirty feet of 3/8-inch nylon rope.
3. Assorted cords, twine or shoelaces.

Directions. Begin the activity by saying: "Imagine that we're on a trip today—miles into the backcountry. A driving rainstorm suddenly catches us by surprise. You have in your day packs a plastic tarp, some rope and some string. Each team has 30 minutes to set up an emergency shelter.

"When the time finishes, we'll all gather back here for a walking tour of our emergency homes. We'll ask each construction crew questions such as 'Why did you choose this location? How does this shelter protect you? How would you improve it if you had to stay here for several hours?'

"After our tour we'll talk about how you made decisions and what you learned that would be practical for camping or living in this group for a week. Okay? Any questions? Shelter-building time!" Proceed with the activity as you explained it. (For examples of possible emergency shelters, see Camp Notebook 46, "Shelters.")

A variation on the emergency shelter activity (which is particularly effective in staff training) is to create the emergency to include an injury simulation. Increase the group sizes to four to six people, and describe the simulation details—time, place, weather conditions, nature of the injury and available equipment.

Non-Verbal Tent Pitching

This activity helps campers practice focusing, concentrating and cooperating. It's most effective when you're actually ready to set up tents for the first night of camping. You may want to schedule it to follow verbal get-acquainted activities or high-energy get-acquainted times.

Materials. Tents with ropes, poles and stakes. (Include printed instructions if they're available.)

Directions. Prepare in advance all the tents so they're ready to set up after your demonstration. Invite campers who know

accepted tent-pitching techniques to help demonstrate. Or invite an uninitiated camper to join an adult leader for the setup (only one person needs to know correct procedures for the demonstration). Then say: "Today we're going to set up our fabulous homes for the week—without talking. That's right—no words. Not even little ones. Grunting or growling is okay."

Then begin the demonstration. Introduce the two demonstrators, and invite the other campers to form a circle around them as they set up their tent non-verbally. After the demonstration have the campers start setting up their own tents—without any talking. If they have questions, they can signal to the two demonstrators to ask for help.

After all the tents are pitched, take time to talk about what everyone learned from the activity. Answer any questions, and give further verbal instruction about tent technique, tying taut line-hitches, cross-roping and caring for tents.

Chapter 23

Wood-Cutting and Fire-Building

"Can we go tell the ranger? Can we tell 'em to put it out?"

Three junior high campers had just confronted their first lawbreakers in a pristine wilderness area of Oregon's Cascade Range. They were outraged by campers who had built a fire beside a huge glacial boulder.

Before entering the wilderness area, the young campers had learned how to build "no-trace fires" using techniques that lessen a fire's impact on the natural surroundings. Later they built their own fire in a small, established fire pit far back from the lake.

The concerned campers did tell the backcountry ranger. The appreciative ranger talked quite a while with the young campers about the wilderness and how to care for it. He explained how irresponsible campers had used a giant boulder as a fireplace for many years, and he assured the group that he'd talk with these offenders. The next morning the young hikers passed the granite sentinel again. It was blackened not by one but numerous fires.

There are two major steps in helping campers learn safe and responsible fire-building outdoors. First, they must learn to gather wood without injuring themselves

or the wilderness. Second, they must know where and how to build fires with minimum physical and visual impact on the natural surroundings.

Gathering Wood Safely

The ax, saw and knife are considered the three basic outdoor tools. They have many different uses, but no other activity requires them more than fire-building—which calls for all three.

Campers of all ages and both sexes enjoy the feel of cutting wood and the immediate sense of accomplishment it brings. However, unless they observe strict safety guidelines and use the tools properly, serious and tragic injury can result.

Safety First

The primary consideration in using saws, axes and knives is safety. We'll discuss specific techniques and safety rules for each tool later in the chapter, but first let's discuss three general factors that contribute to safe tool use:

Sharpness. To be safe, all camp tools should be very sharp. Though it may sound like a contradiction, dull tools are more dangerous. Because they're not sharp enough to cut deep and true, they're more likely to slip, glance or bounce back.

You don't need to teach campers how to sharpen tools before they learn to use them, but be sure all tools are sharp and in good condition the first time campers use them.

Condition. Using a tool in poor condition is inviting trouble. Before using a tool or letting a camper use a tool, make sure it's in good working order. Ax heads should be secure. Cracked handles should be replaced. And all the sharp edges should be covered by a strong leather or canvas sheath when they're not in use.

Wood-cutting area. Designate a wood-cutting area at every campsite. Having this area prevents other campers from accidentally stumbling into someone with a sharp wood-cutting tool. Use a long cord or twine to rope off the area between four trees, and tie surveyor's tape to the cord between each tree so it's easily visible. Then allow only one camper inside the cutting area at any time—unless the saw is made for two people. Station another camper or counselor next to the cutting area to act as spotter. This person should remind the cutter about safety procedures, if necessary. Also designate a tool area where you store all cutting tools.

It's important to remember that a cutting area will be highly impacted by boots and wood-cutting. Choose an area that can withstand the impact. Avoid areas with grasses, flowers or small shrubs. When you leave the campsite restore the area to its natural state. Use the wood chips in the area in your last campfire, or disperse them widely.

Using Saws

A camp saw needs to be lightweight and easy to pack and store. Some of the best saws for campers include:

Folding saw. Available from many hardware stores and camping departments. It's specifically designed for camping and packing.

Bow saw. An excellent tool for campers when packing and storage aren't problems. Always carry a bow saw with a cover.

Cutoff handsaw. Professional outfitters in the north woods often use a standard handsaw that they cut off to fit in a pack. They make leather sheaths to guard the blade.

Pruning saw. Some professional outfitters use a pruning saw from a garden shop.

Saws require technical setting and honing to sharpen. Most hardware stores or saw shops will do this for you at a minimal cost.

The primary danger with saws is sawing at angles and accidentally scraping or cutting a leg, knee or thumb. To avoid these common errors, teach campers to visualize their bodies and the saw as a right angle so that all parts of their bodies are behind or beside the saw blade. After cutting, replace the blade cover and return the saw to the designated tool area.

To further ensure camper safety with older campers, two campers should do all sawing beyond the designated cutting area. One person cuts; the other acts as a spotter.

Using Axes

While hatchets are popular, they're unacceptable tools for young campers—and they're even very dangerous tools for adults. Why? With a hatchet it's difficult to maintain a safe distance between the hatchet head and the woodcutter's knees, shins or feet.

An ax with a full-length handle doubles or triples the distance between the camper and the ax head. The most practical, lightweight ax for trip camping is a Hudson Bay ax, which has a lightweight head and a wide cutting edge. It weighs little more than a hatchet, and its handle is approximately 22 inches long.

Ax safety. You can't overemphasize ax safety. Most campers and counselors use an ax very little at home, and even those who do often develop lax safety practices. To illustrate the carelessness that sometimes occurs when an ax (or any tool) becomes commonplace, visualize this scene from a western youth camp: Three steps take you to the narrow lodge porch. Snow and ice cover both the steps and the porch. Beside the door at the top of the steps is a large chunk of ponderosa pine. Stuck in the pine is a double-bit ax with two sharp edges. One edge is in the wood; the other is in the open air about thigh-high to any camper making the icy ascent.

The safest position to use an ax is kneeling. From this position, any missed blow will hit the cutting log or the ground—it won't glance. While this technique is best for any camper of any age, it's essential for young, inexperienced campers.

Another safety measure for ax-cutting is to saw the wood you're going to split into "sixth-grade lengths" of 10 to 12 inches. Shorter pieces split easier and faster. Moreover, even the most inexperienced campers can succeed with this technique on their first attempts. Camp Notebook 47, "Using an Ax," illustrates proper ax use.

One longtime camp leader says he even uses these basic techniques at home. "It's not only safer," he says, "it keeps me on a level with my own children. If they choose to split a hickory stump in the ground it's their choice. They're not trying to outdo me just because I can cut bigger pieces of wood."

Sharpening an ax. To sharpen an ax, use the procedure illustrated in Camp Notebook 47, "Using an Ax." Begin by driving a small peg into the ground. Then lay the

ax blade on the peg to give you the tilt you need to keep the blade off the ground while you're sharpening it. Kneel with one knee on the handle and the other knee on the ground.

First use a medium-coarse file to cut down the blade's shoulder, then its edge. You can tell when you've filed down an area when it's silver and shiny. Then reverse the process and file the opposite side. When you've filed both sides, there should be a thin wire edge on the blade.

To hone the edge to a fine finish, use a round whetstone. If the stone has a rough side and a smooth side, use the rough side first. Hold the ax in one hand with your thumb across the handle behind the ax head. Rest the handle on your shoulder. Make circular motions with the whetstone moving the full length of the blade edge. Reverse to finish the opposite side.

Lightly oil the newly sharpened blade. Store the ax in a leather sheath in a designated spot. The safest place to store an ax is flat on the ground under a canoe or nearby log—not sticking up in a log or stump where it could be stumbled over in the dark.

Using Knives

A folding pocketknife, Swiss Army knife or folding sheath knife is adequate for most camp jobs. Use a fixed-blade knife, or a sheath knife, only for specialized jobs— slicing, cleaning fish or other big jobs. Sheath knives should be carried only inside a pack or saddlebag. Like the hatchet, sheath knives pose a serious danger, particularly since few sheaths are lined with metal anymore. An accidental fall or blow over the blade can force the blade through the sheath and into the thigh.

Knife safety. There are four basic rules to using a knife at camp:

1. Use your knife only when you're

Camp Notebook 47

Using an Ax

Youth ax

Hudson Bay ax

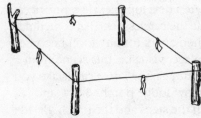

Wood-cutting area

Chopping

Splitting wood
on knees

Log stops any
swings that
miss

Sharpening an Ax

Filing ax head

Peg in ground
elevates ax blade

Edge angle

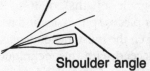

Shoulder angle

Finishing touches
using a whetstone

Move whetstone
in circles

away from the group to avoid accidental contact. A designated area works best.

2. Use your knife only when you're sitting or kneeling.

3. Never walk around with your knife open, and never lay it aside still open.

4. Always open and close your knife away from you.

Sharpening knives. Sharpen knives with a large whetstone. Hold it in one hand, and place the knife blade on the stone at a 20-degree angle. Move the blade across the stone as if you were shaving or whittling the stone—two or three strokes per side until the edge has a fine wire feel. As you sharpen, rotate the stone in your hand to keep from wearing a groove in one spot on the stone.

Finish the blade with a hard Arkansas stone—a fine oil stone—using the same motions (or the side of a leather boot). You can get an even finer edge by "stropping" the blade on a leather belt. Put one end of the belt under your foot, and hold the other end tightly. Wipe the blade backward, up the belt toward you. The belt will remove any remaining metal burrs and wire edges.

Minimum-Impact Fire-Building

In recent years, more and more parks and wilderness areas have begun requiring groups to camp in designated campsites. They've also limited the size of camping groups because of the physical, visual and audible impact on the environment when many people travel together. But these restrictions don't eliminate the need to exercise good judgment when it comes to gathering wood and building a fire. Deciding where and when to build fires requires careful consideration of three factors:

1. Available firewood.

2. Fire danger in the area.

3. The actual fire site's impact on the terrain.

Wood is abundant in many camps, national forests and wilderness areas. We shouldn't assume that campfires will destroy the environment. Timber is our only renewable resource. In many places you can responsibly have campfires for cooking and group enjoyment.

However, there are also many areas where wood is scarce—and they're not just in the West and in high mountain ranges. Even in northern woods, undisciplined wood-gathering has depleted supplies of usable wood around many established campsites. Thus, leaders and campers must make conscientious judgment about how a fire would impact the wilderness where they're camping.

Fire-building guidelines. Here are some guidelines for fire-building to help you preserve the natural quality of campsites you use:

1. Gather wood where it's readily available. If your campsite is depleted of usable wood, gather wood along the route to camp where deadfall or driftwood are plentiful. Send "wood scavengers" deep into the areas where usable wood is abundant, and gather sparingly. Don't concentrate your gathering in one place.

2. Use only downed trees. *Never* cut a living tree.

3. If possible, use an established fire circle. If there's a ring of rocks or an area that's been repeatedly used by other campers, go ahead and use it. This will concentrate the impact in one spot.

4. Plan your campfire for a specific time for cooking and/or group gathering. Don't keep a campfire going "just to have a fire" or just because wood is available.

5. Keep your fire small and intimate. Large fires cause people to move back. Smaller campfires invite people to be close and to talk without raising their voices or

fighting the heat and smoke. Small, concentrated fires also are more efficient for most cooking.

6. If wood is scarce, don't feel obligated to have a campfire. A circle of candles (one for each camper) provides a "warm" circle of light for a friendship circle. That's all you need in mild climates. It can also symbolize your commitment to be careful with nature.

Digging a fire site. Sometimes you'll camp in areas without established fire circles or other fire sites. In these cases, your challenge is to camp "without a trace." Your goal is to leave the site as undisturbed as possible. Thus, in choosing a new fire site, it's important to take every precaution to minimize the fire's impact on the environment.

Here are the steps (also illustrated in Camp Notebook 48, "Minimum-Impact Fires") to choosing and digging a minimum-impact fire site:

1. Choose the area that's least likely to show impact. Avoid fragile areas of moss, flowers and grass. A large, rocky area is ideal, since it allows campers to gather on the rocks where they'll make little impact. Choose a spot that's as level as possible for comfort while cooking or getting warm— and to prevent someone from stumbling into the fire.

2. If the area has living vegetation, use a trowel or shovel to remove the vegetation like chunks of sod. Unearth a spot about 10 to 12 inches wide and 16 to 20 inches long. Place sod pieces out of the traffic so they will stay intact for replacing later. Water it. Also water around the edge of the fire area.

3. Dig through the humus soil until you reach mineral soil. The humus soil is like leaf particles and roots. It's smelly. Mineral soil is sandy, gravelly or pure dirt with no evidence of plant decomposition

in it. Pile all soil from the fire site in one place to replace later. If you run into tree roots, replace the sod and move to another site to start over.

4. Once you've removed the sod and humus, you're ready to dig the actual fire pit. Begin by digging a five- to six-inch-wide trench that's about 12 to 15 inches long. Slope from surface level on one end to about six inches deep on the other. The slope provides a natural draft. The narrow trench also concentrates heat and gives you secure edges to hold pots and pans without a grate. You don't need to circle the fire pit with rocks; in the wilderness, fire scars on rocks are telltale signs of campers.

Another approach used by Louisiana old-timers is the "cross fire." You can adapt this method for smaller fires by following essentially the same steps described above. However, make the trench narrower and intersect it with a second "cross" trench. This technique gives you a cross-shape cooking area. Or you can spread coals in the trench for multiple utensils or foil cooking.

Building your fire. A successful fire has to be carefully laid so the first match will catch and the fire will burn without a lot of pampering. Here are the steps:

1. Before actually building a fire, make sure you have a large container of water near the campsite. (On a backpacking trip, you can use three or four water bottles or a collapsible bucket filled with water.)

2. Insulate your fire pit from dampness with a small cushion of sticks or litter from the forest floor. In snow and rain split a few medium-size dead limbs to expose the dry core. This keeps the fire from burning through to the dampness too quickly.

3. On the cushion of litter and sticks, place tinder wood such as pine needles, fuzz sticks whittled from dry sticks, wood shavings or loose twine pulled apart and fluffed into a ball. You can find dry, flam-

Camp Notebook 48

Minimum-Impact Fires

Cross fire for more ventilation or more pots

Slanting trench creates draft
Natural edges support pots

Set sod aside to save

Feed fuel from sides

Wet-weather fire

mable tinder in the heart of a dead pine snag that's still standing. Resin drippings on the sides of pine trees also ignite easily.

4. Overlay the tinder with kindling. Start with lots of small sticks, then add larger ones. In wet or damp weather, use more small sticks to get a quick bed of hot coals.

5. Then add split wood for fuel on top of the larger sticks. Now your foundation is ready for one match right in the bottom.

6. Once the fire gets going, you can dry more wood on top of or beside the fire. And you can heat a covered pot of water while you're waiting for flames to burn down to coals for cooking. After cooking, return the water pot to the hottest area so you'll have enough hot water for hot beverages and for sterilizing dishes.

Fires for wet, cold and windy weather. Fires for drying out and keeping warm are often necessary for comfort and safety. You can find dry wood even in a downpour. Check dead trees that are still standing or the sheltered limbs and trunks of deadfall. Often you'll spot dry places untouched by rain or snow. Once you spot the lighter-color, dry wood, cut it into short lengths, and split it with an ax to get to the dry and flammable inner core. Sometimes the wood will be decaying, making it easy to break by hand.

If you're building a drying-out fire in a new fire site, follow the same steps listed earlier, except enlarge the area and leave out the trench—especially if getting warm is more important than cooking at the moment. Instead of the trench, build the fire against a back log, and use larger wood than you would for cooking. Lay a "roof" of small logs up against the back log. The slope drains the water while the fire burns up from the bottom. When you use larger wood, make sure the fire is tended until all the wood burns and no charred logs remain.

You can also "pigpen" the fire by stacking wood alternately like a log cabin. This technique creates more air space for drafting.

If possible in rainy or snowy weather, shield the fire from the wet with a plastic sheet pitched at the edge of the fire so that it's high enough for smoke to escape.

If wind is stealing the cooking heat from your fire or stove, shelter it in any of a number of ways:

1. Prop a canoe on its edge nearby, and balance it with paddles.

2. For small stoves use a backpacking utensil roll as a wind-shelter for small stoves. Keep it upright with four long aluminum nails or small sticks.

3. Use an Ensolite sleeping pad as a wind screen. Wrap it around the fire area without getting it too close to be damaged.

No-trace cleanup. The final step of conscientious wilderness fire-building is no-trace cleanup. When a fire is "out-out" (usually the next morning), you're ready to hide the fire site without a trace. To be sure your fire is out, touch the coals with your bare hands, stir and feel again. Add some water and stir just to be sure. (One suggestion: It's easier to clean up the fire site without rush or doubt if you cook your last meal on a stove.)

When you're positive the fire's completely extinguished, scatter big handfuls of the ashes with circular motions over a large area. The scattered particles will disappear soon under falling leaves or needles, or they will be covered by new undergrowth. You even need to scatter ashes in snow; otherwise your fire will be sitting right on top of the earth when the snow melts.

Then replace the soil, humus and sod you dug out for the fire area. Water the sod if necessary. Scatter any remaining firewood on hand. Then copy the natural environment by placing a few limbs, rocks and deadfall over the site. In a few months, no one will ever know you camped there.

Group-Building Through Fire-Building

After fire-building instruction, divide your group into three-person teams. Give each team two matches. Ask teams each to prepare and light a fire as quickly as possible. The test of their fire is when it burns through a piece of yarn or twine that you tie 18 inches above each fire-building site (using two trees or two stakes). Each team that accomplishes its task then cheers other teams until *all* have succeeded—even if it means trying over after running out of matches.

Chapter 24

Food and Cooking

"Food is a gift, a communion, a creation." Dorcas Miller[1]

Food always tastes better outdoors. Campers often discover the foods they didn't like are pretty tasty once they've helped prepare them. Menu-planning, food-purchasing and cooking together reinforce the lifelong process of shared homemaking. Camp meals can also be special times—holy times when campers share their thoughts and express appreciation for sharing life with others in Christian community.

The watchword for cooking and sharing camp meals is "Take Time!" Don't rush. Plan a beverage or appetizer snack to set the tone and slow the group down. Juice or hot chocolate before breakfast, cheese and crackers or a Walking Salad (page 329) before supper are all it takes to give campers a sense of family community. With tents up, canoes racked and a cup in hand, meal preparation time becomes a great socializing event.

This chapter is a common-sense guide to backcountry cooking over fires and small camp stoves. It also contains a few special treats for teenagers. Nutritionist-approved menus for different types of camps are found on pages 76, 91, 132 and 152.

Menu-Planning Guidelines

Budgeting, negotiating menus, making shopping lists and purchasing food for camp can be fun, life-skills training for teenage campers. Planning camp meals can be a special group-building time. Dedicate half an hour of an orientation session to meal-planning by teams of three or four campers. It usually works best, then, to have teams cook the meals they plan and purchase. Those who've never shopped together with eight or 10 people find camp-shopping unusually fun. Groups can purchase and repackage food before the trip—or en route if the trip is a long way from home.

Several factors influence your choice of menus. Let's examine some of the major factors:

Backcountry needs. Plan with your utensils, stoves and fires in mind. Don't plan meals that require more pots and pans than you have available at one time! Explain to food planning and purchasing teams what utensils, fires and stoves they'll have and whether there'll be refrigeration.

Schedule. Adjust menus to fit the rhythm and schedule you plan for camp. For example:

1. Plan quick-and-easy meals (QE) for first nights, early starts and long days. Use any fresh meats the first night. Wrap frozen meats in newspaper for insulation. They'll thaw very slowly while canoeing or backpacking in the summer. And they'll hold for the duration of many winter trips when stored properly.

2. On layover days (LD), plan whole foods cooked from scratch, celebration meals and meals that require leisurely preparation. For example, baking, bean-hole cooking and planking fish require special fires that take time. Long mornings and short travel days with long evenings also provide the leisure needed to prepare special treats.

3. Plan special foods for celebration events at important points on the trip.

4. Plan foods that are easy to package and repackage. When repackaging foods, be sure to tear the cooking instructions from the original package and place inside your new package.

Nutrition. Plan nutritionally balanced meals that include meat and meat substitutes, cereals and grains, milk products, fruits and vegetables. Avoid a steady diet of freeze-dried and dehydrated foods. While a three- to five-day wilderness trip poses no major nutritional crisis for teenagers, it's important to provide meals that allow young people to discover how to plan and prepare balanced meals.

Plan for 3,000-plus calories for summer days and 4,000-plus calories per day in winter. Provide both sources of quick energy (sugars) and slow energy (fats). Be aware that outdoor living is strenuous, and your body requires more calories. Plan daily snacks for midmorning and afternoon snacks to keep energy up.

In recent years, many outdoor schools and church camps have moved toward more whole food cooking on backcountry trips. In her book *The New Healthy Trail Food Book*, Outward Bound instructor Dorcas Miller outlines numerous scratch-cooking recipes and bulk food lists for the backcountry pantry.[2] *NOLS Cookery* from the National Outdoor Leadership School describes backcountry cooking techniques, nutrition considerations, whole food lists and minimum-impact cooking methods.[3]

Chapters 5 to 8 suggest specific menus for different types of camps. To keep track of your camp's menus, keep a camp cookbook. Here's one system: Reserve one page for each meal in a loose-leaf notebook. Put the menu in upper-left corner, the shopping list for entire menu in upper-right corner and recipes in the lower-left. Label menu pages B, L or D for breakfast, lunch or dinner, and number the upper-right corner of the page.

Get campers involved in creating this church camp cookbook. Ask each camper to bring a recipe or menu from home, or work in small groups to invent recipes or menus. Add pages for new treats as you go along, and use those pages that get bad reviews to pad your emergency fire starting kit!

Backcountry Cooking Methods

Having the right fire and cooking when it's ready are the secrets to successful open-fire outdoor cooking. Let's examine five approaches to backcountry cooking you can use when backpacking, canoeing or car camping. Each type of fire is illustrated in Camp Notebook 49, "Backcountry Cooking." Chapter 23 tells how to build a no-trace fire in the backcountry.

Reflector oven baking. Reflector cooking is ideal for leisurely meals when you have abundant wood for fuel. Biscuits, cupcakes and cookies are delightful treats in the backcountry!

When using a reflector oven, build a

bright, blazing fire with flames as high as the top of the oven. To keep the flames hot, feed the fire with small sticks, chips or finger-size wood splits.

Use shallow pans for cakes and cobblers. Pour the batter or mix 3/4- to 1-inch thick; it will cook faster than a deep, wet cake. Small loaf pans are better than the large ones. It takes a small loaf of bread 25 to 30 minutes to bake.

Commercial-made reflector ovens are available from camp catalogs and outdoor shops. However, you can improvise reflector ovens from shiny cookie sheets or by recycling rectangular aluminum pans. Arrange the durable aluminum pieces with rocks or sticks. Cover the ends with aluminum foil. Most important, have the baking shelf level on a firm base and the top and bottom pieces angled to reflect the heat from top and bottom. Other options include:

● Making the reflector oven completely from aluminum foil.

● Cutting a pasteboard box end-to-end along the opposite corners of the box. Cover it with foil to create an oven. Then secure a disposable baking sheet or foil-covered pasteboard shelf in the center. And you're in business!

Dutch oven cooking. Baked beans, Texas chili, peach cobbler and homemade rolls are the Dutch oven delights. While some campers think of Dutch ovens as residential camp utensils, my experience with real bean-hole buffs has been on canoe trips. Lightweight Dutch ovens are even good companions for backpacking.

Cast aluminum Dutch ovens are fairly light and worth the extra weight when you taste the cobbler, rolls and chili. Use lots of hot coals under the oven and on top of the lid. The coals must be hot but not flaming.

Another method is to build a fire over a hole about 15 to 18 inches deep. It will burn down and fill the bottom of the hole with hot coals that you can use on top of the oven as well. This gives you a great chance to make wonderful bean-hole chili with your favorite recipe. Dig out coals to put on the oven lid as well as under it. Lower the oven into the hole and cover it with coals. Then place enough soaked limbs and wet leaves on top of the hole to support the dirt you dug out of the hole. Cover completely the damp limbs and leaves with the dirt until no steam can escape. Let the chili cook for three to four hours (it won't burn in the airtight hole).

Open-fire frying. Flipping pancakes or turning trout to a golden brown over an open fire is classic camp cooking—frying-pan style. You do it just the way you see it in the magazines—hunkering down by the fire.

Use a coated steel pan with a detachable handle for easy packing. Cook on hot coals with small flames. If the flames are too high, it's hard to sit near the fire to cook. Wait and let the fire die down. Use an insulated mitt to protect your knuckles.

Foil-cooking. Cook fresh fish and hobo meals of any type on coals in aluminum foil. It's like a thin Dutch oven. Use hot coals with no flames. Dig out coals, place foiled food on the bottom coals side-by-side and cover the top with the extra coals. To keep foiled food from burning, it must be airtight. Use a "drug store wrap" method: triple-fold the foil end-to-end, then triple-fold each end (see Diagram 46, "Foil-Cooking"). Rolling or wadding foil wrap lets air escape, defeating the purpose.

Bendonn cooking. The Bendonn tote stove is a pair of deep aluminum pans that fit together for baking, boiling or popping corn. The cover pan has a coal ring on top to hold hot coals for baking. You also can use the pans for frying. Both pans

Diagram 46
Foil-Cooking

have removable wire handles. Use hot coals when baking and low flames when frying, boiling or popping corn.

Unusual utensil uses. Most outdoor utensils are multipurpose. Thinking of ways to "make do" with what you have opens up creative, new ways to use different utensils. Here are some ideas:

1. Sierra cup cooking. Cook in a Sierra cup by securing a stick to the handle to keep from burning your hands and face. It's usually best to have the group do it together or to experiment.

If everyone uses the same cup, cooking for eight or nine people in a cup day after day can become boring and tedious. A more useful idea is to use a Sierra cup as a muffin or cupcake mold. This technique was invented by campers who were ready to prepare breakfast—complete with strawberry cupcakes—only to discover they had no oven, no cupcake tin and no cupcake papers. So they invented the reflector oven pot and the aluminum cupcake pans molded on a Sierra cup. Simply mold pieces of aluminum foil over the outside or inside of your cup. Then remove the foil pieces, fill them with batter, and bake muffins or cupcakes in the Dutch or reflector oven.

2. Pot reflector oven. Place a large piece of aluminum foil over the opening of your largest pot with a flat lid. Hold the lid's edge, and slide the lid into the pot to create a reflector oven. Mold the overlapping foil around the pot's edges. Then lay the pot on its side in front of the fire. Use two rocks on either side to keep it from rolling, and let the baking begin.

3. Maytag griddle. Keep your eyes open at garage sales for old Maytag washing machines with cast aluminum lids. The lids make great camp griddles because they're lightweight and thick enough to hold heat. They also have turned edges that hold grease.

4. Warming oven. Place an empty pot on top of the water pot for a great warming spot for cooked food while other items are being cooked. Or use it to help yeast bread rise on a cold day. Put a few small stones under your bread container to prevent the dough from getting too hot on the bottom.

5. Fry-pan baking. Turn a large frying pan upside down over another fry pan to create a shallow oven. Place hot coals on the covering pan just as you would a Dutch oven.

Backcountry Cooking Safety

Safety should always be your first concern when cooking in the backcountry. Common sense is your best guide. A good way to make campers safety-conscious is to demonstrate how to dip and pour water. Then invite the entire group to make a quick oral list of "nevers" for fires and cooking. They'll think of a huge list of common-sense ideas, and everyone will be more safety-conscious. This exercise also impresses campers with the importance of equipment care, and it enhances their ability to make safe judgments on the spot.

Here are a few general guidelines for cooking safely:

1. Always ladle hot water, soups and food. Never pour them. Use a long-handle

Camp Notebook 49

Backcountry Cooking

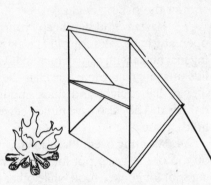

Commercial reflector oven

Homemade aluminum-foil
reflector oven

Open fire cooking

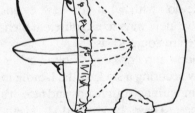

Pot reflector oven

Dutch oven

Stackable pots

Bendonn cooking

aluminum dipper to ladle hot water into a sitting cup. Never hold a cup while pouring. Water spilled or a blob of food dropped on someone's hand can cause painful burns.

2. Always refuel a camp stove before using it—even if you think you didn't use much fuel last time. This routine prevents you from having to stop in the midst of cooking a meal to refuel. If you must refuel a stove part way through a meal or heating water, let the stove cool first. Always use a filter funnel and filler cap when pouring fuel into a stove.

3. Never over-fill a stove with fuel. It makes you pump liquid fuel into the burner, creating the possibility for a dangerous fire. Don't fill the fuel tank completely. Make sure there's enough air space for pressurizing. This allows the fuel to vaporize when it's pumped up.

4. Store camp stove fuel in fuel containers that are different from water bottles and canteens. Label them.

5. Always leave some air space at the top when storing fuel. Seal tightly but not tightly enough to split the cap gasket. Place the bottle in a plastic bag for packing.

6. Always designate an area at camp for fuel storage and for refueling stoves. Set it up away from the fire and cooking area.

Keeping Utensils Clean and Dirty

The days of scrubbing pots to a mirrorlike finish are past. Old-timers have known all along that a blackened pot or pan absorbs heat faster than a shiny, reflective surface. (In the mid-'70s, some companies caught on and started making preblackened camping pots.)

While you don't need to keep pots shiny, you do need to keep them clean inside. Do this by scrubbing them with a handful of pine needles or ashes (duff) and a little water. Dump the residue in the

woods, and dip some water from a creek or lake. Rinse a couple of times, throwing out the dirty water onshore. Then thoroughly rinse in the stream or snow. After utensils are clean and rinsed, rinse them once more by pouring boiling water in and on them. Don't dip utensils in your hot water pot; it contaminates the water that you can use for hot beverages and other hot-water rinsing. Pack pots and skillets in a homemade drawstring bag to prevent soot rubbing off onto gear in your pack or bag.

You can use a plastic pot scrubber on supertough sticks and burned-on foods or grease. However, a plastic scrubber used repeatedly collects bacteria and can contaminate your utensils.

There's one shiny rule: Keep reflector ovens bright and shiny. Reflector oven cooking is effective only if the firelight reflects heat onto the food, so the surface must be as bright and shiny as possible.

Backcountry Cooking Tips

Keeping track of all the kitchen utensils gets rather complicated when your purpose is to live a simple life outdoors. Here are a few tips to make your organization and cooking plans easier:

1. Pack an aluminum measuring cup in the kitchen gear. Place a set of small measuring spoons connected by a ring inside the cup.

2. Carry oil, honey, syrup, mustard, ketchup and such in small plastic bottles to prevent spilling. To be supersafe and to keep your gear from getting sticky, pack the little plastic bottles inside little plastic bags inside the big plastic food bags.

3. Protect aluminum gear by using wooden or Teflon spoons and spatulas. Metal spoons "ding" aluminum pots, making all foods stick to the bottom.

4. Whenever you set up camp, always begin by heating water. Otherwise, waiting

for water to get hot to wash dirty dishes takes forever. Having hot water for drinks, cooking and rinsing dishes after eating is camp luxury. At the same time, don't leave water pots on a stove or fire when the water is low; a pot can boil dry quickly and melt the metal. Always put a lid or pan on top of the water pot to hold the heat and save fuel.

5. Nest all small items inside larger cooking pots—measuring cups, condiments and small utensils. Pad backpacking stoves inside the pots with insulated mitts or potholders before packing to protect the pots' inner surface. Place the pots inside a "dirty bag" to keep your pack clean. When you retrieve the bag at camp, you'll haul out a lot of small gear from your pack at the same time.

6. Backcountry travelers in Minnesota canoe country have a neat way to protect food. They line Duluth packs with large, clear plastic bags and sturdy pasteboard boxes. This gives them a rigid pack to protect bread, eggs and other fragile foods. The boxes hold up for many miles.

Neat Treats for the Backcountry

Here are a dozen favorite backcountry treats for young campers. They've all been tested and approved by teenagers from Millinocket to Missoula. Some can be parts of balanced meals; others are simply fun snacks and treats.

Banana boats. Slit the banana peel on the inside curve. Use a spoon handle to scoop out a shallow trough from the banana. (Eat the excess!) Crush a chocolate chip cookie in your hands, and sprinkle it into the empty trough. Tuck in a dozen minimarshmallows. Then close the peeling, and place the banana treat on hot coals with its ends turned upward. When the peel turns dark brown or black, it's ready to eat with a spoon. Does it remind you of a hot banana split?

Applesauce can cake. Pour a can of applesauce into the bottom of a #10 (one-gallon) can. Then mix a box of gingerbread according to the directions, and pour it on top of the applesauce. Cover tightly with foil. Cook on a camp stove for about 45 minutes at low heat. The gingerbread will absorb the applesauce, filling the can with a rich, tasty cake. Make separate cakes for a double batch.

Terminal Moraine. This is the fabulous first-night favorite for famished football fans and players who leave for camp after the game. The original name was "Stuff"—that's what the football player's father called it. But it was renamed Terminal Moraine when the church group saw the remnants of real glaciers—including medial, lateral and terminal moraines—in Wyoming. (The campers are still experimenting with recipes they'll later call Medial Moraine and Lateral Moraine.)

Brown two pounds of hamburger in a large pot. Dump in two medium chopped onions, followed by an avalanche of canned spaghetti and meat sauce (maybe two 48-ounce cans) and a drift of pork and beans (one or two 53-ounce cans). Give everyone a tasting spoon, and add doses of mustard and ketchup till everyone decides that dinner's ready. Serve with celery stuffed with peanut butter, French bread, beverages, fruit cocktail and gingersnaps.

Doughgirls. (Also called Doughboys, Doughmen, Doughwomen and sometimes Doughpeople.) Find a dead, dry stick. Whittle the end smooth and flat, and scrape away any loose bark. Then heat the stick over an open fire, and put a little flour on its end. Then cover the end and about three inches up the stick with a ball of biscuit mix or a couple of canned biscuits. Mold the dough evenly (no holes). Disregard any dark fingerprints—they'll blend into the brownish color when it's cooked anyway. Hold the stick over the coals (not flames), and patiently turn and wait until the dough turns a beautiful golden brown. Remove the stick, put some butter inside, and fill the hole with jam, jelly, honey or apple butter.

You can also make a Doughpig by first cooking a sausage link speared through the end by a sharpened stick. Then follow the Doughgirl process, covering the sausage with flour and biscuit dough. Add some sweetening, and you've got breakfast!

Customized pancakes. On layover days, make supersize pancakes in a frying pan. Add chocolate chips, wild blackberries or blueberries, bacon pieces or pecan chips to make a special, leisurely morning feast. Cut each pancake in quarters to fill four Sierra cups, then keep on cooking!

Oatmeal patties. Mix rolled oats with honey, cinnamon and brown sugar in amounts that seem appropriate to your sweet tooth. Roll the mixture into balls, flatten, and fry in margarine. Cook enough at breakfast for a midmorning snack and to give to someone you meet on the trail. Maine hospitality!

Stackups. Thinly slice Sierra-cup-size tomatoes. Spread cream cheese and chives on top, and stack like a sandwich. Dip the stack in eggs, roll in cracker crumbs and fry. Turn once and serve right out of the pan.

If it's too much trouble to size the tomatoes or if the ingredients seem too much to carry, save the treat for a canoe trip.

You can also invent your own stackups. Just think of all the things you can slice, spread, dip, roll or sprinkle and cook (or eat raw). Then pass out the fabric markers, and design your own "I Survived Camp Stackups" T-shirts!

Watermelon boats. Here's a treat that's particularly appropriate for a canoe trip (but you can use it for other camps too). Arrange a surprise food-drop with a load of watermelons. Then let campers use their imaginations and artistic abilities to sculpt watermelon boats. Don't let campers get by with simply scalloping the edges of the watermelon half. How about designing a long, skinny melon like a shoe-keel river runner, a raft or a kayak with a removable cockpit cover?

Like canoes, the watermelon boat's design isn't everything. Once you've made your artistic cuts, scoop out the inside in little watermelon balls, or cube it with a knife. Add as many other cut-up fruits (cantaloupes, grapes, strawberries or pineapples) as you can to make tasty, attractive, and healthy salads.

C-P-C. (Translated coconut, pecans and chocolate—or carob.) This is the highest calorie content version of gorp—good old raisins and peanuts. Most supermarkets stock several versions of gorp, which they now call trail mix because it sounds "outdoorsy." Creating your own is really more fun though.

Walking salad. Spread peanut butter and raisins on a cabbage leaf. Roll it up and munch on a transportable, high-protein treat.

Bread. Nothing beats real bread baked outdoors. Dissolve 2 packages of yeast in a half cup of warm water. Mix in a large bowl:

1 tablespoon salt
2 tablespoons cooking oil
3 tablespoons sugar
2½ cups lukewarm water

Add the yeast mixture and 7 to 8 cups of flour. Mix in a plastic bowl. Cover with a clean bandanna and let rise for about an hour and a half. Cut in sections. Knead each piece on foil on a flat rock or canoe bottom. Then put the dough in pans or Sierra cups. Let rise for 30 minutes near the fire or, on a good hot day, inside a zipped-up tent in the sun. Bake reflector, Dutch or Bendonn for 25 to 30 minutes—longer if you use big loaf pans.

Eggs à la goldenrod. Try this easy-to-make breakfast treat on a layover day. Boil eggs until they're firm. When cooled, chop the whites and stir into a white sauce. Finely chop the yolks. Serve white sauce on toast with sprinkled yolks on top.

Notes

[1]Dorcas Miller, *The New Healthy Trail Food Book* (revised) (Charlotte, North Carolina: Fast and McMillan Publishers, 1981), p. 10.

[2]Dorcas Miller, *The New Healthy Trail Food Book*.

[3]Nancy Pallister (editor), *NOLS Cookery* (Lander, Wyoming: National Outdoor Leadership School, 1974).

Chapter 25

Map and Compass Navigation

"Which side of town is your school on?"

"North, near Sandy Springs."

"East or west of Sandy Springs?"

My seven-year-old paused, calculating. "East!" he said, with no hesitation.

"How do you know?"

"How do I know it's east? Because we never eat soggy waffles."

"What?"

"I know it's east 'cause we never eat soggy waffles. Don't you know? Never—north, eat—east, soggy—south, waffles—west. Each letter is a direction."

At seven, Hoke already knew a neat way to remember directions. He learned the "soggy waffle" acronym from a girl scout leader at a church supper. And he has internalized basics for understanding navigation and reading printed maps: Up is north, right is east, down is south and left is west.

Like all backcountry skills, map and compass skills are best taught in small episodes, in practical situations and with a lot of little memory tricks—like soggy waffles. Campers remember a new skill longer when they actually use it.

Using Maps

Groups traveling by van or car have a built-in opportunity to learn basic map reading going to and from camp. Choosing the most direct or most scenic route or locating campsites can be a group experience. Youth can then take turns helping the driver navigate. Drivers for residential camp day trips can contribute to the lifelong travel skill by orienting the campers with a map. Let's look at some of the different maps and the vast information you can gather from them.

Road maps. Many campers don't realize how much information is packed on a one-page road map or atlas. Most map treasures are self-explanatory. Take just five minutes to focus on the map for your trip, and ask yourself and campers, "How many things does a road map tell us?" Using a state road map or a page from a travel atlas, teenagers can easily name 20 or more types of valuable information for camping, such as:

Direction
Distance
Boundaries
Types of roads

Road names and numbers
City and town names
City sizes
City streets
Land area
Population
Mileage calculation
Lakes
Beaches
National seashores
Airports
Winter travel warnings
National forests
Wayside rest areas
State parks
Parks with camping facilities
Wilderness areas and campsites
Recreational and historical sites
Where to write for tourist information
Rivers
Mountain ranges and peaks

Topographic maps. Campers quickly see that topographic maps aren't like state highway maps. They are like close-up photographs of a small area—sometimes as small as eight-by-eight miles. They show detailed curves in roads, lake shores and streams. Green indicates forests, and white areas depict open fields, pastures, and meadows.

But most important on a topographic map is the maze of tiny lines that indicates the area's elevations. Lines that are ¼-inch to 1-inch apart represent gently rising or flat areas. Close-together lines show steep areas. Lines that run almost on top of each other indicate extremely steep areas—maybe cliffs. Mountaintops are easy to identify: The lines get closer and form an oddly shaped circle. V-shaped lines pointing away from a mountain indicate ridges descending to the valley floor. V-shaped lines pointing toward a mountain indicate draws, hollows or ravines between ridges.

Along the map's bottom (south) edge is a mileage scale and the contour interval. The mileage scale allows you to estimate distances, while the contour interval allows you to calculate elevation gain and loss. If, for example, the interval is 40 feet, you gain or lose 40 feet between each set of fine brown-colored lines—or 200 feet between the dark "index lines." The dark lines are marked in feet so you don't have to count lines and multiply.

The U.S. Geological Survey produces numerous topographical maps of areas in the United States. Also many popular national forests, national parks and recreation areas have topographic maps available through their offices. Outdoor stores often supply local topographic maps. If you can't locate topographical maps locally, write the U.S. Geological Survey, Distribution Branch, Denver Federal Center, Denver, CO 80225 where you can purchase maps or order a free map index for your state. The state index is divided into named quadrangles or quads. Once you locate the river, mountains or camp location you're using, ask for the map you need by name.

Topographic maps of your camping area will generate a whole new level of interest for campers. Use the same "learning by exploring" approach you used with road maps. Have campers look at the map and name the type of information the map tells you. Say: "If you see something you don't understand, identify it for us. Guess what it means if you don't know."

You'll need to study the maps ahead of time to answer campers' questions accurately. It's also important to encourage other campers with map knowledge to share it. Here are the kinds of simple questions you can raise for campers to figure out on the map:

● Which is the highest mountain—Old Baldy or Double Knobs?

● How far is it from our campsite to

Green River Lakes?

● How much elevation do we gain between the campsite and Green River Lakes?

● What does the white area along Weaver Creek indicate?

Orienting maps. Locating a map to correspond to the actual directions and landmarks around you is called orienting a map. Orienting a map without a compass can often be done by turning the map to correspond to the visible streams, lakes or mountaintops.

Using a Compass

In addition to maps, the other tool for successful backcountry navigation is an orienteering compass. This compass has three basic parts (see Diagram 47, "Compass Parts"):

1. A circular housing on top with a 360-degree dial and a transparent arrow.

2. A magnetic arrow inside with a colored end that always points to magnetic north.

3. A rectangular base plate with a "direction of travel" arrow.

To simplify compass use for campers, have a compass for each person or have campers pair up. Then lead them through the following exercise:

1. Ask each camper or pair to set the housing arrow north, 360 degrees to match the direction of travel arrow on the base plate. This gives you your direction of travel.

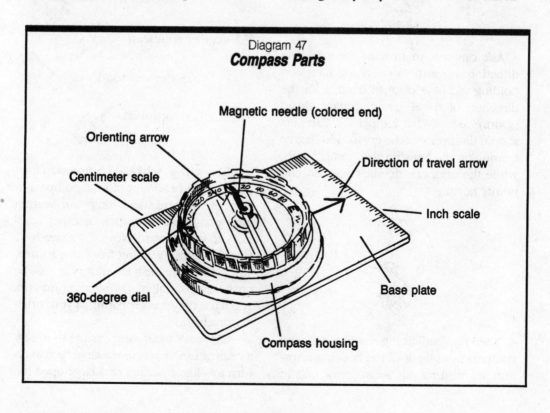

Diagram 47
Compass Parts

Magnetic needle (colored end)

Orienting arrow

Direction of travel arrow

Centimeter scale

Inch scale

360-degree dial

Base plate

Compass housing

2. Then say: "Hold the compass and turn your body until the transparent arrow on the housing corresponds to the colored end of the magnetic needle. The colored arrow will actually fit 'box' inside the transparent arrow outline. Make sure your compass isn't near a metal object such as a belt buckle, since metal objects throw off the magnetic needle." At this point, all campers should be facing magnetic north, compass in hand.

3. Ask campers to turn in the opposite direction. Have them point the direction holding the base plate in hand with the direction of travel arrow straight ahead (south). Ask, "What happens?" Campers should discover that the north, 360 degree bearing on the housing also points south, while the magnetic needle's colored end points north.

4. Then say: "Still facing south, rotate your compass housing until the housing arrow matches or surrounds the magnetic needle.

Now what is the degree of travel?" The answer should be 180 degrees south. Explain that the exercise illustrates the principle of taking "bearings" with a compass.

Then review the steps:

1. Determine your direction of travel by pointing your travel arrow in that direction.

2. Adjust the housing, and box the magnetic arrow inside the transparent arrow.

3. Read the degrees of travel from the housing.

Then let campers practice determining directions by setting their compasses and facing the following directions using compass bearings:

90 degrees east

270 degrees west

45 degrees northeast

135 degrees southeast

225 degrees southwest

315 degrees northwest

Traveling with a compass. Once you've set a bearing, hold the compass in front of you, and sight along your bearing until you find a tree, rock or other landmark to walk toward. Now you're ready to take a bearing. Walking from tree to tree, you can explore the backcountry across the next ridge or valley. On your return trip, you'll use the reverse bearing of your original destination.

Since it's nearly impossible to follow a bearing exactly, choose a large base to return to—like a pasture or a large opening.

If such locations aren't available, use a stream or road as your departure point. On the return trip, set a bearing a few degrees to one side of your original reverse route. Then when you reach your road or stream, you'll know which way to turn (right or left) to reach your departure point (see Diagram 48, "Return Route").

Using a Map and Compass Together

Once campers have learned to orient a map by sight and to set bearings with a compass separately, they can learn to put the two skills together. They'll be able to:

● Find a specific location not marked by a trail.

● Orient themselves in relationship to the terrain.

● Determine where they are on the map.

● Plan a travel route.

● Navigate cross-country to a specific location marked on a map.

Orienting a Map With a Compass

The first step in using a map and compass together is to orient the map with the compass. Magnetic north differs from geographic north. And the variations change over long periods of time, making regular map updating necessary to include new magnetic bearings or declinations (deviation from "true north").

Whenever using a map and compass together, you must compensate for the difference between magnetic and geographic north. The standard way to do this is illustrated in Camp Notebook 50, "Orienting With a Map and Compass." Some other methods include:

1. Draw elongated magnetic north lines several places on the face of a map.

2. Add to (if you're west of the magnetic pole) or subtract from (if you're east) the magnetic bearing according to your location.

3. Some wilderness travelers use a sharp knife or stylus to etch their local mag-

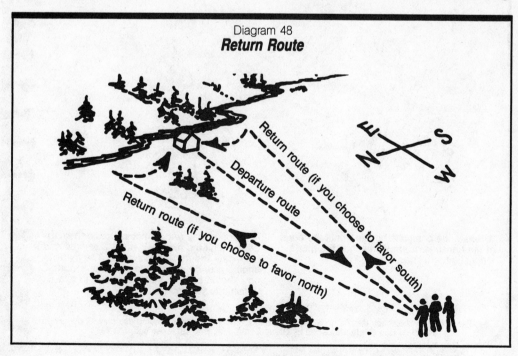

Diagram 48
Return Route

Camp Notebook 50

Orienting With a Map and Compass

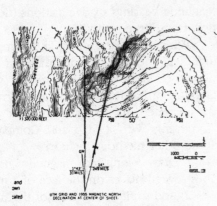

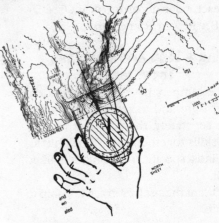

1. To make it easier to work with the map, use a pencil to lengthen the true north and magnetic north lines at the map's bottom margin. Then spread the map on a level spot and continue the process.

2. Place the compass at the bottom of the map with the direction of travel arrow over the true north line.

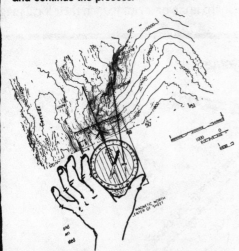

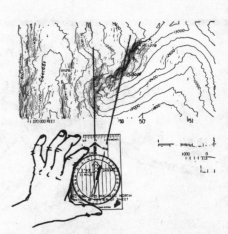

3. Rotate the compass housing until the edge of the transparent arrow matches the map's magnetic north line.

4. Holding map and compass, rotate them together until the magnetic arrow's colored end fits inside the transparent arrow. The map should now be oriented to geographic north. You should see the map accurately in relationship to your surroundings.

netic north bearing into their compass base plate, making it easier to match the housing north point and the magnetic bearing. Accomplish the same goal with stick-on printers lines. You can scratch them off when you use the compass in an area with a different declination.

Using Triangulation to Find Where You Are

Once you have your map oriented, it's easy to find your exact location on the map. Begin by using your oriented map to find two prominent landmarks that you can easily see from where you're standing. (The two landmarks must be visible and recognizable on your topographic map.) Then line up the long side of your compass with one landmark. Draw a pencil line on the map using that aligned edge of the compass. Now, without moving the map, follow the same procedure with the second landmark. Draw another line. Then use your compass as a straightedge, and extend the two lines until they cross. That's where you're standing.

Navigating Cross-Country

The major benefit of using a map and compass is cross-country travel. Hiking or cross-country skiing to find a lake, stream, meadow or access to a climbing route without any marked trail is a major challenge for campers. Their sense of accomplishment when they succeed makes them almost believe in magic! One girl who shared leadership cross-country to a lake half a mile from the trail couldn't believe it when the group emerged at the sparkling blue reservoir. "I never believed we would find it! I just never believed we would!" she exclaimed. The campers spotted a red-bellied turtle and a moose antler along the way. And the campers left behind no trail, footprint or candy wrapper.

Begin by locating yourself on the map using trail markings, triangulation or prominent landmarks. With your map oriented, lay the long edge of the base plate to connect your current location with your destination—the lake, river or mountain peak. Draw a pencil line.

Now rotate the compass housing to box the magnetic arrow inside the housing arrow. The degree mark next to your travel direction marker is your bearing. Remember it—write it down if necessary. You're ready to travel.

Hold the compass steady, away from metal objects. Align both arrows in the compass. Spot a distant tree or rock, and walk to it. You should be able to reverse your compass and check your back trail. Now select another spot using the same direction and bearing. Hold steady and walk again. Look back. With repeated sightings, you can stay on course until you reach your destination.

It's always good to look backward when traveling cross-country. It helps you remember what the return route will look like if you choose to come back by the same route. But still don't depend on memory to guide you back; use your map and compass carefully.

Campers can practice cross-country travel in residential camps just as well as in the backcountry. With imagination and the spirit of discovery, groups can discover new places in familiar surroundings. Or they can use many different routes to rendezvous with other campers for picnics or afternoon gatherings.

Junior highers traveling in separate groups on different routes in the McKenzie lava fields of the Oregon Cascades rendezvous from atop two prominent peaks five miles apart using mirrors at the lunch hour. Sometimes making the mirror signals work takes a lot of concentration. But with patience and persistence (sometimes verging on giving up and returning to camp), the young campers see the flash of the other group's mirror—even though they can't see their friends even with binoculars.

Map and Compass Group-Building Activities

Maps and compasses are great group-building tools for camp. Here are three activities you can use to build community at camp while teaching campers map and compass skills.

Compass Meal

A fun way to practice using a compass is with a real task in mind. Compass meal is a cooperation game in which teams of two to four campers pool their compass knowledge to find the ingredients for cooking breakfast, supper or a picnic that's already prepared and hidden. It's a true "treasure hunt" that's appropriate for both residential and trip camps. Be sure to announce the activity before your basic compass session to intensify campers' eagerness to learn and remember.

Directions. Divide the meal into as many parts as you have teams. Seal parts of the meal in plastic bags. Set up each bearings course in advance. Design the course so that all teams begin and return to the same point. Your area's rocks, trees and streams will determine your courses. Avoid great distances and obstacles to cross. Lengthen or shorten course distances depending on the area.

Write the bearings for each team on 3×5 cards. For example, you might write on one team's card, "35 degrees northeast for 40 steps; 140 degrees southeast for 30 steps; and 80 degrees northeast for 50 steps." Hide parts of the meal at each of the destinations.

Then give each team its set of three to five compass bearings that will lead them to an important part of their meal. All teams must be successful to have a full meal. Help campers be successful in their venture. Precisely following bearings is critical, and groups will need support if they become confused or frustrated. When everyone arrives with the ingredients, prepare your feast!

Dry Camp

Dry camp is an adventure for backpackers or resident campers on a day trip. It has a real objective: to find water to use for a meal or overnight on the trail. Activity leaders *must* go through the activity in advance to check the route and compass bearings and to make sure the water sources contain water at the time of the trip. The water should be drinkable, or you should have a way to purify it.

Directions. Pre-plan a campsite or lunch location on a hiking trail that has no immediate water source. However, keep the site within a quarter of a mile of a stream with potable water that's visible on your topographical map. Carry only drinking water—none for cooking or cleanup. Again, be sure leaders "scout out" the location in advance.

Once the campers reach camp or lunch location and set camp, ask campers to locate themselves on their topographic maps. Then have them identify the nearest water source on the map (the spring, stream or lake must be visible on the map). By orienting their maps and setting a compass bearing for the water source, the group should be able to locate and bring back enough water.

Have each camper take an individual bearing, write it on paper, and give it to you or another leader. (You already know the correct bearing because of your reconnoitering trip.) Then pair campers who

Camp Notebook 51

Backcountry Navigation Quiz

1. Match the following by placing the correct letter from the left-hand column in the corresponding right-hand blank.

a. Quadrangle
b. Scale l:24,000
c. Contour interval
d. Unimproved dirt road
e. Declination
f.
g.
h.
i.

_____ 20 degrees
_____ =============
_____ 1 inch = 2,000 feet
_____ Depression contours—craters
_____ 40 feet
_____
_____
_____
_____ Ophir, Colorado

2. Answer the following questions about your backcountry traveling area. If you were traveling cross-country from _____ to _____ :
a. What direction would you travel?   _____
b. What would be your compass bearing?   _____
c. How far would you travel?   _____
d. Would you gain or lose elevation?   _____
e. How much?   _____

3. Which is steeper: _____
or _____ ?

4. What is the highest point on your map?   _____
                   the lowest?   _____

have the same or similar bearings. Let the pairs compare bearings and set their course using natural landmarks. Leaders should accompany at a distance campers whose bearings were most inaccurate to make sure they don't get too far off course or lost.

Have the team that finds the water source first signal to the others. When all have gathered at the water source, take time to discuss the campers' feelings, learnings and questions. Choose the easiest route back to camp since everyone's carrying water.

A Backcountry Map and Compass Quiz

Camp Notebook 51, "Backcountry Navigation Quiz," tests campers' abilities to read maps and their symbols. Study it yourself, then decide when it's most appropriate to use with campers. They should take

it when they've practiced enough to answer most of the questions. Put their success first.

Questions 2 through 4 are blank for you to fill in with information from the map your campers will be using during their camp. Each participant or team will need a compass and a topographic map. Answers to Question 1 are listed in the box below.

Map Answers for Camp Notebook 51, page 339

The letters in Question 1 should appear in the following order: e, d, b, i, c, h, f, g, a.

Afterword

Lights on the Camping Trail

What are we trying to accomplish in Christian camping? What are the core criteria by which all approaches to camping can be tested and measured? These are good questions—good because they can be answered in dozens of ways, and all answers will be fresh, illuminating and correct.

Recently I've sought some new word that would cast another light on the purposes of church youth camping. These illustrate that the future holds a myriad of shining experiences that will illumine youth camping. I want to conclude with some of the thoughts I rediscovered.

Do Things Kids Can Believe In

I came across an article by Bill Wertenbaker in WoodenBoat magazine. He was reflecting on the loss of Tyehee, his 60-year-old wooden sailing beauty. His children had grown up on the boat and had become teachers for many passengers. In 20 years only one passenger ever took offense at being taught by young people. Wertenbaker writes: "Tyehee gave my sons, and other people's children, too, ways to be useful. They were needed. And if they did something well, this mattered. If they did something wrong, that mattered, too—immedi-

ately, and in ways that did not have to be told about and that they could believe in."[1]

What the Wertenbaker youngsters found in the Tyehee experience can be matched in countless camping experiences—pitching tents, making fires, paddling rapids, cooking meals, or leading campfire songs or cabin devotionals. These are real camp experiences where kids:

- Feel useful and needed.
- Know that what they do matters.
- Learn without having to be told what they've learned.
- Believe in what they do—and hence, in themselves and in God.

Seek to Be Intergenerational

Another recent light fell upon my camping trail when we moved to the Salem community near Covington, Georgia. Our church is on the site of one of the South's oldest camp meeting grounds. Not far away is the oldest state park in the nation, historically popular as a spiritual gathering place for Indians and settlers.

The Salem camp meeting began in 1828 and has been held for 160 consecutive years. Today as many as 1,000 people sing, share fellowship and eat ice cream outdoors during the summer evenings, joining the 300 people who spend all week at the Salem camp. At one evening worship service, the slanting August sun glowed on the cabin fronts, and a grandmother wheeled her granddaughter toward the tabernacle in a stroller. Beside her walked her "spittin' image" daughter—three generations on their way to worship at camp.

I was reminded of Martin E. Marty's emphasis on making camps of the future intergenerational—where eighth-graders and 80-year-olds can learn from each other. This is a worthy goal for any camp. Hopefully, as we move toward the end of the century, we'll see a growing number of our retiring church members involved with young people at church camps.

Always Affirm Campers—Always!

When summer ended, we joined several other parents from our neighborhood in a picnic and awards day at a nearby horseback day camp. Most of our youngsters were beginners—eight- to 14-years old. They had learned to saddle and some basic riding techniques. At the end of each day they groomed their mounts and hauled wheelbarrow-loads of oats and hay to the 30 hungry animals. Work—sweaty, dirty work. And they loved it!

After our picnic in the bunkhouse dining room, the camp director led the campers in games while the parents visited. Then, the awards—patches for those who had achieved a new level and certificates for those who still "had work to do."

How can you help those who haven't achieved feel some success? How can they be motivated to continue when all around them patches are being proudly received? "I don't want anyone who didn't get a patch feeling badly," Linda Green said to the campers. Her voice was strong as she made eye-to-eye contact with the close circle of campers. "Those of you who got cer-

tificates have worked hard too. But you need to know I have standards I go by. They are for your safety. And you can't enter a new level until you've completed all the elements of the level you're on. All of you are close, and a few Saturdays of practice will get you there."

Three kids who didn't get patches nodded, but their eyes only saw the bunkhouse floor.

Then Cliff, the head wrangler, built on Linda's words. "You know," he drawled, "I've been around horses all my life, but I didn't really know how to ride till three years ago when I started taking classes here—from Linda. I've worked my way through several levels, and the level I'm working on now means I have to know all about horses hooves, legs and tendons. You never stop learning."

Then Linda: "That's what I mean—you never get to the place where you can't be taught by someone else."

My last mental snapshot before leaving camp was of one of the campers—the one who seemed most despondent. She was talking one-to-one with Linda, eagerly asking her to enumerate the things she needed to work on to complete the first level. Her letdown was only temporary thanks to Linda's and Cliff's affirming words and ways.

In the end it isn't enough just to learn skills at camp—no matter what they are. It's the care and the community that really matter. When the entire camp celebrates one camper's achievements, when one congratulates all those who tried their best, when everyone can be who they are and be loved—that is camping's "enough."

Notes

[1] William Wertenbaker, "Parting Thoughts," Wooden-Boat (July-August 1988), p. 90.

Camping Resources

Camp Planning and Leadership

Accepted Peer Practices in Adventure Programming. Karl M. Johanson (compiler). Association for Experiential Education, Box 249, University of Colorado, Boulder, CO 80309. A concise book of listings of general program practices for camp administration, staff, participants, activities, equipment and facilities. Covers 22 land and 10 aquatic adventure activities plus emergency procedures.

American Camping Association Catalog of Camping Publications. American Camping Association, Bradford Woods, 5000 State Rd. 67N., Martinsville, IN 46151-7902. An extensive, free camping catalog published annually and distributed to A.C.A., CCI and youth camping professionals in Canada, New Zealand and Australia.

Beautiful Upon the Mountains. D. Campbell Wyckoff and Henrietta T. Wilkinson. Board of Christian Education, Cumberland Presbyterian Church, 1978 Union Ave., Memphis, TN 38104. A how-to Christian education book with several educational models. Included is Groome's "Shared Praxis" Bible study method developed in five practical Bible explorations.

Building Community in Youth Groups. Denny Rydberg. Group Books, Box 481, Loveland, CO 80539. A practical, five-step plan for building relationships in youth groups. Discusses how to establish trust, create freedom, affirm others, experience challenging growth and develop goals in covenant community.

Camp Standards With Interpretations for the Accreditation of Organized Camps. American Camping Association, Bradford Woods, 5000 State Rd. 67N., Martinsville, IN 46151-7902. An indispensable guide for camp boards, administrators and program directors who seek the highest standards for camp facilities and programs. Especially helpful to local churches that conduct travel and trip camps. A smaller pocket version without interpretations is also available.

Christian Camping International's Focus Series. Christian Camping International/USA, Box 646, Wheaton, IL 60189. A series of eight-page papers about camping. Titles include: "99 Ideas for Recruiting Campers"; "The Counselor's Role in Camper Discipline"; "5 Values of Christian Camping"; "Taking the Church Outdoors"; "How to Recruit and Encourage Volunteers"; "How to Lead Small Group Bible Studies With Campers"; "Preparing Your Child for Camp"; "Summer Slump Can Be Risky"; "Age Group Characteristics: Key to Understanding Kids"; "Camping and the Church"; "Creative Discipleship Options for Your Local Church"; and "The Camp Board: Hands-On Implementers or Careful Policy-Makers?"

Christian Religious Education: Sharing Our Story and Vision. Thomas H. Groome. Harper & Row, Publishers, 10 E. 53rd St., New York, NY 10022. An acclaimed, groundbreaking work that focuses on six key areas of Christian education: the nature, purpose, context, approach, stages and leaders' roles.

God's Good Earth. Lloyd Mattson (editor). Camping Guideposts, Whiteface Woods, Cotton, MN 55724. An anthology of Christian values in outdoor education from a variety of writers. The material is grouped in four categories: "A Theology of Outdoor Education"; "Beyond the Nature Trail"; "The Outdoor Classroom"; and "Outdoor Readings and Reflections." The book concludes with listings of outdoor-education resources.

Group Development. Leland P. Bradford (editor). University Associates, 8517 Production Ave., San Diego, CA 92121. Presents a philosophy and theory of group formation and development. Deals with the initial steps toward group life, leaders' and members' tasks, and ways to diagnose group problems and improve decision-making. Though not written from a camping perspective, it provides excellent insights for staff training events.

Helping Youth Interpret the Bible. A. Roger Gobbel and others. John Knox Press, 341 Ponce de Leon Ave. N.E., Atlanta, GA 30365. A step-by-step interpretive approach to teaching the Bible to young people. Uses the themes and experiences of adolescence for focusing questions, models and Bible study activities.

Occasional Papers. American Camping Association, Bradford Woods, 5000 State Rd. 67N., Martinsville, IN 46151-7902. A series of eight-page Occasional Papers on camping philosophy. Titles include: "The Values of Camping"; "A Modern Camp for the New Generation"; "Group Experiences: The Essence of Camping"; "Interpreting Camp to Parents"; "Alternatives to Youth at Risk"; "Year-Round Camping Through Adventure Education"; "Enriching the Camp Experience"; "Whatever Happened to School Camping?"; "Camping Research"; and "Youth Development Through Outdoor Adventure Programs."

Sometimes a Shining Moment: The Foxfire Experience. Eliot Wigginton. Doubleday and Company, 245 Park Ave., New York, NY 10017. The story of a school teacher's 23-year journey from scared classroom instructor to the nurturer and mentor who inspired the Foxfire magazine, Foxfire projects and nine Foxfire books. Provides special inspiration to camp leaders looking for clues for involving youth in experiential education.

Sow Seeds, Trust the Promise, EcuFilm, 810 12th Ave. S., Nashville, TN 37203. A videotape series designed specifically for training outdoor ministry leaders. The four 30-minute tapes are: "Theology and Faith Development," "Community and Self-Understanding," "Outdoor Skills," and "Planning and Resourcing." Tapes may be purchased individually or as a package.

Teaching Through Adventure. Project Adventure, Box 100, Hamilton, MA 01936. Outlines practical philosophy and methods for experiential education. It includes exciting outdoor adventures for teenagers and leaders—action seminars, learning adventures, explorations—all designed to help students internalize their learnings. Though not a church book, it encompasses the major educational concerns of everyone who's committed to making learning exciting for young people.

Transforming Bible Study: A Leader's Guide. Walter Wink. Abingdon Press, 201 Eighth Ave. S., Nashville, TN 37202. Explores all the how-tos of a proven Bible study method in step-by-step, clear and concise terms. Includes more than 20 Bible study outlines as well as guidelines for designing your own Bible studies.

Understanding Teenagers

The Adolescent: A Psychological Self-Portrait. Daniel Offer and others. Basic Books, 10 E. 53rd St., New York, NY 10022. An authoritative study of how adolescents view themselves, their families, friendships and sexual relationships. Based on an 18-year study involving 20,000 boys and girls from normal, delinquent, disturbed and physically ill populations.

Adolescent Spirituality. Charles M. Shelton. Loyola University Press, 3441 N. Ashland Ave., Chicago, IL 60657. Written for everyone who is concerned with the spiritual life of today's teenagers. This book is an in-depth explanation of how adolescents formulate values and construct a self-identity that reflects Christian commitment.

All Grown Up & No Place to Go. David Elkind. Addison-Wesley Publishing Company, 1 Jacob Way, Reading, MA 01867. An appropriate sequel to Elkind's earlier book, *The Hurried Child.* This volume examines the many ways society influences young people and how they often feel emotionally abandoned by the adults who are most important to them.

Being Adolescent: Conflict and Growth in the Teenage Years. Mihaly Csikszentmihalyi and Reed Larson. Basic Books, 10 E. 53rd St., New York, NY 10022. A research-based book that explores the feelings, thoughts and experiences of kids. It enhances the way we understand normal adolescent development.

Determining Needs in Your Youth Ministry. Peter L. Benson and Dorothy L. Williams. Group Books, Box 481, Loveland, CO 80539. A do-it-yourself research kit to help youth leaders uncover the issues facing their teenagers. It comes complete with questionnaires, answer sheets, interpretation guide and program ideas. The easy-to-use tool is invaluable for every youth leader or camp director who wants to base camp programming on campers' needs.

The Quicksilver Years: The Hopes and Fears of Early Adolescence. Peter L. Benson and others. Harper & Row, Publishers, 10 E. 53rd St., New York, NY 10022. Based on Search Institute's survey of 8,000 fifth- through ninth-graders and 11,000 of their parents. Reports on how normal kids from 10 denominations and three youth-serving agencies live—what they value, what they worry about, how they relate to family and church, and their concern for global issues.

Understanding Adolescence. Ronald L. Koteskey. Victor Books, Box 1825, Wheaton, IL 60187. An in-depth, up-to-date resource written for parents but on-target for camp counselors. The author explores cherished myths and opens the way to understanding the tensions teenagers—and their parents—face.

The Youth Ministry Resource Book. Eugene C. Roehlkepartain (editor). Group Books, Box 481, Loveland, CO 80539. A valuable reference book that summarizes current research about all areas of teenagers' lives. Chapters include "Population Trends," "Families," "Sexuality," "Religion and Values," "Social Concerns," "Education," "Substance Abuse" and "Disabilities." The book also includes annotated listings of youth ministry organizations and resources.

Campers With Special Needs

An Introduction to Adventure: A Sequential Approach to Challenging Activities With Persons Who Are Disabled. Christopher Roland and Mark D. Havens. Vinland National Center, 3675 Ihduhapi Rd., Box 308, Loretto, MN 55357. Discusses how to adapt camp activities and adventuring for disabled campers in six steps: awareness activities, group cooperative games, individual initiative tasks, group initiative tasks, low adventure activities and high adventure activities.

Camping With Persons With Handicapping Conditions. Earl H. Miller. Discipleship Resources, Box 840, 1908 Grand Ave., Nashville, TN 37202. Miller—a pastor in Denver, Colorado, and a paraplegic—tells the thrilling story of two annual camps for disabled people. The author includes recommendations for staffing, training, program schedule, dance, music, application forms, health and accident forms, and letters to campers.

Special Education . . . Naturally. Gary M. Robb and others. Indiana University Press, 10th and Morton Sts., Bloomington, IN 47405. A big book of how-to activities for disabled campers. Shows how to individualize activities and how to implement a camp program for campers with special needs and abilities.

Camps in Action

The All New Complete Book of Bicycling. Eugene A. Sloane. Simon & Schuster, 1230 Ave. of the Americas, New York, NY 10020. Describes everything you need to know about bicycle basics, maintenance, repair, riding and touring. Lists many support groups and organizations.

Backpackers' Sourcebook. Penny Hargrove and Noelle Liebrenz. Wilderness Press,

2440 Bancroft Way, Berkeley, CA 94704-1676. A book of preparation tips—from getting permits, maps and trail guides to ordering equipment through the mail. Describes organizations and groups that provide information and support services for backpackers.

Canoeing and Kayaking Instruction Manual. Laurie Gullion. American Canoe Association, Box 1190, 8580 Cinder Bed Rd., Newington, VA 22122. The authoritative book on canoe safety, instruction and lesson planning. Covers equipment, conditioning, strokes, maneuvers, river reading and rescue.

Group Backpacking: A Leader's Manual. Chuck Gormley. Groupwork Today, Box 258, S. Plainfield, NJ 07080. An excellent guide for youth leaders who want to teach a backpacking course. Contains practical information on preparation, gear lists, forms, handouts, menus, first aid, outdoor risks, parental permission, trip evaluation and many other subjects.

The Handbook of Skiing. Karl Gamma. Alfred A. Knopf, 201 E. 50th St., New York, NY 10022. A complete guide to all the essential skiing skills and techniques—both cross-country and downhill. Includes more than 1,400 photographs, drawings and diagrams of ski technique.

L.L. Bean Guide to Bicycle Touring. L.L. Bean, Freeport, ME 04033. Filmed at Maine's Acadia National Park. Features Dennis Coello, a 20-year bicycling veteran who has circled the globe on a bike. Coello tells how to plan a trip, ride safely and perform roadside repairs. The video is fun to watch and is invaluable for bicycle camping workshops.

L.L. Bean Guide to Canoeing. L.L. Bean, Freeport, ME 04033. Canoeing expert and coach Ken Stone and his daughter demonstrate equipment, paddling technique and safety for white-water trips. An excellent video for orientation, workshops and review.

Living on Two Wheels. Dennis Coello. Ross Books, Box 4340, Berkeley, CA 94704. Includes excellent sections on touring, trip planning and packing for the extended adventure. Has lists, step-by-step mechanics and safety.

The New Wilderness Canoeing and Camping. Cliff Jacobson. ICS Books, 107 E. 89th St., Merrillville, IN 46410. Jacobson is a master canoeist, camper and youth leader. His book is chock-full of how-to information—from safety, trip planning and paddling technique to understanding what makes teenagers tick in the outdoors. Profusely illustrated.

River Rescue. Les Bechdel and Slim Ray. Appalachian Mountain Club Books, 5 Joy St., Boston, MA 02108. The first book dedicated solely to white-water safety and rescue. Helps paddlers develop the skills necessary to read the river. Has high-quality drawings, photographs and descriptions of actual rescues and procedures. A must for campers who venture into advanced white-water paddling.

Snow Camping. Nordic World Editors. Anderson World, 1400 Stierlin, Mountain View, CA 94043. Concise chapters by experienced winter campers and cross-country skiers on the winter season, camping techniques, equipment, safety and adventure.

The 2 Oz. Backpacker. Robert S. Wood. Ten Speed Press, Box 7123, Berkeley, CA 94707. A pocket-size book (only 2 ounces) packed with information on keeping fit, walking, camping technique, cooking and navigating.

The Workcamp Experience: Involving Youth in Outreach to the Needy. John C. Shaw. Group Books, Box 481, Loveland, CO 80539. A step-by-step manual for planning a workcamp. Details how to budget, raise funds and prepare guidelines.

Camp Activities and Crafts

Creative Crafts for Camps, Schools, and Groups. Catherine Hammett and Carol Horrocks. American Camping Association, Bradford Woods, 5000 State Rd. 67N., Martinsville, IN 46151-7902. The authors view crafts for their role in camper appreciation and self-development. The book details the specific materials, tools, techniques and terms for many crafts, including braiding, knotting, basketry, ceramics, leatherwork, stencilling, sketching, painting, weaving, whittling and woodworking.

The Foxfire Book of Toys and Games. Linda Garland Page and Hilton Smith (editors). E. P. Dutton, 2 Park Ave., New York, NY 10016. A joyous collection of instructions for indoor and outdoor games, dolls, homemade board games, playhouses and toys. No expense (or electricity!) is necessary. Includes instructions, photos and diagrams.

The Giving Book. Joani Schultz and Paul Thompson. John Knox Press, 341 Ponce de Leon Ave., N.E., Atlanta, GA 30365. A collection of more than 20 activities for recreation, biblical study, community building and experiential learning. The ideas call for active participation.

Group Growers. Group Books, Box 481, Loveland, CO 80539. A collection of 183 group-building activities for youth groups. Includes trust-building activities, discussion starters and other activities that work well at camp.

The Group Retreat Book. Arlo Reichter and others. Group Books, Box 481, Loveland, CO 80539. A complete retreat-planning guide with 34 ready-to-use designs for youth groups. Planning guides cover choosing locations, transportation, budgeting, leadership and the planning process.

Informal Recreation Activities: A Leader's Guide. Phyllis Ford. American Camping Association, Bradford Woods, 5000 State Rd. 67N., Martinsville, IN 46151-7902. Incorporates theoretical principles and practical instruction for camp-activity leadership. Discusses recreational activities, relays, music and rhythm, social recreation and campfires.

More . . . Group Retreats. Group Books, Box 481, Loveland, CO 80539. A collection of 30 youth retreats on self-image, relationships, issues, Bible study and faith.

More New Games and Playful Ideas. Andrew Fluegelman (editor). Doubleday and Company, 245 Park Ave., New York, NY 10017. This sequel to *The New Games Book* is filled with additional ideas about cooperative play. Can be used as a resource guide to publications, organizations and equipment.

Nature With Art: Classroom and Outdoor Art Activities With Natural History. Susie G. Criswell. Prentice Hall, 200 Old Tappan Rd., Old Tappan, NY 07675. A backpack full of art activities that teach campers the fundamentals of natural history while they learn basic art concepts.

The New Games Book. Andrew Fluegelman (editor). Doubleday and Company, 245 Park Ave., New York, NY 10017. A resource with lots of ideas for cooperation and cooperative competition. Deals with the philosophy and attitude of play. Has photos and clear instructions for playing games.

Playfair: Everybody's Guide to Non-Competitive Play. Joel Goodman and Matt Weinstein. Impact Publishers, Box 1094, San Luis Obispo, CA 93406. Sixty games for large and small groups with detailed instructions for leaders. A book that takes play seriously and makes play and cooperation a way of life.

Quick Crowdbreakers and Games for Youth Groups. Group Books, Box 481, Loveland, CO 80539. A collection of more than 200 mixers for youth groups. Includes activities for partners, teams and groups.

Silver Bullets. Karl Rohnke. Project Adventure, Box 100, Hamilton, MA 01936. A fascinating collection of activities by the author of *Cowstails and Cobras.* Includes tested indoor and outdoor activities that teachers, therapists, counselors and church leaders use to build trust in groups.

World of Fun. Harold Hipps and Wallace E. Chappell. Discipleship Resources, 1908 Grand Ave., Nashville, TN 37212. This is the companion book for *Seven Folk Dance and Folk Game Records,* which contains 202 dances from 22 countries. It's one of the most respected folk-dancing texts in America. The records and instruction manual are available individually or in a package.

Youth Ministry Cargo. Joani Schultz and others. Group Books, Box 481, Loveland, CO 80539. Hundreds of ideas using the everyday stuff in a church closet, pantry and variety store to design activities that enhance teenagers' faith.

Nature Awareness

Acclimatization. Steve Van Matre. American Camping Association, Bradford Woods, 5000 State Rd. 67N., Martinsville, IN 46151-7902. Documents a six-day program that introduces young people to the natural world through a combined sensory and conceptual approach. The text is an internationally recognized classic in the field of nature study. The sequel books *Acclimatizing: A Personal and Reflective Approach to a Natural Relationship*, and *Sunship Earth* are equally useful.

Cousteau Almanac of the Environment: An Inventory of Life on a Water Planet. Jacques-Yves Cousteau. Doubleday and Company, 245 Park Ave., New York, NY 10017. No other resource approaches the global concerns of water, natural resources and life like this one. A treasure for camp leaders looking for information to stimulate camp activities. Great for research, displays and nature awareness bulletin boards.

Humanizing Environmental Education. Cliff Knapp and Joel Goodman. American Camping Association, Bradford Woods, 5000 State Rd. 67N., Martinsville, IN 46151-7902. A collection of hundreds of activities designed to give the participant learning experiences in nature education and human relations training.

1001 Questions Answered About the Seashore. N.J. Berrill and Jacquelyne Berrill. Dover Publications, 180 Varick St., New York, NY 10014. This is the book for campers who roam the beaches and wonder about all those creatures washed ashore. Where did they come from? What are they? How do they relate to other sea life? It's all here.

Backcountry Living Skills

Be Expert With Map and Compass. Bjorn Kjellstrom. Charles Scribner's Sons Front and Brown Sts., Riverside, NJ 08075. The classic book on map and compass navigation and orienteering. Continuously revised and updated by the Silva Compass Company.

By Nature's Rules. Safeco Insurance Company of America. Available through local Safeco agents or from Jim Lawless Motion Picture Consultants, 1545 Northeast 130th Pl., Seattle, WA 98125. An excellent film for staff training or for camper orientation before high-country travel.

The New Healthy Trail Food Book. Dor-

cas S. Miller. Globe Pequot Press, 138 W. Main St., Chester, CT 06412. A straightforward book of recipes, menus, food charts and expedition food lists. Focuses on eating simply and eating natural foods on the trail.

How to Survive on Land and Sea. Frank C. Craighead and John J. Craighead (revised by Ray E. Smith and Shiras Jarvis). Naval Institute Press, U.S. Naval Institute Operations Center, Customer Service, 2062 Generals Hwy., Annapolis, MD 21401. This is the classic book for survival on land, sea, desert, tropic and subarctic environments. Covers survival priorities, first aid, signaling, water procurement, shelter, food, travel and environmental hazards.

Modern Outdoor Survival. Dwight R. Schuh. Menasha Ridge Press, Box 59257, Birmingham, AL 35259. A distillation of wisdom and experience for anyone who travels in the backcountry for a day, week or month. Covers weather, clothing, navigation, hypothermia, boating and canoeing safety.

Mountaineering: The Freedom of the Hills. Ed Peters (editor). The Mountaineers Books, 306 Second Ave. W., Seattle, WA 98119. The classic resource on mountaineering, high-country travel and backcountry technique—from camping and snow travel to rope work and rescue.

The National Outdoor Leadership School's Wilderness Guide. Peter Simer and John Sullivan. Simon & Schuster, 1230 Ave. of the Americas, New York, NY 10020. This step-by-step guide to backcountry living and responsible wilderness travel builds on the pioneering ideas of Paul Petzholdt and leaders of NOLS. Covers up-to-date minimum impact techniques, gear and equipment, cooking, first aid, weather and backcountry travel.

NOLS Cookery. National Outdoor Leadership School, Box AA, Lander, WY 82520. A concise discussion of nutrition, rationing, cooking and eating in the backcountry. Covers menu planning and rationing for long trips, stoves, fires, minimum-impact techniques and the mistakes most often made by beginners. Emphasizes whole foods and cooking from scratch.

Safety Brochures for the Backcountry, Tacoma Mountain Rescue Unit, Box 696, Tacoma, WA 98401. A variety of backcountry safety brochures are available for a nominal fee for staff or camper handouts. Titles include: "Four Lines of Defense Against Hypothermia"; "Heatcraft"; "Fatigue Exhaustion"; and "Survival."

The Thermal Wilderness. Safeco Insurance Company of America. Available through local Safeco agents or from Jim Lawless Motion Picture Consultants, 1545 Northeast 130th Pl., Seattle, WA 98125. In the same vein as "By Nature's Rules," this film covers heat-related emergencies. An excellent resource for backpackers.

The Uncalculated Risk. From the American Red Cross, available at Modern Talking Picture Service, 5000 Park St., St. Petersburg, FL 33709. All canoeists, kayakers and rafters should see this film or video before they head down a white-water river. This is one of a dozen films and videos for water and backcountry safety.

Wilderness Medicine. William W. Forgey. ICS Books, 107 E. 89th St., Merrillville, IN 46410. A preventive and emergency guide acclaimed by leading professionals in wilderness travel. Contains medical kit listings, over-the-counter medications, prevention, diagnosis and treatment.

Camp Readings and Reflections

Baptized Into Wilderness: A Christian Perspective on John Muir. Richard C. Austin. John Knox Press, 341 Ponce de Leon Ave. N.E., Atlanta, GA 30365. A vivid and engrossing introduction to a remarkable religious spirit and witness to the neglected voices of nature. Weaves together classical biblical and Christian images and interpretations of Muir's insights.

Earth Wisdom. Dolores LaChapelle. Finn Hill Arts, Box 542, Silverton, CO 81433. A book written with reverence and insight toward the rituals and sacred theology of many religions around the world. Especially helpful for pondering the mysterious experiences discovered in mountain travel and living outdoors.

Gift From the Sea. Anne Morrow Lindbergh. Random House, 201 E. 50th St., New York, NY 10022. A small book of great and simple wisdom. Deals with the profound philosophy of life and love, faith and openness as taught by the sea and the mysterious symbols that are washed ashore.

Grasshopper on the Road. Arnold Lobel. Harper & Row, Publishers, 10 E. 53rd St., New York, NY 10022. Six profound parablelike tales for children, young people and adults. Follows "Grasshopper" through a day. Excellent for reading after mealtimes. *Fables* and other "children's" books by Lobel provide serious, light-hearted moments of truth.

The Lemming Condition. Alan Arkin. Harper & Row, Publishers, 10 E. 53rd St., New York, NY 10022. The story of Bubber and the impending march to the cliffs by his lemming friends and family. This is a clear story about all who follow without questioning. Teenagers can adapt the book into a delightful reader drama.

Life Together. Dietrich Bonhoeffer. Harper & Row, Publishers, 10 E. 53rd St., New York, NY 10022. A discussion of Christian fellowship through Bonhoeffer's sermons and meditations. A classic discussion piece that deals with community, the day with others, the day alone, ministry and confession, and Communion. Useful on backpacking and canoeing trips as well as in residential camps.

The Maine Woods. Henry David Thoreau. Harper & Row, Publishers, 10 E. 53rd St., New York, NY 10022. The three journeys of Thoreau to the Maine backwoods deal with the outer and inner wilderness—the natural and the spiritual. Thoreau found in wilderness "the preservation of the world." His reflection and passion is timeless for the wilderness traveler.

The Man Who Walked Through Time. Colin Fletcher. Random House, 201 E. 50th St., New York, NY 10022. In this spiritual odyssey, Fletcher struggles for two months in the Grand Canyon against heat and cold, lack of water, dwindling supplies and nearly impassable terrain. Highly quotable around backpacking campfires!

Meditating on the Word. Dietrich Bonhoeffer. The Upper Room, 1908 Grand Ave.,

Box 189, Nashville, TN 37202. The final great work of Bonhoeffer. Contains his ideas, sermons and meditations on Psalm 119 and other psalms. Assists campers and counselors in focusing on the importance of God's Word and the life of prayer.

The Outermost House. Henry Beston. Ballantine Books, 201 E. 50th St., New York, NY 10022. No one has captured the sounds of the outer ocean on the beach like Beston. A wonderful book for those who find places on oceans and beaches to listen to their inner rhythms.

Reflections From The North Country. Sigurd F. Olson. Alfred A. Knopf, 201 E. 50th St., New York, NY 10022. A book of reflections on the great harmony of the Earth. Some of the themes include awareness, aliveness, oneness, beauty, simplicity, courage, freedom and immortality.

Roughing It. Mark Twain. New American Library, 1633 Broadway, New York, NY 10019. In his youth, Twain found himself adrift as a tenderfoot in the wild West—traveling, working and camping out in all sorts of serious and hilarious situations. The book is filled with stories that can be read at camp—and some that campers can act out with a little imagination!

Touch the Earth: A Self-Portrait of Indian Existence. T.C. McLuhan (compiler). Simon & Schuster, 1230 Ave. of the Americas, New York, NY 10020. This collection of meditations, reflections and glimpses of Indian life may be as close as some campers will come to learning from Native Americans. Excellent campfire reading.

Walden. Henry David Thoreau. New American Library, 1633 Broadway, New York, NY 10019. The classic book is a record of Thoreau's experiences and thoughts as he experimented with living simply. Although the names *Walden* and Thoreau are familiar, the actual thought and spirit of the man alone on Walden Pond are continuously fresh and renewing.

The Wilderness Reader. Frank Bergon (editor). New American Library, 1633 Broadway, New York, NY 10019. This is a true sampling of the literature of the American wilderness—from John Muir to John McPhee to Rachel Carson.

The Wilderness World of John Muir. Edwin W. Teale (editor). Houghton Mifflin Company, 1 Beacon St., Boston, MA 02108. Muir builds bridges between wilderness mysteries and biblical events—the inner and outer works of God. This collection contains the story of Stikeen, the dog who crossed the glaciers with Muir—perfect to read in three parts on a winter campout.

With Open Hands. Henri J. Nouwen. Ballantine Books, 201 E. 50th St., New York, NY 10022. A pocket-size paperback on how to open your life to God and live prayerfully. Deals with prayer and silence, acceptance, hope and compassion.

Youth Plan Worship. Betty Jane and J. Martin Bailey. Pilgrim Press, 132 W. 31st St., New York, NY 10001. A book designed for young people, teachers and counselors who plan and lead worship services. Contains material on informal worship, a six-session course on worship, outdoor worship and guidance for creating prayers, meditations and hymns. A treasury of scripture selections, readings and thoughts to use in worship.